Additional Praise for *Before* *Nature*

"In the face of the extinctions of our time—indeed, the threat to any human future at all—how are Christians still to pray? Here in our 'twilight,' Santmire invites readers into a practice of contemplative prayer capacious of both personal depth and clear-eyed vision. His Trinity Prayer makes possible a fully ecological immersion in reality, mystery, and hope: a Christian spirituality for life on Earth."

Lisa E. Dahill
Trinity Lutheran Seminary

"For several decades, Paul Santmire has produced a series of groundbreaking books on the theology of nature and the environment. They are rich and indispensable reading for anyone working in this area. Now he has added to his corpus this wonderful volume, *Before Nature: A Christian Spirituality*. In this work, Santmire brings together Christian spirituality, his personal narrative, theology of nature, and mission, in the very best sense of that word. The result is a feast, with all the right ingredients. We will never recover a theology of nature and place without recovering the accompanying practices, and in this work we get a wonderful insight into Santmire's own practices and how to develop a spirituality for and of such practices. It is hard to stress too strongly how important is such a discussion. Even more important is that we learn from Santmire and incarnate such practices into our daily lives. The results would be truly revolutionary."

Craig Bartholomew
Redeemer University College

"In *Before Nature*, Paul Santmire weaves together theologies of nature, both ancient and new, which he persuasively employs to re-frame our understanding of humanity's vital—and humble—role as co-creator and servant. Engaging scientific criticism and illumined by 'fragile faith,' Dr. Santmire journeys into the origin of all things in God as Trinity: Giver, Gift, and Giving. In a narrative combining elements of theological reflection, pastoral experience, and memoir, Santmire calls readers to own their role of theologian/creation-partner through prayer and action. An invitation to vulnerability, wonder, and hope, *Before Nature* is an inspiring and moving challenge to living in God's present—in an 'era of twilight.'"

Br Jonathan Maury
Society of Saint John the Evangelist

BEFORE NATURE

BEFORE NATURE

A CHRISTIAN SPIRITUALITY

H. PAUL SANTMIRE

Fortress Press
Minneapolis

BEFORE NATURE

A Christian Spirituality

Cover image: Wikimedia, Henry Clay Frick, Givoanni Bellini *Saint Francis in the Desert*

Cover design: Laurie Ingram

Library of Congress Cataloging-in-Publication Data

Print ISBN: 978-1-4514-7300-1

eBook ISBN: 978-1-4514-8431-1

The paper used in this publication meets the minimum requirements of American National Standard for Information Sciences — Permanence of Paper for Printed Library Materials, ANSI Z329.48-1984.

Manufactured in the U.S.A.

This book was produced using PressBooks.com, and PDF rendering was done by PrinceXML.

*To my children, Heather and Matthew, and
to my grandchildren, Kaitlyn, Maya, Althea, Maxwell, and Marlow*

The Trinity Prayer

Lord Jesus Christ, have mercy on me.

Praise Father, Son, and Holy Spirit.

Come Holy Spirit, Come and Reign.

CONTENTS

Prologue   xiii
*A Christian Spirituality of Nature for Today's Seekers and Their
Teachers and Pastors*

Part I. Considering the Journey

1. Blessedly Scything with God   3
   You Are Invited

2. Introducing a Way of Prayer   21
   The Practice and the Knowing of the Trinity Prayer

3. The World in Which We Pray   37
   The Eclipse of God and a Fragile Theology of Faith

Part II. The First Steps of the Journey

4. Praying to Jesus   53
   The Revelation of God and the Light of Christ

5. The Ambiguous Case of One Who Prays to Jesus   71
   The Twilight and the Encounter

Part III. Contemplating the Triune God

6. The Heart of the Trinity Prayer   97
   Contemplating the Mystery of the Triune God

7. The Presence of the Triune God in Nature   129
   Contemplating God in All Things

8. The Works of the Triune God in Nature   157
   *Contemplating the Cosmic Ministries of Jesus Christ and the Holy
   Spirit*

Part IV. Calling on the Holy Spirit

9. Calling on the Holy Spirit 187
   The Integrity and the Travail of Nature

10. Sauntering in the Spirit 217
    Practicing the Trinity Prayer

Epilogue 239
   The Trinity Prayer as Spiritual Exercise

Appendix 245
   Possible Seasonal Hymn Tunes for the Trinity Prayer

Index 247

Prologue

A Christian Spirituality of Nature for Today's Seekers and Their Teachers and Pastors

Ours is an era in which "the Nones" represent a growing segment of the U. S. population. As the time of this writing, almost a fifth of all Americans say that they have no religious affiliation. By a recent count, there were more Nones than mainstream Protestants, and it appears that their numbers will continue to grow for some time. About a third of the Nones are in their young adult years, with the highest percentage of them ages thirty to forty-nine. Although the Nones have distanced themselves from institutional religious affiliation, they have generally not abandoned the spiritual quest altogether. On the contrary, their spiritual lives overall seem to be alive and well, if not well defined.[1] Many of the Nones are exploring a variety of spiritual options, especially influences from Asian religions.[2]

In my experience, the Nones do not stand alone. *Within* our churches, as most theology teachers and pastoral practitioners know well, there exists a sizable group whose members are "Nones-Sympathizers." While these individuals still identify themselves with historic Christianity in general, they are more concerned with what they think of as spirituality and less interested in what they consider to be the external, religious expressions of Christianity, such as regular worship attendance. Sometimes, like their spiritual cousins the Nones, they look to Asian or Native American religions for inspiration alongside their primary Christian identification. Think of these Nones and the Nones-Sympathizers as *spiritual seekers*, a term well understood by the aforementioned teachers and practitioners.[3] Together, the Nones and Nones-Sympathizers represent a major and still growing constituency in American religious life today.

This poses a challenge for teachers of Christian theology and Christian pastoral practitioners, as most of them recognize. How can the faith claims of a traditional "religion" like Christianity be communicated—inside as well as outside the churches–to such seekers, a group that is downplaying, sometimes even rejecting, what its members consider to be the external, religious expressions of Christianity? Obviously, there is no simple and surely no single answer to that question. Theologians and pastoral practitioners have experimented with a variety of approaches to this challenge in recent years.[4]

A CHRISTIAN SPIRITUALITY OF NATURE AS COMMON GROUND

I would like to enter this discussion with a proposal of my own. It has to do with *nature*. Could the seekers both outside and inside our churches who are deeply concerned with spirituality, over against what they often perceive to be the arid world of religion, find common ground with the teaching theologians and pastoral practitioners, who are struggling to be faithful interpreters of the classical Christian tradition, in *a Christian spirituality of nature*?

Over the last four decades, as a college instructor, a traveling lecturer, and a practicing pastor, I have encountered an intense interest in nature on the part of a wide range of spiritual seekers, both within church settings and beyond. Long ago, I concluded that the spiritual quest in "the cathedral of the great outdoors" is alive and well, even flourishing.

I am thinking here not only of the deep attraction such spiritual seekers feel for wilderness and coastal areas but also of their more domestic ecological consciousness, expressed in their fascination with proposals for living "closer to the land" and their fondness for urban green places, for bike trails in and around metropolitan areas, for walking, for birding, for gardening, for farmers' markets that sell locally grown produce, for rooftop agriculture, and for organic foods. So it was no surprise for me to learn that, according to one recent study, more than half of the Nones surveyed said that they "often feel a deep connection with nature and the earth."[5] I have every reason to believe that that is true, perhaps all the more so, for the Nones-Sympathizers within our churches.

In the same vein, many spiritual seekers today, notwithstanding escapist tendencies in some quarters, also seem to be committed to political and economic campaigns in behalf of nature, particularly campaigns championing the causes of clean air, restored wetlands and grasslands, and an effective response to global warming. Many of these seekers are also involved in animal rights causes and vegetarianism. In a variety of ways, these seekers care deeply about nature and appear to be open to, if not self-consciously seeking, a spirituality that is engaged with nature.

At the same time, much as these spiritual seekers show signs of a deep-seated love for nature, most also appear to exhibit a deep suspicion of historic Christianity's attitudes toward nature. This suspicion is predicated on the assumption that Christianity not only has little of value to say about nature but also seems to be *hostile* toward nature, particularly toward the human body. How have these seekers arrived at such judgments? On the one hand, it is because those judgments are in some ways factually accurate: historic Christianity has had an ambiguous relationship with the world of nature and with the human body in particular.[6] On the other hand, for various reasons, what might be called the nature-friendly trends in historic Christian life and thought have not always been identified, much less celebrated, by interpreters of the Christian faith themselves, even by professional scholars. How then could grassroots spiritual seekers know about such trends?

Further, the voices of a range of Christian theologians who *have* been extensively involved in ecological theology and ecojustice ethics for the past five decades have simply not been taken seriously by many Christians at the grassroots level, again for various reasons.[7] As a result, what has been called "the ecological complaint against Christianity" (James Nash)—more about this later—has been widely and successfully propagated, even within some church circles. It is no wonder, then, that today's spiritual seekers, who themselves generally feel such a deep solidarity with nature, also regard historic Christianity with an equally profound suspicion. Nor is it any wonder that they have been absenting themselves in large numbers—psychologically if not also physically—from the great indoor cathedrals of their heritage in behalf of the cathedral of the great outdoors.

What if someone were to "attempt the impossible"? What if someone were to show how it is possible to stand in two places at once, to be *bifocal*? By this I refer not to eyeglasses but to the root meaning of the word, having *two foci*. What if we were to imagine the cathedral of the great outdoors engulfing, surrounding, embracing the cathedral of Christian practices, and imagine ourselves standing at the entrance of that Christian cathedral, contemplating the vastness and the mystery and the beauty of the world of nature before and all around us in the cathedral of the great outdoors?

THE LEGACY OF ST. FRANCIS

I have in mind here the justly famous painting by Giovanni Bellini, *St. Francis in Ecstasy* (1480), which I have contemplated many times in the Frick Collection, in New York City, and which I have chosen as the cover of this book.[8] In this painting, Francis has apparently just emerged from a rustic shed nestled in the bedrock of a cliff. Francis's own book, perhaps the book of scriptural readings for the Mass, is on the lectern behind him. He is surrounded by the fecund beauties of the Tuscan landscape and its many creatures——including a rabbit, a heron, a donkey, a flock of sheep, and a lovely laurel tree, whose form mimics the shape of Francis's own body——all transcendentally illuminated by the rays of the sun. Francis himself stands in a kind of cruciform position, with his arms extended horizontally in prayer and his hands showing the stigmata (the wounds of Christ) that he had miraculously received, according to traditional testimony. Francis's eyes are evidently open, as he contemplates the sun, basking in its light, and his lips appear to be moving, as if he is singing.

While we cannot read the mind of Bellini at this point, of course, it appears that he might well have wanted to suggest that Francis, who had been stigmatized by the cross of Christ, has just emerged from his cavelike retreat, as from a kind of spiritual womb, an experience that now allows Francis to see the whole creation with new eyes. If that is, as it appears to be, how Francis's stance is to be read at this point, Bellini's assumption would almost certainly also have been that Francis was there singing the saint's celebrated Canticle of Brother Sun—generally known as the Canticle of the Creatures—which addresses the sun at the very beginning.[9] The received story of Francis's life, which would have been well-known to Bellini, came to its conclusion in two great ecstatic moments: Francis receiving the stigmata and, later, Francis, close to death, creating and thereafter singing his Canticle of Brother Sun and singing it often.[10] That is the kind of bifocal standpoint—behind Francis the book of the scriptural readings and the cave of spiritual death and rebirth, and before him the glorious book of nature—that I am presupposing in this narrative.[11] Francis celebrated the cathedral of the great outdoors, and at the same time he, who made every effort to partake of the Mass every day after his conversion, lived by the revelation he found indoors in the cathedral—or the cave—of Christian practices.[12]

This is what I hope to do in this book: to show before your very eyes (*ad oculos*) that a bifocal Christian spirituality like Francis's is not only possible in our day but even compelling, following in the footsteps of Francis. I propose to do this in a way that speaks simultaneously to two audiences: on the one hand, the spiritual seekers of our time, both outside and inside our churches, who are taken both by spirituality and by nature, and, on the other hand, the cadre of theology teachers and pastoral practitioners who are seeking to enter into conversation with those seekers. I suggest that the two groups can meet amicably and even ecstatically at the place where Francis stands, in a Christian spirituality of nature.

My method will be personal, as any spirituality must be, and bifocal, as this particular spirituality must definitely be. This is the legacy of St. Francis, for me. I want to show my readers that it is not only possible but also possibly enchanting to stand in this one place where the cathedral of the great outdoors and the cathedral of historic Christianity are one world. To the seekers, I will be saying: come walk with me in this enchanted place so that I might show you around. You may be astounded by the spiritual riches you will discover.

To the theology teachers and pastoral practitioners, I will be saying: come along after us and observe us, look over our shoulders, in this enchanted place. See what we are seeing. And then consider whether walking in this place in this way makes sense to you, with a view to your own conversations with the seekers of this world. As you join in this journey, perhaps you will want to revisit your own spirituality along the way. If you do not wish to follow the particular path that I will be exploring, what spirituality of nature will you propose? And how will you communicate that spirituality to the seekers with whom you are in conversation, both outside and inside the church?

THE MEANINGS OF "BEFORE NATURE"

To prepare the way now for the bifocal Franciscan explorations before us, I want to describe in more detail where I am coming from, both professionally and personally, as well as more specifically what this particular book is and what it is not.

As I remember my life, I have always stood *Before Nature*, engaged with nature, as my title for this book suggests. I have been moved, at various times and places, to contemplate the material-vital world of God's good creation, its integrity, its beauties, its terrors, and its mysteries. I recount many such moments of contemplation in this book, beginning with my discussion in chapter 1, "Blessedly Scything with God." Not only have I regularly and, often, passionately stood before nature in contemplation, but I have also written about what I have seen. Five of my six books, starting with my 1970 volume, *Brother Earth: Nature, God, and Ecology in a Time of Crisis*, have been preoccupied with the theology of nature.[13] This current book brings that theological preoccupation full circle, but it does so by stepping back into my own interiority. Thus, it is *Before Nature* in a second—spiritual—sense as well.

In this book, as I stand before nature, contemplating its integrity, its beauties, its terrors, and its mysteries, including the delights and the frailties of my own body and the particular configurations of my own environmental settings, I am preoccupied not with what I see, as such, but with "the eye of the beholder." I reflect about the fragile faith—as I will call it—of the one who has contemplated the world of nature for so long and with such rapt attention.

I explore this fragile faith *before* it consciously connects with nature. This book, in a word, is self-reflective. It is not primarily an account of the objects of my contemplation and all of the related issues, as were my other works on nature. Rather, this book is a spiritual testament.

As such, this book has a particular angle of vision. It tells my own interior story, a story that has been thoroughly nurtured, for better or for worse, by the classical Christian tradition. Hence my subtitle: *A Christian Spirituality*. Everyone has some kind of a spiritual standpoint, and this happens to be mine. To tell the story of my own interiority, I must tell the story of my own particular faith.

I celebrate that faith in its fullness. My father used to say to me, "When you take hold of the rug, you take hold of the whole rug." Similarly, for me, to take hold of a spirituality of nature is, as a matter of course, to take hold of the whole Christian tradition, the faith and life of the Christian church throughout the ages to the present. In my view, there is no such thing as an independent, self-contained Christian spirituality of nature. Hence, readers of this book will encounter a steady stream of reflection about what may be familiar Christian theological and spiritual themes, including, above all, the focus on the classical Christian prayer to God as Father, Son, and Holy Spirit—notwithstanding the problematic shape of some Trinitarian spiritualities.[14] The core of this book is reflection about what I call—and what I want to commend to the reader—"the Trinity Prayer." In some portions of this book, you will find that the theme of nature is muted. This is not a book on nature in the sense that it is the explicit topic on every page.

Hence, well-recognized theological themes *will* permeate the following narrative. For this reason, readers who have little or no theological background may find a few parts of the trail before us a little steep. I hope such readers will do what a good mountain guide once advised me to do: just put one foot in front of the other, and when we get there, it will have been worth it. My intent in this book, in other words, is not to detour around theological essentials, such as the Trinity, however complex or even obscure they might appear to be at the start, but to explore those parts of the trail as carefully and as clearly as I can, precisely because they are essential to the whole story. I own up to this explicit theological orientation at the start, since popular books on the spirituality of nature often tend to avoid or downplay traditional theological language, for reasons that I can understand but which will not work for me. If I were not so explicitly theological, I would not be addressing one of the major purposes of this book: to show that a bifocal Christian spirituality is possible, one that arises from a single place but with dual foci, the cathedral of the great outdoors encompassing the cathedral of historic Christianity.

At the same time, it is important for me to tell the story of my own spiritual passion for *nature* from my own spiritual angle of vision, since many in this generation of seekers are asking whether a viable Christian spirituality of nature, informed by the classical theological tradition, is available or even possible. Emphatically, I believe it is.[15] In this respect, this book stands in continuity with most of my other writings, which have been preoccupied with nature. In the following pages, nature is always on my mind and in my heart, even in the midst of discussions where it may not be mentioned. This book is intended to be a Christian *spirituality of nature* as well as a *Christian spirituality* of nature.[16]

This means, furthermore, that I will *not* explore a whole range of other topics, as I would want to do if I were attempting to offer a more complete account of the fragile faith that so inspires me. Thus, I will consider in detail how, for me, God is present (immanent) in nature, but I will only allude to God's more particular involvement in the dynamics of human history. Likewise, I will accent concrete experiences, such as beholding the lilies of the field, but I will bracket any detailed account of what it means for me to speak with an inmate whom I'm visiting in prison. I will also celebrate the human body, which is essentially immersed in the world of nature, but I won't explore at length "the long struggle to be at home in the body, this difficult friendship."[17]

A SPIRITUALITY OF PLACE

The world of nature, as I have experienced it spiritually, will not only be my chief concern but will also shape how my narrative unfolds. Throughout my life, the natural settings in which I have found myself have always been players or characters in their own right rather than merely some kind of scenery. All my life I have been preoccupied with the natural world as a lived-in experience. Hence, I can only tell my own spiritual story in terms of such settings.

In recent years, I have found a similar self-reflective focus on natural locations in the works of some concerned with *the spirituality of place*.[18] This theme not only offers a language for narrating my own experience but also provides a necessary corrective for anyone, like myself, who is navigating in the currents of historic Christian spirituality, which all too often have pulled the faithful into the interior life, away from the larger stream of experience in and with the natural world, to the disservice of the spiritual life itself.[19]

This is one reason, I now realize after many years, why I have long been haunted by Henry David Thoreau.[20] Thoreau instinctively felt the valence of place. For him, walking, in particular, was a sacred discipline.[21] True, Thoreau never understood how walking in a place like Boston can be just as enlightening as walking in the environs of a Walden Pond. Even less was Thoreau able to imagine how revelatory one's walking in a church procession in a city like Boston might be. But the spirituality of walking—of living in a place and exploring a place and in some sense being at home in a place—is the critical point here. Hence, in the following pages, I will invite the reader to come walking with me, to visit different places of my own experience that have been crucial in my own spiritual life over the years.

A Narrative of Affection, Anxiety, and Vocation

This book is dedicated to my children and my grandchildren, out of great and heartfelt affection, of course, but with a deeper purpose, too. Consider my children, Heather and Matthew, first. By my own reckoning, both are spiritual seekers, albeit in different ways. Both are persons of good character who care about the disenfranchised and about the good earth. On the other hand, both have for many years, if not always, distanced themselves from historic Christian practices. In this sense, they represent one of my two target audiences: the seekers. In this book, I will be conversing publicly with my two children in a way that I have *not* done with them privately. For what are probably understandable reasons, I have never sat them down and explained my own spiritual story: what has kept their father so fixed—fixated, they might have thought now and again—on the world of nature and at the same time so earnestly engaged with the practices of the church. Here follows, then, dear children, that very long conversation in my study that you never had to have with me. I hope you will come along with me on this journey, whenever you are ready to do so.

And my grandchildren? Most of them are not old enough, as of this writing, to read a book like this. But I have their futures in mind. I am imagining them picking up this book in years to come, after they have come of age intellectually, and after they may have heard that their grandfather had dedicated his last book to them, along with their parents. Each may wonder, as he or she holds this book in hand, why this grandfather was so spiritually preoccupied with nature. When that day comes for each of them, I fully anticipate that questions about the spirituality of nature will still be alive in their world, probably more acutely so than today. So I do indeed write this book for them, as well as for their parents, and with much affection.

I also write this book for them with some anxiety. As I now am about to tell the story of my own spiritual engagement with nature, I have noticed that some of them who are old enough to be up and about by themselves have already fallen in love with "the great outdoors," particularly as they have experienced that world in the rural locale in southwestern Maine that I will describe in chapter 1. But I am well aware that they soon will be subjected to strong counterforces, if they have not already encountered them, cultural trends that push children closer and closer to what has been called "nature deficit disorder."[22] According to a recent study by the Kaiser Family Foundation, children in this country ages eight to eighteen spend some *seven-and-a-half hours a day* inside, occupied with electronic media, not playing or otherwise occupied outside. Some evidence also shows that the nature deficit disorder that typically coincides with such habits is not good for their physical or mental health. Nor, in my mind, can it be good for their spiritual health. Will my grandchildren be able to resist such trends and therefore find themselves continually fascinated with the cathedral of the great outdoors? I hope so. And I hope that this book will help them to do that, as they continue to grow in wisdom and in stature.

Furthermore, I write for my children and my grandchildren, and indeed for all of my readers, with a profound sense of urgency. In these times, anyone who cares about the good earth and the poor of the earth must be similarly driven, since the global crisis before us all is so severe and the available options for addressing that crisis so limited. Now, perhaps as never before, is the time for resolute action in behalf of the earth and the poor of the earth. We are facing what NASA scientist James Hansen called a "planetary emergency."

Arguably, therefore, my own lifelong spiritual engagement with nature should at this moment be taking me away from my writing out to the streets, where numbers in my generation ended up during the memorable days of the civil rights movement of the 1960s in the United States. The prophetic environmentalist and theologian Bill McKibben has called on people like me to do precisely that (as he has also shown himself willing to do) because the time for the human species to address the issues of climate change and other related issues is so short, if not already past.[23] I may yet end up out in the streets wearing my clerical collar, with the likes of a Bill McKibben, as I have done before. People in my age bracket, who now are a part of what we used to call "the Establishment," *can* do that kind of street work with some effectiveness, once we have resolved to "put our bodies on the line," to invoke another phrase from the sixties.

But the civil rights movement taught me this, too: we must do everything at once. What if a sizable number of the 2.1 billion Christians on this earth could learn to *love nature* the way that the eminent Christian ethicist James Nash called us to do in 1991?[24] That could make a huge difference in global climate change politics, especially if many American Christians were numbered among them, given the fact that the United States is one of the world's leading climate change offenders. So, whatever else I may feel called upon to do in this era of near-apocalyptic uncertainty, I believe that I must also tend to my own interior garden: to continue, and in some measure to complete, what has been a long-standing vocation for me, laboring in the field of the theology of nature, to try to show my readers why and how they are called, as I believe I have been called, to love nature.

RETROSPECT AND PROSPECT

I offer three last comments now, as we make ready for the first steps of the bifocal explorations before us. First, I know that one is never supposed to say "never," but I am now in my late seventies and this book has the feel of my last. It therefore offers me a kind of closure for more than four decades of writing in this field as well as for just as long of an engagement in random acts of public advocacy in behalf of the earth and the poor of the earth. Hence, I am eager to acknowledge here the names of all those who have helped to make my vocational trajectory possible, including numerous family members, friends, students, teachers, professional colleagues, parishioners, editors, and other coconspirators in many good causes over the years. But I am not going to mention all your names. Such a list would be long indeed. Rather, I must be content here with a generic thank you to all concerned. You know who you are. I am most grateful for your encouragement, your companionship, your insights, and your occasional stubborn insistence on changes in my ways or my thoughts or my wordings. And, of course, I hope that you will read every page of this book, and take it personally, along with everyone else.

Second, I want to address the length of this book. You won't read this volume from beginning to end while you're waiting at the airport for your next flight. The story I want to tell in the terms of my own experience is a long and sometimes challenging narrative. It will take awhile and will require intense effort at points. In some respects, this book is much more like a trek in the mountains than a walk in the park. So I ask you, right from the start, to think about the journey on which we are about to embark in terms not only of Thoreau's penchant for walking but also of Thoreau's onetime commitment to climb Mount Katahdin, Maine's highest peak. This, for better or for worse, is the only way I know how to tell my own personal story.

Third, and finally, I want to note the format of this book. As I explain in chapter 1, I understand spirituality to be *a religious experience that is intense and transforming*. That is what this book is about. That is its character. This book *is* spirituality. It's a personal exploration of faith. It's a confessional expression of a particular constellation of experiences. It is *not* a scholarly study of spirituality.

On the other hand, readers will encounter occasional endnotes, a practice that might be taken to suggest that what follows is *not* the personal narrative I intend it to be. Many books of spirituality do not have endnotes (imagine finding endnotes, say, in Augustine's *Confessions*). Hence, I want to emphasize at the outset that I intend the scattered endnotes along the way to be read as *extensions* of my personal spiritual narrative, as side trips, which I have added to the itinerary to give readers additional options for reflection. I am thinking here especially of the second group of readers whom I am addressing in this book, those who are currently theology students or practicing pastors or seminary faculty or college religion teachers, many of whom will have a passion for such off-the-trail adventures. But other readers, I anticipate, will be perfectly content to go with the main flow of the narrative and to pass by the endnotes. Either way, I will be grateful for your company.

Notes

1. See "Nones on the Rise," *Pew Forum on Religion and the Public Life*, October 9, 2012, http://www.pewforum.org/2012/10/09/nones-on-the-rise/ (consulted February 14, 2013): "A new survey by the Pew Research Center's Forum on Religion & Public Life, conducted jointly with the PBS television program Religion & Ethics News Weekly, finds that many of the country's 46 million unaffiliated adults are religious or spiritual in some way. Two-thirds of them say they believe in God (68%). More than half say they often feel a deep connection with nature and the earth (58%), while more than a third classify themselves as 'spiritual' but not 'religious' (37%), and one-in-five (21%) say they pray every day. In addition, most religiously unaffiliated Americans think that churches and other religious institutions benefit society by strengthening community bonds and aiding the poor." For a thorough analysis of such trends, see Robert D. Putnam and David E. Campbell, *American Grace: How Religion Divides and Unites Us* (New York: Simon & Schuster, 2010).

2. See Peter Berger, "The Religiously Unaffiliated in America" (blog post), March 21, 2012, http://www.the-american-interest.com/berger/2012/03/21/the-religiously-unaffiliated-in-america (consulted January 15, 2013): "The bulk of the 'nones' probably consist of a mix of two categories of unaffiliated believers—in the words of the British sociologist Grace Davie, people who 'believe without belonging.' There are those who have put together an idiosyncratic personal creed, putting together bits and pieces of their own tradition with other components. Robert Wuthnow, the most productive and insightful sociologist of American religion, has called this 'patchwork religion.' This includes the kind of people who will say 'I am Catholic, *but* . . .,' followed by a list of

items where they differ from the teachings of the church. The other category are the children—by now, grandchildren—of the counter-culture. They will most often say, 'I am spiritual, not religious.' The 'spirituality' is typically an expression of what Colin Campbell, another British sociologist, has called 'Easternization'—an invasion of Western civilization by beliefs and practices from Asia. A few of these are organized, for instance by the various Buddhist schools. But most are diffused in an informal manner—such as belief in reincarnation or the spiritual continuity between humans and nature, and practices like yoga or martial arts."

3. The best single scholarly treatment of the multifaceted faith(s) of these seekers is probably the widely read study by Robert Wuthnow, *After Heaven: Spirituality in America since the 1950s* (Berkeley: University of California Press, 1998). While very much aware of the sometimes superficial, "super-market" character of the seeker's quest (as implied by Peter Berger; see the previous note), Wuthnow also identifies a deeper authenticity in the quest of many seekers (3): "A traditional spirituality of inhabiting sacred places has given way to a new spirituality of seeking—that people have been losing faith in a metaphysic that can make them feel at home in the universe and that they increasingly negotiate among competing notions of the sacred, seeking partial knowledge and practical wisdom." And (4): "A spirituality of seeking is tabernacle religion, the faith of pilgrims and sojourners; it clings to the Diaspora and to the prophets and judges, rather than to priests and kings. . . . The one is symbolized by the secure life of the monastery, the cloister, the shtetl, the other by peregination as a spiritual ideal."

4. In my judgment, the popular works of the highly sophisticated and knowledgeable Catholic Elizabeth A. Johnson are exemplary in this respect. She knows how to give voice to the classical Christian narrative in a way that is both substantive *and* responsive to the questions of many seekers. See, for example, her religious bestseller *Consider Jesus: Waves of Renewal in Christology* (New York: Crossroad, 1990). In the arena of pastoral praxis, a variety of "seeker sensitive" congregations have been launched in recent decades, the best known of them perhaps being Willowcreek Community Church, an independent Protestant megachurch in South Barrington, Illinois, near Chicago. Founded in 1975 by the Rev. William Hybels, the church has been averaging a weekly worship attendance of some twenty-four thousand in recent years. Hybels has championed a two-stage approach to reaching out to seekers: first, often dramatic, professionally choreographed, and highly personalized "seeker sensitive" worship services, and second, a carefully organized ministry of small groups geared to instruct and nurture the seekers who are attracted to its worship services. Many other, smaller "seeker sensitive" congregations have also been developed. A good example of the latter is the "Spirit Garage" in Minneapolis, Minnesota, which meets not in a traditional church building but in the "Music Box Theater." It advertises itself as a church yet "not as an organization, institution, or place" but, rather, as a gathering of "people following Jesus." Visitors report that the Spirit Garage is a kind of "funky" place, with "hip music," issue-oriented sermons, and a worshiping congregation of great diversity. Deeply buried in its website is the information that this church maintains ties to the five-million-member mainline denomination the Evangelical Lutheran Church in America (ELCA), insofar as its pastor is ordained in the ELCA, and that its ministry is sponsored financially by Bethlehem Lutheran Church of South Minneapolis (an affluent ELCA congregation).

5. See note 1, above.

6. I trace historic Christianity's sometimes problematic attitudes toward nature in my book *The Travail of Nature: The Ambiguous Ecological Promise of Christian Theology* (Minneapolis: Fortress Press, 1985).

7. I review these developments in Christian ecological theology and ecojustice ethics in my book *Nature Reborn: The Ecological and Cosmic Promise of Christian Theology* (Minneapolis: Fortress Press, 2000), 6–15.

8. The painting is also sometimes, albeit confusedly, referred to as "St. Francis in the Desert."

9. From Francis of Assisi, the Canticle of Brother Sun: "All praise be yours, my Lord, through all that you have made, / And first my lord Brother Sun, / Who brings the day; and the light you give to us through him. / How beautiful is he, how radiant in all his splendour! / Of you,

Most High, he bears the likeness." The Canticle here is translated by Eloi Leclerc, *The Canticle of Creatures—Symbols of Union: An Analysis of St. Francis of Assisi*, trans. Matthew J. O'Connell (Chicago: Franciscan Herald Press, 1977), xvii.

10. For more about the meanings implicit in what I call "the Francis event," see my discussion in *The Travail of Nature*, 106–19. For an insightful interpretation of the Canticle of Brother Sun, see the discussion by Leclerc, *The Canticle of Creatures*, especially vii–xi. For a fresh treatment of Francis's life, see Augustine Thompson, *Francis of Assisi: A New Biography* (Ithaca, NY: Cornell University Press, 2012). For insight into possible symbolic meanings of the Bellini painting itself (e.g., the city at the horizon possibly representing, for Bellini, the heavenly Jerusalem), see H. W. Janson and Anthony F. Janson, *History of Art*, 6th ed. (New York: Henry M. Abrams, 2001), 427–28.

11. Whatever else it might mean, the skull on the lectern behind Francis may well have been intended by Bellini to allude to the traditional baptismal theme—here accented by the stigmata reference—of dying with Christ in order to rise again with Christ.

12. Thompson, *Francis of Assisi*, 61, states the matter quite sharply: "The locus of Francis's 'mysticism,' his belief that he could have direct contact with God, was in the Mass, not in nature or even in service to the poor." But that, I think, is to *overstate* the point. The Mass and all that it implies, especially the humiliation of the incarnate Son of God, surely *is* a locus of Francis's mysticism, but Francis's encounter with the world of nature is *also* a locus of his mysticism. Francis's mysticism was bifocal, as the Bellini painting suggests. See also the remarks of LeClerc, *The Canticle of Creatures*, xii, commenting on the vision espoused by that historic poem:

> There can be no question . . . of playing down the properly cosmic, realistic aspect of the text. To do so would be to go counter to everything we know about Francis's attitude to creatures. His love for them was real, deep, and religious. In his eyes, each of them in its own way and by its very being was a manifestation of the power or the beauty or the goodness of the Most High, and the manifestation sometimes caused him to fall into ecstacy. There can be no doubt that Francis experienced the sacred in the cosmos and entered into communion with God through the medium of created things and indeed in the very depth of created things. It is this aspect of his religious experience that the *Canticle of Brother Sun* expresses.Real though it is, however, this aspect of his experience cannot be separated from another: his union with God along the lowly ways established by the incarnation of the Most High Son of God. In fact, all that is original in Francis' religious experience derives from the synthesis he effected between an interior and very personal evangelical mysticism and an ardent cosmic mysticism. Francis unites, in a wonderful way, a life of union with the person of Christ and the profound religious feeling [which] pantheistic religions entertain toward the cosmos. He unites the Sun and the Cross.

This bifocal spirituality (my term) of Francis is strikingly reflected *in Francis's own language*, as LeClerc points out (*The Canticle of the Creatures*, 76). Throughout his career, Francis was preoccupied with a campaign to instill ecclesial respect for the reserved elements of the Mass, for him, the Body and Blood of Christ. He regularly calls the place for that reservation "precious." He uses the same term several times in *The Canticle of Brother Sun* to refer to various creatures, whom he is calling to praise God. As LeClerc comments: "In Francis' writings, the 'precious' quality of things emerges in close relation with a sacred reality. . . . In using the adjective 'precious' in his Canticle and applying it to the moon and the stars, Francis is giving these cosmic elements a religious value and telling us that for him these cosmic elements have power to express the sacred or constitute a language for uttering the sacred."

13. *Brother Earth: Nature, God, and Ecology in a Time of Crisis* (New York: Thomas Nelson, 1970); *The Travail of Nature: The Ambiguous Ecological Promise of Christian Theology* (Minneapolis: Fortress Press, 1985); *Nature Reborn: The Ecological and Cosmic Promise of Christian Theology* (Minneapolis: Fortress Press, 2000); *Ritualizing Nature: Renewing Christian Liturgy in a Time of Crisis* (Minneapolis: Fortress Press, 2008). I recount the story of these publications in my theological autobiography: "Ecology, Justice, Liturgy," in *Theologians in Their Own Words,* ed. Derek R. Nelson, Joshua M. Moritz, and Ted Peters (Minneapolis: Fortress Press, 2012), 217–32.

14. Later in this book, I will discuss at some length in what sense it is possible to affirm a postpatriarchal understanding of the Trinity, particularly of God the Father.

15. In my book *The Travail of Nature,* I identify two major trends in historic Christian thought about nature, what I call "the spiritual motif" and "the ecological motif." In worldviews shaped by the former, nature tends to be left behind in the quest for God. In worldviews shaped by the latter, nature is always at the heart of things: God is to be found in, with, and under nature. My discussion in this book takes the critical importance of the ecological motif in Christian life and thought for granted. The spirituality I am talking about in this book is down-to-earth; it is ecological. It is a spirituality that has eschewed "the spiritual motif" of rising above nature as I described that motif in *The Travail of Nature.*

16. Works on nature and spirituality abound, many bookshelves of them, written from theological, metaphysical, ecological, literary, historical, phenomenological, interreligious, and many other perspectives. But books that approach this theme *self-consciously from the particular angle of the classical Christian tradition* are relatively rare. Among the best of the latter is Steven Chase's richly rewarding study *Nature as Spiritual Practice* (Grand Rapids, MI: Eerdmans, 2011). This work and my own here might be read as complementary explorations, perhaps as friendly amendments to each other. See, further, Steven Chase's companion volume, *A Field Guide to Nature as Spiritual Practice* (Grand Rapids, MI: Eerdmans, 2011).

17. Jane Kenyon, quoted in Stephanie Paulsell, *Honoring the Body: Meditations on a Christian Practice* (San Francisco: Jossey-Bass, 2002), xiii. Paulsell's book is a good place to begin focused spiritual reflections about the meaning of the human body.

18. For an entrance into this discussion, see the comprehensive study by Craig G. Bartholomew, *Where Mortals Dwell: A Christian View of Place for Today* (Grand Rapids, MI: Baker Academic, 2011), and the literature to which Bartholomew refers. More generally, see Steven Bouma-Prediger and Brian J. Walsh, *Beyond Homelessness: Christian Faith in a Culture of Displacement* (Grand Rapids, MI: Eerdmans, 2008). For the increasingly popular "agrarian" understanding of the theology of place, see Norman Wirzba, *The Paradise of God: Renewing Religion in an Ecological Age* (New York: Oxford University Press, 2003); and for my own take on that approach, see my review of Wirzba's book: "Farming for God," *Christian Century* (December 27, 2003), 23–25.

19. In an early writing, the *Soliloquies* (1.2.7), St. Augustine famously stated that he desired to know *only God and the soul.* In later writings, however, Augustine had many good things to say about God and the beauties of the whole creation. In ensuing centuries, during which Augustine's theology became enormously influential, the focus of the early Augustine on God and the soul alone, over against the rest of God's creation, was highly influential. Some, however, above all St. Francis and his followers, like St. Bonaventure, held the inward and the outward spiritual ways together in a mutually reinforcing balance. For them, it was not God and the soul that was the spiritual center, but God and the soul in the midst of the whole creation. For a review of such trends, see Santmire, *Travail of Nature,* chaps. 4–6.

20. Thoreau figured prominently in my 1970 book, *Brother Earth.*

21. Henry David Thoreau, *Walking* (Memphis: Bottom of the Hill Publishing, 2011).

22. Richard Louv, *The Last Child in the Woods: Saving Our Children from Nature Deficit Disorder* (Chapel Hill, NC: Algonquin Books, 2005).

23. See Bill McKibben, "Disobedience: Direct Action on Global Warming," *Christian Century* 128, no. 1 (January 11, 2011): 10–11.

24. James Nash, *Loving Nature: Ecological Integrity and Christian Responsibility* (Nashville: Abingdon; in cooperation with the Church's Center for Theology and Public Policy, Washington, DC, 1991).

PART I

Considering the Journey

1

Blessedly Scything with God
You Are Invited

During the journey before us, I want to take you to many ordinary places. This story begins in a field at Hunts Corner, in rural, southwestern Maine, in the foothills of New Hampshire's White Mountains. For me, this is a place of knowing. I invite you to join me in that field.

BLESSEDLY SCYTHING WITH GOD: A PLACE OF KNOWING

My grandchildren who are old enough to be aware of such things know that I love to scythe. My children know that for sure. They all have seen me swinging my scythe out on the backfield that separates our plain nineteenth-century farmhouse from the wooded slopes beyond. Every fall, I scythe that swath of variously sized and elegantly configured ferns and purple asters and goldenrod and yarrow and meadow rue and daisies and black-eyed Susans and evening primroses and the differentiated patches of stunning grasses and the innumerable seedlings of white pine, ash, maple, birch, and meadowsweet—and I do so with a passion.

Why this passion for scything? The exercise itself, to begin with, is good. I work hard to take care of this tired old body. There is something, too, about scything that focuses the mind and quiets the heart, notwithstanding all of the physical effort required. In fields that have not been tilled for many years, such as ours, the scyther must carefully attend to the sometimes bulging contours of the land, so as not to jam the carefully sharpened blade into the coarse, rocky soil. As one attains a rhythm with the swinging scythe, one must see through the jungle of plants in front of one's feet and adjust the course of the scythe in flight, so as to be able to cut the plants as closely as possible to the earth and yet to avoid that jarring experience, that dull thud, that clanking, which results from faulty swings when the blade jams into the soil. When the swing is right, however, and the blade is sharp, the cutting feels effortless. In my experience, the scyther is then attuned to the rhythm of the field. Such moments always leave me contented. But there are other benefits of scything, too.

Scything keeps our backfield from turning into part of the forest, as it would quickly do without that kind of yearly attention. I do not mean to demean the forest by any means. The trees on those slopes north of our field have their own awesome standing, without a doubt, especially the colossal, hundred-year-old white pines. Over the years, some of us have explored the edges of those woods, which sweep far beyond our property to the north. One time, my wife, Laurel, and I took our two kids—then not yet teenagers—in tow and ventured up into the heart of the forest. With compass in hand, we bushwhacked our way to the top of neighboring Round Mountain, a small hill compared to the Presidential Mountains twenty miles to the west but still a remarkable capsule of wilderness in its own right, with no trails at that time or logging roads. That adventure, modest as it was, tested the four of us and inspired us for the better part of a day, particularly when we contemplated the vistas of the westerly mountains from a break in the trees near the summit.

Family members and friends know, too, that I have carved out some ascending and descending trails along the edge of the woods at the base of Round Mountain. I love to walk there, and to think about what lies beyond and above. For me, that forest has its own compelling majesty.

But the field has its particular kind of meaning, too, which I want to help preserve. Hence, my scything. Without that work, the forest would overtake the field in no time—with ash trees, for example. During the first few weeks of the spring following my fall scything, hundreds of ash seedlings soon sprout up to a height of maybe ten inches. They are already tiny trees by the time the next fall rolls around. So, if you want to have a field, as I do, you must care for it, lest the forest take over.

The field as I see it—a thought that reflects the perspective of some New England transcendentalists—mediates between our house, on the one hand, with its perennial and vegetable gardens and its modest lawns, and the forest beyond, on the other hand, where one can catch signs of the bears and moose and foxes and other creatures of the wilds that sometimes edge their ways toward our house, or where one can contemplate the red-tailed hawks and the crows, the swallows and the goldfinches, the hummingbirds and the doves, the grouse and the wild turkeys, and the occasional purple grosbeak or downy woodpecker, all of which soar above or fly nearby or otherwise announce their presence from time to time. A few years ago, up the hill road about a mile from our house, my daughter even encountered a lynx. That great cat was crossing our road as my daughter drove along at dusk. She was dumbfounded. As she slowed her car and watched, that astounding creature stopped and looked back at her for a moment before disappearing into the woods. The whole area where I scythe is a rich meeting place for many creatures, myself included.

I will not say much about other creatures from the wild side of things that occasionally invade what we like to think of as *our* space on *our* side of the field, including the deer that sometimes blatantly stand there in mutual contemplation with us as they munch our hostas, and the woodchucks that devour too many of our kohl seedlings and delphinium buds (over the course of one summer, I caught three woodchucks in our have-a-heart trap as well as a cat; one other summer I caught a skunk), and the raccoons that feast on our corn the day before we intend to harvest it.

I don't want to have to tell you about the vicious thoughts that sometimes occupy my mind when I witness what I consider the havoc those wild animals wreak on *our* gardens—thoughts that do not fit well with the image of the gentle grandfather that I like to believe my grandchildren hold. Notwithstanding my occasionally violent thoughts about such "invaders," though, I do love the field, as well as the woods beyond. So I scythe the field once a year in contentment, not just for the exercise but also for the sake of reaffirming its right to be and its larger meanings.

THE DARKER SIDE OF SCYTHING

Scything brings with it more than good exercise and the preservation of beautiful spaces between our house and the woods. You need to understand this, if you don't already. In our part of the world, the scyther must contend with blackflies or mosquitoes or ticks, all messengers of pain in their own ways, depending on the season and the rain. Once, more ominously, my scythe dislodged a nest of mud daubers, a kind of wasp that is called a black-faced hornet by the locals, tucked at the base of some high, thick grass. When I instantly realized what I had done, it was already too late. They were upon me in droves.

In response, I ran faster than I think I have ever run, at least since the days I played soccer in high school. I ran as urgently as I did not only to avoid the onslaught of the wasp stings, which already were painful enough, but also to save my life. Many years before, when I was in my thirties, I had been stung on my leg by three such creatures in a New Hampshire forest and had had to limp back to my car and drive to an emergency room, twenty miles away, in shock. I could have died, due to what I learned for the first time to be a severe allergy to insect bites. So, as I ran away from those mud daubers whose hive I had unknowingly sliced in half with my scythe, I was well aware that that dash of mine to safety might have been (but, thankfully, was not) my last. In this respect, in addition to the good exercise and honoring the integrity of the field, scything also keeps me honest about the world of nature. All of the wonderful creatures of God's good earth are not always our friends. Only people who never leave their homes or their automobiles or their offices can believe such a fantasy.

This brings me to a still darker truth that I sometimes ponder while I am scything, with particular reference to *our* field. We call that field "the pipeline." For me, that bland expression is not bland at all. It affects my consciousness like the thunder and lightning that occasionally roll over our house and gardens and the field and on into the woods beyond and above. Our field covers, in very small measure, a pipeline that day and night delivers oil hundreds of miles from Portland, Maine, to Montreal, Canada. Sometimes helicopters from the pipeline company shatter the silence of the field as they roar by at low altitudes and high speeds, inspecting that pipeline. It can be frightening. So, on any given day as I scythe, I think of that fateful black gold pulsing through the pipe buried beneath my feet, and I realize how deeply my own world in rural Maine is bound up with the dynamics of globalized industrial society everywhere, with the threats and the realities of warfare in the Middle East, in particular, and with global warming, more generally.

An image then sometimes hovers over my mind, especially in the aftermath of one of those helicopter flyovers: the grim reaper of death of course carries a scythe! Forces are at work around the globe in our times that threaten the very existence of human life on this planet and the lives of many other creatures as well. Don't those forces—which New Testament Christians thought of as the "principalities and powers" of death—dwarf in significance anything that transpires in one minuscule life like mine, hidden away at times out in the field and surrounded by what some think of as nature's "pristine beauty"? What is my scything, however good and beautiful it might be in my own eyes, and by extension for the lives of those near and dear to me, compared to that global scything by those principalities and powers?

Still, I typically scythe in peace—how this is humanly possible in these times of global crisis and cosmic alienation is one of the underlying themes of this book—and I hope to continue to do so as long as I have the strength that this idiosyncratic practice requires, because when I scythe, in addition to everything else, beyond the good and the beautiful and the ominous and the portentous, I am blessedly engaged with *God* in nature. As I look down the sloping field as it flows westward toward a valley, beyond which the White Mountains—some of the oldest of this nation—rise into view, and as I then lift up my eyes to those mountains themselves—especially on a clear fall day, when the bright colors of the maples and birches and beeches and the more somber hues of the oaks stand over against the dark figures of the white pines and the hemlocks—I see the grandeur of God.

SCYTHING AND GARDENING

There is more. My family members have seen me raking up all those cuttings from the scything year after year and wheeling them to stack in large piles near our gardens. They have heard me refer to those piles as our "green manure." That is what those piles become. In a year or two, they decay into good nutrients for our vegetable garden, where I spread them and dig them in. In this way, the field serves the garden by helping its plants to flourish, along with the other natural nutrients we occasionally add to the soil, such as cow manure and green sand. When I lift and push wheelbarrows of green manure from the pipeline toward our gardens to be composted or when I spread the cow manure or scatter the green sand, and thereafter, in due course, when I kneel down on the earth to weed the vegetable seedlings, I am lifting and pushing and spreading and scattering and weeding in prayer—because "the earth is the Lord's and the fulness thereof" (Psalm 24:1) and the Lord is there, I believe, in, with, and under every furrow of the soil and every glorious green shoot, both the seedlings and the weeds. I am kneeling there on holy ground.

I am particularly grateful for our vegetable garden. Sometimes, scythe in hand, as I catch my breath out on the field, I look across the little stream that runs between the field where I'm working and marvel at that vegetable garden. It has a life of its own, just like the field where I scythe. The growing season in western Maine is short (neighbors still repeat the story of a killer frost in July a hundred years ago), but after decades of work, our soil is good and the fruits of that good earth are usually plentiful.

It's a joy, too, to eat from the garden, in due season. For us, it is akin to a liturgical calendar. There are the salad season, the zucchini and yellow squash season, the tomato season, the potato season, and the kohl season, each with its own eating rituals. The word *fecundity* comes to mind. I have a photograph on my desk of Laurel holding a huge armful of chard, half as big as she is. She freezes the harvest of those seasons, as much as she can, and so we eat from our garden virtually the whole year.

I have no illusions that we could get by "living from the land." But that vegetable garden is nevertheless a gift of unmerited grace. Not the least of such a grace, for us, is the "veggie feasts" that we host for family and friends, three or four times during the growing season. Those feasts, with all their homegrown and home-cooked delicacies covering our table and all the personal warmth around that table, are unmerited grace multiplied. Laurel does the cooking, and I do the cleaning up when all have gone home, with the responsibility of finding a way to store the plentiful leftovers in the refrigerator or the freezer. For me, those quiet moments are like the times after the Sunday liturgy when I have washed the chalice and cared for the bread and the wine that remained after that meal and felt the holy silence envelop me.

Scything with God

From time to time, my grandchildren, when they were young, have wandered out to the vegetable garden where I was kneeling or to the field beyond to visit with me while I scythed, maybe to pick blueberries while we chatted. At such times, I have often been reminded that Jesus taught that a little child shall lead us. I have seen God in the faces of my grandchildren. I aspire, as a matter of fact, to see nature through a child's eyes. A spirituality of nature developed in the Christian tradition wants to be childlike, as Jesus announced, to be innocent as a dove, as well as to cultivate its own worldly wisdom, like a fox, as Jesus also taught.

In this and many other ways, I am blessedly engaged with God in nature at Hunts Corner, especially when I scythe. It may be the face of a child or the faces of the mountains or even the black-faced hornets. By the grace of God, in those moments I am almost always enthusiastic, according to the root meaning of that word, "in God" (Greek, *en theos*). I love scything with God. I'm elated all the more at such times, too, because I often self-consciously see myself as part of larger, interconnected worlds, of the ecology of that place in western Maine, and more particularly of the fructuous vegetable garden and of Laurel's small but elegant perennial garden celebrating the colors yellow, blue, and red, a garden into which she pours enormous energies, and of our Hidden Garden (more on this later). I then contemplate beyond in every direction the fragile biosphere, which is so preciously layered around this earth, and the domains of our sun and our galaxy all around us, among the billions and billions of other galaxies—and God, in, with, and under it all, hovering, giving birth to all things as this universe's creative and life-giving Spirit.

But which God is this? To respond to this question, my bifocal narrative must now shift from contemplation of "nature and nature's God," as I scythe with God and survey our gardens, which are gifts of grace from the hands of God, to the knowledge of this God that had already been graciously given to me by God *before* I began to scythe and to contemplate the world in which I scythe. This gift, as I have experienced it, in a certain sense precedes my contemplation of nature and nature's God. It is thus a gift in the second sense of my title, *Before Nature.* Long before I ever stood before nature in contemplation at Hunts Corner, engaged with nature, my life had been claimed by the very God with whom I there was blessedly scything.

SCYTHING WITH THE GOD OF MY BAPTISM: NAMING THE GOD OF THIS BLESSEDNESS

Since this is a personal story, it will naturally have many personal points of reference. The narrative of my scything with God begins in the middle of my life (*in media res*). The historic beginnings of my spiritual story are to be found many decades before that, at Resurrection Lutheran Church, in Buffalo, New York, where I was baptized in 1935, "in the name of the Father and of the Son and of the Holy Ghost." (This archaic "ghost" language was standard back then, and it is still used in some hymns and prayers today. I use it myself, on occasion.)

If you were to ask me about the God with whom I scythe, this would probably be what I would say on most occasions: the God whose grandeur I contemplate reflected and refracted in nature as I encounter that grandeur in and around Hunts Corner in southwestern Maine is none other than the God in whose name I was baptized as an infant. I am not proposing to justify this statement here but, rather, simply to describe what it means to me. This is the way things have worked, and continue to work, for me spiritually. My spirituality was bifocal, in the sense that I have been using that word in this book, long before that kind of descriptive language was available to me. So, when I tell you about my blessed engagement with nature, know that I believe that the God of my Hunts Corner world and the God of Resurrection Lutheran Church, in Buffalo, New York, are the same God, and that I have so believed for as long as I can remember.

For Calvin – nature is "the theater of God's glory"

A BAPTISMAL MYSTICISM

Baptism was a major event in churches like the one in which I was splashed, in the name of the Father and of the Son and of the Holy Ghost, in 1935. It was celebrated robustly, both in the life of the infant's family and in the life of the congregation of which that family was a member. This was not just for ceremonial reasons. Whether or not they could readily find the words to say it, the members of such congregations knew in their bones that a baptism was much more than a name giving or the mere celebration of the birth of a healthy child or a way of doting on the cuteness of a baby. Many of the members firmly believed that some profoundly gracious and irrevocably lifelong transaction between God and the child, and the community of faith, was being established by the sacrament of Baptism, with the water and with God's word of promise.

I grew up with that heritage, and then I found it enriched in my seminary years when I was exposed to the baptismal theology of the sixteenth-century protestant reformer Martin Luther, the patriarch of the tradition according to whose canons I myself had been baptized. Luther, as I will note often as this story unfolds, had a profound sense for the immediacy of God in nature. For Luther, nature was a *mask* of God (*larva Dei*), but it was surely for him also a mask *of God*. God was deeply and pervasively "in, with, and under" the world of nature. For Luther, nature was not quite "the theater of God's glory" as it was for Luther's fellow protestant reformer John Calvin, nor was it the world revealed by the ecstatic visions of the modern Jesuit poet G. M. Hopkins, for whom the whole creation is "charged with the grandeur of God." Still, for Luther, nature was astoundingly permeated, through and through, with the powerful presence of God. If you truly were to understand a grain of wheat, Luther once observed, you would die of wonder.

Strikingly, Luther gave voice to that same kind of profound sense for the presence of God in nature when the reformer talked about Baptism. For him, the very God who is in, with, and under all things is also revealingly and graciously present in the waters of Baptism. In those waters, according to Luther, when God's word of promise is spoken, God discloses Godself not just as an immediate and powerful presence but all the more so as a self-giving, gracious, and faithful presence. For Luther, these two themes—God in nature generally and God in Baptism particularly—are thoroughly and inseparably wedded. Such thoughts sometimes percolate to my own consciousness when I am scything. The God whom I encounter in nature when I am scything, as I have said, is for me the very God in whose name I once was baptized.

And there is more. Since my seminary years, drawing on a lifetime's fascination with water and inspired by Luther's spirituality of God in, with, and under nature, a certain baptismal mysticism has found a home in my soul. It began with a kind of love for water when I was a child. Maybe I never got over that "oceanic feeling" that Sigmund Freud postulated that infants feel in the womb. Freud thought that religion has its roots in this feeling. Be that as it may, I have loved water for as long as I can remember. I was a good swimmer as a child, and later swam competitively in high school and college. In my youngest years, I eagerly spent countless hours during summers, floating and paddling and submerging myself in the shoreline waters at nearby Lake Erie or at inland ponds and streams, where my parents often took me and my siblings. I found a kind of peace and solitude and sense of ultimate well-being in such experiences.

As a boy, moreover, I was tutored by my parents in gardening. It was often my chore—in fact, much more than a chore for me—to water what in those World War II days we called our "victory garden." To this day, I am the one in the family who drags the hoses around our Maine home to water the gardens. I still relish the experience. In the privacy of my own soul, indeed, I sometimes imagine myself to be a kind of latter-day Adam caring for the garden of God, as the biblical Adam was called to do. For years, I have also savored all the biblical texts—and there are many—that envision God's salvation coming to renew the face of the earth through the blessings of water.[1]

BAPTISM AND THE AMBIGUITIES OF WATER

On the other hand, who can think about such blessings of water without pondering their maldistribution and their desecration in our global society today? The are such precious blessings but so often hoarded by the rich and the powerful and then left despoiled for the poor! More than a billion people do not have enough water to drink in our time, and waterborne diseases afflict the poor around the world more than any other threat to their well-being. Thus, I cannot think of water these days without bringing to mind and heart the deep-seated injustices of our global society.

The theme of water also brings with it the challenges of confronting the occasionally profound destructiveness of water gone wild. I have rarely found myself romanticizing the experience of water and its blessings. Water, in general human experience, has often been larger than life, sometimes a force of death and destruction. My family visited Niagara Falls frequently when I was a boy—a story that I will tell at length later—and I learned at an early age not only to stand in awe of those waters but sometimes, when I carefully positioned myself behind the wire fence at the edge of the top of the falls, to stand in terror.

It is no wonder that the many biblical references to the primeval waters of the creation and the flooding of the cosmic waters registered so deeply in my soul when I began to ponder those texts in my seminary years. Along the way in my studies, too, when I discovered the powerful idea of the wrath of God in Luther's spirituality and, more particularly, in his teachings about the hidden God, I began to speak not only about the beauties and mysteries of nature but also about the terrors of nature. I think of such things frequently when I wander along the forbidding rocky coasts of Maine most summers. I do believe that the Spirit of God is working powerfully in those waters, as the towering waves slam against the ancient rocks, but the vista still terrifies me.[2] I know that I have to keep my distance.[3]

All of these apperceptions of water have surrounded me spiritually, I have no doubt, when I have been called upon to baptize, particularly when, as part of the baptismal liturgy, I have been privileged to recite Luther's great "Flood Prayer":

Holy God, mighty Lord, gracious Father: We give you thanks, for in the beginning your Spirit moved over the waters and you created heaven and earth. By the gift of water you nourish and sustain us and all living things.

By the waters of the flood you condemned the wicked and saved those whom you had chosen, Noah and his family. You led Israel by the pillar of cloud and fire though the sea, out of slavery into the freedom of the promised land. In the waters of the Jordan your Son was baptized by John and anointed with the Spirit. By the baptism of his own death and resurrection your beloved Son has set us free from the bondage to sin and death, and has opened the way to the joy and freedom of everlasting life. He made water a sign of the kingdom and of cleansing and rebirth. In obedience to his command, we make disciples of all nations, baptizing them in the name of the Father, and of the Son, and of the Holy Spirit. . . .[4]

As I recite—or, rather, incant—those words while the water is being poured, a strange and stirring sense of the immediacy of God and God's grace often overwhelms me. When I am all the more privileged to baptize by submersion, as I was for my own son and his sons, I can only describe my sensation as being charged with the very energy of God.

And there is still more. In, with, and under those waters and those sacramental actions, announced by the word of God, I believe that the "God of grace and God of Glory" that one of my favorite hymns announces is bonding eternally with the person being baptized. At such moments, I do not worry about such more or less abstract theological questions as whether all *have* to be baptized in order to be saved (the gracious answer to that question, to which I wholeheartedly subscribe, is no). I am simply overwhelmed by the love and power and gentleness of God's presence and God's promise at that moment. Such are some of the configurations of what I think of as my own baptismal mysticism, rooted as they undoubtedly are in the contemplative moments with water that I have experienced all my life.

So, it makes perfect inner sense to me, and I feel that it could be no other way for me, to say that the God whom I encounter scything in a field in southwestern Maine is the very God who once claimed my life in Baptism and who charges my soul whenever I officiate at the Baptism of another. Hence, the story of my blessed engagement with nature is a narrative of a *Christian* spirituality of nature. My story, as I stressed at the outset, takes the classical Trinitarian faith of the Christian church for granted. It presupposes that, *for me*, there is no other God than the God of my Baptism, who is addressed as Father, Son, and Holy Spirit.[5]

THE AMBIGUITIES OF BAPTISM

Still, I know that Christian particulars like Baptism and the Trinitarian name of God sometimes rub the spiritual seekers of our world the wrong way.[6] The very subtitle of this book, *A Christian Spirituality*, may sound to some like a contradiction in terms. What does the Christian teaching about the Trinity have to do with spirituality, and vice versa? The culture of the spiritual seekers that I discussed at the start more often than not takes for granted that matters such as Baptism and its Trinitarian language are somehow narrow or even destructive expressions of "religion" over against what are perceived to be the more general and more humanizing insights and practices of "spirituality." I have discussed this popular passion for spirituality over against religion in the preceding pages as well as elsewhere.[7] Here, I simply want to observe that, for me, the two are inseparable, spirituality *and* religion (if we are going to use those terms). It could not be otherwise for the bifocal perspective that I am presupposing in this narrative. I ask the spiritual seekers whom I am venturing to address in this book to hear me out on this one, and then only to decide whether it does indeed make sense, as I believe it does, to speak of—as in my subtitle—"*a Christian spirituality.*"

Ponder this question. Do not those of us who are Christians have the right, and indeed, in these times when the whole earth is "groaning in travail," the obligation, to set forth the spiritual meanings of our own encounters with nature, just as much as Native Americans, Buddhists, Hindus, and others undeniably have the right and obligation to do? Indeed, on a more global scale, how will any genuine kind of "interreligious dialogue" about the earth groaning in travail ever emerge if all the conversation partners in such a dialogue are not encouraged to set forth the diverse particularities of their own religious traditions?

In this spirit, I am inviting you who are spiritual seekers to join me on a pilgrimage of exploration guided by the baptismal trail markers of the classical Christian tradition, which have been so critically important for my own spiritual life from its very beginnings.[8] And, I am inviting those of you who are theology teachers and pastoral practitioners to come along, too, to do your best to assess whether this kind of journey is indeed faithful to the classical theological tradition and whether it will help you in your own conversations with the spiritual seekers and perhaps also with your own, personal spiritual journeys.

This particular and self-conscious attention to Christian trail markers is all the more poignantly necessary given that, in the eyes of some, and perhaps many, such a journey must be begun under dark clouds of historical suspicion. It is widely taken for granted these days by those whom the great protestant theologian of the nineteenth century Friedrich Schleiermacher called the "cultured despisers of religion," as well as by numerous popular proponents of various kinds of "post-Christian" spiritualities, that Christianity bears what historian Lynn White Jr. famously—or infamously—called in 1966 "a huge burden of guilt" for the global ecological crisis today. This is the ecological complaint against Christianity to which I referred at the outset. More than a few in our time are sure that Christianity is ecologically bankrupt and therefore that Christianity can have little of substance and value to say about nature, spiritually or in any other way.

This is not the place to explore and assess this ecological complaint against Christianity. Much of my previously published theological work can be read as a response to that kind of criticism of the Christian tradition.[9] But since the thought that the Christian faith has nothing of value to say about the world of nature is "out there" in our culture, shared by many spiritual seekers and even taught in some university departments of environmental studies, it does makes sense—and it is only fair—to ask that the Christian tradition be allowed to speak with its own voice, to have its own day in court, before jumping to any conclusions about what it does or does not have to say about nature.[10]

GUIDEPOSTS FOR THE JOURNEY:
ON THE MEANINGS OF "NATURE" AND "SPIRITUALITY"

To facilitate understanding of these spiritual explorations, I want to say something about the meaning of two key terms in my title, *nature* and *spirituality*, lest these historically loaded constructs end up being a barrier, rather than a gateway, to understanding.

NATURE

Regarding the first term, *nature*, I would like to say simply this: *nature is the world I encounter when I am scything*. But that is obviously too compact of a definition. So let me unpack it, as best as I briefly can. By "nature," I do *not* mean what the natural scientists generally mean by that term: a self-enclosed universe (or a self-enclosed world of universes) that may or may not be emergent or in process and which more or less runs by itself, unfolding according to its own laws. Methodologically, if not personally, most natural scientists shy away from or resolutely resist any idea of the divine in conjunction with the idea of nature thus understood. I readily accept that kind of a definition as valid for the natural sciences, as predicated on a methodology for research. Indeed, the theological definition of nature that I will soon propose is intended to be "consonant" with this kind of scientific usage of the term.[11] In other words, I believe that scientists and theologians are talking about the same world but that each discipline sees that world from its own perspective.

Nor do I take the term *nature* to mean what some romantic poets and philosophers have meant when they have thought of "Nature" (capitalized) as a kind of self-contained (albeit open-ended) yet thoroughly divine universe, sometimes thought of as "Nature giving birth to itself" or "Nature naturing" (*Natura naturans*), a world that is replete with great mysteries and resplendent with profound beauties, a world in which you can lose yourself. For romantic thinking, generally, God *is* nature and vice versa (*Deus sive natura*). With the classical theological tradition, I reject that kind of pantheistic thinking, which essentially identifies God with the world. On the other hand, I deeply appreciate what might be called romantic sensibilities. Thoreau would be a case in point.

I believe that the theological definition of nature I will propose has a certain consonance with romantic apperceptions of nature, as it also does with scientific encounters with nature. The vision of God depicted in these pages points to a God who is magnificently and powerfully and beautifully in, with, and under, as well as beyond, all things.

Nor again am I employing the term *nature*, not even implicitly, to refer to that alleged world of "resources" imagined by both capitalist and socialist societies—sometimes under the quasi-theological rubric of "the stewardship of nature"—a world whose chief raison d'être is to serve as "the means of production" that will, in turn, undergird what is sometimes thought of as "human progress."[12] Nature is not that so-called world of materials, which gains its meaning solely when it is mined or otherwise transformed for human purposes. On the other hand, I by no means think that appropriate human engagement with the world we call nature should be scorned. On the contrary, with many others, I am deeply convinced that humans, especially in this era of global crisis, must work with nature proactively, effectively, and carefully—in the root sense of the latter word, with caring—for the sake of promoting justice for all of the oppressed human and other creatures of this good earth.

Rather, I am using the term *nature*, as it can be configured theologically in light of the Trinitarian, creedal traditions of the church, to refer—as I noted at the very beginning of these explorations—to *the material-vital aspect of God's good creation*, what the Nicene Creed speaks of as "all things visible."[13] This, in the end, brings me back to my preferred, more compact definition of the term: nature is the visible, tangible world I encounter in and around my home in southwestern Maine, charged as that world is with the grandeur of God and also showing as it does telltale signs of human use and abuse—the house, the gardens, the field, the pipeline, the forest, the mountains, the sky, the "starry heavens" beyond, and my own bodily engagement with it all. Nature thus understood also refers to my own bodily interaction with other, similarly embodied humans—picking up and hugging a three-year-old grandchild, for example.

I want to emphasize two parts of this definition. First, I am assuming that material human artifacts—such as our Maine house and, of course, my scythe—are part of nature. This world of human artifacts is sometimes called "the built environment."[14] Second, I am also assuming that the human body is part of nature. From the air we humans breathe and the water we drink and the food we eat to our sexuality, our DNA, our evolutionary history, and our ecological interrelatedness with the biosphere more generally, as bodily creatures we humans are essentially and inextricably and wondrously immersed in nature. Water, for example, which covers some 70 percent of planet Earth, also constitutes some 70 percent of our bodies. Nature, in other words, is not just the world of our gardens and the fields and forests and mountains and the vast expanses of the universe beyond. Nature is *everything material and living that God wondrously creates* (sometimes working through human intelligence and human-made machines and human hands). This inclusive theological understanding of the term *nature*, I know, does not answer all of the questions that surround it, but at least it points us in a direction that I hope will facilitate rather than hinder meaningful explorations of the theme of this book.

SPIRITUALITY

"Spirituality" is a different kind of construct. Unlike "nature," the word itself does not have explicit, centuries-old layers of meaning, although spiritual practices, such as praying in solitude or in small groups, and reflections about those practices have of course been common in Christianity as well as in other religions in all eras. While the word *spirituality* has deep and ancient roots, in other words, it has become a widely used *term* mainly in our own era. Moreover, it appears that, due to its relatively recent popularization, if for no other reason, the word *spirituality* can mean many different things to many different people.[15] I propose a relatively simple definition of the term, mainly to allow us to get under way in these explorations and to not have to take a long terminological detour at the outset. I understand the term *spirituality* to mean *religious experience that is intense and transforming*.[16]

Please note what this definition does *not* do. It does not frame the term in opposition to "religion," a familiar practice in our culture today that I have already discussed. Spirituality, as I am employing the term, *could* mean the individual testimony of the proverbial guru sitting alone on top of a mountain where he or she voices a worldview and champions a variety of practices solely on the basis of his or her own private intuitions, and perhaps in reaction to the claims of one or more traditional religions. Or it *could just as readily* be—as indeed I am taking it to mean in this narrative—the testimony and the practices of a believer that arise out of a particular religious tradition and the communal expressions of that tradition. In other words, the definition I am proposing is large enough to encompass what is popularly thought of as "religion." Hence, I am quite comfortable discussing Baptism—that central rite of the Christian religion—as the heart of my own spirituality. The first-person religious discourse of this book, and the intense, transformative experience it presupposes, has that particular religious source and inspiration.[17]

Our next step as we continue to consider the journey before us will be to examine the general importance of *practices* for the spiritual life and, more particularly, to review the emergence in my own life of a single practice that I call "the Trinity Prayer." This prayer is deeply rooted in baptismal meanings, beginning with the classical biblical witness to those meanings in the Gospel of Matthew, where the disciples hear from the risen Lord that they are to "make disciples of all nations, baptizing them in the name of the Father and of the Son and of the Holy Spirit" (Matt. 28:19).

Notes

1. For a helpful, short introduction to such biblical texts, see Steven Bouma-Prediger, "Water in Biblical Reflection," *Word and World* 32, no. 1 (winter 2012): 42–50. For an insightful study of water in the context of worship, see Benjamin Stewart, *A Watered Garden: Christian Worship and Earth's Ecology* (Minneapolis: Augsburg Fortress, 2011).

2. This discussion steers around the even more difficult challenge of dealing with the enormities of "natural disasters" like tsunamis. I will take up this issue of "natural evil" later in this narrative.

3. One place I like to visit along the southern coast of Maine is Pemaquid Point. I read a few years ago about two young parents who had taken their two preteen children to that place and how they all had innocently wandered far out onto the point at low tide to get closer to the waves. Sadly, the two children somehow fell into the incoming tidal waters and drowned, and the parents did so, too, in their futile efforts to save the children.

4. *Lutheran Book of Worship* (Minneapolis: Augsburg Publishing House, 1978), 122.

5. I will suggest alternate, albeit subsidiary, ways of speaking of the Trinity, in particular the functional expressions *Giver, Gift,* and *Giving,* in chapter 6. But praying to the Father, Son, and Holy Spirit remains for me the primary way to address God, the Father of the Son, made known to me by the Holy Spirit. See Ted Peters, *God as Trinity: Relationality and Temporality in Divine Life* (Louisville, KY: Westminster John Knox, 1993), 54: "To recognize the metaphorical dimensions to 'Father, Son, and Holy Spirit' does not make these symbols exchangeable with other terms. . . . There is only one Trinitarian formula: Father, Son, and Holy Spirit. This is because it is tied inextricably to the event of revelation and salvation itself. . . . To bypass the biblical terms in favor of some substitutes is to identify with a God other than the God of Jesus Christ."

6. During the same period in my life when I was learning to scythe, I was also serving as the chaplain of a women's school, Wellesley College, Wellesley, Massachusetts. Early on in those years, I arranged for a young scholar from the theology department of Boston College, Mary Daly, to preach in the Wellesley College chapel. Daly was just then in the process of writing a book that would become a classic of feminist theology, provocatively entitled *Beyond God the Father: Toward a Philosophy of Women's Liberation* (Boston: Beacon, 1974). Since those days, I have wrestled with what Daly called the patriarchal language of classical Christianity. One of my first published articles argued that the "Our Father" of the Lord's Prayer should, according to the best canons of scholarly translation-praxis, be rendered "Our Parent" (H. Paul Santmire, "Retranslating 'Our Father': The Urgency and the Possibility," *Dialog* 16, no. 2 [spring 1977]: 101–6.) On the other hand, in those days and to the present, I have made it a practice to keep baptizing in the triune name, Father, Son, and Holy Spirit, given its biblical roots its historic, theological

particularity, and its centrality in classical Christianity. I would like to think, however, that this practice represents postfeminist, rather than prefeminist, understandings. I am, in any case, very much aware that the discussion of patriarchal language in Christian life and thought must continue. As a framework for that continuing discussion, see Ted Peters, "Is Trinitarian Language Hopelessly Sexist?" in *God as Trinity*, 46–55. Peters quotes Patricia Wilson-Kastner (51) in order to point the discussion in the direction that he wants to recommend: "Trinity is more supportive of feminist values than is a strict monotheism. . . . Put very simply, if one imagines God as three persons, it encourages one to focus on interrelationship as the core of divine reality, rather than on a single personal reality, almost always imagined as male."

7. See H. Paul Santmire, *Ritualizing Nature: The Ambiguous Ecological Promise of Christian Theology* (Minneapolis: Fortress Press, 1985), 57–78.

8. The reader may well wish to explore, in due course or in parallel, the pathways forged by other religions or other spiritual worldviews. A good place to begin such religious studies is the multivolume series on religion and ecology edited by Mary Evelyn Tucker. See Tucker and Duncan Ryuken Williams, eds., *Buddhism and Ecology: The Interconnection of Dharma and Deeds* (Cambridge, MA: Harvard University Press, 1997); Tucker and John Berthrong, eds., *Confucianism and Ecology: The Interrelation of Heaven, Earth, and Humans* (Cambridge, MA: Harvard University Press, 1998); Tucker and Christopher Key Chapple, *Hinduism and Ecology: The Intersection of Earth, Sky, and Water* (Cambridge, MA: Harvard University Press, 2000). While demanding for those who are just beginning to explore such things, these volumes generally present balanced pictures of the religious traditions under discussion.

9. See the preface, note 13.

10. For a brief and accessible but also comprehensive theological statement of a biblically oriented ecological theology for today, see the essay by the New Testament scholar and long-standing church activist David Rhoads: "Reflections on a Lutheran Theology of Creation: Foundations for a New Reformation," *Seminary Ridge Review* 15, no. 1 (autumn 2012), 1–49.

11. I have learned much over the years about the relationships between theology and the sciences from Ted Peters, who has made much of the conceptuality of consonance. See, for example, his introductory essay in *Cosmos as Creation: Theology and Science in Consonance* (Nashville, TN: Abingdon, 1989), 11–27.

12. For my reservations more generally about the stewardship construct, see my book, *Ritualizing Nature: Renewing Christian Liturgy in a Time of Crisis* (Minneapolis: Fortress, 2008), 251–258.

13. For a more detailed discussion of this definition, see my book *The Travail of Nature: The Ambiguous Ecological Promise of Christian Theology* (Minneapolis: Fortress Press, 1985), 11f.

14. See T. J. Gorringe, *A Theology of the Built Environment: Justice, Empowerment, Redemption* (New York: Cambridge University Press, 2002).

15. Consider the following popularizing definition, which appeared in a Mayo Clinic newsletter, *EmbodyHealth*, December 2009, 2 (distributed by the Board of Pensions, Evangelical Lutheran Church in America): "Spirituality is the way or ways you find meaning and purpose in your life, and for many, it's a connection to something greater than yourself. Spirituality can be nourished through many different traditions or rituals." More succinctly, see also Roger S. Gottlieb, *Spirituality: What It Is and Why It Matters* (New York: Oxford University Press, 2013), 5: "In its broadest terms, spirituality is an understanding of how life should be lived and an attempt to live that way." The sharpest generic definition of spirituality that I have encountered is by Sandra M. Schneiders, "Christian Spirituality: Definition, Methods and Types," in *The New Westminster Dictionary of Christian Spirituality,* ed. Philip Sheldrake (Louisville, KY: Westminster John Knox, 2005). She distinguishes between spirituality as a lived experience (which is my concern in this book) and spirituality as an academic discipline. This is her definition of the former: "Spirituality as lived experience can be defined as conscious involvement in the project of life integration through self-transcendence toward the ultimate value one perceives" (1).

16. If I were to be more specific at this point, I would want to identify *Christian* spirituality as a particularized expression of the generic definition I am proposing. This is done very well by Richard McBrien, *Catholicism* (San Francisco: Harper Collins, 1994): "Spirituality has to do with our experiencing God and with the transformation of our consciousness and our lives as outcomes of that experience. Since God is in principle available to everyone, spirituality is not exclusively Christian. Christian spirituality is life in the Holy Spirit who incorporates the Christian into the body of Jesus Christ, through whom the Christian has access to God the creator in a life of faith, hope, love, and service. It is *visionary, sacramental, and transformational*" (1058, italics in original). On the motif of intensity, see Lawrence S. Cunningham, "Catholic Spirituality: What Does It Mean Today?" *Commonweal* 133, no. 4 (February 24, 2006): 12. The theme of intensification is also suggested by Louis Dupré in his historical study, *The Common Life: The Origins of Trinitarian Mysticism and Its Development by Jan Ruysbroeck* (New York: Crossroads, 1984), 53: "The mystical life does not consist in an abrupt alteration of consciousness, but rather in an evermore intensively conscious recurrence of the same divine rhythm. It is a rhythm of which every devout person has had a least some experience."

17. For a more analytical discussion of this topic, see Sandra M. Schneiders, "Religion vs. Spirituality: A Contemporary Conundrum," *Spiritus* 3:2 (fall 2003), 163-185. She makes a case for understanding religion and spirituality in partnership, which is the approach that I am taking here.

2

Introducing a Way of Prayer
The Practice and the Knowing of the Trinity Prayer

St. Francis, that great medieval lover of nature, attended Mass every day throughout much of his life. Dorothy Day, that great American witness to peace, nonviolence, and justice for the poor, did the same. As we continue to consider the journey before us, I will not ask you to emulate such saintly practices—at least, not exactly. But I will ask you to think about the importance of spiritual practices more generally and of one spiritual practice in particular: saying the Trinity Prayer. Why? Because, we can learn from great spiritual forebears like Francis and Dorothy Day. And, more particularly, because today most of us live in a culture of secularity, which makes it difficult for many to pray.

Yes, in the United States we have our megachurches, bursting at the seams with members who love to talk about praying. We have our television evangelists who command audiences in the millions and who have the habit of offering highly dramatic public prayers. Our presidents also generally like to be thought of as champions of prayer. They make a practice of attending highly publicized prayer breakfasts now and again. That presidential practice sends a message: we are a nation at prayer. Or so we are led to believe by media reports and, sometimes, by our own observations. Even 20 percent of the religiously nonaffiliated in the United States, the Nones, report that they pray every day.[1] I would imagine that the percentage of Nones-Sympathizers in our churches who pray every day may be even higher.

Still, the truth is that it is not easy to pray, at least not for many Americans today. Even in the ranks of those who like to think of themselves as persons of prayer, finding the time to do so appears to be a monumental challenge. This spiritual problematic is sometimes said to be the result of the hectic pace of our lives. How can you say your prayers when you're still on the crowded commuter train at 7 p.m., and when what you really want to do when you get home is have a cocktail and collapse into bed? How can you say your prayers when you have just finished seeing two additional clients and your supervisor wants you to see yet another, never mind the fact that your two young children are waiting at home for their supper, with a frustrated babysitter who should have departed long before? How can you say your prayers when you've just finished another day of job searching and you don't seem to have any inner energy left for anyone or anything? How can you say your prayers when you have a term paper due tomorrow and you know that you're going to have to stay up all night to finish it?

Others look beyond the hectic pace of our lives to explain the difficulty of praying by pointing to the much discussed materialism of our culture. We are in love with things, not with God, they observe. Why should we pray to God? Still others maintain that ours is a "culture of narcissism" (Christopher Lasch). Why should we look to God with full devotion in prayer when we're so preoccupied with looking at ourselves in the mirror? Then, some observe, there is the agnosticism, even the atheism, that some prominent natural scientists seem to think is necessary if they are to be true to the scientific method. Doesn't that agnosticism and perhaps that atheism leach into the minds and hearts of many of those who study science? How can you pray if you're under such influences?

Finally, there are the perennial questions about the goodness of God, which have been hugely amplified in our time, in the wake of the Holocaust and the Killing Fields of Cambodia and the global hunger crisis and other monstrous evils. How could a good God permit such things? Perhaps, some think, there is no God who cares enough to hear our prayers. So why pray? I will return to this last wrenching question—technically, it is called the issue of "theodicy"—in some detail in the following pages.

First, however, in this chapter I invite you to bracket thoughts about the spiritual dynamics of our era, which make it so difficult to pray, and to think about something much more mundane. Consider the truth of this simple spiritual maxim: *practice makes possible*. This is not an original thought on my part, by any means. Practices have been celebrated by many Christian spiritual guides (and by many in other religions as well) for centuries. Just think of the *Spiritual Exercises* of St. Ignatius of Loyola, a work that has shaped Jesuit spirituality ever since the sixteenth century. But the theme of practices has perhaps become more popular in our own time, spiritually speaking, than ever before.[2] Here, however, I don't want to survey the variety of religious practices, past or present, or review theories about them. Instead, I want to share with you my own take on the matter, what it has come to mean to me personally, because this is an essential theme in my own spiritual story.[3]

I must stress at the outset that to highlight practices in this way is not to suggest that our practices somehow can call God to us, so that we can then know God. On the contrary, left on our own, however much some of us might want to "work at our spirituality," we still live under the sign of the eclipse of God, a condition that I will explore at some length in chapter 3.

I want to suggest something quite different here: not that our spiritual practices open the door to God for us, but that, now and again, the Holy Spirit works to channel the self-disclosure of God to us *through our practices*.[4] That is one way the divine initiative claims our minds and hearts.[5] And that is why this account of a journey of a thousand miles begins by proposing this small practical step. I invite you to consider what spiritual practices generally can mean for you, even if you've already given this matter some thought, and, more particularly, to reflect about how the practice of a single prayer, one that has been critically important for my own spirituality, may be just what you need.[6]

I believe that this particular spiritual practice, the Trinity Prayer, was given by the spirit of God. But this divine gift was *a gift of the obvious*, from a classical Christian perspective. In fact, there's nothing new in this prayer, as far as the ancient faith of the church is concerned. As far as I know, only the *form* of the prayer has not been used in practice ever before. This is what I am calling the Trinity Prayer:

> *Lord Jesus Christ, have mercy on me.*
> *Praise Father, Son, and Holy Spirit.*
> *Come Holy Spirit, come and reign.*

My purpose in this chapter is to persuade you to begin to practice this prayer without any further delay, whether or not you're confident that you understand its meanings or the value of its practice. Don't worry about whether or not you're being "authentic."[7] Just do it. This is the meaning, I think, of a line drawing produced by the Catholic artist Corita Kent a half century ago. In her own handwriting, she quotes a traditional Jewish (Hasidic) saying that depicts an unidentified holy one at prayer: "He repeated the letters of the alphabet over and over, beseeching the Almighty to arrange them into the appropriate words for the prayer." The practice of praying, just doing it, counterintuitive as it might seem, makes the praying itself possible.

HOW TO PRAY: PRACTICE MAKES POSSIBLE

The best way to learn how to ride a bicycle is to get on a bicycle and start to ride. The best way to learn how to swim is to plunge in. The best way to learn how to dance is to get out on the dance floor and start to dance. The best way to learn a new language is to go to the country where that language is spoken and start speaking. Likewise, I believe, the best way to blessedly engage God, in, with, and under nature, as a seeker or a teacher or a pastor, is to start praying in the name of Jesus or to devote more attention to that practice.

Don't assume that you can't do it if you haven't tried it. Experience the surprise! Don't assume that this prayer won't work for you, because it may sound so familiar, if it does. Many have learned to ride a bike or to swim or to dance or to speak a new language or to pray, notwithstanding their initial assumptions, sometimes strongly held, that none of that adventurous stuff would ever work for them. Practice will not make perfect, in other words. But, as my own experience has taught me, practice can make possible. And, it can make possible in many places. You can be on the subway as well as in church. You can be walking down an old country road as well as attending a monastic retreat.

Sure, for the swimming and the dancing and the foreign language speaking and the praying, it is often best to have a guide. That is what I'm proposing to be for all of my readers, especially for those who are beginners but also for those who are already in some measure under way. Having a guide or not, however, the most important thing for the reader who is with me thus far is this: to begin, to take "the leap of faith," as the nineteenth-century Danish theologian and spiritual master Søren Kierkegaard invited his readers to do.

Many years ago, I read somewhere about a traditional rabbinic legend concerning the exodus, the biblical story of God's deliverance of God's chosen people from Egypt through the Red Sea waters. This was the scenario. The children of Israel were hastening to the Red Sea in order to escape. The Egyptian army, with all its worldly might, was in hot pursuit. When the Israelites got to the edge of the sea, however, the promised miracle of the parting of the waters did *not* happen. Was all lost? No. According to the legend, it was only when a single Israelite jumped into the sea that the promised miracle occurred and the people of Israel were delivered through the waters.

REFLECTING ABOUT PRACTICES

This anecdotal approach to the theme before us—practice makes possible wherever you find yourself—can now be complemented by a certain kind of descriptive (or "phenomenological") analysis. An instructive example of this kind of approach isoutlined in an unpublished paper by the Cornell University biblical scholar and ethicist Richard A. Baer Jr.[8] He juxtaposes Quaker silent worship, Pentecostal speaking in tongues (*glossolalia*), and high Anglican, Catholic, or Lutheran liturgy. These seemingly dramatically different forms of worship, Baer argues, actually have a similar, even identical, spiritual function. They make it possible for the practitioners of these rites to "break with the tyranny of the cognitive mind."

Contrary to uninformed speculation and opinion, Baer observes, speaking in tongues, in particular, is not typically a form of religious hysteria, nor is it usually an uncontrolled expression of emotion. The glossolaliac is typically fully aware of what he or she is doing and can also stop at will. Striking parallels exist between the practice of speaking in tongues, Baer points out, and Quaker silence. "At its best," he explains, "Quaker silent worship involves a kind of letting go, a lack of strain or effortful attention, a willingness to 'flow' with the leading of the Spirit and with the larger movement of the entire meeting." Further: "It is almost universally felt in Quaker circles that rational analysis and argument over what is spoken 'out of silence' is inappropriate. . . . As in the case of glossalalia, the process of speaking out of silence and of listening in silence involves a resting of the analytical mind, a refusal to let deliberative, objective thinking dominate the meeting for worship."

Does "high liturgical worship" fit into the same pattern? Baer's answer: yes. Just as glossolalia and silent Quaker worship may at first be puzzling, frustrating, or even irritating to the non-initiate, so to many outsiders the practice of liturgical worship sometimes appears to be little more than a mechanical exercise in futility. What good can possibly come of the repetition week after week of the same prayer of confession, word of absolution, intercessions, and petitions?

But all of this is not surprising, Baer observes, and is not unlike the person first learning to dance. *Thinking* how to follow the proper dance steps does not help all that much. But, when one "has mastered the dance steps, a kind of 'wisdom of the body' takes over which indeed permits the analytical mind, the focused attention, to rest. One begins to 'flow' with the beat of the music, the rhythm of the dance." So it is with the liturgy, says Baer. As beautiful as the music and the stained glass windows might be in a liturgical setting, he observes, "there is yet a deeper movement of the human spirit as it encounters the Spirit of God [and] the presence of the risen Christ. . . . The analytical, objectifying mind is permitted to rest and thus the [human spirit] is free to experience reality on a new level."

Baer is careful to acknowledge that the varying expressions of speaking in tongues, Quaker silence, and high liturgy that concern him the most are all intended by those who practice them to give expression to the mind of Christ, as we know that mind from Scripture, in particular from texts such as Philippians 2, in which Paul celebrates the servanthood of Christ. It's easy, in contrast, to think of radically different examples of practices that may also help people break with the tyranny of the cognitive mind but which can prompt them to act and believe in dysfunctional, even demonic, ways. Consider, for example, something as apparently mundane as the binge drinking practices on some college campuses today. Such practices, when they break with the tyranny of the cognitive mind, may make it possible for the "initiates" to engage in a range of abusive behaviors, such as date rape. Consider also the public rallies of the Nazis in the 1920s and 1930s in Germany, when a kind of mass psychosis settled upon ordinary people, in the context of huge and extended rallies, prompting them to endorse a demonic leader and to follow his ways. Such practices *did* break with the tyranny of the cognitive mind, but with disastrous results. Not just any practice that breaks with the tyranny of the cognitive mind, in other words, should be celebrated.

Notwithstanding these counterexamples, Baer's thesis is insightful and instructive. To enter into a sustainable life of prayer in our time, one must, indeed, find appropriate ways to break with the tyranny of the cognitive mind, to let that mind rest now and again, as Baer suggests, in order to engage a different dimension of reality, what the English spiritual writer Evelyn Underhill regularly called "the Real."

The practice of the Trinity Prayer, I believe, can be one helpful way to break with the tyranny of the cognitive mind. As I have experienced it, it can be like dancing, when, if you are so graced, you get carried away to new and invigorating levels of experience—in this case, a blessed engagement with nature. Practice will surely never make *perfect*, in this sinful world. But practice can make *possible*. And practice can make possible, as I have already observed, in different places. You don't have to be in a cathedral or at a Friends' meeting. You can be on the job, on a walk, or on an airplane; you can be weeding the garden or backpacking in the Rockies.

The Emergence of the Trinity Prayer: A Personal Story

Here is precisely how the specifically Christian dimension of the story I am telling emerged in my own life. I began a practice of prayer that was new to me, with the distant but, for me, critically important guidance of a tradition of prayer that I had never heard of before. I took that plunge. Knowing very little about this way of praying, I simply began to pray this way, as best as I could, by the grace of God. At first, it was like learning to swim or learning to dance or learning to speak a new language. But, in due course, I was enabled to "go with the flow" in a way that I eventually realized was liberating.

When I was a young theological student, a friend introduced me to what he called "the Jesus Prayer." He had learned this prayer at a retreat led by an Eastern Orthodox priest who himself had been influenced by a movement in traditional Orthodox spirituality that focused on the Jesus Prayer. This was the idea. You say the Jesus Prayer—"Lord Jesus Christ, have mercy on me" (or words like that)—repeatedly, even constantly, day in and day out. In this way, you respond to the injunction of the apostle Paul that we are to "pray without ceasing" (1 Thess. 5:17). You practice the presence of Jesus Christ in this unfolding temporal sense—just the way my own family always says at meals, "Come Lord Jesus, be thou our guest. And let these gifts to us be blest," but still more frequently. You keep saying the Jesus Prayer, again and again, until it becomes part of the stream of your own spiritual consciousness, to the point where you may not even be aware that you are saying the prayer anymore. You begin to pray subliminally or unconsciously. And by this practice, Jesus Christ himself, the incarnate, crucified, and risen Son of the eternal Father, will dwell in you and you in him, in the power of the Holy Spirit. That is the promise that is given with the practice of the Jesus Prayer, according to the orthodox masters.

I never investigated the Jesus Prayer movement in Orthodox spirituality, either in practice or from a scholarly point of view.[9] Nor did I stay in touch with the friend who once told me about that retreat. But the thought of such a practice set me thinking on my own. Before too long, variations of the Jesus Prayer found a place in my own spiritual practices, which had to that point been shaped not by the orthodox tradition but primarily by the ways of faith bequeathed to me by the baptismal theology of Martin Luther and by his vision of every Christian's vocation as a kind of prayerful walk through one's everyday experience.[10]

For some time, I experimented with different ways to give voice to the Jesus Prayer, and this was what was eventually given to me, not by my own invention, I believe, but by the Spirit of the God who is the Father of Jesus

Christ—not just the Jesus Prayer but something larger and much more explicitly baptismal, predicated on a vision of God as Father, Son, and Holy Spirit. Certainly, this prayer does not belong to me, since its words are so self-evidently expressions of classical Christian meanings, but I do not know whether any other Christian soul speaks these meanings, or has done so, in precisely this way.

These are the simple words of the prayer that gradually devolved upon my soul in those years. I quote this prayer often in this book, in one form or another, since repetition, as sages throughout the ages have opined, is the soul of wisdom.

> *Lord Jesus Christ, have mercy on me.*
> *Praise Father, Son, and Holy Spirit.*
> *Come Holy Spirit, come and reign.*

I hope it will become evident as my narrative unfolds why this prayer took on its threefold shape in my spiritual life, moving as it does from Jesus to the triune God then to the Holy Spirit—why it could not, in fact, have been otherwise for me. As I recall, I was not consciously aware of this spiritual logic as I first began to find a way to identify and then to practice the petitions of this prayer. Such an awareness was to emerge only later.

THE HERITAGE AND THE PRACTICE OF THE TRINITY PRAYER

There was, of course, ample traditional precedent for this threefold shape of the Trinity Prayer, beginning with the words of the apostle Paul: "The grace of the Lord Jesus Christ, the love of God, and the communion of the Holy Spirit be with all of you" (2 Cor. 13:13). More to the point, the words of this blessing by Paul were the very words (in a slightly different translation), spoken by the pastor-presider, that began every Sunday liturgy in which I had participated since the days of my earliest conscious liturgical experiences as a child—and to this very day. Thus, if I may speak figuratively of these moments of my own spiritual pilgrimage, I did not discover the Trinity Prayer. It discovered me. As a lifelong participant in the church's liturgical practices, it was no wonder that a prayer concerning the mercy of Jesus, the glory and the mystery of the triune God, and the power and the enlightenment of the Spirit so deeply claimed my soul.[11]

I will explore ways to practice this prayer, in some detail, in chapter 10 and in the epilogue and appendix. But I do want to say something right away about practicing it, in order to give you a sense for how it "works" for me, before I begin to delve into its rich meanings. Whenever I use the prayer, I repeat each line four times, this in order to speak with the cadence of many traditional hymns of the church, such as "The Doxology" (Old Hundredth).[12] I then repeat the whole prayer (again, each line four times) as often as circumstances and spiritual stamina will allow. In addition, in the morning and the evening, at the beginning and the ending of the prayer, I always make the sign of the cross, in order to begin and to conclude the day by reminding myself of the prayer's baptismal meanings and of my own Baptism.

This prayer, where circumstances require, can be spoken, either aloud or in the silence of the heart. I opt for singing it, whenever possible, almost always in settings of solitude,[13] in order to give a more resonant, physical voice to the fragile faith within me. The singing helps me to invest my whole embodied self in the praying. If you do choose to sing the prayer often, as I recommend, you may also wish to vary the music from season to season of the church year.[14]

On the other hand, I don't want to give you the impression that this Trinity Prayer is complicated to practice. You only need to call to mind the three simple lines:

> *Lord Jesus Christ, have mercy on me.*
> *Praise Father, Son, and Holy Spirit.*
> *Come Holy Spirit, come and reign.*

Begin with these silent words in your heart, if that suits you best. Take the plunge. You can add the variations later, if you are so moved. It has "worked" for me, very simply, for a long time and in many places.[15]

For decades, I have said or sung the Trinity Prayer numerous times during any given day and, almost without exception, every morning when I have awakened and every evening as I have been ready to retire. I have prayed this prayer when leaving on a trip and upon my arrival. I have prayed this prayer when I have been peacefully weeding the garden or when I have been cut to the quick by a professional crisis. I have prayed this prayer as I have been walking in the woods, full of contentment, or walking along city streets, full of excitement or sometimes righteous indignation. I prayed this prayer when, a few years ago, my wife went into a coma after a stroke and when, a day later, thankfully, she suddenly awoke and began to make a full recovery. I have prayed this prayer when the news of the day has prompted me to recall the witness of saints like Francis of Assisi or Dietrich Bonhoeffer or Dorothy Day or Martin Luther King Jr. or Nelson Mandela, and when I have encountered the influence of the principalities and powers of death in the lives of "good Christian people" who have in word or deed taken stands that have contradicted the acts and the witness of such saints.

As I have reflected about this regular practice, I think I have begun to understand that apostolic injunction to "pray without ceasing." Experienced practitioners of the classical Jesus Prayer – "Lord Jesus Christ, have mercy on me." — have reported the emergence in their souls of what sounds to me like a subliminal consciousness that somehow undergirds the conscious awareness of the person praying. That subliminal consciousness, it seems to me, is where the oft-repeated Jesus Prayer dwells. I have experienced something like that with the Trinity Prayer, even though this prayer is longer and therefore less amenable to uninterrupted repetition than the Jesus Prayer is.

For me, the petitions of the Trinity Prayer—or, perhaps more often, fragments of them—seem to float constantly in the chamber of my subliminal mind—here an image of the divine mercy of Jesus, there a glimpse of the giving of the Father, here a sense for the presence of "Christ beside me," there a sense for the renewing power of the Holy Spirit. This produces a kind of near-constant mindfulness of the triune God in my life, even though the thoughts and images and affections may be fleeting.[16]

Explicit and regular repetition of the whole Trinity Prayer seems to keep my subliminal mind supplied with those fragmentary images that always seem to be there in one form or another. I suppose that it is no surprise, then, that I have occasionally had dreams about the Trinity. I am not sure what to make of that fact, but it does not seem to be surprising in a life given to regular repetition of the Trinity Prayer.

THE TRINITY PRAYER AS A WAY OF SPIRITUAL KNOWING

But just going through the motions, even with classically cast words, as in the Trinity Prayer, is obviously not enough. Practice does make possible. But that practice must be claimed by the self-disclosure of God if there is to be genuine spiritual knowing. When, by the grace of God, that happens, what then is that spiritual knowing?

I hope to show you that the Trinity Prayer, once practiced, offers us a way to engage, however imperfectly, some of the imponderable mysteries of the triune God. In the explorations in spirituality that follow, therefore, you will be invited to think and feel your way into this prayer as an exercise in spiritual insight. Pray this prayer often with your eyes closed, as it were, and then open them prepared to see the world anew, charged all around with the glory of God, Father, Son, and Holy Spirit.

Consider my scything, once again. *How* I see my world when I scythe makes all the difference. It's not simply a matter of going out to the field to "commune with nature." When I arrive in the backfield with my scythe, the eyes of my faith have already been opened by use of the Trinity Prayer, so that I can then see more readily what is given me to see. The Trinity Prayer is for me, in this spiritual sense, before nature. This is why I treasure the oft-quoted bon mot of Marcel Proust: "The voyage of discovery is not in seeking new landscapes, but in having new eyes." The Trinity Prayer gives me the insight that allows me to see with new eyes. And I want to commend this way of seeing to all of my readers in the following manner.

In the next chapter, chapter 3, I explore what it can mean to enter into a life of prayer in a twilight world like ours in the late modern or postmodern West, where perhaps the most haunting spiritual experience for many—some believers among them—is the experience to which I have already referred: the eclipse of God.

In chapter 4, I then reflect about what it can mean to contemplate the light of Christ in such a twilight world, how God can be known addressing us in the word made flesh, in the life, death, and resurrection of Jesus Christ. So, in that chapter, I invite you to pray:

Lord Jesus Christ, have mercy on me.

In chapter 5, I raise the question about the turmoil and the trust in my own soul. What is the truth of my own existence? If I am a soul in turmoil, as I am, in what sense am I a believer? In what sense is the grace of the Lord Jesus Christ real for me? I raise such questions as an encouragement for my readers to do the same, as we continue to pray:

Lord Jesus Christ, have mercy on me.

In chapters 6 through 8, I explore a refracted vision of Godself—the "seeing through a glass darkly" that the apostle Paul talks about (1 Cor. 13:12)—which that encounter with the word incarnate makes possible: the vision of the triune God who dwells in, with, under, and beyond all things, from alpha to omega, from the first things of the universe, before "the Big Bang," to the last things of the universe, after the cosmic death of all things. This God, I also suggest, works in differentiated ways in this world, corresponding to God's own eternal being and becoming, as Giver, Gift, and Giving. In this context, I also seek to explore the parameters of a vision of the ministries of the cosmic Christ and the cosmic Spirit. So, you are invited to pray:

Praise Father, Son, and Holy Spirit.

In chapter 9, I consider what it means to call on the Holy Spirit to come and to enact the purposes of the triune God the world of nature. I suggest that, in doing this, the Spirit works with and responds to the integrity of nature and the travail of nature. This vision of the brooding of the Spirit over all things then makes it possible, I believe, as you practice this prayer in any place, to hope in the future of God, to see with your inner eyes in some fashion that future which the Spirit is calling forth each day in order to sanctify and finally to consummate the life of every individual creature and indeed the whole creation. In this context, I commend the following petition to you:

Come Holy Spirit, come and reign.

With this petition in mind and heart and, I hope, on your lips, I return to the heart of the story in chapter 10, praying the Trinity Prayer itself, with practical suggestions and with celebrations of the blessed engagement with God in nature that can be ours. Call these exercises sauntering in the Spirit, as we pray once again:

Come Holy Spirit, come and reign.

PRAYING THE WHOLE TRINITY PRAYER—WITH NATURE IN MIND

At the very end, once I have concluded my narrative, I hope you will have discerned that, although the Trinity Prayer has a beginning, a middle, and an ending, its three parts presuppose one another spiritually and, indeed, that their meanings interpenetrate one another. It is not as if I'm asking you to climb a ladder with three steps so that you will be asked to leave the first step and then the second behind, as you ascend to the third. On the contrary, although the first petition of the Trinity Prayer—*Lord Jesus Christ, have mercy on me*—is the necessary existential point of departure, in my experience the whole prayer won't "work" spiritually if the one who is praying it tries to move on to the second petition with the assumption that he or she is passing beyond personal engagement with the Lord Jesus Christ, as if the second petition, focused as it is on the great and ineffable mystery of the Trinity—*Praise Father, Son, and Holy Spirit*—is somehow a "higher stage" of the spiritual life.

Likewise, when you come to the petition that invokes the Spirit of God—*Come Holy Spirit, come and reign*—it is not as if, in that moment, you will have discerned the ultimate moment of the spiritual dynamic I am describing, as if, somehow, you are now to enter into some halcyon clarity of a "pure spirituality," whatever that might be. On the contrary, while there are three utterances, there is only one—rich and complex—spiritual meaning. It all holds together or it all falls apart. That's one of the reasons I recommend constant repetitions of the whole prayer.

Be assured, finally, that in each of the chapters ahead, *I will regularly pay explicit attention to my blessed engagement with nature,* whenever that is appropriate, since that is the underlying theme of this whole narrative. So, for example, when I am reflecting about my own sinfulness, I will confront at some length the patriarchal spirit that engulfed my soul and distorted my own relationship with nature for a number of years. More positively—as another example—when I am invoking analogies to help us contemplate God as Trinity, I will narrate how I have found it not only possible but also necessary to envision the Trinity through the lens of nature.

Notes

1. "Nones on the Rise," *Pew Forum of Religion and the Public Life*, October 9, 2012, http://www.pewforum.org/2012/10/09/nones-on-the-rise.

2. In recent years, a number of philosophers, sociologists, and historians—as well as theologians and ethicists—have given considerable attention to the importance of *practices* in a variety of settings. For an entry into these wide-ranging discussions, see the essay by Craig Dykstra and Dorothy C. Bass, "A Theological Understanding of Christian Practices," in *Practicing our Faith: Beliefs and Practices in Christian Life*, ed. Miroslav Volf and Dorothy C. Bass (San Francisco: Jossey-Bass, 1997), 13–32, and the literature cited in that book. More particularly, see Martha Ellen Stortz, "Practicing Christians: Prayer as Formation," in *The Promise of Lutheran Ethics*, ed. Karen L. Bloomquist and John R. Stumme (Minneapolis: Fortress Press, 1998), chap. 4. Practices have also become a central concern for a number of evangelical protestant churches, particularly so-called "emergent churches," such as the Vineyard Churches. For an overview of the latter trend, see T. M. Luhrmann, *When God Talks Back: Understanding the American Evangelical Relationship with God* (New York: Knopf, 2012). For a sociological appreciation and recommendation of spiritual practices in American life, see Robert Wuthnow, *After Heaven: Spirituality in America since the 1950's* (Berkeley: University of California Press, 1998), especially 168–98.

3. I am encouraged in this narrative by Wuthnow's recommendation of practices as being of critical importance for the seekers of this world—to whom this book is addressed along with the theological teachers and pastors who are in conversation with those seekers. See especially, Wuthnow, *After Heaven*, 16: "In my view, the ancient wisdom that emphasizes the idea of spiritual

practices needs to be rediscovered; indeed a practice-oriented spirituality should be considered seriously as an alternative both to dwelling and to seeking." I particularly value Wuthnow's accent on the construct of place (17): "Practice oriented spirituality preserves some of what has always attracted people to a spirituality of dwelling, for it too requires the setting aside of a space in which to meditate, to pray, and to worship, and in the confusion of everyday life such a space may be possible only by carefully demarcating it from its surroundings. Yet these spaces are negotiable, changeable, and the point of engaging in spiritual practices is not merely to feel secure in a sacred space but to grow increasingly aware of the mysterious and transcendent aspects of the sacred as well."

4. Those among my readers who are theologically trained may wish to pursue the thoughts under discussion here, at length and in depth, in James J. Buckley and David S. Yeago, eds., *Knowing the Triune God: The Work of the Spirit in the Practices of the Church* (Grand Rapids, MI: Eerdmans, 2001). Particularly instructive in that volume is the essay by Susan K. Wood, "The Liturgy: Participatory Knowledge of God in the Liturgy," 95–120. What she says about the liturgy—the communal prayer of the faithful—is particularly instructive: "We experience the knowledge of faith in our lives before we reflect upon it. Knowledge is an activity, a process, and we literally act our way into knowing by entering into the relationships constituted by the liturgy. Liturgy becomes the ritual action by which we live and enact the faith" (109). The knowing of faith, she maintains, is kinesthetic first and foremost, not theoretical. For some reflections on the interrelationship between communal and individual practices, such as the Trinity Prayer, see note 6 below.

5. What *God* does with our spiritual practices is, we hope, much. Thus Paul takes it for granted that the first-century Christian congregation at Rome is engaged in such practices. He states that they cry out, "Abba, Father." And presumably, they do that regularly, perhaps often. Such a practice, says Paul, is "the very Spirit of God bearing witness with our spirit that we are children of God . . . and joint heirs with Christ" (Rom. 8:15b-17). As they are thus crying out, I take Paul to mean, they don't really, in the fullest sense, know what they are doing or what God is doing. So Paul tells them that that very Spirit who is bearing witness by their shouts of "Abba, Father," also is, at once, interceding for them with God through their sighs that are too deep for words (Rom. 8:26). Which is to say that, for Paul, the practices (the shouts) and the deep communion with God go hand in hand, thanks to the working of the Spirit, who is involved in both.

6. What is true of individual prayer, which is my focus here, is all the more true of the communal prayer of the church, that is, the church's worship. To explore this theme, in addition to the essays in the volume cited in note 2 above, readers may wish to consult my study *Ritualizing Nature: Renewing Christian Liturgy in a Time of Crisis* (Minneapolis: Fortress Press, 2008), in which I argue that the liturgy is the church's mode of identity formation. In a word, the truth of the matter is this, from the perspective of faith: not "I think, therefore I am" (*cogito ergo sum*), the famous philosophical declaration of human identity proposed by Rene Descartes at the beginning of the modern era, but "we worship, therefore we are" (*laudamus ergo sumus*). In the case before us here, that of individual prayer, the formative identity statement would be "I pray, therefore I am" (*oro ergo sum*). In my view, the communal practice (*laudamus*) and the individual practice (*oro*) are closely interrelated, with the communal being the most fundamental and the most formative. This is why it makes perfect sense to me that the church's worship "in the name of the Father, and of the Son, and of the Holy Spirit," should also and constantly draw forth my own individual voice, every day of the week, every hour of the day, in the Trinity Prayer.

7. See the words of the Carmelite sister Ruth Burrows in "Prayer Is God's Work," *Christian Century* 129, no. 7 (April 4, 2012): 10f: "Many people think they have no faith because they feel they haven't. They do not realize that they must make a choice to believe, take the risk of believing, of committing themselves to live out the commitment. Never mind that they continue to feel that they do not believe. Under the cover of being 'authentic' we can spend our lives waiting for the kind of certainty we cannot have."

8. Richard A. Baer Jr., "Quaker Silent Worship, Glossolalia, and Liturgy: Some Functional Similarities," 1972 (unpublished). A shortened, published version of this essay is available in *Perspectives on the New Pentecostalism*, ed. Russell P. Spittler (Grand Rapids, MI: Baker Book House, 1976), 150–64. The quotations here are from the longer, unpublished essay.

9. I learned later that the literature on the Jesus Prayer is enormous, far too large even to summarize here. Should the reader wish to begin to investigate these rich materials, the classic spiritual narrative by an anonymous nineteenth-century Russian spiritual practitioner, *The Way of the Pilgrim,* is perhaps the best place to begin. Most helpful, too, from both reflective and practical perspectives, is the short essay by Kallistos Ware, *The Power of The Name: The Jesus Prayer in Orthodox Spirituality* (Oxford: SLG, 1974 [10th printing, 2005]).

10. This is not to suggest that the Orthodox tradition does not bring a penumbra of baptismal meanings to its understanding of prayer. See these illuminating comments by Kallistos Ware, *The Power of the Name*, 3: "For the overwhelming majority [of Christians] . . ., Baptism is something received in infancy, of which they have no conscious memory. Although the baptismal Christ and the indwelling Paraclete [the Spirit] never cease for one moment to work within us, most of us—save on rare occasions—remain virtually unaware of this inner presence and activity. True prayer, then, signifies the rediscovery and 'manifestation' of baptismal grace. To pray is to pass from the state where grace is present in our hearts secretly and unconsciously, to the point of full inner perception and conscious awareness when we experience and *feel* the activity of the Spirit directly and immediately."

11. For this reason, this volume, *Before Nature*, stands in the most intimate of relationships with my immediately preceding work, *Ritualizing Nature*. Spirituality and liturgy go hand in hand, in my view and in my experience, and cannot be understood in isolation from each other. As I hope will become apparent as the narrative of this volume unfolds, the liturgy of the church has been the mother, the matrix, of my spirituality. For a short but most enlightening account of the relationship that can obtain between liturgy and spirituality, see Susan J. White, "Spirituality, Liturgy and Worship," in *The New Westminster Dictionary of Christian Spirituality*, 44–48.

12. Given voice in the so-called "Long Meter." See, further, the appendix.

13. I did lead a retreat once that focused on the Trinity Prayer, and in that context we did use the prayer communally. I have also taught the Trinity Prayer to counselees. But most of my usage of the prayer has been as an instrument of private devotion.

14. I will give examples in the appendix.

15. As I developed the Trinity Prayer, I did so with the general awareness that I was navigating in waters than had been traversed often by Christian spiritual practitioners throughout the ages, especially in traditions influenced by monastic "keeping of the hours" and, more particularly, by many Anglicans' commitments to observing the Daily Office, especially as that was offered in its twice-daily form by Thomas Cranmer in the *Book of Common Prayer* (1549). For an overview of this tradition, see George Guiver, "Office, Divine," in *The New Westminster Dictionary of Christian Spirituality*, 471–73. But those multifaceted traditions of devotion—often, although not always, rooted in monastic or ecclesial settings—never spoke to me the way the simplicity and mobility of the Jesus Prayer did. For reasons that I have not understood even to this day, I have needed a simple prayer form that can be a part of every hour of every day, at any time and in any place—a portable prayer, as it were—in the midst of my mundane experience. That is what I eventually found, or was given, in the Trinity Prayer.

16. See the comment by the eminent Quaker spiritual writer Thomas R. Kelly in *A Testament of Devotion* (New York: Harper, 1941), 122: "There is a way of life so hid with Christ in God that in the midst of the day's business one is inwardly lifting brief prayers, short ejaculations of praise, subdued whispers of adoration and of tender love to the Beyond that is within."

3

The World in Which We Pray
The Eclipse of God and a Fragile Theology of Faith

Of course, practicing the Trinity Prayer is not enough in itself. Spiritual practices must be suffused with spiritual knowing if our spirituality is to be for real. Once the tyranny of the cognitive mind has been overcome, what is to become of the deeper mind and the thirsting heart? This question returns us to a mundane observation that I made at the beginning of chapter 2: in these times, it is not easy to pray.

That observation, in turn, presupposes a much more telling question—about *God*. This is the issue that we must now confront. Never mind our spiritual practices for a moment, important as they are. Let's deal with the underlying challenge. How is it possible to know God in the midst of the profoundly confusing world in which we live today? How is it possible to be claimed by God, to be thrown to our knees in awe, in a world where spiritualities seem to be a dime a dozen? We must confront this kind of question because, without that overwhelming knowing, all of our practices would obviously be for naught.

In this chapter, therefore, I will cautiously venture to explore the contemporary question of God in terms of my own experience. To this end, I will follow a way—focusing on Jesus—that was identified by a number of Christian thinkers of the past century, foremost among them the theologian and martyr Dietrich Bonhoeffer, who forged his spirituality in the midst of the crisis of the German church and the German resistance to Hitler during World War II.[1] Instructed by Bonhoeffer, I will identify this part of our journey under the following rubric: the eclipse of God and a fragile theology of faith. Along the way, I will review—and then reject—what I consider to be perhaps the most plausible approach to "the God question" in our time, which I will call a rigorous theology of facts. I will engage this topic in conversation with an eminent American theologian of our own era, a former teacher of mine, Gordon Kaufman.

I regard the fragile theology of faith that I will be recommending as an *implausible plausibility*, particularly when it is juxtaposed to a theology of facts such as Kaufman's. It is predicated not on a self-contained human logic but on what might be called a self-disclosing divine logic, the revelation of the eclipsed God in the person of the one who is said to have proclaimed (John 8:12), "I am the light of the world"—Jesus. Having identified what is for me this implausible plausibility, I will then venture in chapter 4 to explicate some of its meanings, again in terms of my own experience, beginning with the story of Mary Magdalene.

THE ECLIPSE OF GOD AND THE TWILIGHT OF OUR TIMES: A PLACE OF KNOWING

The great German novelist Thomas Mann, lamented in the early twentieth century how easily the word *God* crosses over human lips. I do not take that thought lightly. A domesticated God is no God at all. God is either wholly other, an inscrutable and unspeakable mystery, as an equally great Swiss theologian of Mann's era, Karl Barth, said, or God is nothing but a construct of the human imagination, born perhaps of desperation. God is either, in the words of a hymn I have sung all my life, "Immortal, invisible . . ., In light inaccessible hid from our eyes," or God is an abstract, unifying idea for our worldviews, hardly worthy of our worship. Or, perhaps the idea of God would be some kind of a spiritual opiate, good for nothing but dulling the pain of human existence, as the nineteenth-century philosopher of history Karl Marx claimed.

I want to honor the wholly other God as I tell my story. Indeed, I want to acknowledge that the challenge of faith in this God has become all the more acute for many people in the Western world today, since the time of Mann and Barth. If we do not live today in total darkness, as far as faith in the wholly other God is concerned, we surely do live in twilight times, when, for many, nothing ultimate is certain or even of much concern anymore, even in a time when there are many spiritualities competing for our attention. As you sometimes cannot see the forest for the trees, so in today's world, you often cannot see God for all the spiritualities being proffered in the public marketplace, whether at your local big-box bookstore or online. Wandering among the trees in near darkness: this is the kind of situation that Martin Buber, writing in the era of Thomas Mann and Karl Barth, and well aware of the message of critics like Karl Marx, called "the eclipse of God."[2]

EXPERIENCING THE TWILIGHT

If you, my readers, are truly to hear the story I am telling about my blessed engagement with God in nature, you must come with me without delay into the twilight, even into the darkness, of our times, in full awareness of what you are doing. The place is Boston, Massachusetts. I am privileged—in both the positive and negative senses of that word—to be able to spend much time in rural Maine from spring through fall, but the urban world of Boston is my home and has been for some time.

It is early in the morning, before dawn. It is a bitterly cold winter day, and I am walking along the Charles River, my shoes cracking through the hardened surface of the snow. I have to pull my fur cap tightly to my skull and bend my head to protect my eyes from the blowing snow. This is not the beautiful world I sometimes encounter during the fall season in rural Maine when I am scything with God. Nor is this the world of promise that comes to mind when I think of my own Baptism more than seven decades ago in Buffalo, New York. This is something else. At a time and a place like this in the frigid twilight, the thought of the eclipse of God is chillingly plausible.

The idea of the eclipse of God was bequeathed in my lifetime to those who would believe in God by one of the most traumatic events in the history of the human species—the Holocaust. Six million Jews, and many others, among them gypsies, gays, and disabled persons, were calculatedly and ruthlessly put to death in Adolf Hitler's Germany. As a young boy during those times living a conventional middle-class existence in Buffalo, I was protected. Later, after World War II, I did see newsreel films about the liberation of some of the camps. The photos of the piles of bodies and of the emaciated survivors horrified me. But I must have completely repressed those experiences. As I recall, I never talked about them with anyone. Nor was I ever called upon, at home or in school or at my church, to discuss what I had seen in those films. I am not sure when the very expression "the Holocaust" gained currency in my own social and religious world. Remarkably, I remained consciously oblivious to the Holocaust until the end of my high school years in 1953.

This all changed when I was an undergraduate, not far from where I was walking in that chilling snowstorm along the Charles River. It happened in a university lecture hall, during a course in German history. There, a crisis of faith was thrust upon me, from which, I think, I have never fully recovered. I discovered the Holocaust existentially.

The instructor began to review the story of the Holocaust and then to narrate how many "good Germans" looked the other way when the Jews were carted off to the camps. He talked, too, about Lutheranism's long tradition of hostility to the Jews in Germany, beginning in a most ugly fashion with Luther himself. He also described the Lutheran tradition's doctrine of unquestioning obedience to the state, predicated on a reading of Romans 13 (see v. 1b: "the powers that be are ordained by God"). Many German Lutherans, accordingly, simply let the state do whatever it chose to do, he said, since they believed that it had been established by God.

But those were *my* people! I grew up in a German Lutheran immigrant community. That was the church in which I had been baptized, and which had so powerfully nourished me since I had been a child! Not a few Lutherans in Germany had become "German Christians," said the instructor. They celebrated the rise of Hitler as a gift of God. Me? World War II had long been over, but I had never even thought about the meaning of the Holocaust before! Why hadn't we discussed it at my church? Why hadn't church bodies or speakers at youth rallies or Bible camps addressed this issue? In that lecture hall that day, I found myself at the edge of tears. I still feel those tears.

Providentially, in due course, I was befriended during my crisis of faith by a pastor, Henry E. Horn, who touched the lives of countless students in my generation. It was he who first introduced me to the life and works of Bonhoeffer. That encounter with Bonhoeffer, in turn, opened my mind and heart to engage the theology of the Confessing Church in Germany during the Nazi era. That church stood up against Hitler, imperfectly, but publicly. In the midst of a certain intellectual incoherence about such matters for a number of years, I was subsequently assigned to a gifted history tutor, whose name I can no longer remember. He took me under his wing and respected my own questions, notwithstanding the fact that he was an agnostic and that his reading of Lutheran history in Germany was much more critical than even mine had come to be.

I wrote my 1957 undergraduate honors thesis on the German resistance to Hitler. My research focused on a number of leading lights of the resistance movement, among them Bonhoeffer. In those studies, I discovered for myself many inspiring accounts of individual Christians who put their lives at risk in order to stand in the way of the Nazi behemoth. On the other hand, I also learned that the Nazis themselves were champions, in their own way, of the theology of nature! A heroic, nordic wilderness-ethos of "blood and soil" (*Blut und Boden*) permeated much of their propaganda. This cast a pall over my then burgeoning theological and spiritual interest in nature, a pall that remains to this day.

This is why Karl Barth's proclamation in his early public years of the wholly other God appealed to me so profoundly as a young theological student. Barth established, in no uncertain terms, that the God of *Blut und Boden* was no God. Barth refreshingly proclaimed, too, that the God whose place was at the apex of Western bourgeois civilization was in fact an idol. This is why, at the same time, I found Martin Buber's announcement of the eclipse of God so compelling. On any given day of my life, I can readily call to mind the chilling visages of those piles of dead bodies in the camps. And I can readily hear the voices of survivors, like Elie Wiesel, who cried out: where was God during the Holocaust?!³ That is why, in a starkly strange and perhaps deeply self-contradictory way, I *do* feel at home in the darkness from time to time, as when, on a frigid, snow-driven, predawn morning, I make my way through the crusty snow on the path along the Charles River, with my fur cap pulled down as far as it will go and with my head bowed to keep the snow particles from cutting at my eyes. I think I know, in some small measure at least, what the eclipse of God means in our time.

But, of course, looking back, even on horrendously evil events like the Holocaust, is in fact just that—looking back. If we are to think of our times as an era of twilight, if not darkness, we will have to be as clear as we possibly can about the present as well. Most of my readers will know all about such matters, so I will only mention them here. If current global trends continue, the human species is facing a bleak future indeed. Climate change threatens all manner of devastating global disruptions, rising seas, shrinkage of agricultural lands, increasingly chaotic weather patterns, vast destructions of forests, and more, all of which will in all likelihood unleash massive social struggles, huge migrations of peoples, and wars over shrinking resources like water. The countless millions of poor around the world will continue to get poorer. Mass starvation and epidemics will become much more commonplace. And then there is always the possibility of nuclear war, intentional or accidental, unleashed perhaps by some rogue state or by a terrorist act of madness. It is a chilling picture—and no wonder that films and novels about nuclear winter or other global catastrophes are so popular in our times.

Call this the existential challenge of historical evil, pondering what humans have wrought—and may yet wreak—against one another and against the life-support systems of our planet. But this historical evil is embedded in a virtually infinite universe of cosmic destruction that in some ways is even more troubling, at least to anyone who takes the time to think about it. Schoolchildren today are, more often than not, well acquainted with images of our incredibly immense universe, with its billions and billions and billions of galaxies, all of them apparently going—nowhere. Five billion years from now, our own galaxy, the Milky Way, will collide with another, producing an unimaginably colossal event of cosmic destruction. What's more—or less—our entire universe, after many more billions of years, is heading toward some kind of a final heat death, according the Second Law of Thermodynamics.

The story of the evolution of life on this spec of cosmic dust that we inhabit—planet Earth—is no more encouraging. Evolutionary violence drives the story of every species on the earth, and the law of that massive violence is suffering, destruction, and death, the fabled world of "nature red in tooth and claw" (Alfred, Lord Tennyson). Further, that world, bloody and deadly as it is, is itself often disrupted by geological and meteorological events of massive scope, the earthquakes and the tsunamis, not to speak of extraterrestrial interventions of even larger scope, such as the earth being impacted by enormous meteors or comets, some of which have changed the whole history of terrestrial evolution with massive, global impacts.

Where is God in all of this? If, in some sense, God permitted the Holocaust, many thoughtful souls are asking in our time, will God now also permit humans to undermine the ecological support system of the biosphere, which makes life on this planet possible? And what about the pervasiveness of evolutionary violence on this earth? What, furthermore, are we to make of the picture we have of the whole cosmos lurching, violently but silently, toward a state of virtually infinite, dead frigidity? Along with countless Christians and others around the world today, I take such questions very seriously.[4] Where are believers to stand in these twilight times? How are we to walk in hope? How are we to keep faith alive? How are we to muster the spiritual energies we need to love the earth community of which we are a part? Has God truly been eclipsed in our times?[5]

Responding to the Eclipse of God (I): A Rigorous Theology of Facts

Many theologians and spiritual writers of stature, of course, have attempted to address this profoundly existential challenge. Some have stepped back to read the "signs of our times" dispassionately and to reflect critically about received theological traditions in order to ascertain whether faith in God is possible anymore in this our secular era, and, if so, what kind of faith that might be. Among these critical thinkers, I find the works, and the life story behind those works, of one of the most distinguished American theologians of the last generation, Gordon Kaufman, to be highly instructive. That Kaufman also happened to be my dissertation advisor probably has made my own continuing engagement with his thought and his life story over the years inevitable. Kaufman's appeal for me—more than a number of other major theologians of his era—was his sometimes brutal honesty.

Kaufman's project can be called a rigorous theology of facts. He looks at the world in which we live realistically and fearlessly and then asks what we can legitimately believe about God, if anything, anymore. Kaufman's works are demanding, and his thought may seem abstract to some who have not studied theology. But I ask all of my readers to do at least this much: experience the rigor of his thought, even if some steps along the way may feel too demanding. It is clear to me, in any case, that *I* can only take my readers on the spiritual journey I am proposing if we walk together through this theological valley of the facts, for the fragile theology of faith that I am taking for granted in this narrative—which I will address in the following section—presupposes that a sometimes brutally honest theological argument such as Kaufman's *is* plausible, even if it is, as I believe, profoundly inadequate.

THE PILGRIMAGE OF A THEOLOGIAN OF FACTS

For our purposes here, we can best approach Kaufman's theology by listening to what he has to say in his own theological autobiography.[6] Strikingly, as he recounts the story of his theological development, Kaufman does not even mention the Holocaust. He does not have an argument with God, as Job once did, or as I have had, in my own mundane way, since my college years. Kaufman's theological autobiography is not predicated on any Jobean struggle to justify the ways of God, addressing the question of "theodicy," of how a good God could allow a horrendous evil like the Holocaust to happen. Kaufman clearly knows about the evils of this world, especially in recent years, but that is not the theme that has driven his own thinking. Rather, Kaufman found himself, from his earliest years, claimed by what he believed was a logically prior question: does the idea of God itself make any sense in today's world?

Kaufman tells us at some length about his own Mennonite upbringing. An offshoot of the Protestant Reformation, Mennonites sought to return to what they perceived to be the life of the earliest church, above all, to its pacifism, its commitment to avoid violence and seek peace in all things. Mennonites also believed in adult Baptism, or "believer's Baptism," for the sake of developing mature discipleship. "Religious faith," Kaufman explains, "was a matter of thoughtful personal conviction and mature decision and commitment about how one's life was to be led, not something to be taken for granted as part of the general socializing process through which we all go from infancy to adulthood."[7] Indeed, thinking for himself, critically and clearly, characterized Kaufman's own spiritual pilgrimage all his life.

Spiritual experience, however, is not a theme that looms large in Kaufman's theological autobiography. He tells how he "looked into studies of mysticism" during his formative theological years. But he says that his interest in mysticism "has always been from a distance." Then we hear this striking self-revelation:

> I seem to be "tone deaf" with respect to so-called religious experience. When others speak of their "experience of God" or of "God's presence," or the profound experience of "the holy" or of "sacredness," I simply do not know what they are talking about. Perhaps this is one reason why the problem of God has been, throughout my life, so baffling and difficult.[8]

Kaufman not only tells the story about the absence of any significant "religious experience" in his own life but also explains that early on in his life he "concluded that talk about *experience* of God involves what philosophers call a 'category mistake,' and should not, therefore be engaged in."[9]

Kaufman began to develop what I am calling his theology of facts in his 1968 book, *Systematic Theology: A Historicist Perspective.*[10] There, on the basis of his commitment to see only what can be seen through human eyes, especially through the lenses of the natural sciences or of historical scholarship, Kaufman concluded that it is "not plausible today to hold that the historical Jesus had come back to life again after his crucifixion" and therefore that "christian hope should no longer be understood as involving life after death for us mortals."[11] Behind such assertions was Kaufman's increasingly rigorous understanding of theological method: that theology is first and foremost a human construction, not primarily an interpretation of some (alleged, in his view) divine revelation.

This idea of theology as a human construction, based on what is scientifically and historically plausible, was further reinforced for Kaufman, along the way, when he made extended trips to India and encountered the plurality of religions there and when he participated, at the highest levels, in the global Christian-Buddhist dialogue both in Japan and in the United States. It seemed plausible to him, indeed, that humans around the globe, in all cultures, were responding to the challenges of theological construction, thus creating their own view of things.

In due course, Kaufman's engagement with the issues of evolution and the ecological interrelationship of all things led him to conclude that "the personalistic side of the traditional christian conception of God" was no longer valid. Kaufman rejected various themes, including one that, like a father, God has purposes he is seeking to fulfill and that God invites all peoples to identify with those purposes, in personal communion with God. Kaufman saw, he tells us, that there is a conceptual and a logical incompatibility "between, on the one hand, the traditional personalistic understanding of God, and of God's intimate relation to humanity, and on the other hand, our growing awareness that human existence is essentially constituted by, and could not exist apart from, the complex ecological ordering of life that has evolved on planet earth over many millennia."[12] Kaufman also concluded not only that the traditional theologically personalistic way of seeing things was no longer credible but that it was, in some profound senses, dangerous. Kaufman argued that "the notion of God's providential care was getting in the way of our taking seriously our full human responsibility for the nuclear crisis in the midst of which we were living."[13]

But, if all this is true, if there is no resurrection, if there is no providential care of a heavenly father in which to trust, if there is no personal God in any traditional sense to whom to turn in prayer, who—or what—is God? Kaufman responded to this question at length in his mature writings, such as his major 1993 book, *In the Face of Mystery: A Constructive Theology.*[14] There he argued that the humanly constructed symbol "God" refers in fact to what Kaufman had come to think of as a universal process of "cosmic serendipitous creativity."

Wherever one looks, according to Kaufman, at all levels of reality, from the cell to the brain to the galaxy, one sees signs of an inexplicable and often wondrous creativity, and so it has been throughout the whole long and highly complicated processes of cosmic evolution. That creativity we may call "God," Kaufman believed. On the earth, furthermore, we can see "evolutionary and historical trajectories of various sorts, working themselves out in longer and shorter stretches of time."[15] Those trajectories, Kaufman held, such as human history in general or the history of religions in particular, are exemplary expressions of that universal phenomenon of serendipitous creativity.

Kaufman, however, did not want us to think of this serendipitous creativity as some kind of a force at work in the cosmos. He was not substituting the idea of an impersonal force, he stressed, to replace the traditional idea of the providential workings of a personal God. Rather, Kaufman held that he was merely describing what in this narrative I have called the facts: "Creativity happens; new and novel realities come into being in the course of temporal developments. This is an utterly amazing mystery."[16]

RESPONDING TO THE ECLIPSE OF GOD (II): A FRAGILE THEOLOGY OF FAITH

At one level of my own mind and heart, I find Kaufman's constructions compelling.[17] Like Kaufman and many others, I have an impulse to let the facts speak for themselves. And I am inclined to think that many other thoughtful souls in these times, perhaps including some, if not all, of my readers, may feel the same way.

But I would not be true to my own experience if I were to sign off on this theology of the facts as if it were the whole truth. For better or for worse, I am driven by a theology of faith as well as informed by a theology of facts. I cannot do otherwise than give voice to my own experience. For me, religious experience is not a contradiction in terms, as it is for Kaufman. Religious experience is, rather, a joy that I cannot restrain.

What if "serendipitous creativity" has spoken? I asked Gordon Kaufman this question whimsically in a private conversation, toward the end of his life, as we were driving to a faculty seminar of the Boston Theological Institute one evening. He replied: "No, that's not possible. We can't believe that anymore." But that was a serious as well as whimsical question on my part.

So, I now ask: what if the word of the wholly other God has addressed my mind and heart in a way that now allows me to see with new eyes, to see, indeed, more than the facts? What if my mind and heart have been enlightened by the revelation of God? What if I can now, in some sense, "see through a glass darkly," as the apostle Paul once stated (1 Cor. 13:12)? Dietrich Bonhoeffer pondered such things when he was in prison, just prior to his execution. It was the season of Advent, when the church traditionally celebrates the coming of God, in Christ, into this world. Bonhoeffer observed that being in prison is like his Advent hope. You have to wait for someone to open the door from the outside.[18]

What if the wholly other God *has* opened the door to our world of facts from the outside? To use the traditional language of theology, what if the wholly other God has *revealed* Godself to us—we who have "no hope and [are] without God in the world" (Eph. 2:12)—from the immeasurable and inscrutable beyond to us here and now? What if someone *has* walked into our twilight time from beyond the limits of our factual thinking and enlightened us?[19] Indeed, what if that someone is the light of the world (John 8:12)? These questions point to what I have learned to think of as hearing and seeing in faith. In the midst of the twilight, the door is opened from the outside, and you hear the voice of Christ and, in due course, you see the figure of Christ—and, indeed, much more. Let me anticipate, as if with the blink of an eye, what that much more can be, to give you a glimpse of where I want to take you next in this journey.

FROM THE TWILIGHT TO THE LIGHT OF CHRIST

It turns out that I am treading through the snow in the early-morning darkness along the Charles River because I am going somewhere. In recent years, I have made it a practice on Thursday mornings to walk from my apartment a couple of miles along the Charles River to participate in the Eucharist offered by the Society of St. John the Evangelist, in the elegant, basilica-style chapel of its Cambridge monastery. I typically leave my home those Thursdays in the morning twilight. Since I'm not usually an early riser, nor do I have anything like a clear mind at such an hour, that twilight walk, for me, is sometimes depressing, a feeling that is exacerbated during the cold winter months, when I may have to contend with ice and snow along the way. But, now and then, and repeatedly so over the years, that depression has given way to elation. This has happened on rare occasions when, as I walked along, the winter storm has subsided and, just at those moments, the rising sun has begun to come into view. See that amazing ball of fire now, that very brother sun so intensely celebrated by St. Francis, reflected on the river, shining just on me, or so it seems. No wonder I am elated!

I know a good deal about seasonal affective disorder (SAD), to be sure. Many years of experience as a pastoral counselor have taught me that many people suffer from that malaise. Sometimes, what a counselee needs is not to learn how to pray more regularly or to engage loved ones more responsively but to purchase one of those expensive lightbulbs that mimic sunlight, which can work wonders with people's seasonal depressions when regularly used, say, as an evening reading light. My elation at seeing the sunrise may well be attributable to the fact that I myself may suffer, at least to some degree, from SAD. But I believe that it's more than that.

On those Thursday mornings, when the morning sun begins to shine, dispelling the twilight whatever the season of the year, I know, in faith, however feebly, that I am on my way to behold the light of Christ. The sunrise along the way, I believe, is claimed by the Spirit of God to announce that prospect to me in the midst of the twilight. Especially on the coldest of winter mornings, the rising of the sun reminds me where I am heading: to enter into the joys of the people gathered around the altar, as if around a hearth, announcing and contemplating the light of Christ, graciously revealed to us by God the Father, in the power of the Spirit. That the God who, according to the testimony of Genesis, created the light itself is revealed to me personally in that communal eucharistic rite is profoundly moving.[20] No wonder, then, that, when I am walking toward the monastery in the frigid early-morning twilight, and when the wind and the snow die down and the sun then begins to shine, with its beams reflected across the river as if they were shining only on me, I experience moments of elation in the midst of my otherwise depressed pedestrian existence.

These are some of the contours of the fragile theology of faith that I want to commend to you in this narrative, which is for me a spiritually compelling implausible plausibility. Now I want to explore the deeper dynamics of this faith as we can see them in the story of a single biblical witness, Mary Magdalene. I will do so by attending to that story's particular historical setting, which was to become rife with what I will refer to as apocalyptic meanings.

Notes

1. Scholarly studies and popularizations of Bonhoeffers life and thought are legion. Among the best of the former is the insightful work by Clifford J. Green, *Bonhoeffer: A Theology of Sociality*, revised ed. (Grand Rapids, MI: Eerdmans, 1999). For an important study of Bonhoeffer's spirituality, seen through the eyes of theological feminism, see Lisa Dahill, "Reading from the Underside of Selfhood: Bonhoeffer and Spiritual Formation," *Spiritus: A Journal of Christian Spirituality* 1:2 (fall 2001), 186-203.

2. Martin Buber, *The Eclipse of God: Studies in the Relations between Religion and Philosophy*, (Amherst, NY: Humanity Books, 1999), 23, 127.

3. Once, when he was in a Nazi concentration camp, Elie Wiesel witnessed the SS guards hang two men and a young boy. Since the boy was not heavy, it took a long time for him to die. A bystander cried out, "Where is God now?" Wiesel later wrote that that experience had "murdered my God and my soul and turned my dreams to dust" (Elie Wiesel, *Night*, trans. S. Rodway [Harmondsworth, UK: Penguin, 1981], p. 45; cited by Paul S. Fiddes, *Participating in God: A Pastoral Doctrine of the Trinity* [Louisville, KY: Westminster John Knox, 2000], 154).

4. Consider the words of the Polish poet and Nobel Prize winner Czeslaw Milosz: "If nature's law is murder, if the strong survive and the weak perish, and it has been this way for millions and millions of year, where is there room for God's goodness? Why must man, suspended on a tiny star in a void, no more significant than the microbes under a microscope, isolate his own suffering as though it were different from that of a bird with a wounded wing or a rabbit devoured by a fox?.... Such questions plunged me, sometimes for weeks, into a state bordering on physical illness" (Czeslaw Milosz, *Native Realm: A Search for Self-Definition* [Berkeley: University of California Press, 1981]. Quoted by Douglas Burton-Christie, "The Weight of the World: The Heaviness of Nature in Spiritual Experience," in *Exploring Christian Spirituality: Essays in Honor of*

Sandra M. Schneiders, ed. Bruce H. Lescher and Elizabeth Liebert [New York: Paulist Press, 2006)], 153).

5. In discussing the eclipse of God in our time, I have not considered the so-called "new atheists," who have been much in the press in recent years. They are surely a highly publicized part of today's cultural milieu. I have not mentioned them for a reason. The writings of Samuel Harris, Richard Dawkins, and Christopher Hitchens, who are, as it were, "evangelizing atheists," are, as far as I can see, mostly superficial responses to the twilight times in which we live. Some wag has called them "atheism lite."The problem is that the new atheists extend the claims of the natural sciences beyond the limits of the sciences. If the natural sciences are empirical, and if the existence of God can be neither empirically proved nor disproved, why try the disproving anyway? Unless one has an ax to grind, as these writers evidently do, such a venture is self-contradictory. They don't like historical religions for a number of reasons, some of them fully justified. Think of the Crusades or 9/11. But those human evils, perpetrated in the name of religion, hardly prove or disprove that God does or does not exist. For a discussion of the new atheists, in contrast to the classical modern atheists—Karl Marx, Sigmund Freud, and Friedrich Nietzsche—whom I take very seriously, see John F. Haught, *God and the New Atheism: A Critical Response to Dawkins, Harris, and Hitchens* (Louisville, KY: Westminster John Knox, 2008).

6. Gordon D. Kaufman, "Theological Autobiography—My Life and My Theological Reelection: Two Central Themes," *Dialog: A Journal of Theology* 40, no. 1 (Spring 2001): 43–60.

7. Kaufman, "Theological Autobiography," 45.

8. Kaufman, "Theological Autobiography," 46.

9. Kaufman, "Theological Autobiography," 46 (italics in original).

10. Gordon D. Kaufman, *Systematic Theology: A Historicist Perspective* (New York: Scribners, 1968).

11. Kaufman, "Autobiography," 51.

12. Kaufman, "Autobiography," 53.

13. Kaufman, "Autobiography," 54.

14. Gordon D. Kaufman, *In Face of Mystery: A Constructive Theology* (Cambridge, MA: Harvard University Press, 1993).

15. Kaufman, "Autobiography," 55.

16. Kaufman, "Autobiography," 56.

17. This is not to suggest that Kaufman has said the last word about these matters. There is surely room for discussion and debate within the theological context that Kaufman made his own. My point here is that the kind of argumentation that Kaufman projects *must be taken seriously.* I myself have done that for some time, since long before I encountered Kaufman and his theology. The theological approach that he has taken has been part and parcel of my own spiritual history, for better or for worse, since I was a college undergraduate. And, as I have indicated, I don't think I am alone in this respect. Readers who want to pursue some of the complex issues with which Kaufman was preoccupied for many years may wish to explore the parameters of a kind of second-generation discussion that has recently emerged, emanating from a forum sponsored by the Center for Theology and the Natural Sciences (Berkeley, CA) and the Vatican Observatory, under the rubric the "Divine Action Project." For an entree into these discussions, see, first, Wesley Wildman, "The Divine Action Project," *Theology and Science* 2, no. 1 (April 2004): 31–73. In his own trenchant way, Wildman gives voice to the kind of argument proposed by Kaufman. Then see the forceful responses to Wildman in the ensuing issue of *Theology and Science* 2, no. 2 (October 2004): 186–201. Those responses, by Philip Clayton (186–90), John Polkinghorne (190–92), William R. Stoeger (192–96) , and Thomas Tracy (196–201), take issue with Wildman's approach (and thus, implicitly, with Kaufman's, too).

18. Dietrich Bonhoeffer, *Letters and Papers from Prison*, enlarged edition, ed. Eberhard Bethge (New York: Macmillan, 1971), 135: "Life in a prison cell may well be compared to Advent; one waits, hopes, and does this, that, or the other—things that are really of no consequence—the door is shut, and can be opened only *from the outside*" (italics in original).

19. I am comfortable using the language of "enlightenment" in order to articulate some of the meanings of the faith I am describing, even though that term brings with it a variety of connotations that could take these explorations in radically different directions. The term has been at home in my own spiritual life for many years. As a thirteen-year-old confirmand, I was asked to memorize Luther's explanation of the Apostles' Creed in his *Small Catechism*, including these words: "The Holy Spirit has called me by the Gospel, enlightened me with His gifts." More generally, the imagery of light and darkness, hence the theme of enlightenment, permeates the thought-world of the Gospel of John, which has shaped my own spiritual life ever since I can remember, above all in the context of my lifelong liturgical experience. That dependency on the spirituality of the Fourth Gospel, and the imagery of light and darkness in particular, will become immediately apparent in these explorations and will be evident all the more so in chapter 4, in my discussion of Mary Magdalene.

20. Along with texts from the Gospel of John, Paul's proclamation in 2 Cor. 4:6 has fascinated me for many years: "For it is the God who said, 'Let light shine out of darkness,' who has shone in our hearts to give the light of the knowledge of the glory of God in the face of Jesus Christ."

PART II

The First Steps of the Journey

Lord Jesus Christ, Have Mercy On Me.

4

Praying to Jesus
The Revelation of God and the Light of Christ

As I begin now to explore some of the meanings within the Trinity Prayer, and with the first petition in particular—*Lord Jesus Christ, have mercy on me*—I invite you to return with me to a setting we visited in the previous chapter: walking along the Charles River. By now, you may have noticed that I love that river.

HEARING AND SEEING IN THIS FRAGILE FAITH: A PLACE OF KNOWING

The Charles River was the butt of jokes four or five decades ago. It never caught on fire the way the Cuyahoga River once did as it flowed through the industrialized neighborhoods of Cleveland into Lake Erie. But the Charles was bad enough in those years. It was a kind of huge sewage ditch. Industrial poisons leeched into those waters, too. Although the river is now much cleaner than it once was, it's still a conduit for overflowing sewage during heavy rainstorms, and eating fish from its waters is officially banned. On the other hand, the U. S. Environmental Protection Agency (EPA) gave the river a "B" grade in 2011. The river met EPA water quality standards for boating 82 percent of the time and for swimming 50 percent of the time. Be that as it may, I love the Charles. As a token of my affection, I join in the popular riverbank cleanup once a year, and I do whatever lobbying I can in the river's behalf year-round. I rejoice, too, in the flora and fauna of the river and its banks and have written about that joy elsewhere.[1]

However much I love the Charles River, however, I love the monastery of the Society of St. John the Evangelist, which is situated along that river's edge, just as much. I want to take you to that setting once again. See me, then,

53

contemplating the river, not on the bitter-cold winter morning where I took you in the last chapter, but now in the much warmer, but still brisk, early-morning spring darkness. It's Easter Eve, and the time is 3:30 a.m. My wife and I have made our way to the monastery—accompanied by any venturesome souls we've been able to persuade to come with us, sometimes including a grandchild or a child with spouse—to participate with the monks in the Great Easter Vigil at 4:30 a.m. We are standing outside the doors of the striking monastery chapel, located right at the river, in the early spring morning, waiting for the Vigil to begin, with many other eager souls who have come early to ensure they have seats.

The liturgy commences in the dark in the monastery garden, where the monks call us to gather. More often than not at that time of the year and at that early hour, the weather is indeed on the cold side and forbidding. In the midst of that dark chill, one of the monks lights a fire, others bless it with incense, and still others read biblical proclamations about fire and the Spirit. Next, led by one of the monks, who is carrying the towering paschal candle, we all process into the chapel, each carrying a lighted candle and all chanting, "The light of Christ."

Inside, the liturgy proceeds with readings that recall the whole history of creation and salvation, according to the Scriptures. Each reading is framed by the communal chanting of a psalm, which further lifts up the Easter promise. The climax of all those readings is the Gospel for the day, the biblical narrative of the resurrection of Christ. On any given Easter Eve, that Gospel reading could be the narrative of Mary Magdalene at the tomb of the crucified Christ, as that story appears in the twentieth chapter of the Gospel of John.

I always eagerly look forward to hearing that narrative read in that kind of a charged liturgical setting. I am aware that Mary Magdalene has become a kind of cause célèbre for some spiritual seekers as well as for spiritual entrepreneurs in the past decade.[2] But this is a text that has claimed my own mind and heart for more than forty years. As a practicing pastor, I may have preached on this Easter text more than fifteen times across the span of my ministry. During those years, I immersed myself in some of the great Johannine commentaries of the church, from Martin Luther to Raymond Brown.[3] While at other times in my preaching on the Gospels I accented the themes of liberation of the poor (Luke), the cost of discipleship (Mark), and the formative power of the Christian community (Matthew), for many years and to this day my mind and heart have always come back to the Fourth Gospel and to the story of Mary Magdalene, in particular, in order to explore the personal dimensions of my own relationship with Jesus, the word made flesh (John 1:14), who called his own by name (John

10:3b-4).[4] The figure of Mary Magdalene has haunted and inspired me for my entire professional life.

THE REVELATORY PARTICULARITY

I invite you to join me in pondering this story now, presupposing what for me is that powerful liturgical setting at the monastery along the river, in the darkness, but with the first dim rays of the dawn beginning to make themselves known, through the stained-glass windows above.[5] This Johannine narrative lucidly discloses the revelatory concreteness and the personal particularity of the first moments of the fragile faith that has so deeply claimed my own life and which comes to expression so movingly, for me, in the first petition of the Trinity Prayer: *Lord Jesus Christ, have mercy on me.*

Contrast this with the way that many theologians in the past approached their work. Many took a kind of God's-eye view of things—*sub specie aeternitatis.*[6] In the unfolding of the traditions fostered by John Calvin, for example, some theologians imagined "the eternal decrees of God," before the creation of the world: God the purposing Father resolves to create the world and then to send the Son to save the world, by drawing all the redeemed into fellowship with the Son in the power of the Holy Spirit. While in Gordon Kaufman's view that kind of universal personalistic divine decreeing is not plausible in our evolutionary age, Kaufman nevertheless continues to think in the same kind of universalizing terms. The issue for Kaufman is whether it is possible to take seriously the idea of a personal God of the whole cosmos, as we now understand the cosmos scientifically. Kaufman assumes, as did many previous theologians, that theology primarily has to do with the larger questions of God and the world.

The story of Mary Magdalene at the tomb represents, for me, a radical reversal of that kind of thinking. The ultimate concern here is not abstract and universalizing but concrete and particularizing. What is ultimate is disclosed in the relationship between Jesus and a single person at a particular time and a particular place.[7] This is clear to me, especially when I encounter the story of Mary Magdalene on Easter Eve.

THE EXEMPLARY STORY OF MARY MAGDALENE

The story of Mary Magdalene as it appears in John is relatively brief and somewhat confusing when analyzed closely. It shows signs of considerable editing in its various settings. Also, the question "What really happened?" hovers at the edge of any interpretation. But for our purposes here, we can focus on what clearly are the main lines of the narrative while judiciously bypassing the question of appropriate historical verifiability.[8] I will also bracket discussion of the meaning, if any, of the resurrection of Jesus as it might be viewed from the vantage point of the natural sciences today. I do that based on the assumption that we are hearing here an utterance of faith that can be neither demonstrated nor disproved on empirical grounds.[9] It will be sufficient for our explorations to observe that what we have preserved for us here is a narrative that many early Christians understood to be a trustworthy account of Jesus' own history as the risen Lord in such situations and of the relationship of his closest followers with him.

The two main characters of this dramatic sequence in John 20 that I want to focus on are Jesus and Mary Magdalene. In John's Gospel, Mary appears here for the first time. Presumably, John assumed that his readers would know who she was. From the Gospel of Luke, we know that she was part of a larger group of women who helped support Jesus and the Twelve. Some of these women likely had been healed of various ailments. According to Luke, Mary was one of those who had been restored to health by Jesus (Luke 8:2).[10] She was also one of a group of women from Galilee who went with Jesus to Jerusalem and witnessed his crucifixion. Her relationship with Jesus must have been close, even intimate, in terms of her gratitude to him.

The Gospel of John tells us that at this moment Mary alone came to the tomb, early in the morning, while it was still dark. She sees that the stone that had been placed in front of the tomb where Jesus had been buried had been removed. She then runs to tell Peter and the Beloved Disciple (the latter appears only in the Gospel of John) about the news. They, in turn, run to the tomb and make the same discovery. Then they return to their homes, "for as yet they did not understand the Scripture, that he must rise from the dead" (John 20:9).

But Mary remains. And here we witness one of the most poignant narratives in the whole Bible. Mary stands weeping outside the tomb in the predawn twilight. Then she bends over to look inside the tomb. The story tells us that she sees two angels, who ask her why she is weeping. With profound grief and affection, we may imagine, she says, "They have taken my Lord, and I do not know where they have laid him" (John 20:13). The body of one who had healed her, whom she loved, and who had been brutally killed before her own eyes had now apparently been desecrated. All that was left to her was her grief.

Just then she turns around, the story tells us, and there she sees a figure, Jesus. But she does not recognize him. Why? Presumably, she, like the other disciples at that time, had not yet understood that the crucified Jesus was to rise from the dead.[11] In a touching irony, the story tells us that she mistakes Jesus for the gardener, a thought reminiscent of the Genesis creation narrative, where we hear about "the Lord God walking in the garden at the time of the evening breeze" (Gen. 3:8). She mistakes Jesus for the gardener, even after she hears his voice when he questions her: "Woman, why are you weeping? Whom are you looking for?"(John 20:15). Does the evangelist now expect us to assume that there was a moment of silence, allowing the two to contemplate each other? Be that as it may, Jesus then addresses her with the compassion that, based on widespread Gospel testimony, only he could extend. He calls her by name.

I want to underline the theme of compassion here. Jesus is the one who is the light of God in a dark world, as the Gospel of John proclaims, not just in terms of the revelation of God but all the more so in terms of the love of God, as the oft-quoted proclamation of John 3:16 attests: "God so loved the world that he gave his only begotten Son."[12] The communities for whom John wrote were steeped in lore about the love of God and the compassion of Jesus. In John's Gospel, this theme is expressed most dramatically in his vision of Jesus as the Good Shepherd, who lays down his life for the sheep (John 10:1-18). That image would have been vivid in the minds of community members as they pondered the story of the resurrected Christ appearing to Mary: "He calls his own sheep by name and leads them out. When he has brought out all his own, he goes ahead of them, and the sheep follow him because they know his voice" (John 10:3b-4).

The other Gospel writers often use the word *mercy* in this kind of context (John does not use this particular word). Luke, for example, has the account of a blind man near Jericho sitting by the roadside and begging (Luke 18:35-43). The man calls out to Jesus repeatedly, "Have mercy on me." And Jesus responds by healing the man. The difference between such accounts and the narrative of Mary Magdalene is circumstantial. Mary had been healed and then befriended by Jesus. So he can call her by name. The blind man, in Luke's account, had, before his encounter, been unknown to Jesus. We can imagine that the blind man subsequently might have become a follower of Jesus and would therefore also have been befriended by Jesus. But, in this respect, the picture of Jesus is the same in the Gospels of both John and Luke: Jesus is the one who embodies the love of God or the mercy of God for those who are lost.

The story of Jesus speaking to Mary at the tomb then continues in the following manner. John probably intends to have us assume that when Jesus spoke to Mary, asking her whom she was seeking and why she was weeping, she once again was staring into the tomb with her back to Jesus, deeply feeling both her loss and her love for Jesus—while not knowing that it was he who was speaking to her. At that moment, with her back to him, Jesus calls her by name: "Mary." She turns around, we're told, and immediately recognizes the one who is speaking to her. She says "Rabbouni!" (John 20:16), which, the text tells us, means "teacher." This, in fact, was a rarely used word at the time, which may well be read, as the Catholic biblical scholar Raymond Brown suggests, as "my dear Rabbi," a term of personal affection.[13]

Mary apparently then reaches out to Jesus, the text tells us. But Jesus says to her: "Do not hold on to me, because I have not yet ascended to the Father. But go to my brothers and say to them, 'I am ascending to my Father and your Father, to my God and your God.'" So Mary then goes and announces to the disciples, "I have seen the Lord" (John 20:17f.).

We witness here in this poignant story, however brief its scope, the deepening of an intimate relationship, which John surely understood in terms of Jesus' friendship with his disciples, one of John's central themes. At first, like the other disciples, Mary had no grasp of what had unfolded in Jesus' resurrection. Then, overjoyed when she once again heard Jesus' voice and realized that it was he, while still thinking in terms of the world that had existed before Jesus' resurrection, she reaches out to touch him. But he will not allow that, since, with the resurrection, a new era had begun.[14] He is now not to be known as he was in former days.

Jesus then reveals that he must return to the Father. Still, Jesus stands there, face-to-face, with Mary. For John, this surely means that the revelation of the new eon has begun, in Jesus. The evangelist presumably wants us to know that at that moment Mary was the first believer—indeed, the first apostle—in the new age, inaugurated by the resurrection, for he tells us, in words that resonate with other Gospel accounts of disciples who had encountered the risen Lord for whom he was, that Mary said, "I have seen the Lord" (John 20:18). In other words, she finally "got it." But she was the first to "get it," according to John. She testified to what had happened to her, when Jesus had revealed himself to her as the risen Lord. She was indeed the first apostle.

THE PERSONAL PARTICULARITY OF THIS FRAGILE FAITH

Spiritually, this is where the fragile theology of faith begins—not with some universal vision of God creating and redeeming all things, nor with some universal vision of the "creativity" that lies behind and in all things, but with a single self's personal encounter with the risen Lord.[15] This is the radicality of what Paul Tillich once called "biblical personalism."[16] The vision of the Bible is not first and foremost universal. It is first and foremost particular, indeed, personalistically particular. It begins "in the middle of things" (*in media res*). Of course, once this particular has been encountered, universal implications are revealed in every direction. We will explore a number of those implications later in this chapter as well as extensively in other chapters.

For now, I want to invite you to imagine yourself standing in the chapel at the monastery with me on Easter Eve. Imagine that I or my wife has invited you to that great Easter Vigil. Imagine that, while the world outside is still full of darkness, the priestly procession, carrying the gospel book and candles, has now arrived at the center of this holy place, by the baptismal font, where the paschal candle now stands. Imagine that the story of Mary Magdalene is now being read. Can you also imagine that when Jesus says "Mary," he is also saying *your* name? Can you dream with Dietrich Bonhoeffer that the prison door of this world's twilight times is now being opened from the outside, and that, as you hear the word of Jesus calling you by name, his light is flooding into your world, so that your heart and mind are being enlightened?

This is the spirituality of what I am calling a fragile faith, announced by John in the first chapter of his Gospel: "And the word became flesh and dwelt among us, and we have seen his glory, the glory of a father's only son, full of grace and truth" (John 1:14). To be sure, John presupposes a universalizing frame for this announcement that the word made flesh is indeed the word of the Father-Creator (John 1:1). But John is clearly eager—already in his first chapter, compactly, and then dramatically throughout his Gospel—to identify that word as the one who dwells in the midst of the community of believers.[17] This is even suggested by John's choice of words. "And the word became flesh and dwelt among us" could be translated more literally, as has often been noted, as: "And the word became flesh and *tented* among us." This word calls to mind the pilgrimage of the ancient Israelites in the wilderness on their way to the Promised Land. They lived in tents in the wilderness, and their faith was in the God who tented with them.

Luther was therefore right in his interpretation of John's Gospel when he, Luther, insisted that the word spoken of by the evangelist must regularly be understood as being given "for us" (*pro nobis*). In his preaching and teaching, accordingly, the reformer invited his hearers, as I am inviting you here, to allow a story like Mary Magdalene's to become *their* story, to hear Jesus calling them by name also and then to begin to see things with new eyes. Luther believed—as do I, instructed by him—that when the gospel word is read and proclaimed in such settings, Christ himself is really present, no less really present than in the sacramental ministrations of the eucharistic bread and wine.[18] I hope that you also can be informed by Luther in this way, so that you can hear in the gospel address the risen Lord speaking to you, as he spoke to Mary Magdalene at the tomb, thus inviting you to be open within to his indwelling mystical presence.

From Mary Magdalene to the Apocalypse

After the narrative of Mary Magdalene runs its course, we hear no more about her, either in John's Gospel or elsewhere in the canonical New Testament. We have no record of what became of her, notwithstanding the fact that she remained a subject of intense interest, mainly in a few circles where an alternative faith, known as Gnosticism, flourished.[19] But we do know something about what became of the Johannine communities that had claimed her as a hero of the faith. Things changed. The powers of darkness—which Jesus had overcome, according to Johannine belief, by his life, by his being lifted up to the cross, and by his glorious exaltation to the eternity of the Father—had not defeated Jesus. But neither had those powers been banished from the world of his disciples.

Indeed, very soon after the time of Jesus' death, communities of his followers, who kept rejoicing in his resurrection, were beset by the principalities and powers of death with a new vehemence. An age of persecution was at hand. Both Peter and Paul, according to church traditions, were martyred in Rome. By the time of the Emperor Domitian (81–96 a.d.), the political demand for emperor worship in the whole empire had been promulgated and fierce persecutions of Christians had commenced.

In this new situation, the traditions that came to expression in the Gospel of John took on a different, "apocalyptic" form in the Book of Revelation. The word *apocalypse* means "unveiling." The Book of Revelation is not about predictions. It is concerned with the unveiling of the stories of two world-historical powers—"the Beast," that is, the Roman emperor, and "the Lamb," that is, the crucified and risen Christ. This unveiling shows us a kind of cosmic struggle between the self-asserting brute force of the Beast and the self-giving spiritual force of the Lamb. The themes of darkness and light, of struggle and death, that were in evidence in various muted but moving ways in John's Gospel now are projected onto the unfolding history of the times, particularly onto the machinations of Roman power, for example, in words like these, spoken of the triumphant saints: "These are they who have come out of the great ordeal; they have washed their robes and made them white in the blood of the Lamb" (Rev. 7:14b).

John the Seer, who wrote the Book of Revelation, saw himself as "a prophet." From the earliest days of the first generation of Christians, there may have been believers who felt called to prophesy, in the sense that their function was to receive and announce visions of things to come.[20] As one of these, John the Seer may have been part of a network with which John the Elder, the author of the Fourth Gospel, was also associated. John the Seer's vision reached its most dramatic intensity in chapter 13 of the Book of Revelation, the vision of the two "beasts," one of whom he may have understood as the emperor Nero, then with the vision of Christ as the victorious Lamb, and the fall of Rome, called Babylon, in chapter 14.

Much has been made of such themes in recent years in the United States by the so-called rapture-theology movement. But predictions of the imminent salvation of a few believers being "raptured" up to heaven and the condemnation of everyone and everything else hardly represent John the Seer's meanings.[21] On the contrary, what we meet in the Book of Revelation are themes of light and darkness, first encountered in the person and "the signs" of Jesus, now writ large and with dramatic intensity on the history of those times. The one whom Mary Magdalene personally encounters as the light of the world, the one who overcomes the darkness of her world, is now viewed in world-historical, even cosmic, terms as the victorious lamb of God, who stands over against the powers of this world, above all against Rome, and who calls those who would follow him to be ready to accept martyrdom nonviolently in his name, as all await the arrival of the new heavens and the new earth, the renewal of the whole creation (Rev. 21:1ff.).

This is why I find it instructive to view what we know about Mary Magdalene through the lens of Dietrich Bonhoeffer's story. As he reflected about such things in his prison cell, Bonhoeffer knew that nothing about faith is self-evident, indeed that much in this world stands against any kind of viable faith. He knew that the door to God must be opened by God Godself, from the outside. Bonhoeffer believed that the tears of our grief can only be assuaged if they are addressed by the voice of the wholly other God in the word-made-flesh, if authentic faith and hope and joy are to be ours and our hearts and minds are to be enlightened.[22]

But that does *not* mean that the one who encounters the divine word entering into our world in and through Christ and who rejoices in being called by name will be spared the fate of Christ himself, as Bonhoeffer's case shows, a narrative akin to the stories of many early Christians: the fate of death at the hands of the still rampant principalities and powers of this world. The Christ who spoke to Mary at the tomb, after all, was the same Christ who, according to John, was immediately also to appear to Thomas, with the other disciples, behind closed doors, and then to ask Thomas to touch his, Christ's, wounds (John 20:19-29). Those wounds announced the still reigning ruthlessness of Roman powers in those times, as well as witnessing to the birth of the new body of Christ, the church, by the sacramental signs of blood and water—Eucharist and Baptism—flowing from the side of the glorified Savior.

This Fragile Faith and the Existential Trauma of Suffering

The theme of apocalyptic end-times and the struggle against the powers of death and darkness brings me full circle to my own engagement with the horrendous story of the Holocaust, in particular, and also to the sobering facts of evolutionary history more generally and all its suffering, the spilling of animal blood for eons and of human blood for millennia. If I begin with the personal self-disclosure of the ineffable God in the person of Jesus to the likes of Mary Magdalene, and if I end with the apocalyptic vision of the new heavens and the new earth, as the consummation of the mission of Jesus, what about the middle of the story?

What, indeed, are we to make of human tragedies like the Holocaust, on the one hand, and of the evolutionary vision of nature red in tooth and claw, on the other hand? Can I somehow make sense of the groaning of the whole creation now that I have been claimed by Christ personally and inspired by his life, death, and resurrection to a new hope for all things at the very end?

At this point, we encounter the profound issue of "theodicy" with its full force. This somewhat abstruse word points to, what for faith, can only be regarded as an existential trauma. Such is the question that has echoed painfully in human hearts at least since the time of the Book of Job to our own era, especially in the hearts of witnesses to the Holocaust like Elie Wiesel. How could a good and loving God allow all of the evils of human and natural history to happen? After many years of pondering this question, following in the train of many thinkers much more insightful than I am, I have long ago decided that the best way to respond is to say that *there is no rational answer*. There is no way, finally, to *explain* all of the stark facts of human and natural suffering from the perspective of faith. Attempts to develop a "theodicy," to "justify God's ways," have never been fully successful, in my view. Valiant efforts have been made, but almost all of them end up, in one way or another, trivializing evil or domesticating God—or even demonizing God.[23]

For such reasons, I believe that it must be sufficient for our fragile faith, to begin with, to state the intellectual and theological *impasse* of the theodicy question and then, as I learned at my mother's knee, to trust in the Lord. So, spiritually, I recommend that believers and those who are seeking to be believers should confront the existential trauma of this problem and then, in due course, hold firmly to the revelation of the ineffable God in Jesus Christ—that God is indeed love.[24] I choose to rest, then, with the prophet III Isaiah's profession of faith: "For my thoughts are not your thoughts, nor are your ways my ways, says the Lord. For as the heavens are higher than the earth, so are my ways higher than your ways and my thoughts than your thoughts"(Isa. 55:8-9). And in that rest, I affirm that the final word for human and natural history, notwithstanding the enormous and outrageous facticity of human and natural violence, is the love of God in Christ Jesus, perfected finally by the Holy Spirit.

Hence, in my view it is profoundly wrong to say or even to imply that God, the Father of our Lord and Savior, Jesus Christ, "permitted" the Holocaust. We do not know the reason for all of that suffering and death. But we do resolve to engage the evils of this world like the Holocaust and to resist them. We also give thanks that the wholly other God has entered into our history, in the person of Jesus Christ and in the power of the Spirit, to struggle with, to be wounded by, and yet to overcome the principalities and powers of death, even as this God speaks to us personally and calls us by name, through the same Jesus Christ and by the power of the same Spirit, as all of us are called upon to take up our own crosses to follow Jesus (see Matt. 16:24).

I recommend a similar approach to the issue of theodicy as it arises in our encounter with the evolutionary violence in the unfolding history of nature. This is a question of particular interest to persons, such as myself, who are committed to see the works of God in natural history as well as in human history. Violence in nature is a phenomenon readily acknowledged in the Bible, in the Old Testament in particular, although obviously not in our scientific terms of evolutionary history.[25] Indeed, the Book of Job can be read as an exemplary encounter with both the vitalities and the bloodletting of natural history.[26] But, as I understand Job, those issues are never resolved rationally, with suggestions perhaps that God "*had* to do" or "*had* to permit" such-and-such in order to have a history with cosmic reality in the first place. Rather, Job is called by God to contemplate nature red in tooth and claw, knowing that God has purposes with the cosmos that he, Job, can acknowledge, and even in some respects celebrate, but never understand. When all has been said and done, the lesson we learn from Job, I believe, is this: we are to trust in the goodness of God, the often brutal facts of nature to the contrary notwithstanding.[27]

Another reason I want to avoid any attempt to resolve the theodicy problem rationally has to do with the particular culture in which we live today in the United States, a culture that tends to shape our minds and hearts so that we will underestimate or even whitewash the radicality of evil. This tendency is all too common in the ranks of those who would explain evil: they tend to explain it away. Some traditional Christian thinkers have even spoken of the "happy guilt" (*felix culpa*) of human sin, the idea being that sin and disruption of the creation were somehow something good because they "merited" the wonderful redemption that God provided in Jesus Christ.[28] I consider that a dangerous theological assertion, since it implies—theological protests to the contrary notwithstanding—that the darkness of human experience is somehow good because it leads to the greater good of the light of Christ.

THE DARKNESS: TELLING THE WHOLE TRUTH

I am instructed at this point by a book written some years ago by the Canadian theologian Douglas John Hall, *Lighten Our Darkness: Toward an Indigenous Theology of the Cross*.[29] Hall describes a misplaced optimism in North American culture, the view that all problems can be solved if we keep on living the way we are, continuing to neglect the real suffering of the world. The world's darkness, in other words, isn't really dark. It is being overcome by business as usual.

In this respect, Hall talks about a different kind of light, call it an intramundane light, a false light of human invention. This is not the light of the suffering Christ, who was condemned by the Romans. This is the so-called light of the eighteenth-century Enlightenment, the light that allegedly radiates from human rationality and human achievement and the belief in inevitable progress. It is the light, in America, of so-called Manifest Destiny. This light shines so brightly in our culture that Manifest Destiny's dark underside—the destruction of Native American peoples, the history of slavery, the rape of the good American land, the bombs dropped on Hiroshima and Nagasaki—is scarcely visible and is therefore not usually discussable:

> This high-minded witness to the light; this preoccupation with the positive; this readiness to see in every new invention its potential for serving God and [humanity]; this mostly uncritical acceptance of the electronic age as though it were bound to release [people] from boring work and set them on the path of true leisure; this celebration

of space flights and the extensions of their already extravagant scientific aims by the addition of spiritual and religious dimension. . . .—this so characteristic behavior of the adherents of cultural Christianity in North America indicates how wedded our Christianity is to the spirit and method that Luther called *theologia gloriae* [the theology of glory].[30]

Hall wrote this in the late 1970s. What would he have said about our hypermedia culture today, driven by the so-called information revolution, with its fixation on computer-generated "realities," on "virtual" electronic friendships, on constant texting and tweeting? What would he think of death by drones in Afghanistan and elsewhere, so directed by "pilots" sitting in air-conditioned comfort in California, who go home at the end of the work day and watch their kids play soccer?

In response to such trends, Hall argues that it would be better if, instead of following the familiar description of the church's mission as a witness to the light, "we said that an indigenous theology of the cross would call forth a people who could bear witness to the darkness."[31] Karl Barth made much the same point when, early in his theological career, he insisted not only that God must be thought of as wholly other but also that Christians must stand ready to say no to this world as well as yes to Christ. Dietrich Bonhoeffer, also, spoke in the same vein when, in his book *The Cost of Discipleship*, he distinguished between "cheap grace" and "costly grace." The time has come to tell the whole truth about the darkness of this world, which shrouds even "the best and the brightest" of the world.

I take all this into account, with as much focus as I can muster, whenever I repeat the first petition of the Trinity Prayer: *Lord Jesus Christ, have mercy on me.* I think of both Mary Magdalene and the Apocalypse—the gift of this revelatory and intimate personal relationship with Jesus Christ and his love, on the one hand, and the call of the same Christ to walk with him as he communicates his love to the downtrodden and so contends with the principalities and powers of this age, on the other. I have heard the voice of Jesus, and I have seen his light. He has befriended me and enlightened me. But I also know that the one who calls me by name is the same one who has come into the world to identify and then to overcome all of the powers of violence and death in the creation, and who calls those who follow him to tell the truth about those powers and then to engage and resist them, wherever possible and however feasible, with passionate, nonviolent, and self-giving love, sometimes even at the cost of their own lives.

Notes

1. H. Paul Santmire, *Ritualizing Nature: Renewing Christian Liturgy in a Time of Crisis* (Minneapolis: Fortress Press, 2008), xi–xvi.

2. For this mostly popular and, on occasion, scholarly discussion, see the thoughtful essay by Pheme Perkins, "The Search for Mary Magdalene: First Apostle," *Christian Century* 123 (May 16, 2006): 26–29, a review of five recent books. For the celebration of Mary by a number of gnostic and New Age groups, whose members often see Mary as the bride of Christ and, indeed, as co-redemptrix, see the essay by Mary Ann Beavis, "The Deification of Mary Magdalene," *Feminist Theology* 21, no. 2 (January 2013): 145–54.

3. Martin Luther, "Sermons on the Gospel of John," *Luther's Works* [hereafter *LW*], ed. Jaroslav Pelikan et al. (Saint Louis: Concordia Publishing House, 22 [1957], 23 [1959], 24 [1961], 69 [2009]); Raymond E. Brown, *The Gospel According to John* (Garden City, NY, 1970), 2 vols.

4. I only came across the long-established work of Sandra M. Schneiders on the Fourth Gospel in recent years, well into my retirement. A student of Raymond Brown, she offers what I consider a fascinating—and in many ways compelling—account of the whole Gospel of John, particularly of the central role played by Mary Magdalene in that Gospel. See, especially, her study *Written That You May Believe: Encountering Jesus in the Fourth Gospel*, revised and expanded edition (New York: Crossroad, 2003). But the overall account of Mary Magdalene I am presenting here, for better or for worse, is mainly mine, based on my own textual encounter with her over the course of many years. Those who may wish to pursue recent scholarly thought about Mary Magdalene can consult the instructive essay by Mary Ann Hinsdale, "St. Mary of Magdala: Ecclesiological Provocations," *Catholic Theological Society of America Proceedings*, 66 (2011): 67–90, and the literature she cites, especially on pp. 73–78.

5. Although this narrative focuses on my relationship with Jesus Christ seen through the prism of the Mary Magdalene story, I hope it will be clear to all of my readers that this is a relationship that is real for me only insofar as my fragile faith is rooted in the milieu of the life of the church and sustained by that life–as, in this case, I hear the word about Mary Magdalene proclaimed in the context of the church's liturgy, the Easter Vigil, in particular. This is the context in which I know Jesus most fundamentally, not primarily in any kind of private setting or any other kind of solitary encounter with him. I came to know Jesus consciously, already as a child, in the stories proclaimed and taught in the midst of the church's gathered life. And I still know him there first and foremost. Hence, when in an April 9, 2012, cover story, *Newsweek* magazine announced, "Forget the Church: Follow Jesus," I have no idea what the editors, or the writer of that cover article, could be talking about. I learned to know the love of God in Christ Jesus in the life of the church already as a child. I know Jesus today, first and foremost, only as I hear of him and hear his words in the proclamation of the church and encounter him in the eucharistic ministrations of the church. That I also know him elsewhere, beyond the life of the church, in my daily life, for example, or as the cosmic Christ, is a knowing that is dependent on that primal knowing in the life of the church.

6. This expression – meaning "from the perspective of eternity" – has been used in a variety of ways in modern philosophy and theology. For its theological use, cf. the affirmation by the historian, Christopher Dawson, *Dynamics of World History*, ed. John J. Mullow (Wilmington, DE: ISI Books, 2002), 248: "For the Christian view of history is a vision of history *sub specie aeternitatis*, an interpretation of time in terms of eternity and of human events in the light of divine revelation. And thus Christian history is inevitably apocalyptic, and the apocalypse is the Christian substitute for the secular philosophies of history." While not wanting to take issues with such a

universal approach to the meaning of cosmic history, that is not where the fragile faith I am discussing here *begins*. For me, faith begins from the perspective of the particular, sub specie particularis.

7. Those familiar with the history of theology may suspect that at this point I have been influenced by the spiritual reflections of the nineteenth-century Danish theologian Søren Kierkegaard, and indeed I have. For much of his vocational life, Kierkegaard took issue with the speculative philosophy of one of the greatest German philosophers of the nineteenth century, Georg Wilhelm Friedrich Hegel. Hegel's universalizing metaphysics of world history influenced many in that era and beyond. Kierkegaard once observed, however, that Hegel understood everything but himself! Better to begin with the particular event of Jesus, Kierkegaard believed, and with your relationship to that event, than to begin with some universal vision of reality that is fated to leave you without your own existence in the process. In the twentieth century, Kierkegaard's theological focus on the believer's encounter with Jesus was sometimes called, even by those who affirmed it, "the scandal of particularity" (Emil Brunner). And that expression, at that time, still had a substantial theological purchase, since, in the twentieth century, the approach to theology exemplified by Hegel, against whom Kierkegaard had so passionately argued, was still taken for granted by many. Since the turn of the twenty-first century, however, things apparently have changed. With the widespread emergence of so-called postmodern ways of thinking in this century, the generalizing ("foundational") worldview of thinkers like Hegel has been called into question. Postmodern thinkers have argued, in one way or another, that all we have as a basis for philosophical or theological thought is a world of multitudinous particulars. In a word, the era of Hegel—for many, although not for all—has, in this respect, come to an end. For this reason, therefore, "the scandal of particularity" now appears to be much less scandalous than it did in the twentieth century, since all thinkers today, it is assumed, are working only with the particulars of their own experience. For a short but informative review of these developments, see Philip D. Clayton, "Systematic Theology and Postmodernism," *God and Contemporary Science* (Edinburgh: Edinburgh University Press, 1997), chap. 1. On the other hand, in my experience, awareness of such recent trends in philosophy and theology is often restricted to the ranks of those with relevant academic interests. Many citizens of our "postmodern world," even some of the most intelligent among them, still continue to think in modernist terms. Hence, for them, the scandal of particularity is still very much an issue. A case in point: juxtapose the generalizing claims of the natural sciences—for example, that our entire cosmos is headed toward a colossal "heat-death" some day—with the particularistic claims made by some persons of faith today, such as myself, that the resurrection of Jesus is the beginning of a cosmic era that will finally, beyond this epoch of cosmic history, give way to a "new heavens and a new earth in which righteousness dwells"(2 Pet. 3:13). Such a claim can sound scandalous even to those who affirm it, such as myself.

8. I am passing by a range of highly complex interpretive problems here. To begin with, I use the expression *appropriate* historical verifiability to signal that historical research into the life of Jesus should be held to the same standards—no higher, no lower—than research into any event in any comparable era, for example, Jesus' public entry into Jerusalem before his crucifixion compared with Caesar's crossing the Rubicon. The best we can say is that it is highly probable that each of those events happened in the terms that we have come to know them. Of course, claims for the resurrection of Jesus are singular; no comparable claims are made about Caesar, for example. But the singularity of events in the past does not necessarily imply that they "did not happen." Narratives of singular events may or may not correspond to what "actually happened."Of interest in this respect is the rigorously historical argument of New Testament scholar N. T. Wright, spun out over many hundreds of pages of analysis, that, as far as the resurrection of Jesus was concerned, *something* profoundly dramatic, akin to the New Testament resurrection stories, *must* have happened; otherwise, we could not explain historically the dramatic rise and spread of early Christianity around the Mediterranean basin after the death of a "failed Messiah." See, for example, N. T. Wright, *The Resurrection of the Son of God* (London: SPCK, 2003). Finally, if I were to explore these matters in more detail at this point, I would want to draw on Paul Tillich's theological approach to such questions. This is the challenge. Given the fact that the Gospel

accounts of Jesus' life do not always agree with one another and even that there are contradictory reports, on occasion, within individual Gospels, how are we to determine historically "what really happened"? There is also the possibility, and indeed the probability, that early Christian communities exaggerated or even invented some accounts about Jesus' miracles, for example. Tillich invoked the idea of an "analogy of the image" in this context: the notion that the narratives about Jesus that we have in the New Testament *correspond in some measure* to what really happened, notwithstanding a whole range of varying and sometimes conflicting details given by the New Testament. Theologian Paul Lehmann adopted a similar approach; he maintained that there is an "empirical substratum" to the stories about Jesus in the New Testament.

9. This is not to say, however, that this is the end of the discussion. Some theologians, who are also natural scientists or at least scientifically literate, have explored how it is possible to conceive, although not to demonstrate, how the resurrection can be integrated into a scientific picture of the cosmos in a way that does not violate the canons of science. See, for example, Robert John Russell, *Cosmology: From Alpha to Omega: The Creative Mutual Interaction of Theology and Science* (Minneapolis: Fortress Press, 2005), chap. 10.

10. Later church tradition identified Mary Magdalene with the sinful woman of Luke 7:36-50, but there is no historical evidence for this. Fatefully and sadly, however, that mistaken identification then opened the door to dysfunctional, sexist speculations about Mary as a "dangerous" eroticized figure, a theme that was then vividly expressed in Western art. For an introduction to those trends, see Robert Kiely, "Picturing the Magdalene: How Artists Imagine the Apostle to the Apostles," *Commonweal* 137, no. 15 (September 10, 2010): 14–19.

11. In a careful and insightful study, "Touching the Risen Jesus: Mary Magdalene and Thomas the Twin in John 20," *Catholic Theological Society of America Proceedings* 60 (2005): 13–35, Sandra M. Schneiders argues that, for John, Mary represents one who is still living with pre-Easter apperceptions of Jesus, whereas Thomas represents one who is working—struggling?—with post-Easter apperceptions of Jesus.

12. The importance of this theme of love throughout John's Gospel is underlined by Sandra M Schneiders in her illuminating article "Johannine Spirituality," in *The New Westminster Dictionary of Christian Spirituality*, ed. Philip Sheldrake (Louisville, KY: Westminster John Knox, 2005), 385–87.

13. Brown, *The Gospel According to John (xiii–xxi),* p. 1010.

14. Sandra M. Schneiders explores this theme in her essay "Touching the Risen Jesus."

15. See Martin Luther, *LW* 29:111: "Those who want to ascend advantageously to the love and knowledge of God should abandon the human metaphysical rules concerning knowledge of the divinity and apply themselves first to the humanity of Christ. For it is exceedingly godless temerity where God has humiliated Himself in order to become recognizable, to seek for oneself another way."

16. Paul Tillich, *Biblical Religion and the Search for Ultimate Reality* (Chicago: University of Chicago Press, 1955).

17. Another biblical writer rooted in the traditions of the Johannine churches, whom we know as the author of the Epistles of John, gives us an even more emphatic statement about the incarnate Word being known in the community of believers: "We declare to you what was from the beginning, what we have heard, what we have seen with our eyes, what we have looked at and touched with our hands, concerning the word of life—this life was revealed, and we have seen it and testify to it, and declare to you what we have seen and heard so that you also may have fellowship with us; and truly our fellowship is with the Father and with his Son Jesus Christ. We are writing these things so that our joy may be complete" (1 John 1:1-4).

18. Luther, *LW* 36:340: "Again, I preach the gospel of Christ, and with my bodily voice I bring Christ into your heart, so that you may form him within yourself. If now you truly believe, so that your heart lays hold of the word and holds fast within it that voice, tell me, what have you in your heart? You must answer that you have the true Christ. . . . How that comes about you

cannot know, but your heart truly feels his presence, and through the experience of faith you know for a certainty that he is there."

19. For this, see Schneiders, *Written That You May Believe*, 244.

20. See Richard Bauckham, *The Theology of the Book of Revelation* (Cambridge: Cambridge University Press, 1993), 3: "Since Christian prophets normally prophesied in the context of worship meetings, we must assume that this is what John usually did. The reading of this written prophecy [the Book of Revelation] in the worship service (1:3) was therefore a substitute for John's more usual presence and prophesying in person."

21. See Barbara Rossing, *The Rapture Exposed: The Message of Hope in the Book of Revelation* (Boulder, CO: Westview, 2004).

22. Bonhoeffer worked out these ideas in terms of the traditional theological construct of Christ "the Mediator," which Bonhoeffer construed to mean Christ "the middle" or "the center." For this, see Green, *Bonhoeffer: a Theology of Sociality*, 220ff.

23. The public discussion of the theodicy question in our era is complex—and enormous. Readers who wish to pursue it more fully, from the perspective of Christian theology and spirituality, can do no better, I believe, than to begin by pondering the thorough and thoughtful discussion by Paul S. Fiddes, "The Vulnerable God and the Problem of Suffering," in his book *Participating in God: A Pastoral Doctrine of the Trinity* (Louisville, KY: Westminster John Knox, 2000), chap. 5.

24. Over the years, my own spirituality has been enriched, as I have already indicated, by my continuing encounter with Luther. While he is not addressing the theodicy issue specifically in the following statement, for example, I have found such affirmations by the reformer profoundly helpful when I have thought about this challenge: "You cannot believe, you must entreat God for faith. This too rests entirely in the hands of God. . . . However, you can spur yourself on to believe. First of all, you must no longer contemplate the suffering of Christ (for this has already done its work and terrified you), but pass beyond that and see his friendly heart and how this heart beats with such love for you that it impels him to bear with pain your conscience and your sin. Then your heart will be filled with love for him, and the confidence of your faith will be strengthened. Now continue and rise beyond Christ's heart to God's heart and you will see that Christ would not have shown this love for you if God in his eternal love had not wanted this, for Christ's love for you is due to his obedience to God. Thus you will find the divine and kind paternal heart, and, as Christ says, you will be drawn to the Father through him. Then you will understand the words of Christ, 'For God so loved the world that he gave his only Son, etc.' [John 3:16]. We know God aright when we grasp him not in his might or wisdom (for then he proves terrifying), but in his kindness and love. Then faith and confidence are able to exist, and then [we are] truly born anew in God" (Martin Luther, *Luther's Works* 42, Devotional Writings I, ed. Martin O. Dietrich [Philadelphia: Fortress Press, 1969], 13).

25. See, especially, Terence E. Fretheim, *Creation Untamed: The Bible, God, and Natural Disasters* (Grand Rapids, MI: Baker Academic, 2010).

26. See Fretheim, *Creation Untamed*, chap. 3.

27. One of the best studies of evolutionary violence and the theodicy issue is by Christopher Southgate, *The Groaning of Creation: God, Evolution, and the Problem of Evil* (Louisville, KY: Westminster John Knox, 2008). This is the question: how could a good God create, or even permit, such a blood-drenched history? While such an investigation is surely worth the effort, and while Southgate develops his arguments thoughtfully and carefully and with full awareness of the huge challenge he is addressing, in my view he ends up with an image of God as a kind of human problem solver writ large. If God decided to have a history with a diverse, evolving creation, so the argument seems to run, there had to be room for widespread death and suffering along the way. To me, such a reasoned approach to these matters, even one so modestly proposed as Southgate's is, does not do sufficient justice to the overwhelming mystery of God. Missing is the testimony of Job to the awesomeness of the Creator: "Where were you when I laid the foundations of the earth?"(Job 38:4). Better to say nothing, or very little, about resolving the issue

of theodicy, in other words, and live with the—substantial—rational tension than to end up with arguments that tend to domesticate God.

28. The phrase *felix culpa* has typically been sung during the historic Easter Vigil: *"O felix culpa quae talem et tantum meruit habere redemptorem"* ("O happy fault that merited such and so great a Redeemer"). Thomas Aquinas cited that phrase in agreement in his *Summa Theologica* (3.1.3 ad 3).

29. Douglas John Hall, Lighten our Darkness: Toward an Indigenous Theology of the Cross (Philadelphia: Westminster, 1976).

30. Hall, *Lighten Our Darkness*, 222.

31. Hall, *Lighten Our Darkness*, 223.

5

The Ambiguous Case of One Who Prays to Jesus
The Twilight and the Encounter

Am I ready to do that? Am I ready to live "between the times," between the particular experience of Mary Magdalene and the universal faith of the Apocalypse—on the one hand entering into communion with the crucified and risen Lord, while on the other hand standing ready to lay down my own life at any time, in the name of the same Lord, in this apocalyptic era, as I await the coming consummation of the world? Am I ready to be both a personal disciple and a public advocate of the way of Jesus Christ in this twilight world, wherever I can? I eagerly want to answer such questions in the affirmative. I surely do not seek martyrdom, in any historic sense. Nor did Dietrich Bonhoeffer, as a matter of fact. But I would like to think that, by the grace of God, should such extraordinary circumstances arise, I would be ready.[1]

THE TWILIGHT OF A SINGLE SOUL:
A SPIRITUALITY OF ORDINARY PLACES

I know myself too well, however, to jump to any such conclusion. The twilight of our times, indeed, is not just around us, it is *within* us. It is within *me*. If this book is really to be of any lasting help to my readers, therefore, I must do my own public self-assessment: to be frank with you about my own sinful shortcomings, insofar as I am aware of them, especially as they pertain to nature. I must tell the truth about myself, as best as I can. This is the ambiguous case of one who has no other spiritual recourse than to call to Jesus and ask for mercy, wherever I may find myself, because I so urgently need that mercy.

71

However, I do not want to tell you just about my sinful shortcomings. Rather, I want to affirm the whole truth about myself. Yes, I live in the twilight of this world and that twilight does indeed dwell within me. Nevertheless, I believe that I have been touched by the risen Christ also, reminiscent in some ways of Mary Magdalene's experience when she was staring into the empty tomb. By the grace of God, it has been given to me to know the one who is the light of the world (John 6:12). That very Jesus to whom I cry out for mercy has been merciful to me. How?

I have already spoken of hearing the voice of Christ himself addressing me in the story of the Magdalene when the Easter Vigil Gospel was being read. I have known in faith, too, that he is the one who presides at the table in that liturgy and offers himself to me in the bread and the wine. Now, after I venture to describe the twilight within me, I want to tell you, as well, how the same Christ has touched me not only in the life of his gathered community but also in various other ordinary places.

THE DARK NIGHT OF THE SOUL?

I chose the expression "the twilight of a single soul" deliberately. As I have reflected about my life, I have realized that, to date, I have never really encountered that "dark night of the soul" that masters of the spiritual life talk about. Luther, for example, when he was a young monk, went through a wrenching time of *Anfechtung*, a German word that is not easily translated. The English expression "trials and tribulations" only begins to convey its meaning. Luther's whole, deeply felt world of faith, his very identity as a profoundly devout Christian, collapsed, and he felt himself in spiritual free fall. To this point in my life, I have never been swept down into such depths of despair.

Nor have I ever been overwhelmed by the chaos of a society that was falling apart. When Jürgen Moltmann, the great twentieth-century theologian of hope, was seventeen, for example, he experienced firsthand the mass annihilation wrought by the Allied fire bombing of Hamburg, Germany. This was an incomprehensibly dark night of the soul for him, as he remembers that evening. Some forty thousand men, women, and children in Hamburg were burned to death; he himself barely escaped that inferno, for no apparent reason.[2] Myself? I have only read about such experiences.

Nor, again, have I sought out spiritual trials in deserts or mountains or elsewhere that might have simulated profound spiritual isolation or even the threat of death, as a way to step into the presence of the living God. I have done some mountain hiking in New England, but I have never aspired to be a spiritual child of the wilderness. I traveled once to the edge of a desert in Namibia, but I did not venture any further. I have pondered the mysteries of the ocean from the Maine and Cape Cod coastlines, but I have never gone sailing on the open sea. I have touched the edges of monastic spirituality in the region where I live, which has been very important to me, but I have never traveled afar to immerse myself in, say, the life of an isolated Mt. Athos in Greece, above and beyond the world of mundane experience. As a matter of fact, I have never been much of an adventurer at all, spiritually or in any other sense of that word. I am secretly reassured, then, by this thought: Henry David Thoreau, that great champion of living with wildness, took his laundry home to his mother every week during the time when he was living alone at the edge of things, in the liminality of Walden.

Do not get me wrong. I have learned much from the traditions of those classical Christian spiritual masters who focused on the extraordinary, the ways of the desert or of barren mountain heights or of the open seas (for the latter, in particular, I have pondered Celtic monastic traditions extensively over the years). Theirs is an indispensable spiritual witness for every epoch.[3] Their efforts to trek beyond the ordinary, particularly to move beyond what I earlier called the tyranny of the cognitive mind, in search of the extraordinary, whether in the desert or in the mountains or on the open seas, have inspired countless souls to seek to do the same and then to return enriched. In Christianity, those traditions have been kept alive historically by monasticism and its ascetic practices, defined particularly by the classical monastic vows of poverty, chastity, and obedience. For that reason, as well as for many others, most serious-minded Christians today are indebted to monasticism, whether or not they recognize that fact.

A Spirituality of Ordinary Places

But I have been just as much inspired, if not more so, by what might be called the spirituality of ordinary places that came to expression in the life of Luther in his middle years. Reared spiritually as a Augustinian monk and devoted passionately to that tradition's asceticism, in 1525 Luther forsook his monastic vows—and took a wife. Subsequently, he developed a vivid spirituality of ordinary places, by which and in which he passionately affirmed God in everyday life, in the marriage bed, to be sure, but also in the carpenter's shop, at the judge's bench, before the altar, in the tavern, down on the farm, or walking through the primordial forests.[4]

This has been the primary milieu of my own spiritual life over the years, the world of ordinary places, concretely rooted in what early on in my adult life I learned to call "the holy estate of matrimony." I have had my own crises, to be sure, but nevertheless I have lived mainly on the surface of things for most of my life. So, for me, the meanings suggested by the image of the twilight are much more telling than those of any dark night of the soul, critically important as the latter has been in the history of Christian spirituality.[5] I suspect that many others also find themselves in ordinary places and are either unable or unwilling to reach out for the extraordinary represented by the classic spiritual quest in the desert or on the mountain or surrounded by oceanic infinities.

WHO AM I? AN AMBIGUOUS NARRATIVE

Be that as it may, whether a spiritual narrative is about the dark night of the soul or about times of existential twilight, the story of our sin and grief must be told, along with accounts of the healing and the enlightenment. A Christian spirituality, in one way or another, is a narrative of a searching self who, in addition to everything else, confronts his or her own brokenness, however pedestrian that brokenness might appear to be. Here are some of the details of my own story.

MY DISPUTE WITH GOD

I begin this account by referring once again to moments when I have had my own personal dispute with God. In my own conventional manner, thousands of miles and many decades removed from the historic Holocaust, living my own bourgeois life in America, I still have moments when I am deeply disturbed by what I perceive to be the providence of God and the issue of the Holocaust. How could a good God create and govern a world in which the Holocaust could happen?

Although, as I have already said, I know in my mind that the best answer to this theodicy question is to pass beyond the question itself and to trust in the Lord, whose ways are higher than our ways—to hear the voice of the wholly other God from the whirlwind, as Job did, "Where were you when I laid the foundations of the earth?" (Job 38:4) and then to come to rest in trustful silence—in my heart I *still* sometimes raise the question with a cathected seriousness. I consider this bent of my soul to be a spiritual weakness, a failure of trust in the God who has revealed Godself to me in the person of Jesus Christ.

Now resolving to trust in the Lord when confronted by the outrageous facticity of evil in this world – as I already have had occasion to observe —may sound like a cryptic response to this enormously complex question. But, along with countless other Christians of many walks of life, I have been wrestling with this issue for years, and I have concluded that this is how the faith that I want to claim should rightly be allowed to claim me. Luther once observed that faith is like taking the hand of a guide while blindfolded and following that guide over a high and narrow bridge.[6] Faith, of course, is much more than that. But, at its roots, I think that the theodicy question is most fundamentally a question of trusting in the goodness of God made known to me in Jesus Christ, the facts of this world to the contrary notwithstanding. And I fault myself frequently in this respect, for not letting go of my own questions and then simply taking hold of the hand of the guide, in order to cross this particularly high and narrow bridge.

MY ATTRACTION TO THE THEOLOGY OF FACTS

Like my mundane wrestling with the theodicy question, I have also mentioned how what I have called the theology of facts, as espoused by Gordon Kaufman, appeals to me at times. I wonder on occasion, for example, whether I should simply let go of my fascination with the story of the risen Christ speaking to Mary Magdalene and deal with the facts as Kaufman interprets them. Can I really believe in the resurrection? Doesn't it seem more likely that, in the aftermath of Jesus' death, his first followers dealt with their own profound grief and disappointment by somehow allowing themselves to be subjected collectively to spells of psychic projection, consoling themselves with a desperately devised fiction that Jesus had been raised from the dead? I also consider this occasional bent of my soul to be a spiritual weakness, a failure of loyalty to the revelation of God in Christ.

Still under the rubric of the theology facts, I am one of those who is taken, sometimes to the point of spiritual fatigue, by the dark pessimism that cosmological physics brings with it in our time—the images, for example, of our earth being sucked into the sun in a few billion years and the whole universe stalling in a state of dead frigidity billions and billions of years thereafter, according to the Second Law of Thermodynamics. Is that how all of the struggles for survival on this earth and the occasional heroic human quest to find a flourishing, beautiful, and self-giving life are eventually to be resolved? Did the life and death of Jesus mean nothing? Does the Bach B-Minor Mass mean nothing? Was Bonhoeffer's martyrdom only a historical accident? Is the whole multibillion-year history of this universe's space and time continuum nothing more than a tale told by an idiot? Insofar as I allow such questions to flood into my soul, now and again with real force, is this not yet another spiritual deficiency of my own, an unwillingness to grasp the fullness of the hope that is given to me with God's word of promise in Jesus Christ?

My Relationality—Especially with Women

Then there are the disturbing phenomena that I can discern when I examine my own relationality. As a son, well into my young adult years, I often distanced myself, stubbornly and unkindly, from my parents. As a pastor for more than forty years, I was aware that a number of public positions I took in the name of justice and at least some of the confidential consolations I offered in the name of love were motivated by self-aggrandizement as well as by self-giving. As a husband in two successive marriages, moreover, one short, the other enduring, I have been aware of a range of petty habits and sometimes irrational acts of my own that have been hurtful to each of my spouses, in differing ways, sometimes deeply hurtful. As a father, I have not always been engaged with my two children as I think I ought to have been, especially when they were moving into and through their teenage years, which coincided with the era in my professional life when I was zealously working inordinate hours.

I want to go into more detail, in this context, about *my relationship with women* in my adult years and its inner meanings for me, since that has had significant implications for my spirituality of nature. I was brought up in the eerily halcyon days of the 1950s in patriarchal America. I was taught, at home and elsewhere, that the "man of the house" is "the breadwinner," and that the woman of the house is the caretaker and the child rearer. My parents exemplified that social ideal, and it worked for them, as far as I could tell. In retrospect, however, I am convinced that that ideal was disastrous for me both personally and spiritually.

But before that thought ever dawned on me, I had found a way to idealize *nature* in terms of "the feminine" (Mother Nature) and vice versa. In my late twenties, I made a wood carving of Mary, the mother of Jesus, and the result was a kind of mother earth goddess figure. My journals from my early seminary years are full of allusions to losing myself in nature, sometimes in only slightly disguised sexual terms. As a matter of course, spiritually I was attracted in those years to theologies of "the Eternal Feminine," as exemplified by the thought of the great Pierre Teilhard de Chardin.[7]

Still, I regard that whole chapter of my personal and spiritual life to have been a disaster. The proper theological word is *sinful*. It took me awhile, and considerable pain, to discover that fact. My first marriage fell apart in those years, doubtless for many reasons. But it did not help that I tended to approach my first wife—in the most sophisticated theological terms, of course—as an ideal exemplar of "the feminine" and of "the natural." I would call to mind visits I had made to remote wilderness places like the Grand Tetons in Wyoming as I contemplated her figure. But she would have none of it, to her credit.

My second wife would also have none of it. Had I not learned anything from the dissolution of my first marriage? But she was—and is—an amazing truth teller. Look at *me*, she would say, in various ways: don't look at "the feminine." By the grace of God, I eventually began to do that. Although I was thoroughly confused at the time about such matters, what she put me through, kicking and screaming, as it were, was a painful demythologization of "the feminine." And with that went a certain subtle but thoroughgoing deromanticizing of nature in my own mind and heart.

It helped at that time, too, that I happened to be serving as the chaplain of an all-women's institution, Wellesley College. There, women ran the show, in every respect and at every level. Often, in free-flowing, small-group discussions with students, I was the only male present and more often than not was totally ignored. The women sometimes talked about "the problems of men," historically and personally, as if I were not in the room.

Not without a sense of self-preservation, I decided that it might be a good idea to get ahead of the curve as far as the then-emerging wave of theological feminism was concerned. So I became a leading scholarly advocate on campus of the writings of theologians like Mary Daly and Rosemary Radford Ruether. I also invited them, and other feminist theologians, to preach in the college chapel where I presided, and I welcomed them into our living room to engage dozens of eager, bright young women. Whether by inspiration or by foolishness, I once cooperated behind the scenes with Mary Daly when she walked out of "my chapel," which turned out to be a practice session for her later, much more successful walkout at Memorial Church, Harvard. That was her final "exodus" from patriarchal religion, she believed.

More substantively for me, at that time I eagerly read theological feminists, especially the works of Ruether, which provided me with the conceptual clarity about the dangers of identifying nature and "the feminine" that I had earlier lacked. It was also my privilege in those days ("the sixties") to work with a number of visionary student leaders on social justice issues, among them the impressive president of the student government at that time, later to go on to some national fame, Hillary Rodham. Such real women trumped whatever lingering images I still consciously harbored in those days about nature and "the feminine." But I still sometimes wonder how much my heart and soul have been fully exorcized of that sinful, patriarchal spirit that had for such a time commanded my ways of relating to others, with such personally destructive results.[8]

A case in point. Once, at Wellesley College, during a class I was teaching on the theology of nature, the students and I were discussing an essay by Ruether. In her discussion, Ruether mentioned what she called "the rape culture." One of the students, who happened to be from West Virginia, expressed puzzlement about Ruether's meaning. We explored the matter. The dominant culture, run by powerful men—other students explained to her—depicts both women and nature as objects for exploitation. Accordingly, the rape of women and the rape of the land are brutal expressions of the same ideology, the objectification of "the other." At one point, I innocently (or so I thought) said to the student who had first asked the question: "You should be able to tell us all about that. You're from the land of the coal mines and the rape of the earth." At the time, I thought that that was a good pedagogical point. But she gasped, bowed her head, soon began to cry, and then left the room. I assured the other members of the class that I would talk with her without delay when that particular class was over, which I did.

It turned out that there was a history of sexual abuse in her extended family, as well as a history of loss of loved ones in the mines and illnesses induced by the mines' pollution of the air and the land. She told me that the class discussion had been a shocking discovery for her. She later chose to talk with the class about her personal history. As a participant in that discussion, I realized how easy it had been for me to intellectualize "the concept" of rape of the land, whereas for her it had been a matter of personal experience. I sometimes wonder how much I continue to intellectualize such things, oblivious to the anguish of those who experience them firsthand.

And these are, in all likelihood, only some of the dysfunctional relational patterns in my life of which I have been consciously aware over the years. I assume that there have been and are, in fact, others, perhaps many others, unknown to me. Then there is my own interiority to consider.

MY INTERIORITY

It is sobering for me when, now and then, I peer into the dark recesses of my own soul and there encounter signs of seething rage that no therapy—psychiatric or pastoral—has seemed equipped to heal. This is an emotional turmoil that only rarely emerges consciously, but which, when it does, overwhelms me: when, for example, my beloved wife, now of almost fifty years, happens to probe my feelings at some vulnerable point and I explode; or even, much more conventionally, when I let loose raw utterances of "road rage" in the privacy of my own vehicle. When I'm alone, I regularly utter loud juvenile profanities when I accidently knock anything over, like a stack of books. I'm also troubled sometimes, by fragments of my own dream life that I happen to remember, some of which are strange images of uninhibited aggression or faceless sensuality. So, I can dream about the Trinity! But do I carry within my own soul the kind of seething anger reflected in the Cain and Able story? Deep within, am I somehow driven by the forces of evolutionary violence and libidinal instinct? Was Sigmund Freud right about the all-consuming, amoral powers of the human unconscious? How powerful is my spiritual life, in fact, compared to such native, inner forces?[9]

And what have I done, on the positive side, to foster spiritual growth over the years? Here, I think that the answer must be mixed. This whole book is about my prayer life. You will have to judge this for yourself. As far as I can remember, I was a good pastor. I poured my life into helping others with their spiritual challenges, in confidential conversations. Through the years, I also presided over a number of weekend retreats for students and other church groups. But I have rarely allowed myself much time to deal with my own spiritual challenges. I sometimes think that I might have been helped along the way had I participated, with some regularity, in spiritual retreats, the way many Jesuits do for a month every year.

But, justifiably or not, I felt pressured—or, rather, I deeply desired over the years—to spend every available moment of time apart from my work with my wife and two children. I don't blame myself for this. I have often asked myself, as a matter of fact, whether husbands or wives who take the call to marriage and parenthood seriously and who also work full-time can practice spiritual disciplines in any other way than the occasional manner I have typically adopted. Still, I do look wistfully over my shoulder sometimes and wonder how my spiritual life might have been enriched over the course of my adult life had I found a way to make a directed, silent retreat, say, once a year.[10]

Now, if the overall state of my interiority troubles me—as it sometimes does—*why haven't I asked for help?* Some of the monks at the monastery I frequent are experienced spiritual directors, but I have yet to speak to any of them. Nor did I seek out a spiritual director in earlier chapters of my life. In contrast, over the years, I have found mentors in other areas of my professional and personal life that have needed attention. I have sought out professionals to help me with my preaching, with my liturgical leadership, and with my scholarly writing. And I have found time to talk with psychiatrists or with pastoral counselors when that was necessary. So, why have I not asked for professional help with my prayer life?[11]

I would like to think that this is due to a justifiable vocational decision, one to which I have just alluded. As a husband, my most intimate of relationships—akin only to my relationship with God—are with my wife. For me, this existential reality has barred the door to intense personal sharing with any other, such as, for example, with a spiritual director or even with the most treasured of my friends. I have not pledged my life to any other person in this world the way I have pledged my life to my wife. Nor has any other person pledged his or her life to me the way that she has. I wear the ring she gave me and she wears the ring I gave her when we were married. There are no other rings. And I consider my relationship with her profoundly spiritual, as when we hold hands to say our table grace at every meal or in seasonal moments of devotional practices, when, for example, she and I sing the first stanza of "O come, O come, Emanuel" together every day for four weeks as we light the candles of our Advent wreath. Then there are the times, often late in the night, when we share our deepest vulnerabilities with one another, sometimes with tears. Maybe married people, for the sake of putting first things first, shouldn't generally have spiritual directors.[12]

On the other hand, doesn't all this sound like special pleading? Might not my decision not to seek out a spiritual director be predicated simply on spiritual sloth? Or on a refusal to take the next step in my spiritual life? More profoundly, have I perchance simply been afraid to put myself in a position of increased spiritual vulnerability? To this day, I'm not really sure why I have not asked for help from a spiritual director, especially since such a step has become a popular protocol in recent years for many who are specialists in spirituality. But I do think that my reluctance reflects some significant spiritual ambiguity, if not sinful avoidance of deeper truths about God and myself.

MY SOCIAL LOCATION

Beyond all this, and perhaps the most troubling, I often ponder the ambiguities of my own social location. I have been able to hold my life together the way I have done, with some success, because for my whole adult life I have bought into a system of social privilege that presupposes the oppression of others, near and far. I have already alluded more than once to the comforts of my own economic status. I can "get away" to rural Maine in the warmer months and be warm at home in a spacious urban condominium during the colder months as well as be well fed and well cared for medically in every season.

My ethics of eating, in particular, is by no means stellar.[13] I eat relatively modestly and low on the food chain, for health reasons, except for festival meals. But I am not a vegetarian, which, of course, must be the eschatological ideal for faithful Christians, as we look for that day when the lamb will lie down with the lion. I do believe in an ethic of nonviolence, but many of my habits belie that belief, particularly regarding meat eating and more generally regarding my well-protected affluent American existence, which presupposes the exercise of sometimes brutal economic, political, and ecological power around the world. Nor am I deceived when, before a Thanksgiving Day meal, for example, I remind myself that neither the first disciples of Jesus (for Peter especially, see Acts 11:7) nor St. Francis were vegetarians. I know I am caught up in an ethos of violence, notwithstanding my own self-justifications. And I am a follower of the Prince of Peace?

With all that goes the many advantages of gender and race and social status that I mostly have taken for granted. Being white and male and heterosexual and middle-class in America has given me all manner of educational, economic, personal, and ecclesiastical advantages over the years, which I have by and large accepted, notwithstanding some conscious commitments to challenge the hegemony of such structures of injustice.

NATURE—A CASE IN POINT?

My own lifelong fascination with the world of *nature* may be an egregious case in point. It is a fact often noted, particularly by American historians, that nature in itself—especially the wilderness—only became a subject of widespread public esthetic or spiritual interest in the modern era when a class of people who had the leisure and the economic wherewithal to "visit" or "travel to" the world of nature had emerged and had solidified its social position. It was the wealthy, after all—the people who lived in the huge mansions along the Hudson River valley and other such retreats of the rich in nineteenth-century America—who provided a market for the characteristically huge and dramatically romanticizing paintings of the Hudson River School.

Although the financial resources of my own family were quite modest compared to those available to the barons of the Hudson River world, I did nevertheless grow up in a picturesque, semirural, and financially secure environment at the edge of Buffalo, New York. And my parents made it a point to introduce their three children firsthand to the august beauties of the

American national parks, an opportunity that many of the poor members of our society have never had.

As a matter of fact, I only became acquainted with "the other side of Buffalo" when I was a college student and worked one summer at Bethlehem Steel in Lackawana, New York, next to Buffalo, a chapter of my life to which I shall return later. There I met and labored with crews of mostly African American men, a group of people I had never encountered before with any immediacy. So even my ostensibly innocent passion for nature, which I have carried with me since I was a child, has undoubtedly been shaped, at least in some measure, by the realities of social class. In those days, I felt much more at home visiting a national park than I did visiting the other side of my own city. I still wonder, decades later, how much my passion for God in nature has been driven, or at least shaped, over the course of my life by the—unjust—assumptions of my own social class and its position of power.

I can therefore readily identify with the man of high standing who once approached Jesus and inquired about the way to eternal life. I am captivated by such theological issues. Ask me what eternal life is or, perchance, what the wilderness means to me, and I will launch into a disquisition whose length will be determined only by the limits of your auditory patience. At the end of that biblical conversation, however, Jesus said to the man: "Sell all that you own and distribute the money to the poor, and you will have treasure in heaven; then come, follow me." When the man heard this, we are told, he was very sad and he went away, for he had many riches (Luke 18:22-23). I feel precisely that kind of sadness whenever I recognize the inertia of my own social location.

WHO AM I?

I thus know my deeds and my misdeeds, my sins of commission and my sins of omission, or at least some of them, and the Lord and others whom I have encountered over the years surely know many more. My life, as I recollect it, particularly from the perspective of its dark inner recesses, has been wracked with contradictions. Call this the unfaith of a life of faith. This is why the famous prison poem of Bonhoeffer—"Who Am I?"—continues to speak to me more than fifty years after I first read it:

> Who am I? They often tell me.
> I stepped from my cell's confinement
> Calmly, cheerfully, firmly,

Like a squire from his country-house.
Who am I? They often tell me.
I used to speak to my warders
Freely and friendly and clearly,
As though it were mine to command.
Who am I? They also tell me.
I bore the days of misfortune
Equally, smilingly, proudly,
Like one accustomed to win.

Am I then really all that which other men tell of?
Or am I only what I myself know of myself?
Restless and longing and sick, like a bird in a cage,
Struggling for breath, as though hands
were compressing my throat,
Yearning for colors, for flowers, for the voices of birds,
Thirsting for words of kindness, for neighborliness,
Tossing in expectation of great events,
Powerlessly trembling for friends at an infinite distance,
Weary and empty at praying, at thinking, at making,
Faint, and ready to say farewell to it all?

Who am I? This or the other?
Am I one person today and tomorrow another?
Am I both at once? A hypocrite before others,
And before myself a contemptibly woebegone weakling?
Or is something within me still like a beaten army,
Fleeing in disorder from victory already achieved?

Who am I? They mock me, these lonely questions of mine.
Whoever I am, Thou knowest, O God, I am Thine![14]

Who am I? I urgently want to answer that question the way Bonhoeffer did, by entrusting myself to God, and often I do. But I can only do so when I plead, again and again: *Lord Jesus Christ, have mercy on me.*

Given the ambiguities of my life, given my habitual residence in the world of the rigorous theology of facts even as I aspire to be claimed by what I have called the fragile theology of faith, and given my noticeable spiritual deficiencies and personal failures and foibles and confusions, I can do no other than throw myself at the feet of Jesus and say, as the apostle Peter did: "Go away from me, Lord, for I am a sinful man" (Luke 5:8). I can do no other than begin every prayer and indeed every moment when I happen to have God in mind and heart, implicitly if not explicitly, by asking Jesus to have mercy on me—for, if the truth be known, I have nothing of my own, spiritually or in any other way, to bring to the table or to the public forum or to some wilderness retreat or to the pulpit or to the kneeling bench or to my home or to a book like this or to any other setting, nothing that isn't corrupted by my own sins.

Hence these words have been critically important for me for so many years: *Kyrie eleison, Christe eleison, Kyrie eleison.* As a matter of course, as I developed the Trinity Prayer over an extended period, early on I held firm to that initial petition that I had learned from the liturgy, from the New Testament, from Luther, and from the Orthodox practice of the Jesus Prayer itself, with this traditional translation: *Lord Jesus Christ, have mercy on me.* For me, that was and is the only possible way I could—and still can—enter into the presence of God.[15]

Who am I, then? "I believe," I say, making the New Testament text my own; "help my unbelief" (Mark 9:24). Notwithstanding all my sins, known and unknown, and notwithstanding my numerous moments of unbelief, I am this child of faith, by the grace of God. I can be no other. I cannot stop being overcome by these childlike moments of faith, nor do I desire to do so.

ENCOUNTERING THE RISEN CHRIST: TESTIMONIES OF A POSTCRITICAL NAÏVETÉ

That it makes profound sense to me to throw myself at the feet of Jesus before I think or feel or do anything else spiritually may sound *naive* to some. But, as I have said, this is the only way into the spiritual life that I know. Still, I do owe my readers an explanation of what I mean by this action, overlaid as it is by the rich texture of biblical metaphor. To that end, I want to address the issue of my naïveté and then share some personal testimony.

MY NAÏVETÉ?

Throwing myself at the feet of Jesus? Do I actually believe that that is what I am doing or what I must do in order to enter in communion with God, by the grace of God? I do. But I want to remind my readers: there's naïveté, and then there's naïveté! In fact, if the word is rightly used to describe my own spiritual orientation, I welcome it. I would like to think of my personal point of departure with Jesus in the Trinity Prayer—*Lord Jesus Christ, have mercy on me*—as what has sometimes been called, somewhat abstractly, "postcritical naïveté." This terminology may not be immediately helpful to a number of my readers.[16] For this reason, I want to translate it, without delay, into the more concrete language of biblical faith.

I will invoke an image that I have already highlighted and describe the spiritual orientation I am narrating and recommending in this book as *a childlike faith*, which has been given to me as a gift. Yes, I would like to think that my faith, such as it is, is not *childish*. That would be precritical naïveté. But mine is indeed a fragile faith, and in that sense, when all has been said and done, it is essentially and unavoidably—as well as postcritically—naive. That is how one enters the kingdom of God, according to Jesus, to become as a little child.[17]

A PERSONAL TRAUMA AND THE TOUCH OF CHRIST

What is this naive faith like? To respond to this question, I want to offer some personal testimony. Moments of childlike faith bring with them, in my experience, different kinds and different degrees of intensity, from episodes of anguished struggle and moments of quiet contentment to occasional times of near ecstasy. Children, of course, are given to such mood swings, from the sometimes terrified crying in the night and the placid daytime preoccupations of play or learning to the momentary heights of joy, as when a parent comes home from work and sweeps the child up into his or her arms. I know such spiritual mood swings well, as I hope the following stories will illustrate.

One summer, just before my last year in college, when I was staying with my uncle in Syracuse, New York, I took off in my 1950 Chevy for what I thought was going to be a wonderful weekend. My destination was a resort at the end of Cape Cod, in Chatham, Massachusetts, where my beloved, a young woman whom I had dated off and on during our college years, was working for the summer. As I drove, my heart was suffused with high hopes of seeing this relationship move toward engagement and then marriage. But that was not to be. This was a case of misplaced expectations on my part. So, one tearful, rainy night, we "broke up." I was devastated. Mine was a young love that had had no perspective, I now realize. She was my first and, I had imagined at the time, my greatest and most lasting love. I had never experienced such a love or such a loss before.

Rather than spend the night in a nearby motel, as I had been intending to do, I dropped her off at the resort where she was working and turned away into the rainy night to return home. I drove through the early-morning hours back to Syracuse, sometimes sobbing, sometimes screaming, with no other sounds than the constant tempo of the windshield wipers. When I finally entered my uncle's apartment, I found a note from him that he would be away for a couple of days. I was still shivering in the aftermath of those tears and cries of grief that had filled my soul on the way home.

As I walked into the living room, I saw the sizable crucifix that my uncle had on the wall. He had purchased it in Spain, I believe. It was made out of a mahogany-type wood. More than a foot in height, it emitted an aura of serenity. The body of the crucified Jesus, head down, was in silent repose. I could see the nails in the hands and the feet and the wound on the side. Without a thought, I fell to my knees, made the sign of the cross, looked up, and whispered, "Lord, have mercy." And I kept repeating that frantic whisper, for how long I do not remember. But I was there, on my knees, for some time.

Then there was a deep and astounding silence, and in the midst of that silence a touch, or so I thought. I felt the presence of Jesus standing behind me, and I felt his hand on my shoulder. It could have been a figment of my imagination. But to this day I believe that it was much more. And as I felt that hand on my shoulder, I was at peace. The Lord had reached out, somehow, someway—perhaps by means of a figment of my imagination, if that is what it was—to touch me when my young heart was in its deepest need.[18] At that moment, my grief began to heal.

That experience has stayed with me over the years. It regularly comes back to me when I kneel before a crucifix, at home or in church. When I recall how I thought I felt the hand of the Lord on my shoulder, that experience has a way of repeating itself and I am at peace all over again, in the presence of the Lord.

As Mary Magdalene stood staring into the empty tomb in that early-morning twilight, and as the risen Lord, standing behind her, addressed her by her own name, did he also reach out and gently touch her shoulder? The biblical narrative is silent about this possibility. And there is much in the long and all too often sad history of relationships between men and women that would have inhibited Jesus from doing that. What, after all, would have given *him* the right to touch *her*? On the other hand, he had more than likely mediated some form of healing to her on one or more earlier occasions. Had he ever touched her along the way, not like a patriarch claiming what he thought belonged to him but as a brother touching a sister in her grief, or as a mother consoling a frantic child? Perhaps he had. But at this moment in the story, I would prefer to think of the gentle resonance of *his voice*, not even the softness of his familiar hand, touching her—so that there would be no tension of any kind "in the air." His voice touched her! Whatever might have happened between the two of them at that moment, when she stood staring into the empty tomb and then heard his voice, she was surely deeply touched. I can testify to that kind of experience of my own, in some small measure.

AN ENCOUNTER WITH DEATH AND THE TOUCH OF CHRIST

Another memory of this kind comes to mind, too. I must have been ten years old. I remember my mother and father waking me and my brother in the middle of the night. Come, they told us, we have to go to your grandfather's house because he is very ill. I had never experienced a deathwatch before. No one close to me had ever died, and I had no idea what death was. But I was overwhelmed by the sadness in that house. My mother burst into tears when she entered her childhood home and embraced her own mother. Then my mother sobbed all the more when she embraced our pastor. I had never seen her cry like that before. But there was something profoundly reassuring to me when the pastor placed his hand on my shoulder, even if only for a moment, without speaking, as he then turned to speak in hushed tones to other members of the family in that dimly lit living room.

Three days later, it was time for the funeral. By then, I was thoroughly drained by all the mourning around me and by the busy preparations for the wake at my grandparents' house. Sitting there in the quiet nave of the only church I had ever known at that time, the neogothic stone edifice where, I had often been told, I had been baptized, it was as if the whole sanctuary were shrouded in black.

I remember kneeling at that altar with my father to my right and then to his right my mother and my brother. I had knelt there with my family many times before, even though I had not been allowed to receive the bread and the wine in those years, since I had not yet been confirmed (the practice of many Lutheran churches in those days). But this time was different. I was touched by what I imagined to be the strength of my father's faith as he knelt beside me and as I made sure that I was physically close to him. I felt secure in his strength. Then I was literally touched by our pastor, after he had offered my father the bread. I did not have words for that experience at the time, but that was the calming reassurance of a warm embrace, conveyed by the gentleness of the pastor's face and by his firm touch on my shoulder, once again.

Looking back at that deathwatch experience and that kneeling at the altar rail next to my father and being so touched by our pastor on both occasions, I am sure that that was the comfort of the crucified and risen Jesus, then and there, that so deeply moved my young heart. I am grateful that I now have the words to say this much.

A SPRINGTIME ENCOUNTER WITH CHRIST—AND MORE

Then again, there's another Resurrection Lutheran Church in my life. Not the one where I was baptized in Buffalo, but the one where I currently worship, in Boston's historic Roxbury neighborhood. Founded by Swedish immigrants a century ago, it is a thriving, albeit struggling, African American congregation. It's in the heart of things. Close by are the regional centers of the neighborhood, the Boys and Girls Club, the library, the police station, and the headquarters of the Urban League. Down the street a block is Dudley Station, a hub for public transportation in Boston. Some thirty thousand souls pass through this station on any given day.

Roxbury suffers from all the ills of most inner-city neighborhoods. Several congregation members knew the young man who was gunned down at Dudley Station when that happened a few years ago. More recently, the young son of one of our members was inadvertently shot to death on his porch, an innocent victim of a neighborhood crossfire. The very streets by our church tell their own sobering story, with their potholes, the fast-food detritus, the broken glass, the discarded condoms.

One spring Sunday morning, as my wife and I hurried to church, we noticed that one of the congregation members had planted a score of mums in the eight square feet of earth visible at the front entrance of the church. The sun was shining on them, and they were brilliant. My wife proceeded on into church in order to give someone a message. I stood there for some time, contemplating those gorgeous yellow flowers in that ugly street setting. Long before, I had learned from the venerable American theologian of nature Joseph Sittler to translate Jesus' saying about the lilies of the field with the word *behold* rather than the usual term *consider*: "*Behold* the lilies of the field, how they grow; they neither toil nor spin, yet I tell you, even Solomon in all his glory was not clothed like one of these" (Matt. 6:28).

I stood there, beholding those mums, transfixed. At that moment, it was as if the noise of the streets, the horns and the sirens, and the hip-hop resounding from passing cars, had subsided. All was quiet in my soul. I then imagined Jesus, standing next to me again, this time gesturing toward those mums. And I heard his voice in my heart: "Behold!" Some would say that I was projecting on the basis of a treasured text. But I don't think that I was. I believe that Jesus, the crucified and risen Lord, was standing there right next to me, gesturing and speaking. And I believe that he remained there, gesturing and speaking to passers-by, as I went into church, also to meet him there in faith. Was his presence outside by the mums any less real than his presence inside, in his word addressed to us that morning or in the meal at which he presided?

I can also tell about other experiences like this one, of spiritually encountering the crucified and risen Christ. I have already told you about my sense of being touched by the light of Christ along the Charles River and then in the midst of the great eucharistic feast of the Easter Vigil at the monastery. I tell these experiences to lead you into a sense of real presence, an experience of the living Lord, in many and various forms, an experience of the Lord who first spoke to the apostles, among them Mary Magdalene, and who has continued to touch lost souls like mine, throughout the ages.

THE INSPIRATION OF TWO HISTORIC SPIRITUALITIES

The witness of two historic spiritualities—the classical Celtic and the traditional African American—has so deeply moved me over the years. Both have been popularized in recent decades, sadly, sometimes to the point of spiritual blandness. But both—notwithstanding their obvious historical differences—are, in fact, profoundly rooted in a deep and immediate spiritual communion with the risen Christ.

So, on occasion, and always deeply touched, I sing with the members of Resurrection, Roxbury, these words, the English adaptation of the traditional Celtic song "St. Patrick's Breastplate":

> Christ beside me, Christ before me,
> Christ behind me, king of my heart;
> Christ within me, Christ below me;
> Christ above me, never to part.

My wife and I made a pilgrimage to Ireland some years ago, which I have described in some detail elsewhere.[19] That journey opened up grand spiritual vistas for me, for which I have been profoundly grateful ever since.

My soul is just as moved when, as often happens, I am caught up in the voices of the same congregation, with words like these, from the traditional spiritual:

When I'm in trouble, Lord, walk with me;
When I'm in trouble, Lord walk with me;
When my head is bowed in sorrow,
Lord, I want Jesus to walk with me.

I will have more to say about my life in this congregation in a later chapter. Here, I mainly want to acknowledge my gratitude for the witness of both of these two powerful spiritualities. In some small measure, my own experience with the risen Lord resonates with both of them and indeed has been inspired all the more so by both.[20] I realize that "I have many miles to go before I sleep," that my own encounter with the risen Christ is just the beginning of a relationship that I hope will grow and deepen, informed by such stirring witnesses, until I die and then, whenever the time is right, meet him face to face in the day of the new heavens and the new earth.

YOUR OWN SPIRITUAL JOURNEY?

For now, however, I ask you to consider this question. Can you affirm this kind of fragile, childlike faith—this postcritical naïveté—as a promising point of departure for the next step of your own spiritual journey? Or can you reaffirm that faith? Notwithstanding your own personal or public failures or what you may consider to be your own inability to believe or perhaps the inertia of your own social location, and notwithstanding whatever kind of pain you may be experiencing at the moment, can you hear the voice of Jesus calling you by name, as he spoke to Mary Magdalene at the tomb? Feel what you may take to be his hand upon your shoulder. Imagine that he's standing next to you, in the midst of the lilies of the field, saying, "Behold!"

Then throw yourself at his feet and call on his mercy. Literally, as I will explain in the epilogue of this book, I have found it helpful to collapse on my knees sometimes, as I once did as a young man in Syracuse, New York, in the midst of a personal trauma. Then, when the time is right, stand and walk in his light, wherever he might lead you, however depressing or ominous the twilight might be, within you as well as around you. Walk with him even to the point of being willing to put your own life on the line for his sake. And every step of the way, keep praying, as often as you can, the first petition of the Trinity prayer: *Lord Jesus Christ, have mercy on me.*[21]

Notes

1. Christian spirituality was shaped from its earliest days by a theology of martyrdom. True, that word means "witness," but its connotations of physical suffering and physical death cannot be avoided. Regarding the first expressions of this martyriological spirituality, see Rowan Williams, *Christian Spirituality: A Theological History from the New Testament to Luther and St. John of the Cross* (Atlanta: John Knox, 1980), chap. 1, especially his discussion of the life and death of Ignatius of Antioch (d. c. 110), pp. 15–21. Ignatius, in contrast to Bonhoeffer, *did* seek martyrdom.

2. This is how Moltmann describes that experience: "That was not a 'normal' experience of suffering; these were the extreme and excessive burnings of hell. At that time the eclipse of God descended on my world, and the dark night of the soul took hold of my heart and destroyed my spirit. It was the unfathomable experience of annihilating nothingness" (Jürgen Moltmann, *A Broad Place: An Autobiography*, trans. Margaret Kohl [Minneapolis: Fortress Press, 2009], 190).

3. For a short but rich introduction to these traditions, see Andrew Louth, *The Wilderness of God* (Nashville, TN: Abingdon, 1991).

4. In this new spirituality of ordinary places, comprehensive as it was, I believe that Luther's decision *to marry* was the paradigmatic moment. The move into the world beyond the established monastic life had begun in earnest already in the early thirteenth century, as Bernard McGinn has shown (*The Presence of God: A History of Western Christian Mysticism*, vol. 3, *The Flowering of Mysticism: Men and Women in the New Mysticism—1200–1350* [New York: Crossroad, 1998], see especially 12–30). That trend "made possible a growing conviction that God could be found anywhere and by anyone, if the proper dispositions were present and grace was given"(13). As far as I can see, however, on the basis of McGinn's discussion, this new spiritual movement into the world of ordinary places in the thirteenth century was still largely, if not totally, predicated on the older monastic assumption that the disciplined and therefore the authentic spiritual life and *celibacy* are inseparable. Surely, this was the case for the most famous role models of this "new mysticism," such as Francis and his partner, Claire. Seen in this respect, Luther's public and therefore exemplary decision to marry (and *not* to live a celibate life in a "marriage," as more than a few cohabiting couples were said to have done, as a spiritual discipline) was a radical, if not unprecedented, event in the history of Western spirituality. That he also celebrated marital existence as ordained by God, and did not view marriage merely as a concession to the weakness of the flesh, as even Paul had done, was also a critically important and therefore exemplary factor. For a short but helpful historical overview of Christian thought and practice in this respect, see Wendy M. Wright, "Marriage, Family and Spirituality," in *The New Westminster Dictionary of Spirituality*, ed. Philip Sheldrake (Louisville, KY: Westminster John Knox, 2005), 419–21.

5. For a vivid, first-person introduction to some of the attractive features of a spirituality predicated on going beyond the limits of ordinary experience toward "the liminal," see Belden C. Lane, *The Solace of Fierce Landscapes: Exploring Desert and Mountain Spirituality* (New York: Oxford University Press, 1998). Lane points out instructively that "biblical religion, from ancient Israel to the early Church, takes shape in a geographical context dominated by desert–mountain topography" (43). He also shows how profoundly desert and mountain imagery has shaped the history of Christian spirituality (46–50). Lane then summarizes his own spiritual quest: "There is an unaccountable solace that fierce landscapes offer to the soul. They heal, as well as mirror, the brokenness we find within. Moving apprehensively into the desert's emptiness, up the mountain's height, you discover in wild terrain a metaphor of your deepest fears. If the danger is sufficient, you experience a loss of competence, a crisis of knowing that brings you to the end of yourself, to the only true place where God is met" (216). In contrast to the solace of fierce landscapes, I am committed to exploring what might be called the solace of Jesus in the mundane world. This does not sound very heroic, I know. But that may well be an advantage, at least for some of us. We may have been called by God to find our way, with God, precisely in the here and now of ordinary experience. This touches on a complex theological point in our understanding of ourselves as persons of faith living in a world created, redeemed, and consummated by God, a point that I can

only mention here. In his major study *Eccentric Existence: A Theological Anthropology* (Louisville, KY: Westminster John Knox, 2009), 2 vols., David H. Kelsey has argued that the best way to think of humans theologically is precisely as "quotidian" creatures, understanding ourselves primarily in our "lived world in its concrete everydayness" (1:190–214). To draw on Kelsey's terms, in this book I am exploring a spirituality of the quotidian, which, for me, yields a blessed engagement with nature.

6. Martin Luther, *Luther's Works,* ed. Jaroslav Pelikan (St. Louis: Concordia, 22 [1957], 23 [1959], 24 [1961], 69 [2009]), 22:305: "We are like a person who is subject to attacks of dizziness. If he is to climb a high tower or cross a bridge with deep water flowing underneath, he must be blindfolded, have his head covered with a coat, and be led and carried across. Otherwise he will fall from the tower and break his neck, or he will fall into the water and drown. Thus, too, if we are to be saved, we must follow our Leader; then we are safe. We, too, must simply close our eyes and follow our guide, the divine Word, and say: 'I will let myself be wrapped in swaddling clothes, have a cloak placed around my head, and be led to the point where I believe without seeing. On this I am willing to live and die."

7. Later, I was to approach Teilhard critically as well as appreciatively. See my *Travail of Nature: The Ambiguous Ecological Promise of Christian Theology* (Minneapolis: Fortress Press, 1985), 155–81. For the "eternal feminine" in Teilhard's thinking, see Henri de Lubac, *Eternal Feminine: A Study on the Text of Teilhard de Chardin*, trans. Rene Hague (New York: Harper and Row, 1968).

8. The dynamics of gender bias are relatively well understood from a scholarly point of view, particularly with regard to spirituality. But I find them incredibly complex in terms of my own lived experience. I do not know whether I have ever come out of the forest so that I can see the trees. For an excellent discussion of such issues from a scholarly perspective, a discussion rich with implications for self-analysis, see Lisa E. Dahil, "The Genre of Gender: Gender and the Academic Study of Christian Spirituality," in *Exploring Christian Spirituality: Essays in Honor of Sandra M. Schneiders*, ed. Bruce H. Lescher and Elizabeth Liebert (New York: Paulist, 2006), 98–118.

9. The English theologian and spiritual writer Sarah Coakley recounts similar moments in "How My Mind Has Changed: Prayer as Crucible," *Christian Century* 128, no. 6 (March 22, 2011): 32–40: "Anyone who has spent more than a short time on her or his knees in silence will know of the almost farcical raid that the unconscious makes on us in the sexual arena in such [times of silent] prayer, as if this is a sort of joke that God has up God's sleeve to ensure that 'ourselves, our souls and bodies,' are what we present to God and not some pious disembodied version of such" (37). Coakley seems to suggest, however, that such farcical moments can be regarded as stages along the spiritual way, to be integrated into some more comprehensive spiritual synthesis and thus surpassed. I wish that that were so, in my case. Maybe it could be if I were more disciplined. But, for now, well into my seventies, having wrestled with such things for many years, I find that even in some of my most intense spiritual moments, in the blink of an eye, I can be back in the midst of my adolescent sexual fantasies, in their primal rawness, as if I had never gained any perspective about them whatsoever. My strategy at such times has been this: "Okay, Lord, now help me get beyond this." And that has usually worked. But the underlying problematic has remained unchanged.

10. When I read the spiritual memoir *The Cloister Walk* (New York: Riverhead, 1996) by Kathleen Norris, who is married, I was sobered to learn about her two extended stays at St. John's Abbey in Minnesota. I had never even investigated whether such spiritual adventures might be possible for me.

11. The practice of spiritual direction has a long and sometimes circuitous history. See Janet K. Ruffing, "Direction, Spiritual," in *The New Westminster Dictionary of Christian Spirituality*, 243–45.

12. In contrast, for a warm and self-authenticating firsthand affirmation of the importance of spiritual direction, written by a married Methodist pastor and theologian, see L. Roger Owens, *Abba, Give Me a Word: The Path of Spiritual Direction* (Brewster, MA: Paraclete, 2012).

13. I have given some thought not just to my own eating practices but to the spiritual meaning of food more generally. However, most of these thoughts have been tentative and incomplete. For a coherent and well-informed discussion of these matters, see Norman Wirzba, *Food and Faith: A Theology of Eating* (New York: Cambridge University Press, 2011).

14. Dietrich Bonhoeffer, *Letters and Papers from Prison*, enlarged edition, ed. Eberhardt Bethge (New York: Macmillan, 1971), 347f.

15. There are other ways to enter into the presence of God. For example, in her autobiographical essay "How My Mind Has Changed: Prayer as Crucible," Sarah Coakley commends the classical spiritual way of waiting for God in silence and thus confronting one's own nothingness in "the dark night of the soul." What has "worked" for me all along the way, in contrast, has been to recognize the merciful touch of Jesus at the earliest possible moment of any spiritual exercise and then, and then only, to confront the darkness of my own soul and of the world around me. For me, it is necessary to begin with the *words* "Lord Jesus Christ, have mercy on me," and then to enter, as one who has been embraced by the mercy of Jesus, into the crucible of the *silence*.

16. I use the expression "postcritical naïveté" in the general sense it has taken on in theological discussions over the past few decades. See the statement by the New Testament scholar and theologian Marcus Borg, in the lecture "Spirituality and Contemporary Culture," National Forum of the Center for Progressive Christianity, Irvine, CA, June 1–3, 2000, *http://www.religion-online.org/showarticle.asp?title=1639* (consulted February 9, 2010): "Post-critical naivete is not a return to pre-critical naivete. It brings the critical with it, but integrates it into a larger paradigm. So it can bring the historical critical method with it. Post-critical naivete is the ability to hear the Christmas stories once again as true stories, even though you're pretty sure that Jesus was born in Nazareth and not in Bethlehem, even as you're pretty sure that the magic star and the wise men themselves come from an exegesis of Isaiah 60, rather than reflecting historical memory. You know all of that, but you're still able to hear these as true stories, as metaphorical narratives using ancient archetypal language to make, among other affirmations, that Jesus is the light coming into the darkness, to make the affirmation that the Herods of this world constantly seek to destroy that which is born of God. The struggle between the kingdom of Herod and the kingdom of God as known in the Lordship of Christ goes way back to the beginning. You hear all of that as true."I would want to specify, however, that the narratives of Scripture, according to the "analogy of the image" (Tillich), reflect "what really happened" in history. For a more extended, technical discussion of postcritical naïveté, see Paul Ricoeur, "Preface to Bultmann," in *Essays on Biblical Interpretation*, ed. Lewis S. Mudge (Philadelphia: Fortress Press, 1980).

17. The New Testament image of Jesus with the children has fascinated me for many years, together with his saying that his followers must be dovelike but not dovelike alone. This is the first text: "'Let the little children come to me; do not stop them; for it is to such as these that the kingdom of God belongs. Truly, I tell you, whoever does not receive the kingdom of God as a little child will never enter it'" (Mark 10:14b-15). That's the *naïveté* of the faith that I'm narrating and recommending. This is the second text: "'. . . so be wise as serpents and innocent as doves'" (Matt. 10:16b). Doves who are as wise as foxes—that's the motif of *postcritical* naïveté.

18. I am aware that a sizable percentage of humans in our society experience what are often referred to as "hallucinations." See the study by Oliver Sachs, *Hallucinations* (New York: Knopf, 2012). But I see no reason to rule out the thought that God works, at times, through hallucinations in the human self, particularly centered on currents in the human brain. This would be the spiritual process in such a case: as the risen Lord draws near, the brain responds to that presence with hallucinations of that presence.

19. H. Paul Santmire, *Nature Reborn: The Ecological and Cosmic Promise of Christian Theology* (Minneapolis: Fortress Press, 2000), chap. 7.

20. African American spirituality was reinforced for me along the way when I was able to spend a spiritually, liturgically, and politically charged month with a group of other American Christians, visiting black lutheran churches in South Africa at the height of the apartheid crisis. I

told that story in my book *South African Testament: From Personal Encounter to Theological Challenge* (Grand Rapids, MI: Eerdmans, 1987).

21. Readers who are familiar with the classical Christian tradition will have recognized along the way that in highlighting my relationship with Jesus and his mercy so existentially, which means, for me, so passionately, I am obviously not saying anything new. From New Testament times forward, the classical tradition of the Christian faith has always presupposed this kind of focus on Jesus as the primary way to know the transcendent God. This, for example, is how Rowan Williams, formerly archbishop of Canterbury, has described the faith that came to expression in the life and works of St. Athanasius, the great Christian theologian and bishop of Alexandria, in the fourth century: "We do not begin from innate or intuitive ideas of the absolute or the transcendent; we are drawn into a transformed life, speech, and activity in which the inexhaustible resource of the God who draws us in is gradually discovered. And the agent of that 'drawing' is the historical figure of Jesus, through the relations with himself which he establishes in church and sacrament" (Rowan Williams, *Christian Spirituality: A Theological History from the New Testament to Luther and St. John of the Cross* [Atlanta: John Knox, 1979], p. 50). In the fifth century, St. Augustine also predicated his thought about knowing God on the assumption that the unknowable God has become knowable for us in Jesus. This is James K. A. Smith's reading of Augustine in this regard: "When the 'Word became flesh' (Jn 1:14), the transcendent God descended into the realm of immanence(finitude), but without thereby denying or giving up his transcendence. . . . God's transcendence is inaccessible to us, but the way in which this is remedied is precisely by God's humiliation and descent to the order of the (fallen) creature. It is God who moves toward finitude, rather than lifting up (as an operation of *Aufhebung*) the finite" (James K. A. Smith, "Between Predication and Silence: Augustine on How (Not) to Speak of God," *Heythrop Journal* 41, no. 1 [January 2000]: 76). In our own time, as is well known, Karl Barth reaffirmed, sharpened, and extensively developed the classical Christian focus on Jesus as the primary way to know God, above all in Barth's multivolumed *Church Dogmatics* (London: T&T Clark, 1995), 14 vols.. Likewise, Dietrich Bonhoeffer's thought focused on Jesus as the primary way to know God. For an entry into Barth's theology, see his American lectures, *Evangelical Theology: An Introduction* (Grand Rapids, MI: Eerdmans, 1979). For a first encounter with Bonhoeffer's writings, see *The Bonhoeffer Reader*, ed. Clifford J. Green and Michael P. Dejone (Minneapolis: Fortress, 2013).

PART III

Contemplating the Triune God

Praise Father, Son, and Holy Spirit.

6

The Heart of the Trinity Prayer
Contemplating the Mystery of the Triune God

Under the rubric of full disclosure, I want to issue this warning here, in the midst of my narrative. I'm about to take you into the central mystery of this fragile faith: engagement with God as Trinity. Stand ready, therefore, to take a quite different turn in our journey, into a spiritual territory where there are few tangible guideposts to provide existential bearings. If you have ever done any mountain hiking, encountering such a challenge will come as no surprise. Often, it's the last parts of the trail, as you draw nearer and nearer to the summit, that are the most difficult—and the most rewarding.

Claimed by the light of Christ now, in the midst of the twilight of this age, I invite you to come with me to contemplate the wholly other God, Father, Son, and Holy Spirit, who is disclosed to us through Christ, in the power of the Spirit.[1] Then, in the following two chapters, we will begin to contemplate the presence and the works of this God, in, with, and under the beauties and the mysteries and the terrors of nature.

Our mantra for this part of our journey will be the words of the second petition of the Trinity Prayer: *Praise Father, Son, and Holy Spirit.* I ask you to cling to these words with heart and mind—and, indeed, to speak them often—as we encounter together some of the most alluring vistas of these chapters of our spiritual journey.

CONTEMPLATING THE TRIUNE GOD: THE RATIONALE

The New Testament witness to God as the Father of Jesus Christ, with the Spirit being the one who variously realizes the works of the Father and of the Son, does not explicitly address what it means to praise God, Father, Son, and Holy

Spirit as "one God in three persons." That language came to the fore after the New Testament era, and it has provoked much discussion ever since.[2] Some theologians and spiritual writers therefore advise that we should *not* explore the meanings of divine mysteries like the Trinity. Focus on tangible things, they maintain, such as the life and claims of Jesus, and avoid the intangible wherever possible.

But, as anyone who has ever taught the New Testament to teenagers knows, the question of what it means explicitly to talk about one God as Father and Son and Spirit is irrepressible for almost anyone who wants to take the Christian tradition seriously. The language of the New Testament overflows with references to these divine "persons."[3] The traditional worship of the church—above all, the widely used confessions of faith such as the Apostles' Creed—is thoroughly and sometimes technically Trinitarian.[4] As a result, in practice, the challenge of addressing God as Trinity *will* be raised whenever Christians think about their faith, whether deeply or superficially. Further, and much more important, the challenge of addressing God as Trinity *should* be raised because of the very character of our relationship with the God revealed to us in Jesus Christ by the power of the Spirit.

God is personally related to us. That is a premise of biblical faith and of ensuing Christian testimony.[5] And a personal relationship, by its very nature, grows and deepens over time, or at least it can, if it is a good and faithful personal relationship. So, as a matter of course, we can hope that our knowing of God will grow in depth and breadth as it evolves. On the other hand, our relationship with God is not symmetrical. It *is* personal. It *is* an I-Thou relationship (Martin Buber). But it is a unique personal relationship. God is our Creator, Redeemer, and Sanctifier. We are created, redeemed, and sanctified creatures. And God in Godself is inscrutable and unfathomable, wholly other, even though God discloses Godself to us personally. How, then, do we grow in knowledge of the ineffable one who addresses us personally in Jesus Christ, in the power of the Holy Spirit?

HOW TO CONTEMPLATE THE TRIUNE GOD:
ANALOGIES AS REFRACTED LENSES

One thing we can do, instructed by the practice of Jesus himself, is to tell stories or parables. As we prayerfully explore what it means for us to know God, we ask one another: What is God like? Or who is God like? Is God perchance like a father, who rushes out to welcome his prodigal son as that son is making his way home after a long and disreputable absence? (Luke 15:11-32). The language of knowing God more intimately as a matter of course is the language of metaphor or parable, of story or analogy.[6] To say this much is only to say what learned theologians from ancient times like Gregory of Nyssa, to Thomas Aquinas in the Middle Ages, to Sallie McFague in our own era have said, in many and diverse ways, and said much more forthrightly, extensively, and compellingly than I can say here.

In other words, figurative thoughts about God are unavoidable. They're all we have, as a matter of fact.[7] Better that we articulate those thoughts self-consciously, therefore, rather than lapse into a simplistic, literalistic kind of thinking—precritical naïveté in our postcritical era—that presupposes that God *is* a good shepherd, rather than that God *is like* a good shepherd, or which assumes that God dwells in heaven above, as if the earth were flat and heaven were literally located upward.

Hence, when we seek to deepen our personal engagement with God, Father, Son, and Holy Spirit, we are well advised to consider the analogies—as well as the images, the parables, the metaphors, and the stories—at our disposal to help us grasp, however imperfectly, what the God revealed to us in Jesus is like or who that God is like. One of the best Christian witnesses to thinking about Father, Son, and Spirit in such terms, the fourth-century Eastern theologian Gregory of Nyssa, was quite deliberate about these things, and instructively so.[8] He was well aware that we humans will invoke analogies to understand what and who God is as Father, Son, and Holy Spirit. Better we do this self-consciously, Gregory believed, in response to the witness of the Bible and to the witness of all the faithful who have gone before us, than not to embark on this kind of spiritual quest and thereby to be denied the grace of knowing God, Father, Son, and Holy Spirit more fully.

I remember driving from Boston to my parents' home in Buffalo, more than forty-five years ago, to tell them that I had committed my life, in my own mind and heart, to the woman whom I would eventually marry and to whom I have been married ever since. Their first excited question was, of course, "What is she like? Tell us about her." So I told stories about Laurel. Had I been able to recall the sonnet by Shakespeare at that moment, I might also have said: she is like a summer's day, but "more lovely and more temperate"; her "eternal summer shall not fade." Almost five decades later, the word *temperate* would not readily come to my mind. She now appears to me more like a lovely rose—with thorns. This is an image that she wholeheartedly welcomes these days. But you get the point. Persons are sometimes best described by such images. So it is with our personal relationship with God. Hence I want to tell you what—and who—I think the God I know personally in Jesus is like, so that you, too, can find ways of deepening your own personal relationship with God in terms that make sense to you.

Whatever spiritual knowing of God may be, then, it involves "pondering the analogies," separating the metaphorical wheat from the metaphorical chaff and perhaps invoking many different kinds of analogies—some of which may not be totally "in sync" with others—in order to give the richest possible account we can of God's self-revelation to us.[9] Consider good analogies as akin to a certain kind of lenses: as ways of seeing God and God's ways as clearly as we possibly can, even though we know that all of our seeing, in this case, will be refracted.[10] Good analogies, then, are not instruments for building up any kind of a coherent system of theological truth. Rather, they make it possible for us, who have been claimed by Christ and inspired by the Spirit, to approach and to contemplate the divine mystery.[11]

This is no idle matter for me, no casual or curious thinking about a God who is said to be one-in-three and three-in-one, as if I were working on some kind of mathematical puzzle. For me, these analogies are powerful personal images that have taken hold of my soul at the deepest levels. They help me to contemplate the mystery of the Trinity. In the words of the old hymn, "I once was blind, but now I see." The analogies I am about to discuss are spiritual lenses that allow me to contemplate God, however imperfectly, much more clearly than I might otherwise have been able to do without them. Apart from such lenses, everything about the God who discloses Godself to me through Jesus Christ as Father, Son, and Holy Spirit would be out of focus, even stirring around in some grand confusion. Insofar as I see the Father, Son, and Holy Spirit spiritually in any sense, I see through such images.[12]

PREPARING TO ENVISION AND TO GUARD THE MYSTERY

Some additional brief comments are necessary here, however, before we begin to explore the analogies I propose to highlight. This, after all, is a complicated subject, so I want to identify the path along which I will be taking you as clearly as I can at the outset.

First, I am retaining and, indeed, affirming the use of the traditional name of God, Father, Son, and Holy Spirit in these explorations. This is the name in which I was baptized. And this is the name in which I have baptized innumerable souls throughout my more than four decades in the ministry. But I do not want to invoke this name uncritically. I have learned some things in this respect during the past forty years, both from ecofeminist theologians and from others, personally as well as theologically.

The word *father* covers a multitude of sins. Often in Christian history, the image of "the Father Almighty" has been interpreted in profoundly dysfunctional ways. This image has frequently served as a kind of ideological cornerstone that legitimatized the evils of patriarchy, both in the church and in society more generally. In my reflections about my own sinfulness in chapter 5, I described how I too had been captive to the patriarchal mind in my early years (I will leave it for others to judge whether or in what respects I still am). I do not want to perpetuate patriarchy by championing uncritical theological practices.

This is one reason I have been so grateful for the insights of Jürgen Moltmann over the years, particularly for what he has called "the new Trinitarian thinking." This approach does not begin with the abstract idea of monotheism ("the Father Almighty"), with "God, the Father" understood as the heavenly patriarch and owner of all things. Rather, it begins with the concrete images of God, Father, Son, and Holy Spirit as we meet those images in the Scriptures. As Moltmann explains, compactly but forcefully:

> The new Trinitarian thinking has to do with Jesus the Son, and with God whom [Jesus] exclusively calls "Abba, my dear Father," and with the Holy Spirit who in fellowship with him is the giver of life. The differentiation between Father, Son, and Spirit describes the rich relations of the divine reality of the biblical history of God: the Father reveals the Son, the Son reveals the Father, and sends the Spirit of life from the Father. The Father communicates [*begets* is the creedal term] the Son, and the Son reveals the Father, and the Spirit of the Father radiates from the Son into the world.[13]

Gone in this new Trinitarian thinking is the traditional view of "the Father Almighty" considered in himself, alone, as the absolute patriarch. Rather, the Father is the one who "begets" the beloved Son, who, in turn, is sent by the Father to save the world by preaching and teaching the nonviolent kingdom of God, by giving up any claim to power over anyone or anything, especially by dying on a cross, and by being raised from the dead by the Spirit of the Father, in vindication of the coming and the final, eternal realization of the kingdom of God.

This approach to Trinitarian language—interpreting "the Father" first and foremost in terms of "the Son," as we know the Son in the Scriptures—does not answer all of the questions raised in this respect by ecofeminists and by other critics, but I do believe that, if rigorously pursued, it does point us in the right direction, away from the evils of patriarchy in church and society.[14] Later in this narrative, I will also draw on another of Moltmann's theological insights and will portray the first person of the Trinity as "the motherly Father." That is also a critically important point to make for this spiritual journey, which I very much hope will take us away from the thinking, the behaviors, the rites, and the institutions of patriarchy.

Second, and closely related to the first observation, not only am I retaining and affirming the divine name, Father, Son, and Holy Spirit, as we encounter it in the New Testament and as its meaning has been received by the new Trinitarian thinking, but I also do not want it to stand alone. Therefore, I will also, and often, refer to the Trinity in more self-evidently functional terms, in order to identify more specifically the identity of each of the divine persons. I hope this will have the effect of holding the meanings of "the Father," in particular, within the orbit of the new Trinitarian thinking, and of keeping that reference from drifting, in the reader's mind, into the orbit of traditional images of God the Father as the divine patriarch who rules over all things by domination. Although a number of such parallel functional "names" are available, the following makes the most sense to me spiritually: Father, Son, and Holy Spirit as *Giver, Gift,* and *Giving.*[15]

The reasons for this practice will emerge much more concretely, I hope, as we explore what I will call analogical narratives of the Trinity. All of these narratives will share one thing in common: their Trinitarian structure. I will identify that structure—beyond simply invoking the divine name, Father, Son, and Holy Spirit—with the metaphors of *Giver, Gift, and Giving.*[16] These metaphors took root in my own spiritual life over the years, nurtured as I was from childhood by faith in the God who abundantly gives and the gift of grace from the giving God, in the preaching and teaching and worship of the church of my forebears.[17]

Still, in the abstract, as it must be at this point, the theme of God as Giver, Gift, and Giving does not mean a great deal. But I hope that you will find this way of envisioning the Trinity illuminating, alongside the more familiar "Father, Son, and Holy Spirit," once we have begun to probe more deeply into the following analogical narratives. Call this theme—Giver, Gift, and Giving—an *integrating analogy.* I will invoke this integrating analogy in each of the three analogical narratives now before us. It is in this kind of narrative context that such an integrating analogy gains its full spiritual purchase.

Third, I will be offering you what you immediately will recognize to be three roughly hewn analogies, so perceived because of their narrative form, if for no other reason. I will do this in order to foster a deeper kind of contemplation of the Trinity: a Thanksgiving dinner experience, encounters with Niagara Falls, a traumatic but lifesaving moment in a steel plant. I take my cue here from some of the teaching moments of Jesus, such as the parable of the prodigal son, or, as it might more accurately be called, the parable of the waiting father (Helmut Thielicke). For Jesus, the God whom he calls father (*abba*) is like that waiting father who runs out to embrace his prodigal son. My own stories will be quite different, to be sure. They will be longer narratives rather than concise and thereby compelling parables. But they still will be analogical in some of the ways that Jesus' parables are. Hence I'm calling them roughly hewn analogies.

This all may sound formidable. But these roughly hewn analogies—or analogical narratives—have advantages. In "seeing through them" as lenses, you will *not* be tempted to think that you are seeing God directly or clearly, as, for example, more abstract language about God as "Being Itself" (Paul Tillich) or more traditional theological language like "person" or "substance" or "perichoresis" might lead you to think. Gregory of Nyssa himself valued analogies precisely for this reason.[18] God in Godself is ineffable and incomprehensible. God in Godself is wholly other. We know God only as God has disclosed Godself to us, indirectly, in the midst of our own fragmentary experience. This is why we use analogical language to talk about our experience of God.

On the other hand, and this is my fourth preliminary comment here, I do *not* believe that these analogies, roughly hewn as they are, are arbitrary.[19] In my own life, they have emerged in the midst of decades of experience with the Trinitarian faith of the church, in liturgy, prayer, and theology, especially in the wake of the remarkable revival of Trinitarian theology in the second half of the past century.[20] They have also arisen out of my decades of encounters with a number of well-attested motifs in the Scriptures. In concluding this discussion, as a matter of fact, I will suggest that the roughly hewn analogies that have come to have such a central place in my own spiritual life are intimately related to a number of prominent biblical themes: the divine banquet of redemption, the majestic power of God in nature, and the universal, sacrificial love of God.

Fifth, and by way of anticipation, I want to signal to the reader here that I have found these analogies to be most helpful in focusing the mind and touching the heart as I regularly give voice to the Trinity Prayer itself. I will discuss this and related matters in the epilogue of this book, but I am eager at this point for you to have a sense where I want to take you eventually. Although each of these analogies is indeed roughly hewn, I understand each one to also refer to *a quality of the triune God.*

When I think of the Trinity as festive communal process, I imagine *the joy of God.* When I think of God as majestic torrential flow, I imagine *the power of God.* When I think of God as self-sacrificing savior, it is easy for me to think of *the love of God.* The analogies I will be depicting, in other words, *are* roughly hewn. But from them can emerge in the mind and heart of the one who claims them, when praying the Trinity Prayer, simple but powerful images of the life of the triune God in Godself as joy, power, and love.[21]

Sixth, and finally, in all of these considerations I want to do everything I can not only to approach the mystery of the Trinity analogically but also to *guard that mystery.* I have already attempted to do that by making it as clear as possible that the analogies I am invoking are indeed that—analogies. They are not precise concepts, by any means. Nor are they in any respect photographic. Moreover, even as analogies, I understand them to be roughly hewn. I have also recognized that these analogies, when taken together, are not only complementary and self-correcting but also, in some respects, mutually contradictory. All this helps to guard the mystery of the Trinity. But I want to say still more at this preliminary point in order to guard the mystery in yet another way.

Consider these two themes, which I can only allude to here but which, even so, I find helpful in guarding the mystery of the Trinity: the *divine infinity* and the *divine fecundity.* The first one I learned to think about when I was once deeply engaged with the writings of the great eighteenth-century American theologian Jonathan Edwards. Somewhere, I recall, Edwards notes that, according his understanding of mathematics, there are two kinds of "infinity." The first is static. God is infinite, according to this meaning of the term, in the sense that God is larger than any finite creature known to us or even larger than all finite creatures taken together. The second, in contrast, is a dynamic kind of infinity. Infinity, in this sense, means *always* growing larger. So, God is indeed larger than all finite creatures taken together, according to this understanding of the word, but God is also constantly expanding, becoming ever larger, eternally. Edwards opted for this second kind of infinity, as do I, following him, as the most fitting way to envision God in Godself. This construct, then, not only guards the mystery but also affirms the majesty of that mystery. With this image, God's being and becoming are an eternally expanding infinity.

I learned to think about the second theme, the divine fecundity, when I once explored the thought of the thirteenth-century theologian St. Bonaventure while working on my historical reflections about Christian thought and nature.[22] Whereas a number of theologians, prior to his time, thought of God as "the Good," presupposing a kind of static vision of God, for Bonaventure it is much more fitting to affirm that God in Godself is "Overflowing Goodness." The image of God as a fountain of goodness *in Godself* easily comes to Bonaventure's mind. He calls God the "Fountain Fulness" (*fontalis plenitudo*). The inner life of the Trinity has this kind of profoundly overflowing eternal dynamism. For Bonaventure, the life of God in Godself is thus one of incomparable beauty and unimaginably rich fecundity.

In approaching the mystery of the Trinity, therefore, while I do find it spiritually helpful and, indeed, for me, necessary to invoke roughly hewn analogies in order to deepen my own fragmentary knowledge of God given to me in Christ by the Spirit, I find it just as helpful spiritually to guard the mystery, not only by recognizing the limitations of analogies of any kind but also by recalling the witness of theologians like Edwards and Bonaventure to the mystery of God, envisioned in terms of the eternally expanding infinity and the eternally rich fecundity of God in Godself.

ROUGHLY HEWN ANALOGIES: PLACES OF KNOWING

At the outset, I noted how important the theology of place has become for me over the years. Thus far in these exploration, accordingly, I have narrated my experience in a number of contexts, scything in Hunts Corner, for example, or walking along the Charles River. Places of knowing have been no less important for me as I have endeavored to engage the mystery of the Trinity. I now want to depict the existential meaning for me of three other places of knowing, as I seek to configure three roughly hewn analogies for the Trinity.

THANKSGIVING DINNER: THE TRINITY AS FESTIVE COMMUNAL PROCESS

It's Thanksgiving Day some years ago. Around the large, expanded table in our home is gathered a motley crew—including a number of "strays," as my children used to call them, privately. The group includes not only my wife, Laurel, and me, our two children, and other relatives and friends but also a random college student or two not able to go home for the holiday, a recently divorced father whose children are elsewhere with their mother, and a young woman from Zimbabwe whom we know through church.

As I finish circulating the several sumptuous dishes to our guests at the table, my inner eye is focused on Laurel, opposite me, at the far end of the table. Although she has been cooking all day, she is now engaging everyone energetically with stories about the food and its preparation or perhaps interjecting herself into a discussion about the president of the United States. Once the platters have made their way around the table, she interrupts the several lively conversations under way and announces that it is time for grace. I motion for everyone to take hands. After my prayer, we all sing "the Doxology" at the top of our voices—ending, "Praise Father, Son, and Holy Ghost." The joy around the table is palpable. As everyone smiles at one another, uplifted by the singing, I look down the table through the candlelight and contemplate Laurel once again. In my eyes, she's radiant.

In a down-home way, something threefold, something *Trinitarian*, is going on here in this single Thanksgiving meal. *Three* distinct acts are unified as *one* and, dare I say, unified in love? I'm thinking now of the Giver, the Gift, and the Giving, of Father, Son, and Holy Spirit. This is how I would like you to read this dinner analogy. Laurel and I called this ragtag crew together. She worked all day preparing the meal. I did the housecleaning and set the table. We both were intensely involved in the preparations, in one way or another, for hosting this gathering. But for the sake of my story here, let's imagine that *she alone* is the host of this celebration. Think of me as out of the picture, for a moment. Think of her as *the* host. Picture her, accordingly, as *the giver.* Imagine that she is the one whose party this is.

Call the food itself, in turn, *the gift* to everyone, especially as the wine is served and the platters are passed around the table and received with gratitude by our guests and by ourselves. Someone once said that it's a feast when there's more than enough. This is a feast indeed! The platters are plentiful and colorful, aromatic, and, indeed, much more than enough. The slowly roasted turkey, whose alluring aromas filled our apartment all day. The spiced stuffing, the bright Hubbard squash, the fresh bread (brought by a guest), the buttered mashed potatoes, the rich gravy, the tart cranberry sauce, the fresh brussels sprouts, the "jug wine" (as we call it), and the plain but indispensable ice water. Each dish, each glass bespeaks its own giftedness, food for the soul as well as for the body.

In addition, there's the process of sharing those platters with one another and sharing the conversation at the same time. Call this *the giving.* The people around the table all seem eager to offer the platters to one another, and all seem just as eager to receive the fruits of that giving with gratitude. Even more, they all appear eager to touch and to smile at one another as each, again and again, holds a platter for the person next to him or her so that the neighbor can take as much food as desired. The excited conversation around the table is another form of giving. People share themselves as they share their stories and ask questions that draw others out, so that they can give in return.

These *three* focal points of the meal—the giver, the gift, and the giving—are distinct yet inseparable, so that that meal, by the grace of God, is *one* great feast, a single festival of thanksgiving on Thanksgiving Day, as the vibrant unison voice of our doxology announced. God—Father, Son, and Holy Ghost—is *like* that, in everything that God is and does.

It's an imperfect analogy, as are all analogies, especially those construed to illuminate the mystery of the Trinity. Not without reason did the great St. Augustine—who, in the early fifth century, wrote what was to become one of the most influential treatises on the Trinity from that point on, in which he proposed a number of analogies to claim some meaning for that mystery—often suggest that he only wrote what he did in order not to say nothing.[23] I am well aware of the difficulties of saying anything about the Trinity. On the other hand, I must say something, for richer for poorer, about the Trinity, rather than nothing, if I am to tell the story of the fragile faith that is within me, as I believe God is calling me to do in this book.

So I offer this humble analogy of the Thanksgiving meal at our home in order to share how this one simple soul seeks to contemplate this great mystery that is at the heart of things. For me, knowing the God disclosed in Jesus Christ, in the power of the Holy Spirit, is like that festive meal I have described here. I find that this imperfect image illuminates the mystery of the Trinity and, in particular, *the joy* of the triune God. The classical Christian tradition can be read as depicting God in this manner as a kind of an eternal festival processing: God as the *Giver*, the *Gift*, and the *Giving*, *three* focal points of divine energy yet *one* God. God as Trinity, in other words, means God as a single loving community, with three differentiated, vital, and integral centers of activity interacting and communing—the theological tradition uses the phrase "mutually interpenetrating" (*perichoresis*) at this point—with each other, all distinct yet all at once remaining one eternally bonded community.

THE NEED FOR AN ANALOGY FROM NATURE

But the image of the Trinity as a festive communal process is not enough. It points us to the interdependent and personal character of the God who is Giver, Gift, and Giving, and in that respect, such an analogy is indispensable. The triune God is, in many ways, essentially like that Thanksgiving celebration I just depicted. But that analogy does not do full justice to what some theologians and mystics throughout the Christian ages have thought of as the overwhelming mystery and incomprehensible power of the God who is wholly other.

Here, I have in mind Luther, in particular, to whose mystical passion I am much indebted, as will become clear in chapter 7. For Luther, the God who is Father, Son, and Holy Spirit is wondrously and majestically in, with, and under the whole cosmos and its history. God permeates the beauties and the mysteries and the terrors of nature. Hence, the interpersonal analogy of the festive community we just considered must be complemented—and in some ways corrected—by another. It looks something like this: the Trinity as a powerful torrential flow. From this angle of vision, God is still Giver, Gift, and Giving, but in a way that overwhelms the imagination.

It is no accident that this analogy of the Trinity as a powerful torrential flow appears prominently in this book, which is concerned with a blessed engagement with God *in nature*. The communal meal analogy, which we have just considered, and the crucified God analogy, which we will consider soon, are at home in the world of recent Trinitarian discourse. Rarely, however, has that discourse highlighted such an image from nature, an image that, for me, is spiritually necessary.

Think, for example, of the size and age of our universe, populated as it is with some 500 billion galaxies, some 13 billion years old and still expanding. Our reflection about God must be commensurate with a universe like this. This is why the theme of torrential divine power is so important. Much theological and spiritual reflection these days, I have observed, is much more limited. It has a default terrestrial, if not totally anthropocentric, focus when nature is being discussed, as if God were chiefly the God of human life on earth (such discourse often suppresses, as well, reference to gargantuan terrestrial phenomena like tsunamis, earthquakes, or volcanic eruptions). On the contrary, the triune God is a God of astounding power, in, with, and under all the cosmic immensities. To be sure, the theme of divine power is in some respects highly problematic, particularly when it is construed abstractly in terms of "omnipotence."[24] My meanings here, however, are concrete. Divine power, in my view, means that the triune God, as the God of all things, has an all-comprehending cosmic reach.

This brings me back to the primary point I want to make here. For me, *the triune God is natural as well as personal.* God must therefore be thought of in terms of a nature analogy as well as in terms of a social analogy or, as we will soon see, the personal analogy of self-giving love. Unless nature is a primary analogy for God, as a matter of fact, nature—especially when it is understood cosmically, that is, in terms of the whole universe (or universes)—will essentially remain something distant from God or even alien to God. On the contrary, I believe, the "living God" confessed by biblical traditions is as much akin to nature and its immensities (a biblical theme I review in the next section) as this God is akin to communal interpersonal relationships or personal self-giving love. So let me show you a way now to imagine how the God who discloses Godself to us in Jesus Christ, in the power of the Spirit, is natural as well as social and personal.[25]

NIAGARA FALLS: THE TRINITY AS POWERFUL TORRENTIAL FLOW

I have already referred to my Baptism, many years ago in Buffalo. That location was, in some sense, a historical accident, as is every Baptism. But, already as a young boy, I drank deeply in the spirit of that city and its environs. Lake Erie, one of the majestic Great Lakes in North America, was very much part of that world, and I was keenly aware of it from an early age and was often drawn to contemplate it as a young boy.[26]

My grandparents owned a summer home almost at the edge of that lake, and from there I would walk down to the lake and wander around its beaches and inlets. When I was a college student, I worked one summer for Bethlehem Steel, right at the edge of the lake. My family also took weeklong cruises on that lake and, beyond, on all the Great Lakes, all the way to greatest of them all, Lake Superior, which gave me still broader perspectives on those waters. But it was the easterly egress of Lake Erie that fascinated me the most in my early years, as its waters poured into the Niagara River, propelled themselves toward and over the magnificent thundering of Niagara Falls, and then flowed through the huge and gaping Niagara River gorge and on into Lake Ontario.

Living as close to the Falls as my family did, we visited them often, both because they were such an astounding sight in themselves and because friends and family members from around the country found that our home was a convenient station on *their* way to visit the Falls. When I was a teenager, too, in the midst of the sometimes oppressive summer heat, my friends and I would on occasion jump into someone's car and head for the Niagara River. Our destination was only halfway between Lake Erie and the Falls, but we thought of the Falls intensely as we plunged into the surging river waters far above the Falls to see if we could make any headway swimming upstream. We couldn't. Obviously, we were horrified by the thought of being carried too far downstream. Images of helpless human bodies, being swept along by the torrents and then over the Falls, filled our minds. But it was safe enough for us, all accomplished swimmers, as we flailed our arms at the height of our powers against the currents, only to remain stationary. In retrospect, I think that that swimming was a kind of (safe) adolescent dancing with death.

Who can describe Niagara Falls, this icon of the historic American consciousness? Many writers and countless painters have tried. I will only tell what little I know. The Falls were formed at the end of the last ice age. Waters from three of the bodies we now call the Great Lakes carved out these Falls, leaving the gigantic river gorge before them, as those waters made their way forward, eventually, toward the Atlantic Ocean and as they relentlessly chiseled away at the bedrock underneath, inching the Falls ever closer back toward Lake Erie.

Today, over the two separate branches of the Falls, the American and the Canadian, more than 6 million cubic feet of water fall every minute. They plunge over heights that reach as high as 170 feet, and they extend more than a half mile wide. *Thundering* is indeed a good word to describe the impression they make when you stand on the observation platform, feet away from the apex of the Falls. My brother remembers feeling the ground tremble under his feet at that point, on the Canadian side, when he stood there as a boy. Sometimes, looking down from that point, he and I would watch a little ship, far below in the gorge, often obscured by the mist—it was called the "Maid of the Mist" in those days—making its way toward the Falls, with yellow-coated tourists packed on its decks, and then turning around, just in time it seemed to me.

Often, when my family had visitors and we motored down to see the Falls, after we had come home I would go to bed at night astounded. I would lie there thinking: never mind whether *I* am awake or asleep, *those tons and tons of water* keep flowing over the Falls and keep carving out the gorge in front of them without ceasing! It was truly an awe-inspiring memory for me as I lay there in the solitude of my bed.

Once, as a young man, Paul Tillich—who, after he emigrated to the United States, was to become one of the nation's leading theologians during the middle of the twentieth century—visited a steel mill in his native Prussia. It was my privilege to study six years with Tillich as an undergraduate. The visit to the steel mill was a story he told more than once in my hearing, although I am not sure whether he ever wrote about it. With youthful passion and spiritual abandon, he recounted, he looked at the flowing molten steel and said, "That is God." Tillich would later qualify such statements carefully. But I know what he had meant. Had I had the same kind of inspiration in my own youth, I could have easily looked at the Falls and the gorge and the turbulent waters below and said, "That is God."

If we consider the mysterious majesty of the Trinity, such exuberant statements can, indeed, readily emerge from the mind and heart. Consider the Falls themselves, ever overflowing, throwing down immense cascades of water every second of the day. *God the Father* is like that, always and ever overflowing with goodness and creativity, always and ever, indeed eternally, being *the Giver*. Whether we humans sleep or not, whether we notice it or not, the Father is constantly the Giver, pouring forth goodness creatively, from alpha to omega of the whole creation and, indeed, in the eternal being and becoming of God in Godself.

Notice, further, that those waters that pour over the Falls are thereafter channeled for a number of miles. The cliffs lining the river below the Falls keep those waters moving in a single direction rather than chaotically flooding everywhere. The cliffs give a kind of good order to the waters below. The cliffs, as it were, channel the overflowing divine goodness and creativity in a specific direction and give them a certain kind of form as these move toward the vast basin of Lake Ontario.

Early on in the Christian tradition, the "word" (*logos*) referred to in the first chapter of John, where the Son of God was being envisioned as co-creator with the Father, was interpreted in the metaphysical categories of the day as the logos of the creation, that ontological structure which "holds all things together" (see Col. 1:17). The *Son of the Father*, called the logos of God, was understood to be the divine agency that gives form and good order to all things and sustains them in their being. Thus I imagine the cliffs of the Niagara River gorge, on either side of the river below, as a gift in a certain sense: a gift of order and direction.

So we have this image thus far. The eternally overflowing creative goodness of the Father is akin to the waters cascading over the Falls. The shaping and directing function of the cliffs downriver from the Falls are akin to the workings of the eternal Son or logos, holding all things together, shaping and directing all things toward their future consummation in the eternal kingdom of God, as the river flows on into the vast reaches of Lake Ontario.

But do not overlook the turbulence of the waters, especially at the base of the Falls, as they cascade down into virtually immeasurable currents and eddies and countercurrents and countereddies. Contemplate that turbulence.

That apparently chaotic churning appears to be what moves those waters downstream and works to carve out ever new ways for the pulsating river to rush on toward its resting place in Lake Ontario. That turbulence, we may think, is like the work of the *Spirit*, the "lifegiver" announced in the New Testament and in traditional images. That, in turn, is akin to the vision of the chaotic "tongues of fire" that fell down on humans and drove ordinary men and women to become saints and martyrs. It suggests to me also the impulsive life force of God that draws the evolutionary history of our cosmos forward toward its eternal resting place in God. It recalls, likewise, the image of the breath or spirit of God "hovering" creatively—giving birth is what the text suggests—over the primeval waters of the first days of creation depicted in Genesis 1. Christian interpreters of that Genesis text by the second century already understood that "breath" or "spirit" of God to be the Spirit of the triune God.

Sometimes, when I was a young boy and had just returned from a visit to the Falls, I would spend an inordinate amount of time in my bath just before going to bed. I would use all the force available to my boyish arms to swirl those waters in what I imagined to be a hundred different directions. As I did, I would contemplate all the currents and eddies, insofar as I could see them. And, in doing so, I would recall the turbulence of the Niagara River at the base of the Falls and beyond, and I would marvel at its complexity and power and mystery.

I now believe that the Spirit of God once worked, in many times and in many ways, on the soul of that young boy as he contemplated the overflowing waters—ever flowing, it seemed, in his mind and heart—and the work of the river walls below that captured and channeled that overflowing, even as those currents were astoundingly turbulent, moving in ways that no mortal mind could predict or understand. So I thought in those days—and so I still think.

Is it a surprise, then, that five or six decades later, when I am scything in a verdant field in southwestern Maine overlooking the mountains of God to the west in New Hampshire as they are clothed in the brilliant colors of the fall foliage, it makes deep sense to me to think of the Trinity as eternal Giver and Gift and Giving? Isn't it in reach of at least a few mortal souls to think of God not only as a festive communal process but also as one who is, at once, resplendent with the glory of eternally overflowing creative goodness, a God of immeasurable and indeed inconceivable power, holding and shaping every creature and all creatures at once in being, for countless millennia, channeling all creatures wondrously toward the end for which they were first created, in their becoming, and at the same time moving them forward by the turbulence of this process to their final fulfillment, on the day when God will be all in all?

Analogies for the life and works of God as Trinity are, as I have stressed, imperfect. It is not easy to hold together in our minds even the two analogical narratives that I have thus far proposed for interpreting who the God is who is revealed in Jesus Christ, in the power of the Holy Spirit. But, as I throw myself at the feet of Jesus Christ and allow him to be for me the light of the world, this is the refracted vision of God that comes into the view of my fragile faith, as I open my eyes anew, insofar as I can see through a glass darkly and ponder the God who reveals Godself to me in Jesus Christ, in the power of the Holy Spirit. And I invite you as well to see with the eyes of such a fragile faith. There is still more to see, magnificently more.

THE TRINITY AS THE SELF-SACRIFICING SAVIOR

The Crucified God is an expression given currency in our era by Jürgen Moltmann, especially in his book with that title.[27] Moltmann believes, as do other major interpreters of the Trinity in our time, that God as Trinity cannot be understood in the abstract, apart from the history of salvation, which culminates, for faith, in the life, death, and resurrection of Jesus Christ. It is as if the Trinity is an icon and the image at the heart of that icon is the cross of Jesus Christ.[28] Numerous classic Christian paintings of the Trinity depict God precisely in that manner, with the eternal Son on the cross, positioned at the center of the figure of God, the Father.

In the *Crucified God* and elsewhere in his writings, Moltmann introduced a new accent in thought about the Trinity or, more accurately, he lifted up a theme that had not previously been highly visible in the history of Christian reflection about the Trinity: the suffering of the Father.[29] Moltmann, as we have already seen, rejected the traditional image of God the Father as a kind of heavenly patriarch.[30] That (false) God, in Moltmann's view, presided over a hierarchy of hierarchies: spirit over matter, political rulers over those ruled, the rich over the poor, males over females, whites over persons of color. On the contrary, Moltmann argued, God the Father is not a heavenly patriarch, but a "Motherly Father."

Moltmann graphically underlines this point by referring to some traditional language of the church used at the Council of Toledo in 675, which announced that the Son was born "out of the womb of the Father" (*de utero Patris*).[31] We know God the Father, in other words, only as the Father of the one whom he painfully handed over to die, the Son, Jesus Christ. In eternity, indeed, the Father in some manner begets the Son and then, with anguished, empathetic love, sends the Son on his fateful mission in the midst of cosmic history. The pain of the Father is as much a part of this picture as is the suffering of the Son.[32]

That way of imagining God has been profoundly important for my own spiritual life ever since I first read *The Crucified God*. I have not been able to think about God as Father, Son, and Holy Spirit, nor begin to contemplate any image of that divine mystery, without seeing *the Cross*, the eternal Giver's act of becoming the Gift of salvation for me and the world by the Giving of that Gift to me and the world. Nor have I subsequently been able to envision God the Father, in particular, in any other terms than as the eternal Giver, who suffered in begetting and then also in sending the Son.[33]

I have claimed the image of the motherly Father, in particular, as my own because, as I have already confessed, I was taken—no, overwhelmed—as a young pastor and theologian by the feminist critique of patriarchy that I first met in the writings of and conversations with Daly and Ruether, among others, as well as by my own personal experience with women more generally, as a husband and as a teacher and chaplain at Wellesley College.

Along the way, I also had come to treasure a spiritual intuition that I first self-consciously met in Luther's writings and then in Old Testament studies of the motif of blessing. This is the theme, then, that I have taken for granted for many years now: God the Father is eternally the Giver, constantly overflowing with goodness and blessings throughout the whole creation, and even feeling the anguish of the Son, who had to suffer the throes of death. This view of the Father liberated my spirituality, I believe, from any conscious remnants of that thinking that depicts the Father as the domineering, all-transcending One, who lords it over nature, and who creates humans in his image to do the same with nature, as well as lording it over one another throughout the millennia of human history.

This means, more particularly, that the roughly hewn analogy we are about to consider is a necessary clarification, and in some respects a necessary correction, of the roughly hewn analogy that we have just explored: the triune God as powerful torrential flow. As necessary as the latter is, especially for a spirituality of nature, it cannot stand alone. The God who has disclosed Godself to me in Jesus Christ is definitely not a God of mere power, nor, surely, a God of absolute, unqualified power. The God whom I confess is the God whose power is made perfect in weakness (2 Cor. 12:9), particularly in the scandalous, self-giving weakness of the Cross. I have already signaled this understanding of the power of God in my rejection of the monotheistic understanding of "the Father almighty" as a "god" of dominating power. The power of God, as many theologians and spiritual writers in our era have stressed, is always—however inscrutably—the power of God's love.

So, as I tell my story in this volume, and in line with innumerable Christian pilgrims throughout the ages, I am more than eager to expand on and strengthen my testimony to Jesus Christ as the Savior of the whole world and to the Father of Jesus Christ, who held him to his bosom in eternity and was willing thereafter to surrender him to suffering and death for the sake of the whole creation. In this sense, God is love (1 John 4:8): "For God so loved the world that he gave his only begotten son" (John 3:16). This is the culminating analogy of the self-giving at the heart of God that I want to propose in order to allow us, with increasing intensity, to engage the mystery of the Trinity personally.

How are we to do that? I have already told you about what I have perceived to have been the risen Lord's encounter with me, in the midst of my own mundane experience, when I pondered the story of Mary Magdalene. Now I want to narrate a different kind of story, another analogy that has also helped me to engage the mystery of the Trinity with my own fragile faith. Here I explore a moment when my own life was at risk.

IN THE HOLD AT BETHLEHEM STEEL

Earlier in these reflections, I have mentioned my experience one summer when I was a college undergraduate, working for Bethlehem Steel, in Lackawana, New York, adjacent to my hometown of Buffalo. I recalled how I was astonished to cross over into that totally new—and alien to me—cultural milieu, the world of urban working-class African Americans circa 1955. What follows is a story from those times that forever molded my own spirituality—although how deeply I was only to realize much later.

Those were the post–World War II times of "peace, progress, and prosperity," the Eisenhower era in the United States. Any able-bodied male in those days could walk in off the streets and immediately be hired to work in the steel plants. So I easily found a job at Bethlehem Steel one summer. I was assigned, for no particular reason of which I was aware, to the ore docks on the night shift. This meant not only that I would have to adjust to the shock of being the only white man in the midst of an all-black crew, laboring among people who spoke in ways that I often could not understand and who came from a cultural world that was totally unknown to me, but also that the ore docks themselves were a brave new world for me.

In the middle of the night, typically, one of the huge ore freighters that traversed the Great Lakes in those days—from the Masabe Range in Minnesota to the steel plants in Cleveland and Buffalo and elsewhere—would sidle up to the dock in Lackawana to have its mountains of ore unloaded. Those indeed were the days of technological giants in the earth. The off-loading from those enormous ships was accomplished by gigantic scoops, usually two of them per ship. Each of those gargantuan scoops was as large as half of a railroad locomotive. Each would devour some sixteen tons of ore as it sank its gigantic teeth into the towering piles of ore in the cavernous holds of the ore ships. Each scoop was operated, moreover, by one driver, whose workspace was built into the lower arm of the scoop itself. That operator would look out a single side window in the body of the scoop to spy out where in the great hold to steer the scoop in order to take hold of yet another sixteen tons of ore.

And those scoops were by no means precision instruments. The operator could only see out one side, so he had to imagine how close the other side of the scoop might be coming to the wall of the hold, lest the scoop slam into that wall and somehow puncture it. From time to time, however, the inevitable happened. One of the scoops would go crashing into the plate-steel wall of the hold, emitting an explosive noise that always made me shudder.

Those of us in the ore crews mostly slept until the next ore boat came in. We were housed in a kind of cabin in the body of the great, sliding machine that held the arm of the scoop. So when a ship came in and the scoops began to work, we would of course be awakened by the force of the whole gigantic apparatus sliding back and forth, from the hold of the ship to the growing great piles of dumped ore on land behind the towering machines. I and an older black man sometimes sat near each other wordlessly at one end of the moving cabin when the scoops were working—it was usually too noisy to talk about anything—and the rest of the crew would play some kind of a dice game, with loud shouts now and again, under a swinging light bulb at the other end. The din and the shouts were, together, sometimes deafening. Then the whistle would blow. It was time to go to work.

All of us would clamber over the rig of the great machine and on to the deck of the ore freighter. From that precipitous location, we would then climb down vertical steel ladders into the hold, with helmets on our heads and shovels in our hands. It felt like some three stories climb from top to bottom. The hold of the ship was larger than a football field, it seemed to me, and totally disconnected from the world high above, from whence the gigantic scoops kept plunging down, in search of yet more ore.

It was our job, once down on the floor of the hold, to hurry over to the corners or edges of the hold, where the giant scoops could not reach all of the ore, and to shovel the ore piled there into the center of the hold. It was also our job to keep our eyes on those scoops, which were plunging in and out of the hold, in different directions, all the time. The scoops could not, in effect, see us much of the time. We had to look out for them, lest we be smashed against the walls.

At one moment, it so happened, I was intensely scraping ore from one of the corners of the hold, with my helmet-covered head bent down over my shovel where a remnant of an ore heap remained. All at once it was if I had been tackled in a football game. A figure came flying at me from nowhere and hurled me aside. Together, we fell in a heap a few yards away. Just at that moment, one of the monstrous scoops came hurtling toward us and crashed into the corner where I had just been shoveling. I would have been killed had I still been working there. That man had saved my life.

Everyone on the crew laughed, and then we all hurried to yet another area of the vast hold to shovel still more ore toward the center. The enormity of what had happened did not hit me at the time. I was too swept up by the shock, I imagine, and by the need to get working again, to do my fair share, in another location. I don't even remember telling my parents about what had happened when I saw them the next day. Maybe I was still in shock. Maybe I was concerned, too, that they would be afraid and would force me to seek other work. Be that as it may, I did not begin to reflect about what had happened in that cavernous hold until some years later.

When I finally did, it began to dawn on me. My life had been saved! And not only that, but my life had been saved by someone I did not even know, by a person who had every right not to care whether I, an affluent white boy from the suburbs, lived or died. The more and more I thought about that act of saving, the more and more the words of an old hymn, written by a repentant slaver, kept coming to mind—"Amazing grace, how sweet the sound, that saved a wretch like me!" That man, whose name I did not even know, had been willing to risk his life to save mine. In my youthful stupor that day, I never even found a way to thank him.

That precious memory of my salvation suggests an analogy to me for understanding the heart of the triune God, the self-sacrificing savior. I have learned a little about urban African-American communities since those days of my youthful ignorance. I served a multiracial inner-city congregation for thirteen years in Hartford, Connecticut. I have been a member of a mostly black congregation in Boston for just about as many years. One of the things I have learned over these years is the critically important role that the black church plays in such settings.

The black church generally offers an alternative reality to its members, many of whom are otherwise defined by the larger society to be of little or no account. At its best, the black church is the community that it takes to raise a child, not just as a bulwark against the larger society but as a support system, as a field of dreams, as a good place for children to grow up with hope and personal aspirations.

Although I have no way of knowing for certain, I would like to believe—and I think it is entirely plausible—that the man who instinctively risked his life to save mine down in the hold of that ore freighter had been nurtured in the black church, directly or indirectly, when he was a boy. He did not have to think twice about what it might mean for him to love his enemies. He acted impulsively—with deep moral roots, I now believe—to save my life while risking his own. In that sense, I am convinced, he was sent to me by that larger community of which he was a part, and he was empowered by the ethos or spirit of that community, subliminally if not self-consciously.

What if my savior had not been successful? What if we both had died? I know how my own family and other loved ones would have responded—with deep grief, of course. But I want to focus here on how the African American community that sent that man forth into the world, to imitate the Savior, would have responded. Their grieving would have known no bounds. The preaching and the hymnody and the tears and cries of mourning would have filled to overflowing their house of worship, where his life and his sacrifice would have been celebrated. Members of that worshiping community would have praised God—with their anguished tears and groans and their deeply moving gospel hymns—that a son of their community had so faithfully responded to his calling to be like Christ.

The analogy works powerfully for me. There was a threefoldness about the act that saved my life that day. There was the giver, the gift, and the giving. There was the giver: the community of faith that, in a sense, had sent the man out into the world and that would have deeply grieved had he died. There was the gift: the man himself, willing to lay down his life for others. And there was the giving: the power that inspired the man to take the action he did at that moment. Over the years, accordingly, that man has become an icon for me of the crucified Jesus Christ in the heart of the eternal God, the motherly Father, empowered by the Spirit.

Dare I believe that that man—whom I, at that time, and the cultural world in which I lived considered to be worth next to nothing—was sent and empowered to offer his life in my behalf so that I might live? I do. And I also dare to believe the same of Jesus Christ, all the more so: that this is the love of God, that the Father was willing to risk the life of his only, beloved Son, that the Father sent that Son to die for sinful me and for the world and to rise again in my behalf and in behalf of the world, so that I and the world might have life and, indeed, life abundant, with the hope that all will gather one day at the bosom of the Father, united with the incarnate, crucified, risen, and ascended Son, and enlivened by the Spirit, transfigured in the triune eternity of God Godself and basking in the joys of a gloriously renewed creation, when the lamb will lie down with the lion.

I hope that you have already taken that leap of faith in order to see that much, too. Or, if you have not yet done so, I hope you will consider it. See the crucified God in the heart of God, and be amazed at what this crucified God has also done for you and for the whole world.

THE ROUGHLY HEWN ANALOGIES IN RETROSPECT: THE BIBLICAL ALLUSIONS

My spiritual life is richly informed by each of these individual fragmentary narratives—sometimes complementary, sometimes contradictory—and by all of them taken together: God as the festive communal process, God as the powerful torrential flow, and God as the self-sacrificing savior. Each analogical narrative, in its own way, witnesses to the God who is Giver, Gift, and Giving. Each, taken together with the others, offers an imperfect but illuminating testimony to the mystery of the Trinity, Father, Son, and Holy Spirit.

Moreover, each of these analogies can serve as a point of entry to further explorations of the Scriptures, as a way to encounter their witness to the triune God in Godself and to the works of the triune God. I want to pause here to sketch how this kind of interplay between these analogical narratives and key biblical themes can work out in practice, in order to give you a firmer sense of direction for our continuing spiritual journey here.

The *analogy of the festive communal process* is enriched by a contemplative reading of texts such as the so-called Little Apocalypse of Isaiah, chapters 24–27, which announce a God who will bring all creatures to fulfillment in one great festival banquet:

On this mountain the Lord of hosts will make for all peoples a feast of rich food, a feast of well-aged wines, of rich food filled with marrow, of well-aged wines strained clear. And he will destroy on this mountain the shroud that is cast over all peoples, the sheet that is spread over all nations, he will swallow up death forever. Then the Lord God will wipe away the tears from all faces, and the disgrace of his people he will take away from all the earth, for the Lord has spoken. It will be said on that day, Lo, this is our God, we have waited for him so that he might save us. This is the Lord for whom we have waited, let us be glad and rejoice in his salvation. (Isa. 25:6-9)

Jesus himself claimed that banquet theme as his own, in all likelihood, being well-known as one "who came eating and drinking," regarded by his critics as "a glutton and a drunkard, a friend of tax collectors and sinners" (Matt. 11:19). Jesus was also remembered in his own time as one who gathered thousands and fed them, as a sign of the world-transforming kingdom of God (see John 6:1-15), and, more intimately, as one who hosted his own disciples in order to feed them with fish and bread (John 21:9-14).

Then there is that later expression of the same underlying theme of eating together festively expanded apocalyptically in the Book of Revelation: a new heavens and a new earth, when death will be no more (Rev. 21:1ff.), a text that echoes the Little Apocalypse of Isaiah, which we have just encountered.

In retrospect, I am sure that these biblical motifs about the festive banquet worked subliminally in my own mind and heart as the roughly hewn image of the Trinity as a family Thanksgiving meal began to take shape in my inner life over the years.

Likewise the *analogy of the powerful torrential flow* can be deepened and made more concrete by reflecting on a range of biblical images. Consider, in particular, this testimony from Psalm 29: "The voice of the Lord is over the waters; the God of glory thunders, the Lord over the mighty waters. The voice of the Lord is powerful; the voice of the Lord is full of majesty. . . . The Lord sits enthroned over the flood: the Lord sits enthroned as king forever" (Ps. 29:3,4,10). Or, Psalm 33: "By the word of the Lord the heavens were made, and all their host by the breath of his mouth. He gathered the waters of the sea as in a bottle; he put the deeps in storehouses" (Ps. 33:6-7). Similar images appear dramatically in the poetic testimonies of the Book of Job, chapters 37–40. So the Lord is presented as saying to Job, memorably:

Where were you when I laid the foundation of the earth . . .? [W]ho shut in the sea with doors when it burst out from the womb—when I made the clouds its garment and thick darkness its swaddling band . . .? Have you entered into the springs of the sea, or walked in the recesses of the deep . . .? Who has cut a channel for the torrents of rain and a way for the thunderbolt, to bring rain on a land where no one lives, on the desert, which is empty of human life, to satisfy the waste and desolate land, and to make the ground put forth grass? Has the rain a father, or who has begotten the drops of the dew? From whose womb did the ice come forth and who has given birth to the hoarfrost of heaven? The waters become hard like stone, and the face of the deep is frozen. . . . Can you lift up your voice to the clouds so that a flood of waters may cover you? Can you send forth lightning. . .? (Job 38:4-35)

I feel the same kind of primal power emanating from the story of the disciples on the Sea of Galilee that we encounter in the Gospel of Mark. A storm comes upon them, and they fear for their lives. The text then shows us Jesus, in the words of the old spiritual, as "the man who stilled the waters"(Mark 4:35-41). Some scholars who have studied this story carefully have spoken of the divine luminosity of Jesus taken for granted by its Markan author, befitting one who is regarded by Mark as the son of the very God who is the Creator of all things. The storm text itself ends with this haunting question: "Who then is this, that even the wind and the sea obey him?" (Mark 4:41).

Such images of God working gloriously amidst the primeval waters and of Jesus as the Lord of those very waters have fascinated me since the earliest days of my biblical studies, doubtless because of my boyhood experiences with water in many forms, particularly with Niagara Falls—and probably for other reasons, too, deeply rooted in my unconscious. I invite you, the reader, now to allow what you can imagine about my Niagara Falls experiences and what you can hear in such biblical texts to speak to each other, in order to lead you with more abandonment into the depths of contemplation of God, Father, Son, and Holy Spirit.

The *analogy of the self-sacrificing savior* is attested in many places in the Scriptures, of course, beginning in the Old Testament—from Psalm 22, regarded by the church as a psalm of the passion of Christ, with its anguished cry, "My God, my God, why have you forsaken me?" (Ps. 22:1) to 3 Isaiah's witness to the "suffering servant of God" (Isaiah 53). In the New Testament, the four Gospels themselves can be read, as has sometimes been said, as "passion narratives with introductions." In the Gospel of John, perhaps most explicitly, the whole story of the God incarnate (John 1:14) comes to its conclusion when Jesus is "lifted up to the Cross" (e.g., John 8:28). Further, for John, Jesus and the Father are one (John 10:30). This suggests to me that, in John's vision, the triumphant Savior on the Cross dwells, as it were, in the heart of God. I cannot see the Father and the Son, in the power of the Spirit, in other words, according to the Johannine vision, without seeing the Cross. A contemplative reading of the New Testament leads me to that conclusion.

More particularly now, like many Christians throughout the ages, I have returned to the testimony of Philippians. 2:5ff. throughout my whole adult life. This text witnesses to Christ Jesus as one who was in the form of God but who "emptied himself," taking the form of a slave, being obedient to the point of death, even death on a cross. For a time, when I was a young theology student, I was taken by a modernizing interpretation of this ancient text: the idea that in the incarnation Jesus "emptied himself" of what in the modern era was thought of as the absolutes of his divinity—the divine omnipresence, omnipotence, and omniscience—and became "purely human," regaining his divinity in the aftermath by his resurrection.

But I soon set such thinking aside, not only on the basis of close studies of the Philippians text itself but also because, during the same years of my theological study, I was being claimed, more and more, by Martin Luther's "theology of the cross." I then came to this conclusion, as Luther had affirmed in many different ways, that there is no other "divine" Christ than the Christ whom we know in the flesh and on the cross, in particular. This is the Christ who was "exalted" (Phil. 2:9) to the heart of the Father, I believe, and who dwells there eternally as the "crucified God." This is the Christ who is to be worshiped and adored "to the glory of God the Father" (Phil. 2:11), the crucified Savior. How this "works," rationally speaking, I do not begin to understand. But that the Crucified is at the heart of the Father, in the glory of the Spirit—that is the only way I now can contemplate God, Father, Son, and Holy Spirit. Claimed by such a vision, then, was it an accident that my own experience of being saved by someone who was willing to lay down his life for me on that ore freighter has for so long vividly lived on in my mind and heart?

RETROSPECT AND PROSPECT

The communal festival of Thanksgiving, the overwhelming majesty of Niagara Falls, and the rescue of my own life by what I now believe to have been a profound act of self-sacrifice—these roughly hewn analogies, for me, resonate with the testimonies of Scripture and vice versa, as I contemplate the mystery of the triune God. I invite you to listen for that resonance now yourself. Imagine moments in your own life like the Thanksgiving festival I described, like my primordial experience of Niagara Falls, like my rescue from the jaws of death in the depths of that ore freighter, and then say to yourself, hesitantly if not yet with complete assurance—*God is like that*. God is like that joy, that power, and that love.

But these analogical narratives—helpful as I hope they are in themselves, and even more helpful when framed by biblical motifs as they can be—are still insufficient for grasping the mystery of the Trinity, as is every analogy, a point that I have already made several times but which I want to repeat here, at the end of this particular discussion. Generally in the spiritual life, but especially when we are contemplating mysteries like the Trinity, this oft-cited mystical saying must be heard regularly and with real force: "Everything comes to rest in mystery" (*omnia exeunt in mysterium*). And the conviction of St. Augustine with reference to his long and complex treatise on the Trinity must be remembered constantly: in such things, we say something so as not to say nothing. The analogies for the Trinity we have just considered—which have given us some images of the mystery of the triune God, consonant as they are, I believe, with the testimonies of the Scriptures—by no means transcend the fragile faith that gives them birth. All things considered, if we *see* in any sense, as I believe we do, we see *through a glass darkly* (1 Cor. 13:12).

In that spirit, keep repeating this prayer: *Praise Father, Son, and Holy Spirit.* And, just as often as mundane circumstances may give you occasion, keep imaging who or what this God is like. Perhaps a festival communal process. Perhaps a powerful torrential flowing. Perhaps a self-sacrificing saving. I hope that analogies like these will make it easier for you to ponder testimonies in your own mind and heart about what or who God is like, as you yourself praise this God, Giver, Gift, and Giving, whenever and however you can.

Now I want to turn to a different angle of vision, still with the middle petition of the Trinity Prayer in mind and heart as well as on your lips. I want to lead you to a place where you can contemplate the majestic presence and wondrous works of this same God in, with, and under the beauties and the mysteries and the terrors of nature and its evolutionary history with God, as we continue to pray, wherever each one of us may be: *Praise Father, Son, and Holy Spirit.*

Notes

1. I have alluded to the problematic character of referring to God as "Father" a number of times thus far. I will discuss this matter at some length in the next section of this chapter.

2. The single best short essay I know of that addresses the origins, history, and significance of Trinitarian thinking is by Catherine Mowry LaCugna, "The Practical Trinity," *Christian Century* 109, no. 22 (July 15–22, 1992): 672–78. If I were teaching a course on the Trinity, this is the article that I would ask everyone to read at the outset. Readers who would like to explore the unfolding of Trinitarian thinking, from the Bible to the ancient creeds of the church and beyond, sketched in much more technical language, may find it helpful to keep the following compact theological schema by David H. Kelsey, *Eccentric Existence: A Theological Anthropology* (Louisville, KY: Westminster John Knox, 2009), 1:120, in mind as a guide to understanding these complex historical issues: "The process leading to discovery of a properly Trinitarian understanding of God began with reflection on triadic liturgical formulas ('In the name of the Father, the Son, and the Holy Spirit') that were perceived to be related somehow to three sets of scriptural stories about the divine economy broadly understood [creation of the world, reconciliation through Christ, and consummation of the world]. It shifted to reflection on the divine economy narrowly understood as the economy of reconciliation [through Christ] and its implications for understanding God formulated creedally. It shifted attention again from the economy of salvation to the immanent eternal life of the triune God imaged as a community in communion of free self-giving love. The One with whom human persons must ultimately have to do is . . . constituted by the communion-in-community of three perichoretic hypostases freely and in love giving and receiving Godself eternally."

3. One example is the eighth chapter of Romans, in which we hear that "the Spirit helps us" (v. 26), that "God searches the heart" (v. 27), and that God "did not withhold his own Son" (v. 32). Another is the first chapter of John, in which John the Baptist announces that Jesus is "the Lamb of God" (v. 29) and "the Son of God" (v. 34), and that he, John, saw "the Spirit descending . . . on him" (v. 32).

4. Consider the last stanza of a hymn that has been popular in both Catholic and Protestant communions in America for many years, "Holy God, We Praise Your Name": "Holy Father, Holy Son, Holy Spirit, three we name you, though in essence only one; undivided God we claim you and, adoring, bend the knee while we own the mystery" (source unknown; trans. Clarence A. Walworth).

5. Coherently summarized by Paul Tillich, *Biblical Religion and the Search for Ultimate Reality* (Chicago: University of Chicago Press, 1955).

6. Although, from a scholarly point of view, careful distinctions can be made to define the meanings of "metaphor or parable, story or analogy," I am taking them, for purposes of this general discussion here, to have overlapping meanings. They all can help us to affirm, in various ways, what or who God is like. For those who are interested in such matters, I am taking analogy to be the most fundamental construct in this discussion, although I understand it in a literary sense, rather than metaphysically. I do not presuppose a metaphysics of ontological participation, such as that assumed by the thomistic construct, "the analogy of being" (*analogia entis*). For the fine points of this kind of discussion, see Eberhard Jüngel, "Metaphorical Truth: Reflections on Theological Metaphor as a Contribution to the Hermeneutics of Narrative Theology," in *Theological Essays*, trans. with an introduction by J. B. Webster (Edinburgh: T & T Clark, 1989), chap. 1; Sallie McFague, *Metaphorical Theology: Models of God in Religious Language* (Philadelphia: Fortress Press, 1982); and Janet Martin Soskice, *Metaphor and Religious Language* (Oxford: Clarendon, 1985).

7. See Jüngel, "Metaphorical Truth," 60: "God is only properly spoken about when we speak of him metaphorically."

8. The use of analogies to interpret the meaning of the Trinity was already in vogue in the writings of Tertullian in the second century—for example, root, tree, fruit; fountain, river, stream ("Against Praxeas," *Ante-Nicene Fathers*, vol. 3, ed. Alexander Roberts and James Donaldson

[Grand Rapids, MI: Eerdmans, 1973], 602f.). For those who would like to explore Gregory's thought about analogical thinking about the Trinity, see Sarah Coakley, "'Persons' in the 'Social' Doctrine of the Trinity: Current Analytic Discussion and 'Cappadocian' Theology," *Powers and Submissions: Spirituality, Philosophy and Gender* (Oxford: Blackwell, 2002), chap. 7. My discussion here draws on Coakley's exposition.

9. This process of imaginative engagement with God is similar to the process of understanding in our perhaps more familiar engagement with Jesus Christ as we know him in the Gospels. Images of Jesus abound in the New Testament, including high priest, lamb of God, and good shepherd. Some of these images even appear to contradict one another—such as Jesus as both the lamb of God and the good shepherd. But each has its own revelatory power and enriches our understanding of Jesus Christ. It is similar for our analogies for the triune God. They sometimes appear to stand in tension with one another, even, in some ways, to contradict one another. But the question is whether such imaginative riches help us to grasp the mystery of God's self-disclosure, not primarily whether they may or may not be logically or literally inconsistent or even contradictory.

10. So the apostle Paul famously observed of the mysteries of the end times, "now we see through a glass darkly"(1 Cor. 13:12). What we see with the eyes of faith, in other words, we by no means see clearly; but we *do* see.

11. See the felicitous statement by Jürgen Moltmann, *Experiences in Theology: Ways and Forms of Christian Theology,* trans. Margaret Kohl (London: SCM, 2000), 160: "The principle of analogy is not an instruction for building up a theological system. It describes a theological movement or train of thought. Knowledge of God comes about in the rhythm of perceived similarity and perceived dissimilarity to God. The more we know God, the more we perceive that we know nothing of God. Analogical knowing of God takes place in approaches to the Divine mystery. But the closer we come to God, or—better—the closer God comes to us, the more unknowable for us he is. Strangeness is a category not of distance, but of closeness, for it is the closeness which first makes the strangeness apparent."

12. For me, images of God are always necessary for faith, precisely because, with the classical Christian tradition, I encounter God as Trinity. And one must have images of some kind in mind and heart in order to contemplate the triune God. Otherwise, the distinctions between the divine persons collapse, and we are left with an experience of undifferentiated oneness or nothingness or darkness. The reader should know, however, that in this respect my own spirituality has parted company with a major trend in Western Christian spirituality— celebrated in our time by some scholarly students of Christian spirituality—which has held that there is *a higher experience than the experience that is shaped by images.* Andrew Louth depicts that tradition clearly in his discussion of the spirituality of St. John of the Cross, *The Wilderness of God* (Nashville, TN: Abingdon, 1991), 106: "When John speaks of contemplation, he is taking for granted a distinction that had become traditional in the West by the end of the Middle Ages (though it has not in fact very deep roots in the Christian tradition): the distinction between meditation and contemplation. According to this distinction, meditation is a form of prayer that depends on images: in my prayer I imagine (say) a scene from the gospels and try to enter into it, see what it means for me, try to respond with love, repentance, and commitment. It is a form of prayer that depends on images: these images inspire my feelings and devotion. Contemplation, on the other hand, dispenses with images, the reason and the imagination are ignored or suppressed, and prayer becomes a kind of alert attentiveness in the darkness where God is. Contemplation is understood to be a higher form of prayer than meditation: meditation prepares the soul for contemplation. For St. John contemplation is the prayer of the night: it is watching in darkness, freed from the distractions of thoughts and images." For me, living within the world of ordinary places, meditation, when it is inspired, *is* contemplation: there is nothing higher, in my view, than inspired meditation, which uses images. This touches on a related issue, more physiological in character than strictly spiritual, but of its own importance nevertheless, given the fact that humans are essentially bodily creatures and that the human brain, in particular, is very much involved in

receiving and shaping our spiritual experience. In emphasizing the essential character of images in our experience of God, therefore, I do not wish to exclude those whose metier is not given to easy visualization, whether due to genetic makeup or cultural conditioning or both. For them, I would make my point this way. For me, there is no higher form of contemplation than that activity of the mind and heart that depends on concrete ideas.

13. Jürgen Moltmann, *Sun of Righteousness, ARISE: God's Future for Humanity and the Earth,* trans. Margaret Kohl (Minneapolis: Fortress Press, 2010), 149–50. For a more systematic argument, see Jürgen Moltmann, *The Trinity and the Kingdom: The Doctrine of God,* trans. Margaret Kohl (San Francisco: Harper & Row, 1981), especially 69–71.

14. See Rosemary Radford Ruether, *New Woman New Earth* (New York: Seabury, 1975), 65–66: "Traditional theological images of God as father have been the sanctification of sexism and hierarchicalism. . . . Jesus, however, refers to God as father in such a way as to overthrow this hierarchical relationship. . . . The fatherhood of God could not have been understood as establishing male-ruling class power over subjugated groups in the Church or Christian society, but as that equal fatherhood that makes all Christians equal, brothers and sisters."

15. I have heard over the years, in both theological and liturgical settings, the following ways of speaking about God used to explicate Trinitarian meanings: "creator, redeemer, and sanctifier" and "lover, beloved, and love." It would take me too far afield, however, to explain here why thinking about God as "Giver, Gift, and Giving" has made and continues to make the most sense to me spiritually, as a way to help me to grasp what the primary symbolic address, to God as Father, Son, and Holy Spirit, means.

16. In the current theological milieu, talk of such matters might well be contested. Students of theology who have come of age intellectually in recent decades will immediately sense a high charge with the mention of these constructs. "The Gift" is now a major theological issue. For an instructive review of this topic, see Risto Saarinen, *God and the Gift: An Ecumenical Theology of Giving* (Collegeville, MN: Liturgical Press, 2005). As Saarinen shows, philosophical and sociological discussions of "the Gift" and its meaning have been under way for many decades. Saarinen's study itself has been hailed as the first systematic treatment of the theme from a theological perspective. I refer interested readers to that work, which clearly summarizes both the earlier philosophical and sociological discussion and more recent theological explorations, as well as making a strong case of his own for the viability of a theology of giving. Also of value in this context are the following works: J. Todd Billings, *Calvin, Participation, and the Gift: The Activity of Believers in Union with Christ* (Oxford: Oxford University Press, 2007), especially chaps 1 and 6; *The Gift of Grace: The Future of Lutheran Theology,* ed. Niels Henrik Gregersen, Bo Holm, Ted Peters, and Peter Widman (Minneapolis: Fortress Press, 2005), especially chapter 6 by Bo Holm, "Luther's Theology of the Gift."

17. The language of giver, gift, and giving was thus a kind of native milieu for my own spirituality for many years. One telling example would be the nineteenth-century Swedish folk tune I often sang, "Children of the Heavenly Father," in *Evangelical Lutheran Worship,* no. 781, stanza 1: "Children of the heavenly Father safely in his bosom gather; nestling bird nor star in heaven such a refuge e'er was given." I only recently became aware of the trends and issues addressed by Saarinen in the 2005 volume *God and the Gift* to which I referred in the preceding note. Soon thereafter, I also became acquainted with the sophisticated and compact study by Stephen H. Webb, *The Gift of God: A Trinitarian Ethics of Excess* (New York: Oxford University Press, 1996). Webb concludes his study by referring to God as "God the Giver who gives us life, God the Given who gives the self in total abandonment, and God the Giving who receives our gifts, which is also God's giving again" (158). See also Robert W. Jenson, "Triune Grace," in *The Gift of Grace* (see preceding note), 23: "If we speak of gift, the Father is thus the ungifted giver. The Son and the Spirit are in different ways the gift." Finally, as this book was about to go to press, I came upon the study published more than a decade ago by Michael Downey, *Altogether Gift: A Spirituality* (Maryknoll, NY: Orbis, 2000). He envisions God as love, which means, for him, that God is "the Giver, Given and Gift/ing" (58). I cite these materials here, however, only to suggest

to the reader an adventure for further exploration. I also mention these things because it now appears to me that the kind of language that refers to God as Giver, Gift, and Giving that I am using here is very much "in the air" of the current Christian theological and spiritual climate. Still, as far as I am aware, my own reflections in this book about Giver, Gift, and Giving are, for richer, for poorer, only my own, born of my own spiritual history.

18. See Coakley, "'Persons' in the 'Social' Doctrine of the Trinity," 121.

19. When I first read the illuminating study by Amy Plantinga Pauw, *The Supreme Harmony of All: The Trinitarian Theology of Jonathan Edwards* (Grand Rapids, MI: Eerdmans, 2002), a few years ago, I found myself strangely reassured about my own mostly private (at that point) musings about Trinitarian analogies. I do think that the analogies that have come to mean so much to me *are* roughly hewn, as I have said, and therefore that they are idiosyncratic, compared to much of the church's long tradition of reflection about the Trinity. Edwards's analogies appear to have been much more elegant and circumspect than mine. Still, in his own way, he seemed to experience some unease and a certain defensiveness about his own inventive use of analogies, as I do all the more so, particularly about how that usage might be received by his critics. I identify with Edwards's unease and defensiveness, expressed in these words: "I expect by very ridicule and contempt to be called a man of a very fruitful brain and copious fancy, but they are welcome to it. I am not ashamed to own that I believe that the whole universe, heaven and earth, air and seas, and the divine constitution and history of the holy Scriptures, be full of images of divine things, as full as a language of words; and that the multitudes of these things that I have mentioned [i.e., images, analogies of the Trinity], are but a very small part of what is really intended to be signified and typified by these things" (*Works* 2:152, cited by Pauw, 38f.).

20. One good discussion of that Trinitarian revival is offered by Stanley J. Grenz, *Rediscovering the Triune God: The Trinity in Contemporary Theology* (Minneapolis: Fortress Press, 2004).

21. At this point, this discussion takes us to the edge of a highly technical theme in the history of Christian theology concerning what has traditionally been called "the attributes" of God or, more recently, "the perfections of God" (Karl Barth). One helpful entry into this discussion is the summary of Karl Barth's exposition provided by Otto Weber, *Karl Barth's Church Dogmatics: An Introductory Report on Volumes I:1 to III:4*, trans. Arthur C. Cochrane (Philadelphia: Westminster, 1953), 85–92.

22. For this material, see H. Paul Santmire, *Travail of Nature: The Ambiguous Ecological Promise of Christian Theology* (Minneapolis: Fortress Press, 1985), 97–104.

23. Augustine apparently did not use exactly these words, but he often said much the same thing in a variety of ways. See James K. A. Smith, "Between Predication and Silence: Augustine on How (Not) to Speak of God," *Heythrop Journal* 41, no. 1 (January 2000): 66–86.

24. For the kind of theological problems given with the traditional theological idea of power understood as omnipotence, see Anna Case-Winters, *God's Power: Traditional Understandings and Contemporary Challenges* (Louisville, KY: Westminster John Knox, 1990).

25. Since God has so often been "spiritualized" in traditional Christian teaching, this statement may sound extreme to some. But, in this respect, I am in good company. This, for example, is how Karl Barth approached the matter, according to the summary of Otto Weber, *Karl Barth's Church Dogmatics*, 83, where Weber is reviewing Barth's discussion of the biblical themes "the living God" and "the God who acts," quoting Barth: "'Acts occur only in the unity of spirit and nature' . . ., and if God is the active agent, he cannot be 'that chemically purified absolute spirit,' as theological and philosophical speculation is so fond of regarding him. . . . He is spirit, 'but just the divine Spirit.' And he is 'certainly also nature, but just the divine nature'. . . . Therefore we cannot comprehend his nature either by elevating to the uttermost our concept of spirit or of nature, and even less by erasing spirit or nature." This is not to suggest, however, that Barth would be in agreement with my own understanding of a Christian spirituality of nature. On the contrary, many years ago when I was a young theological student studying in Germany, I traveled to Switzerland to have what was for me a memorable conversation with Barth about my interests.

And he warned me against them! For my own reading of Barth's theology of nature, see *The Travail of Nature*, chap. 8.

26. Sadly, in recent years, this magnificent body of fresh water has been poisoned by a thick, vast, and growing coat of toxic algae, covering a sixth of its surface and bringing with it a huge dead zone at its lower levels, reducing fish populations drastically. These developments also make large portions of the lake inaccessible for recreational use. Sadly, too, a 2013 study found that western New York (infamous in the past for the poisonous Love Canal) is home to some eight hundred hazardous waste sites that could wreak environmental havoc in Lake Erie and possibly other Great Lakes, too, in years to come.

27. Jürgen Moltmann, *The Crucified God: The Cross of Christ as the Foundation and Criticism of Christian Theology*, trans. R. W. Wilson and John Bowden (New York: Harper & Row, 1974).

28. See Jürgen Moltmann's statement, *Experiences in Theology: Ways and Forms of Christian Theology*, trans. Margaret Kohl (London: SCM, 2000), 304: "The death of the Son of God on the cross reaches deep into the nature of God and, above all other meanings, is an event which takes place in the innermost nature of God himself: the fatherless Son and the sonless Father."

29. Moltmann's most succinct statement of this theme is his brief essay "The Motherly Father: Is Trinitarian Patripassianism Replacing Theological Patriarchalism?," in Johann-Baptist Metz and Jürgen Moltmann, *Faith and the Future: Essays on Theology, Solidarity, and Modernity* (Maryknoll, NY: Orbis, 1995), chap. 14.

30. For a sharply critical statement of Christian understandings of God as Father, see Sallie McFague, *Metaphorical Theology: Models of God in Religious Language* (Minneapolis: Fortress Press, 1982), chap. 5.

31. Jürgen Moltmann, *The Trinity and the Kingdom: The Doctrine of God*, trans. Margaret Kohl (San Francisco: Harper & Row, 1981), 165.

32. See Jürgen Moltmann, *A Broad Place: An Autobiography,* trans. Margaret Kohl (Minneapolis: Fortress Press, 2009), 194f.: "The pain of the Father and the suffering of the Son manifest a single movement of the triune God: the Father in his pain surrenders the Son (Romans. 8:32) and the Son surrenders himself (Galatians 2:20). . . . Through self-surrender to annihilation on the cross Jesus brings the light of fellowship with God into the abysses of annihilating God-forsakenness."

33. Some of my readers may find the theme of God's suffering, particularly the suffering of the Father, troubling. If so, this could be a case where the *preaching* of the church, which forms the minds and hearts of the faithful, has not kept up with the *teaching* of the church. For the latter, see the discussion of Christopher Southgate, *The Groaning of Creation: God, Evolution, and the Problem of Evil* (Louisville, KY: Westminster John Knox, 2008), 57: "The suffering of God has been a common motif in the theology of the last hundred years, especially in the light of the World Wars and more particularly the Holocaust. This motif is in tension with the classical notion of the *apatheia* of God. Platonic formulations insisted that if God truly suffered, God would not be in control of God's life, would not be self-determining. Against that is, first, the biblical witness to a God who is both approachable and responsive, who grieves over the sins of the people and is stirred to wrath by their sin. Second is the discomfort of many theologians at formulations that isolate the suffering of Jesus from that of the Father. Jürgen Moltmann's fine study *The Crucified God* (1973) indicated the riches of Trinitarian reflection that are released by taking leave of the classical doctrine and allowing 'patripassianism,' the real suffering of the Father at the passion of the Son. Third, the extremes of human suffering that became known all over the world from the experience of the Holocaust make a God who did not suffer a hard God to proclaim." Southgate's whole discussion, in this context, serves as a good introduction to these trends. See, further, the excellent study by Paul S. Fiddes, *The Creative Suffering of God* (New York: Oxford University Press, 1988).

7

The Presence of the Triune God in Nature

Contemplating God in All Things

I now propose to walk with you around this spiritual summit in order to contemplate what we can see of the mysterious *presence* and the majestic *works* of the triune God unfolding in every direction. In other words, continue to praise Father, Son, and Holy Spirit, invoking the words of the Trinity Prayer, but now, from these heights, begin to contemplate the same triune God in, with, and under all things and working in all things. In this chapter, I will invite you to contemplate the presence or the immanence of God. In the next, I will explore the works of God.

The theme before us in this chapter, the divine immanence, is critically important for any Christian spirituality of nature. Critics of the Christian tradition who have been concerned with environmental issues and ecological thinking in our time have typically argued—with some justification—that modern, if not all traditional, Christian theology has focused mainly on the human creature, not on the whole of nature also, meaning that it has been thoroughly *anthropocentric*. Those critics have also maintained—again, with some justification—that Christian theology throughout the ages has focused mainly on the *transcendence* of the divine, on the God who is "wholly other," in effect leaving the whole creation, if not the human creature in its midst, desacralized and disenchanted.[1]

Hence there has been widespread theological and spiritual commitment in our time, championed by such theologians as Sallie McFague and Jürgen Moltmann, to reaffirm the immanence of God in all things, so that the whole creation can be encountered as a world of enchantment and divine immediacy.[2]

129

I personally have been preoccupied with the immanence of God in nature since I first began to think about such things in the middle of the past century, well aware of the critique that had been directed against the Christian tradition in precisely this respect but all the more eager to share my own experience of the God who is in, with, and under nature.[3]

CONTEMPLATING GOD IN NATURE: A PLACE OF KNOWING

I want to begin these explorations of the divine immanence in nature by taking you to another place for which I feel deep affection. A five-minute stroll from where I live is located one of the entrances to the historic Mt. Auburn Cemetery. Virtually every week of every season when my wife and I are not away and when the weather permits, we take walks along Mt. Auburn's many miles of roads and paths. This cemetery has its own character, no less inspiring, for me as a walking place than the nearby banks of the Charles River. I want to take you to Mt. Auburn now in order to address the challenge presently before us: to broaden the vision of the triune God so that it comprehends all things created by God, not just God in Godself. I am taking you to this particular place because I do not want the universalizing vision now before us to appear as abstract and removed from our mundane experience.

But a cemetery? I owe you a word of explanation. It *is* beautiful, a wonderful world to explore. I do not want to romanticize the place, however, even though it was established in 1831 with an underlying romantic impulse. Previously in the United States, at least up to the end of the eighteenth century, death was hardly romantic in the popular mind. Fostered by a tough-minded puritan spirituality, cemeteries in that earlier era typically were ugly and often neglected. That all changed, however, with the creation of Mt. Auburn and many other American cemeteries modeled after it. The movement to "beautify death" became a prominent trend in nineteenth-century American culture and beyond.[4] I want to bracket such thoughts here, however, and simply consider Mt. Auburn for what it also is: not just a cemetery but also an impressively designed and imaginatively cared for *arboretum* that affords us the wider vision I want to show you.

The 170 acres of Mt. Auburn, originally a farm, were contoured with a number of small hills over the years and enhanced with several small ponds. Most impressive is the variety of its more than five thousand trees—some seven hundred species, from massive purple beeches to the smaller and softer dawn redwoods (of Chinese origin), from colossal sugar maples standing alone in their own rough-barked grandeur to the more supple weeping willows rooted at the edges of some of the ponds and wafting gracefully in even the most gentle of breezes. I regard the purple beeches, in particular, several of them well over a hundred years old, as if they were my own old friends. I have the impulse to talk with them.[5]

Taken together, all of the trees and shrubs in Mt. Auburn are like a grand chorus for me, each lending its own distinct yet harmonizing voice to the whole, especially during the spring and summer seasons, when the dogwoods and the magnolias and the weeping cherry trees and the azaleas and the laurel and the clethra bushes are in bloom. Likewise, in the fall, when the golden, red, and brown colors of the changing leaves of the soaring Norway maples and the cone-shaped gingkos and the several species of majestic oaks appear, standing in contrast with the scores of dark conifers, I hear the resounding concert of all of these fellow creatures deep within my soul.

Since we usually take our walks during the middle of the day, however, we do not see very many of the innumerable birds that thrive in Mt. Auburn throughout the seasons, although we often hear some of their songs (dedicated bird-watchers from all over the region, who arrive at dawn with their binoculars, typically see representatives of numerous species). Once, to our great surprise, we did catch sight of two owl chicks fluffing themselves high on a thick horizontal branch of a huge oak. Another time, we almost stumbled over two sizable wild turkeys, who scarcely seemed to notice us. On occasion, we will see a loon working one of the ponds, feasting, presumably, on some of the goldfish that inhabit those waters, alongside the bullfrogs and the turtles. A great blue heron will grace the same ponds, now and again, quietly and elegantly making its presence felt. And redwing blackbirds often show themselves near one of the ponds. Then there are the goldfinches in the tall grasses and the bluejays in the spruce trees, along with many other bird species whose names I have yet to learn.

With its rich and diverse flora and fauna, and its elegant design, Mt. Auburn exudes a spirit of peace and fecundity at almost every turn. Even the noises of the city traffic all around the arboretum are muffled when one walks about the place. The dead, of course, do not speak, certainly not from their classically designed tombs or their well-kept graves.[6] On the other hand, there's more than meets the eye in this beautiful, peaceful arboretum. If you look carefully, you can recognize those adorable baby owls as the predators-in-waiting they actually are, and you can catch sight, now and again, of red-tailed hawks flying high above, searching for prey on which to pounce. I once came upon one of those hawks as it stood on the ground next to the carcass of a pigeon that it had apparently just begun to devour. Another time, eerily for me, I happened to have a personal encounter with yet another one of those hawks, perched on the branch of a magnolia tree at eye level, watching me before I noticed it.

Speaking of predators, one morning I even encountered a coyote in Mt. Auburn, whose kind is increasingly establishing its own territory at the edges of cities like Boston. Due to Mt. Auburn's location and design, however, the dark side of evolutionary nature is only rarely seen by pedestrians like me. And thoughts of the occasional destructiveness, mayhem, blood, and gore of nature therefore reside only at the edges of one's consciousness. All is well—or so it seems. That is the message that Mt. Auburn announces at almost every turn.

IN SEARCH OF AN ALL-COMPREHENDING VISION

Where, then, are we to find the all-comprehending vision to which I have referred? That is best afforded from the tower at the center of Mt. Auburn. Located at the top of the tallest of the small, humanly constructed hills in the arboretum, this stately, medieval-looking structure rises some three stories high. You climb up winding stone stairs inside, as if you were within a small cathedral steeple, to gain access to the top. From the castlelike turret of the tower, you can see, a half mile to the southeast, the Charles River, winding its way into Boston. As you then eye the eastern horizon, some twenty miles away, you can observe the Tobin Bridge, a major Boston landmark that carries traffic northward toward the coasts and the mountains of New Hampshire and Maine.

Nearer along the horizon, to the southeast, you can contemplate a resplendent profile of the whole of Boston, a small city by global standards but elegant in its own right, perhaps precisely because of its comprehensible size. As you behold the Boston skyline, you often can catch sight of airliners approaching Logan Airport from the south, gracefully gliding down over the Boston Harbor behind the few but commanding skyscrapers of the city. Further to the south, some thirty miles away, on a clear day you can see signs of the coastline of the great Atlantic Ocean beyond.

I have never been atop the tower in the evening (that is not permitted), but, on a clear night, standing on a nearby elevated bank along the Charles, a place that offers the same perspective as the tower, I once saw at the southeast horizon an enormous harvest moon rising slowing but gloriously over the whole city of Boston, the moon's glow adumbrated below by millions of sparkling city lights. Deep in my heart, that overflowing and omnipresent luminosity called forth images of the city of God and the new heavens and the new earth, in which righteousness dwells. That, for me, was a divine vision. Whenever I'm atop the tower, I can see this stirring nocturnal scene in my mind's eye.

I am well aware that there are many things that such a vision does not permit me to see. I have already alluded to the dark side of nature while I was reflecting about my walks in Mt. Auburn. Darker still is the violence in the streets near my inner-city church, whose steeple—seven miles to the east, in Boston's Roxbury neighborhood—can only be seen from the Mt. Auburn tower with binoculars during the daylight hours. Nor, of course, can one see from such a distance the impact that Boston's historic racism has had all over the city, the jails crowded with young African American men, for example, or the Latino teenagers congregating in parks when they should be in school.

Then, right where I'm standing, contemplating the vision, I am immediately aware of this mortal, septuagenarian body of mine, which sometimes wearily carries me around my walks in the arboretum and up to the top of its tower. Up here, from this vantage point, in addition to everything else, I can survey the large complex of Mt. Auburn Hospital buildings a short distance away, to whose emergency room Laurel once drove me in some haste. The infection I had at that time could have killed me had it not been promptly treated. Of course, I *do* think about such dark things, even in the midst of the serenity of my walks in the arboretum with my dear wife. But my purpose at this point in my story is not to recall, once again, those dark thoughts but to show you the grand vision, the presence and the working of God, Father, Son, and Holy Spirit, in, with, and under everything that I can see from the top of the tower.

But I need to be more specific. It is no accident that I am standing at such an elevation in order to show you the vision. Saints and mystics throughout the Christian ages have often contemplated God with precisely such a perspective before them. They have frequently imagined themselves to be on a spiritual pilgrimage, indeed, climbing up to Mt. Zion or to some other great mountain, in search of a beatific vision. Ordinary believers have often thought of themselves likewise, albeit in more prosaic terms.

When I was a teenager and attended Bible camps, well-intentioned leaders used to refer to this kind of thing as "a mountaintop experience." Later, when I was in college and attended a retreat now and again, that language was psychologized: in those days, we who were the so-called "well-integrated young achievers" were said to be seeking "peak experiences." In one form or another, such experiences have profoundly shaped the Christian consciousness in the past and continue to do so today. Indeed, in my book *The Travail of*

Nature, which is a study of historic Christian attitudes toward nature, I identified "the experience of the overwhelming mountain" as the primordial Christian standpoint before nature.[7] But herein lies a critically important problematic that I want to identify briefly before I try to show you more of what I can see from the top of the tower.

ANGLING THE VISION HORIZONTALLY: DON'T LOOK UP

Standing before nature on such imagined heights, the historic Christian mind has been divided. A dear Sunday School teacher, who urgently wanted this then-young boy to depend on God at every step in his life's journey, once said to me: "Don't look back. Don't look forward. Look up." That made good sense to me in those days, but I have subsequently realized that that was poor spiritual counsel—if one were to adopt it consistently and at the same time desire to envision the presence and the workings of God in, with, and under nature. It is sobering, then, to realize that many past and contemporary Christian spiritualities have been self-consciously focused on looking up to God's dwelling place in the highest heavens or even higher. This aspiration was given its most sophisticated expressions by giants of the tradition like Dante and St. John of the Cross. It has been much more simply expressed, but still movingly, by faithful souls like my Sunday School teacher or my college retreat leaders. I have called this form of spirituality "the theology of ascent."

Think of the Mt. Auburn tower again or the primordial mountain image to which I just alluded, above all Mt. Zion, or even Jacob's ladder, a biblical image of immense spiritual popularity throughout the Christian ages. Think of ascending to any high place and then *looking up* to the heavens above—to God. According to this way of seeing things, God is indeed far removed from this created world below, utterly transcendent, the *mysterium tremendum*, attainable, if at all, only above and then beyond the apex of a grand hierarchy of being. For this way of thinking, God, in Godself, is *akin to the sun*, brightly shining in the heavens vertically above but in itself blinding, being in no way accessible to humans by their own powers.

So in order to enter into mystical communion with such a God, according to this way of thinking, you must rise above every created thing and be carried up to the highest heavens or higher. You must leave all of the levels of the creaturely hierarchy below—the waters, the hills, the trees, the animals, the farms, the arboretums, and the cities of this world—and be elevated to immediate or ecstatic contemplation of the majestic light of God itself, far above the realms of the angels. I recognize that numerous Christians throughout the ages, many of them much more disciplined and insightful and doubtless much more inspired than I, would never have wanted to abandon this way of ascent to the eternal light of God above. But I want to be as candid and as forceful at this point as I possibly can.

I long ago concluded that if one's spirituality is shaped by the theology of *ascent*, then a viable and vital spirituality of *nature* becomes very difficult, if not impossible. When you look up to give glory to God "in the highest," in a word you look *away* from the world of nature below. You no longer stand before nature. Your mind and heart are totally engaged in the project of climbing to the ethereal, immaterial heights above nature.

Hence I want to revise the spiritual counsel that my Sunday School teacher once gave me. I recommend that we should no longer resolve, spiritually, to look up. This is my counsel now, in the same, venerable Sunday School language: "Don't look back. Don't look forward. Look down." This is my angle of vision when I stand before nature, engaged with nature, on the tower of Mt. Auburn. I look down—and all around. I don't aspire to lift up my contemplation to the sun above, over my head.

This, I believe, is how best to contemplate the presence and the workings of God, Father, Son, and Holy Spirit in, with, and under the whole creation. Look down. See your own body and then survey the built environment around you, like the tower and then the cityscape at the horizon. See also all the other manifold and variegated creative processes of God all around you, first the trees and then, as far as your unaided eyes can take you, even to the virtually infinite reaches of the ocean beyond the southeastern horizon. This, I believe, is where God wants to be found, not vertically above. For me, therefore, *there is no up*, spiritually. *There is only down*—and around, and in, with, and under, as I will try to show you more reflectively now as I explore the spirituality of Martin Luther with the thoroughness that it deserves.[8]

GOD IN, WITH, AND UNDER NATURE: THE PARADOXICAL VISION OF MARTIN LUTHER

How do we envision the immanence or the presence of God in nature? Many Christian mystics and spiritual writers throughout the ages have found it easiest to imagine God *beyond* nature or *totally other* than nature. I identify my own spirituality with that angle of vision. In my view, God *is* wholly other, utterly beyond all things. On the other hand, many of the same mystics and spiritual writers *also* have identified God's *beyondness* with the image of God's *aboveness*,

God is the beyond but not the above.

as we have just seen. They have interpreted the wholly other God in terms of the theology of ascent. This stance I reject.

My thoughts here may perplex you. Why do I confess that God is wholly other, *beyond* all things, dwelling in light inapproachable, and thus humanly inaccessible, and yet at the same time maintain that God is *not exalted above* all things? How can I suggest that God is the Beyond but *not* the Above? Further, how can I suggest that the God who is the Beyond is at once the God who is the Immediate, in, with, and under all things? In more traditional theological terms, how can I affirm both the transcendence *and* the immanence of God, in a compelling way, without weakening either experience? This is a classical spiritual question for the Christian mind and heart, and, in particular, very much my own question.

I can venture to make the affirmations I do about God—that God is the Beyond but *not* the Above, *and* that God is the Beyond who is at once the Immediate—because my heart has been thoroughly formed by the spirituality of Martin Luther. I have already used Luther's language often in this narrative, affirming that the wholly other God is "in, with, and under" all things and, more generally, confessing that the God who has disclosed Godself to me in Christ is to be found when I look down—and around—not up. Luther's spirituality, I have discovered, is predicated not on the theology of ascent but on what I have also called in *The Travail of Nature* and elsewhere "the theology of descent."[9] Since this approach to God on Luther's part has been so profoundly important for my own spiritual life, I want to explore it with you, as carefully as possible.

The Limits and the Uses of Some Terminological Conundrums

To set the stage for these explorations of Luther's spirituality, I want to do two things: first, consider some theological boundaries, and second, bring to the fore the spiritual discourse of paradox. I will first highlight some terminological conundrums that my readers with theological training will immediately recognize but that may be new or puzzling for my other readers. For example, I cannot remember a time at my family dinner table when I voiced any of the following words: *deism, theism, panentheism,* or *pantheism.* For some, I am aware, such terms may sound like the proverbial counting of angels on the head of a pin. Hence my avoidance of them in down-to-earth dinner table conversations or in sermons, for that matter.

But I ask for your understanding here. Although these words have their limits, they can be helpful as diagnostic terms, the kind your physician might use when he or she is trying to explain to you how ill or how healthy you actually are. I do believe that such terms can sometimes be useful for technical, scholarly interpretations of historic spiritualities like Luther's. But I will use them here only as needed for clarity.

To frame the discussion to come, I think it is enough to say the following: Luther is neither a "deist" nor a "pantheist." He believes neither that God is totally *separated* from this world (deism) nor that God is totally *identical* with this world (pantheism). The truth of the matter, however—and here is where things get complicated for those trained to use such language—is that *none* of the aforementioned diagnostic terms really "works" adequately when used to describe Luther's view of God and nature, including a term that is increasingly popular in theological circles today, *panentheism*, as I will explain in a moment. It is much better, then, having acknowledged that Luther is neither a deist nor a pantheist, to listen to Luther speaking in his own distinct voice.[10]

Luther offers a vision of overflowing divine power, fecundity, and goodness present in all things.[11] For Luther, in a sense, there is no other milieu known to us where God essentially dwells. We are not privileged to know about God's dwelling place in itself. We do not know where God is in Godself. What we are privileged to know, rather, is that God is a present God, "God with us" and "God with all things," and therefore that the whole creation is profoundly good, even sacramental in some sense. Without compromising the divine transcendence, as we shall see, for Luther, God is wholly and immediately present throughout the whole creation.

LUTHER'S MYSTICAL DISCOURSE OF PARADOX

Luther's theology of the divine immanence has baffled some interpreters. But it is actually quite accessible, as long as readers can understand how Luther invokes the mystical discourse of *paradox*.[12] Paul Tillich, who considered himself to be writing in the Lutheran tradition, held that since theology has to do with both an infinite God and a finite world, there is a logical place for paradox. Søren Kierkegaard, who also was giving voice to the Lutheran tradition in his own way, took the discourse of paradox with utmost seriousness, too. In my own mundane spirituality, I have found the language of paradox indispensable in thinking about *how God is present* in nature, just as I have found the language of analogy indispensable in order to give expression to *who God is* or *what God is like*.[13]

From his earliest years as a monk, Luther was at home with the paradoxical language of mystical theology, particularly as that theology was mediated to him through German theologians like Johannes Tauler.[14] Thus Luther himself saw to it that an anonymous work in mystical theology, the *Theologia Germanica*, was published, and he praised it enthusiastically in an introduction.[15] He felt comfortable with mystical paradoxes, in particular, such as the saying of "the philosopher" Hermes Trismegistus: "God is the circle whose center is everywhere but whose circumference is nowhere."[16] Luther was at home with the experience of the mystics, too, as when, early in his career, he spoke of love for God as rooted in the inexpressible and the unfathomable God, which experience he called a "transport right into the midst of the innermost darkness."[17] For Luther, indeed, faith could be a kind of mystical *rapture*:

> The Christ-faith is a being-taken-away (*raptus*) and a being carried away (*translatio*) from all that is experiential (*fuehlbar*) inwardly or outwardly to that which is experiential neither inwardly nor outwardly, toward God, the invisible, the totally exalted, inconceivable.[18]

Luther's most favored paradoxical practice in this respect was his invocation of *many prepositions* in order to point to the divine immanence and to the divine transcendence, as we now shall see.[19] Luther was by no means satisfied with the use of only a single preposition, such as "above" or "in," or even with the three prepositions that are most frequently associated with his sacramental theology by those who know anything about it, "in, with, and under."[20] But use of those prepositions will suffice in interpreting his mystical and paradoxical discourse, particularly in contrast to other, perhaps more familiar, literalizing uses of a single preposition.

THE PARADOXICAL "IN, WITH, AND UNDER" AND THE LITERALIZING "IN" OR "UP"

Luther's mystical discourse about the divine immanence, using multiple prepositions as he does, places him at the opposite end of the metaphorical spectrum from a number of prominent twentieth- and twenty-first-century theologians, such as Sallie McFague and Jürgen Moltmann, who affirm what they think of as a *panentheistic* understanding of the divine immanence. All things, such thinkers affirm, are "in" God, hence the term pan-*en*-theism ("all in God"). But note: the panentheistic approach is actually a kind of *metaphorical reductionism*; the preposition "in" completely dominates the spiritual discourse.

The paradoxical use of multiple prepositions also distances Luther from a major Western metaphorical trajectory of a more traditional kind: the theology of ascent. This theology—the vision of the Great Chain of Being—is especially evident in the thought of St. Augustine and his successors.[21] This vision presupposes, too, a kind of *metaphorical reductionism*. But in this case, the single most important preposition is not "in," as in the case of those who argue for pan*en*theism, but "above." God is envisioned as "the One," the purely spiritual being at the top of a hierarchy of being. And the way for the believer to encounter God is to "climb the ladder" of creaturely being, to keep ascending higher and higher, contemplating the several gradations of being, from material things, to living things, and thence to the creature of embodied spirit, the human, and, next, to and through the purely spiritual creatures, the angels, up finally to the highest, the One or the Good or God. The dominance of the theology of ascent is especially vivid in works like Dante's *Divine Comedy*.[22]

The same is true for the quite different theological projections of the sixteenth-century Protestant reformer Huldrich Zwingli, which would have radical implications for his discussions with Luther about the real presence of Christ in the Eucharist. For Zwingli, "above"—the focus here is on "heaven"—is the single most important preposition.[23] Although the theology of another major reformer in the same era, John Calvin, differs from Zwingli's in a number of ways, for Calvin the theology of ascent was of central importance, too, as Julie Canlis has emphasized in her study *Calvin's Ladder: A Spiritual Theology of Ascent and Ascension*.[24]

For Luther, in contrast, *there is no "up"*—just as there is no "in"—in any singular fashion. There is only up and down, in, with, and under, around and beyond, all referring to the believer's encounter with the visible creation here and now. Luther assumes, in other words, that we can never have a kind of "God's-eye view" of where God is, as if God were contemplating Godself in a mirror and we were seeing what God sees. From Luther's perspective, we cannot know God's eternal dwelling place at all, whether that place be depicted as high above us like the sun over our heads (Augustine, Zwingli, Calvin) or surrounding us and our world like a womb (Moltmann, McFague). According to Luther's angle of vision, however imperfect our seeing with the eyes of faith may be, we can only know God where we are standing here and now.

LUTHER'S MYSTICAL DISCOURSE AND THE RELATIVIZATION OF SPACE

While using prepositions in his characteristically expansive way, in order to focus our vision on the immediate presence of the ineffable God here and now,

Luther also radicalizes the idea of the divine spatiality itself. Our commonsense spatial categories simply do not apply to God, he believes.[25] Thus the fullness of God can dwell in a single grain of wheat yet be beyond all things at the same time:

God is substantially present everywhere, in and through all creatures, in all their parts and places, so that the world is full of God and He fills all, but without His being encompassed and surrounded by it. He is at the same time outside and above all creatures. These are all exceedingly incomprehensible matters; yet they are articles of our faith and are attested clearly and mightily in Holy Scripture. . . . For how can reason tolerate it that the Divine Majesty is so small that it can be substantially present in a grain, on a grain, through a grain, within and without, and that, although it is a single Majesty, it nevertheless is entirely in each grain separately, no matter how immeasurably numerous these grains may be? . . . And that the same Majesty is so large that neither this world nor a thousand worlds can encompass it and say: "Behold, there it is!" . . . His own divine essence can be in all creatures collectively and in each one individually more profoundly, more intimately, more present than the creature is in itself, yet it can be encompassed nowhere and by no one. It encompasses all things and dwells in all, but not one thing encompasses it and dwells in it.[26]

Strikingly, too, Luther can speak of this paradoxical divine immanence in the good creation in tangibly concrete terms. Thus he can envision the whole creation visibly as the "mask of God."[27] This means, for Luther, that God is hidden there. But it also means that God is powerfully present there, in front of your very eyes, although hidden. In the same vein, Luther thinks of the Creator vividly as being "with all creatures, flowing and pouring into them, filling all things."[28] And God is constantly active. God is "an energetic power, a continuous activity, that works and operates without ceasing. For God does not rest, but works without ceasing."[29] For Luther, therefore, creation is not merely some transcendental event before the beginning of time. Rather, the divine act of creation is also *now*. And that divine act intimately and powerfully permeates the whole visible creation, before us and around us.

Corresponding to Luther's understanding of the whole creation as permeated with the immediate presence of God here and now is Luther's view of the fitness of the whole creation itself to accommodate the divine presence, a view sometimes identified by the theological formula that "the finite is capable of the infinite" (*finitum capax infinitum*).[30] This is an aspect of creation's goodness, in Luther's view.[31] Also corresponding to Luther's understanding of the good creation as permeated with the divine presence and, indeed, radically open to that presence is his consistently lavish praise of the whole creation as a world of wonder and enchantment.[32] If someone really understands a grain of wheat, as we have already heard Luther say, that person will die of wonder.[33]

Although Luther does not generally present us with a view of the creation as "the theater of God's glory," as Calvin did, Luther—like Calvin, and indeed like many premodern Christian theologians—has what can be called an "omni-miraculous view" of the created world. For Luther, once you have eyes to see, you can encounter miracles everywhere: in a seed, in the birth of a child, in a bolt of lightning, no less than in the healings of Jesus or in the Eucharist. Thus, in one exuberant statement, Luther could say that all creatures are sacraments.[34]

Throughout all of his descriptions of the divine immanence, it should probably be noted, in view of the criticism that has occasionally been directed at Luther in this respect, he guards the idea of divine transcendence of the creation very carefully. Luther's use of many prepositions, and his regular observations that God cannot be contained by any creature or in all the creatures combined, guarantees that, for Luther, God is not to be thought of as in any sense being identical with the creation (*Deus sive natura*). God is not in the world as straw in a sack, Luther can say, in his own characteristic manner.[35] As I have already stressed, Luther is *not* a pantheist, although some, especially those who are still thinking under the influence of the theology of ascent, which envisions God's proper place as above all things, sometimes accuse Luther of pantheistic tendencies. Luther's use of many pronouns and his relativization of the construct of divine spatiality decisively distance his spirituality from any thought of pantheism. This is clear in many statements by Luther, such as the following:

Nothing is so small but God is still smaller, nothing so large but God is still larger, nothing is so short but God is still shorter, nothing so long but God is still longer, nothing is so broad but God is still broader, nothing narrow but God is still narrower. He is an inexpressible being, above and beyond all that can be described or imagined.[36]

By the same paradoxical logic, as we have seen, Luther cannot be called a "pan-en-theist" either—an idea, in any case, that was not current in his own time. According to Luther, we do not know God's spatiality in any respect, as the protagonists of panentheism seem to think we do. For them, God's place is around the universe, like a womb; the universe is *in* God. For Luther, we only know God's presence in, with, and under, above and below, beyond and around and within our world. But that is surely enough, more than we could ever imagine asking for, I would say.[37] That leaves us, in faith, with a world that is overflowing with the presence of God, a sacramental world of enchantment, mystery, and wonder.

THE PROMISE OF LUTHER'S MYSTICAL, PARADOXICAL DISCOURSE

Thus far in this chapter, I have taken you to the top of the tower in Mt. Auburn to see a vision of God majestically and mysteriously in, with, and under all things. I have counseled you *not* to attempt to contemplate God as the Above, as if you were looking up at the sun overhead, because if you were to do that, the world of nature would more or less be left below, perhaps even out of sight. To be sure, and emphatically, I also invited you to venture to see that God is the Beyond, that God, in technical terms, is radically transcendent, in every direction, as it were. But here I was not pointing you to some absent beyond. The God whom we are seeking to engage from the heights in this journey is also radically immanent. Hence I have counseled you to seek the Beyond by looking down and around, where the Beyond is to be found as the Immediate.

I have sought to guide your vision in this way with the help of one of my spiritual mentors, Martin Luther. He has provided me with the insight I needed to envision the mystery and the majesty of God in, with, and under all things. His passionate, paradoxical vision has made it possible for me to see God in, with, and under the trees of Mt. Auburn and the waters of the Charles and the elegant cityscape of Boston, framed by the images of the Tobin Bridge and the flights gliding into Logan Airport and, beyond it all, by the prospect of the great Atlantic Ocean. With Luther's guidance, more particularly, I have been enabled to see the life and power of God pouring into the great purple beeches and charging the tiniest seed with divine power and vitality.

Luther has helped me to envision nature as an omni-miraculous world, too, intrinsically open to the omni-active divine presence. Seen in this light, nature is a world of wonder and enchantment, even sacramental in some sense. Are my weekday walks through and around Mt. Auburn, then, all that different from my walking forward toward the altar to receive the eucharistic bread and wine on Sundays? When, as a priestly officiant, I stand behind the altar, holding up the bread and the cup, and at that moment contemplate the people of God gathered under the overarching nave to celebrate the Eucharist, is that standing all that different from those times when I stand before nature at the top of the Mt. Auburn tower? Luther's spirituality of nature prompts me to ask such questions. For, according to this angle of vision, the whole world of nature is charged with the majesty and mystery of the God who is in, with, and under all things.

On the other hand, when I walk around Mt. Auburn and when I then stand before nature on the tower, I also see a world laced with darkness. Luther has helped me to see this aright also. With Luther's guidance, I have been enabled to contemplate the dark side of the vision—with God somehow hovering there as well—including the blood and gore of the predators and the horrors of unjust incarcerations of hundreds of young black men in the prisons of the Boston area, not to speak of the fragility and the mortality of my own embodied self. Luther knew well, from personal experience, that nature, whatever else it might be, is the mask of God. God *is* there. But God is also *hidden* there. According to Luther, when we contemplate God in, with, and under nature, we very much see through a glass darkly. And that darkness, for Luther, is indeed dark. The world we see, good as it is and as overflowing with the presence of a good God as it is, is also a world of sin and death, of suffering and destruction. Luther was not, nor do I want to be, some kind of a romantic who refuses to see the darkness for what it is.

TRACES OF THE TRIUNE GOD IN NATURE: THE *VESTIGIA TRINITATIS*

Luther, in my view, left a number of important things unsaid or understated. I have in mind here particularly his relative silence about what, following a long tradition in Christian spirituality, we can think of as the traces of the triune God—the *vestigia Trinitatis*—throughout the whole creation. Luther took that tradition for granted, but he never made much of it. When he thought of such things, moreover, he tended to focus mainly on the traditional notion of the image of God (*imago Dei*) in the human creature (Gen. 1:26). But I think it is important, particularly when our chief concern in this narrative is the spirituality of nature, to make the effort to draw lines from the triune God to what we can see in the whole world of nature, too.[38]

The first Genesis creation narrative suggests as much. The picture of the God we see there is that of a creative architect who contemplates the whole "building" of the creation and rejoices in the goodness of each step of this universal creative process, seeing in the end that the whole is "very good" (Gen. 1:31). The good and elegant workings of the invisible Creator, in other words, are reflected in the goodness and elegance of the visible creatures.[39] Granted, what we see when we contemplate nature will be, at best, only a dim reflection of the triune God, hence the word *traces*. But that does not mean that God is in no way reflected in the creative works of God's own hands. So we can cautiously, but also expectantly, survey the whole world of nature to see what traces of the triune God we might find there.

Note the direction of this contemplation. This exercise begins *with* God—whom we know as eternal Giver, Gift, and Giving through Jesus Christ, and whom we already have begun to contemplate through the refracted lenses of roughly hewn analogies—and *then* leads us to engage nature in itself and to look for traces of the divine in all things. It is not the other way around, as if we were somehow able to survey nature in itself, see what we might think of as traces of the divine, and then make affirmations about God.[40] No, nature in itself is far too ambiguous, far too freighted with blood and gore, and far too twisted by the powers of death and destruction to offer us anything like a basis for knowing God in any viable sense. It seems fitting, then, to return at this point to what we have already been enabled to see of the triune God, a vision refracted through the lenses of some roughly hewn analogies framed by biblical meanings, and then to look for traces of the Trinity that we might be enabled to see in the world of nature before us.

God is a communal process.

TRACES OF A FESTIVE COMMUNAL PROCESS

First, recall this roughly hewn analogy: God is like a festive communal process. In what sense can we see traces of this aspect of the triune God mirrored in nature? I want to approach this question by dividing the meanings suggested by the analogy: first, by considering the divine festivity or joy, and then, by considering the other element of the theme, God as a communal process.

Traces of the joy of the triune God mirrored in nature? This is a precarious, albeit suggestive, theme for me. For the prophet Isaiah, it was different. This was a robust theme for him. In the temple, Isaiah saw that the whole earth was full of the glory of God (Isa. 6:3). The Psalmist, likewise, calls on all the earth to "break forth into joyous song and sing praises" and also proclaims: "Let the sea roar, and all that fills it. . . . Let the floods clap their hands; let the hills sing together for joy, at the presence of the Lord. . . ." (Ps. 98:1, 7, 8f.). In some ecstatic moments, such as when I've been scything with God or when I've been standing before Niagara Falls in awe, I have had some fleeting sense, I think, of the joy of God mirrored in nature. Was this not an assumption of the Psalmist when that biblical poet celebrated the great sea monster that God created, the leviathan, saying, "to play with it"? (Ps. 104:26).

I also have pondered, from time to time, the phenomenon of what might be called the overabundance of beauty in the natural world. Thus John Muir once came upon a vast field of red poppies in the high Sierras and stood awestruck before their radiant beauty, seeing them as a field of joy. Doubtless there are evolutionary reasons for the colors of such flowers, but, from time to time, one does have the sense that nature has provided much more color than was needed simply for such species to survive. What are we to make, then, of the amazing profusion of colors in a meadow, such as the one my wife cares for adjacent to our place in southwestern Maine?

This applies also to the sounds of all of the birds and insects and other animals in a forest at night, such as the one beyond the backfield of our Maine home. Are those sounds, when heard together, perchance larger than the sum of their parts? Whatever the logic of survival may be for individual species, isn't the whole, at least on occasion, a kind of symphony of joy?[41] Wasn't this the kind of experience the Psalmist drew on when he proclaimed: "Then shall all the trees of the forest sing for joy" (Ps. 96:12). Considering what appears to be the overabundance of beauty in nature generally, was it then mere rhetoric when Isaiah proclaimed: "Sing for joy, O heavens, and exult O earth; break forth into singing!" (Isa. 49:13). Still, for me, such moments of hearing and contemplating the joy of the triune God mirrored in nature, vivid as they have been, have been relatively rare.

On the other hand, seeing traces of God as communal process mirrored in nature is an experience that has come much more easily for me. The technical Trinitarian language traditionally used of God is this respect is *perichoresis*: the divine persons mutually *interpenetrate* one another, all retaining their own integrity. So it is no accident, then, spiritually speaking, that we humans live in a world of *ecological interdependence*. Or in the traditional theological language, nature, as best as we can tell, appears to be perichoretic.

WHAT THE TREES CAN SHOW US

I can see signs of that that ecological interdependence in Mt. Auburn with my own, untutored eyes. The trees of Mt. Auburn are our brothers and sisters because they are fellow creatures of God. We all are created, sustained, and redeemed together, so we are kin. Now, as most school children are presumably taught today, the trees in our neighborhoods are also closely related to us because they serve us, by working with countless other trees around the globe, above all with those that thrive in places like the Amazon basin or in the boreal forests and tundra of northern Canada, as "the lungs of the planet," in order to emit oxygen that we then can breathe. The trees help to make the air breathable for us. And we return the favor by providing them with some of the carbon dioxide that they need to grow, and also by caring for these trees as best we can—or should—so that they may have standing in their own right, not just so that they might serve us. Hence we can glimpse something of the communal process of God Godself in our ecological interdependence with trees.[42]

More particularly, we can see similar traces of the perichoretic God in the interdependent relationship between the oak trees and the squirrels, a phenomenon that most schoolchildren understand. The acorns from those trees provide food for the squirrels and so help them to survive. The squirrels, in turn, bury many more acorns in the ground in the fall than the squirrels need or later can find, and that helps the oak trees to survive as a species, when numbers of those buried acorns send forth the shoots of new trees. This relationship, to be sure, is more complex than schoolchildren usually know.

Some scholarly observers of oak trees over a course of seasons have determined, for example, that, by some as yet to be explained process, the oak trees produce an overabundance of acorns every few years, thus assuring that the squirrels will not devour all or even most of the acorns in those particular years of abundance and thus also making possible a sizable number of new oak seedlings in due course. In that sense, anthropomorphically speaking, the oaks take themselves and their own future as a species seriously, as well as offering their acorns as a food supply for the squirrels. The oaks and the squirrels—the latter may also nest in the oaks—are in this modest but very real sense a community of ecological interdependence, reflecting in some manner, for those who have been given eyes to see, the inner life of the God that is a communal process.

TRACES OF A POWERFUL, TORRENTIAL FLOW

Second, think of the triune God again, but this time in terms of a powerful torrential flow. Atop the tower at Mt. Auburn, we must invoke our imaginations all the more if we are to glimpse traces of this God of majestic power, who, in Luther's words, is "flowing and pouring" into nature and "filling all things." Apart from a very rare hurricane or tornado or a still rarer quaking of the earth, or from the small predators that one rarely sees, Mt. Auburn is a relatively placid place. If you have eyes to see, however, you can look all around and imagine giants in the earth and in the seas and in the heavens, where you can catch glimpses of the works of God's amazing power.

In 2012, a man walking along the Charles River saw (and photographed) in those waters what he later called "a prehistoric, floating dinosaur. Covered in armor." It was a juvenile sturgeon, a species that predates the dinosaurs. Occasionally, a mature sturgeon will weigh as much as eight hundred pounds. Currently protected, sturgeon have now and again been seen in the nearby Merrimack River. But none have been seen, at least not in recent memory, in the Charles. This ancient fish calls to mind the gigantic creatures of the ocean beyond, such as the great white sharks or the enormous right whales that can sometimes be observed off the coast of nearby Cape Cod.

The wildness of the archaic sturgeon also calls to mind the primal storms of the vast Atlantic far beyond, which sometimes toss lobster boats around like matchboxes and whose tumultuous waves crash against the rocky shores of Maine to the north, with sounds akin to thunder. I have been helped to stand in awe of such primordial forces of nature by the witness of the Book of Job, chapters 38–40, to the spectacular vitalities of the Creator's works. I think I have a good sense for at least some of Job's meanings when he celebrates the monstrous and—to humans—alien creatures of the earth, such as the lion, the behemoth, and the leviathan.[43]

I have also imagined being atop the tower of Mt. Auburn on a clear night in the evening. Notwithstanding the light pollution from the city, one can, of course, contemplate the canopy of the stars, or at least some of them, from such a vantage point. Then one can readily imagine the Big Bang, which some 13 billion years ago launched this unimaginably immense, ever-expanding universe of more than 100 billion galaxies and perhaps 500 billion stars (a 2010 study estimated 300 sextillion stars!). One can recall majestic images of some of the galaxies that cosmological physicists have enabled us to see represented against the background of this gargantuan cosmic unfolding. One can also call forth thoughts of whole solar systems disappearing into colossal black holes.

As I have spoken in various church and academic settings around the country during the past four decades, and as I have regularly talked about the meanings of such cosmic immensities, numbers of serious-minded souls have raised questions, in turn, about cosmic and terrestrial evolution. I have always responded that such scientific findings make it easier for me, not more difficult, to be a person of faith. Thanks to the findings of modern physics and astronomy, in particular, we can see visions of God's cosmic magnificence and mystery that ancient Hebrew poets could never even have imagined. On the other hand, these words of the Psalmist have rarely been far from my mind during such conversations:

The heavens are telling the glory of God; and the firmament proclaims his handiwork. Day to day pours forth speech, and night to night declares knowledge. There is no speech, nor are there words; their voice is not heart; yet their voice goes out through all the earth, and their words to the end of the world. (Ps. 19:1-4)

Similarly, I recall the words of the prophet Isaiah spoken in the ancient temple and repeated in every eucharistic prayer that I have ever heard: "Holy, holy, holy is the Lord of hosts; the whole earth is full of his glory" (Isa. 6:3).

For me, the cosmic immensities of God's good creation reflect, however imperfectly, the magnificent and mysterious power of God. The very being and becoming of God, who is like a powerful torrential flow in Godself, are thereby reflected, in a fragmentary way, for me to contemplate in nature. We can, in this respect, contemplate traces of the mysterious presence and majestic works of the triune God in the whole world of nature. To invoke themes we considered earlier, the whole world of nature, with its nearly infinite diversity and its nearly infinite richness of creatures, in some measure thus mirrors the ever-expanding infinity and the eternally rich fecundity of God in Godself.

TRACES OF SELF-SACRIFICE IN NATURE?

Third , think of the triune God yet again, but this time as the self-sacrificing savior. Surveying the whole world of nature from these heights, what traces of the triune God envisioned in this respect can we see? The answer, I believe, is relatively few. While we may readily catch sight of the triune God reflected in the ecological interdependence of all living things and in the enormously powerful processes of nature everywhere, we can identify only a few instances of authentic self-sacrifice in nature apart from the human community.

True, we humans are essentially embodied creatures and we are thoroughly natural in that sense. To the degree that we can identify bodily self-sacrifice among humans, therefore, we can also imagine seeing traces in nature of the triune God as self-sacrificing savior. While such cases of self-sacrifice are surely in the minority when viewed against the backdrop of the whole of human history, which overflows with mindless violence, nevertheless this minority report is profoundly impressive—from the early Christian martyrs like Peter and Paul to witnesses in our own era like Dietrich Bonhoeffer, from solitary peacemakers like St. Francis in the Middle Ages to prophetic champions of justice in our own time, such as Martin Luther King Jr. And this is but to touch on a very few examples from Christian history. It is to say nothing of the history of human self-sacrifice for the sake of others in many other cultures and in many other eras. Such human stories are, each in its own way, reflective, in some measure, of the being and becoming of God viewed as the self-sacrificing savior. For Christians, of course, the greatest of all of these stories is the life history of Jesus of Nazareth and his death, for the sake of others, on the cross.

When we come to the world of nature beyond the human community, however, the examples of self-sacrifice for the sake of others seem to be relatively few. I do remember reading news stories about some companion animals, especially dogs, who appeared to have risked their lives or actually lost their lives in, for example, the process of alerting sleeping family members that their house was on fire. But if there is such a thing as an exception that proves the rule, such stories should probably be considered to be the exceptions. As a rule, we rarely meet traces of genuine self-sacrifice for the sake of others in the wider world of nature.

Sometimes there are indeed touching examples, such as the care given to infants in many species or the acts of mutual self-protection in certain animal groups. A case in point would be what can be called the traditional elephant society, that is, before the era of massive human destruction of such societies. Until recent human incursions, nurturing and protection of the young and of the very fabric of their society, typically over a course of many years, has been commonplace in the elephant world. Signs of self-sacrifice for others among nonhuman animals, however, are perhaps the most evident in primate groups.[44] Probably the most we can say in this respect is that self-sacrifice appears to be one factor among many in the evolutionary history of life, prior to the emergence of the human species.[45]

This is not to say that the self-giving *of God* is not powerfully and pervasively at work in, with, and under the whole world of nature. I will return to this thought later, under the theme of "cosmic redemption." But my point here is that, apart from the embodied human community, the wider world of nature in itself generally reflects the self-sacrificing of the triune God only in the most fragmentary of ways. On the other hand, those particular ways are well worth noting, as long as we keep them in proper perspective.

Celebrating Traces of the Triune God

All in all, then, when we survey the world of nature from atop the Mt. Auburn tower with the imagination of faith, we can indeed contemplate numerous striking traces of the triune God, whom we have already come to know as one who is akin to a festive communal process, a powerful torrential flow, and a self-sacrificing savior. The being and becoming of the God who is Giver, Gift, and Giving are mirrored with some frequency, if irregularly, in nature.

Thus, when the first astronauts on the moon looked back at planet Earth, this precious blue and green jewel glowing in the cosmic darkness, with the knowledge that they were then contemplating an amazingly complex and interrelated, as well as beautiful, biosphere, they were in truth, whether they knew it or not, contemplating traces of the God who in Godself is like a festive communal process. Or when, on a clear night, I gaze in awestruck wonder at the heavens above with a deep sense for the vastness of it all, from the unimaginable Big Bang to our colossally expanding universe as we know it today, I am contemplating a dim but real reflection of the God who is like a powerful, torrential flow. And, similarly, when, many years ago, I contemplated Laurel peacefully—and on occasion painfully—nursing one of our babies, I saw more than the scene that visibly presented itself to my eyes, I saw the self-sacrificing of the triune God reflected there. When it is given me by the Spirit, I believe, I can survey the whole creation and see traces of the joy and power and love of the ineffable triune God mirrored on earth and beyond.

Seeing such traces of the triune God in nature energizes me spiritually. It reminds me who it is who is so pervasively and miraculously and wondrously in, with, and under all things. This kind of reassurance is akin to the much more parochial experience I have when I stand at the door of a certain gallery at the Museum of Fine Arts in Boston. Although I do not know a great deal about the history of art in general, I happen to have some understanding of Vincent Van Gogh's life story and his life's work. I know him, in this sense, before I enter that gallery. No wonder, then, that as I stand at the door of that gallery and look around at all the paintings in the room, I immediately recognize each of Van Gogh's several works hanging there. When I do that I am esthetically gratified. I realize that my knowledge of this great artist is apt, and I am led by such an experience of his works to ponder his life and creativity in new ways.

In a like manner, this is why I am so eager to identify the *vestigia Trinitatis* in the world of nature. This experience is spiritually inspiring. It reminds me who the God of my scything and my Baptism is and prompts me to ponder the inner life of this God all the more. It also calls me to attend still more to some of the elegant configurations of the natural world itself that I might otherwise not fully have noticed.[46] I stand still, before each trace of the Trinity that I identify, lost in wonder, awe, and praise for what the divine artist has given me to see.

Hence you, the reader, I trust, will not be surprised to hear me say the following at the end of this chapter of our journey. Often, when I stand atop the Mt. Auburn tower on a clear day and when I survey the world of nature all around me, I hear myself uttering these words: "Praise Father, Son, and Holy Spirit." Instructed by Luther's faith in the mysterious and majestic presence of God in, with, and under all things and inspired also by the biblical vision of heaven and earth full of God's glory, I find this petition of the Trinity Prayer, at such a time and in such a place, irrepressible. My hope is that you can imagine yourself experiencing the same prayerful impulse each time you stand before and engaged with nature.

Notes

1. For a review of these trends in theological modernity in the West, see H. Paul Santmire, *The Travail of Nature: The Ambiguous Ecological Promise of Christian Theology* (Minneapolis: Fortress Press, 1985), chaps. 7 and 8.

2. Sallie McFague, *The Body of God: An Ecological Theology* (Minneapolis: Fortress Press, 1993); Jürgen Moltmann, *The Trinity and the Kingdom: The Doctrine of God*, trans. Margaret Kohl (San Francisco: Harper & Row, 1981).

3. H. Paul Santmire, *Brother Earth: Nature, God and Ecology in a Time of Crisis* (New York: Thomas Nelson, 1970), especially 117–20.

4. That impulse was still very much in force in the United States, I argued in an early article ("Nothing More Beautiful than Death?" *Christian Century* [December 14, 1983], 1154–58). In the mid- and late twentieth century, it was expressed in sophisticated psychological terms by Elizabeth Kübler-Ross' widely hailed book *On Death and Dying* (New York: Routledge, 1969). She argued that the "highest" way to approach death was *acceptance*. I maintained, in contrast, especially with memories of the Holocaust vividly in mind, that the best response to the culture of the denial of death is not acceptance but *resistance*.

5. In his classic book *I and Thou* (New York: Scribners, 1958), Martin Buber considers the possibility of having an I-Thou relationship with *a tree* but finally decides that such a relationship is not possible because of the absence of speech on the part of the tree. In my first major published article, "I-Thou, I-It, I-Ens," *Journal of Religion* 47, no. 3 (July 1968): 260–73, I responded to Buber's discussion by proposing that we should envision a third kind of relationship we humans have with other creatures, an "I-Ens relationship," as well as the "I-Thou" and the "It-It" relationships. An I-Ens relationship with a tree, accordingly, does not entail speech, but it does entail a profound encounter with, and deep respect for, the tree as a creature with its own integrity and its own place in the greater scheme of things.

6. Dozens of famous personages are buried in Mt. Auburn, many of whose works can still be seen or heard in various ways today, among them Phillips Brooks, Mary Baker Eddy, Felix Frankfurter, Buckminster Fuller, Asa Gray, Winslow Homer, Bernard Malamud, Francis Parkman, B. F. Skinner, and I. F. Stone.

7. Santmire, *The Travail of Nature*, 17–22.

8. I find support for this kind of spirituality not only in Luther but also in the orientation of another spiritual master, whom I discussed at the very beginning of this narrative, St. Francis. See the judgment of Eloi LeClerc, *The Canticle of Creatures—Symbols of Union: An Analysis of St. Francis of Assisi,* trans. Matthew J. O'Connell (Chicago: Franciscan Herald, 1977), 185, writing about the vision that comes to expression in that critically important song by Francis: "[For Francis, there] is no longer a world above and a world below, a luminous world of the spirit and a dark world of nature. The Most High himself is present at the roots of reality and flourishes in all things. The kingdom of God is no longer another world set over against our present world, but is at the heart of even the most ordinary humdrum existence; it is a transforming power dwelling at the core of our present life."

9. Santmire, *The Travail of Nature*, passim.

10. For more on Luther, see my essay "Creation and Salvation according to Martin Luther: Creation as the Good and Integral Background," in *Creation and Salvation, I: A Mosaic of Selected Classic Christian Theologies*, ed. Ernst M. Conradie (Berlin: LIT, 2012), 173–202.

11. See the statement of the Reformation scholar David Steinmetz, "Scripture and the Lord's Supper in Luther's Theology," *Interpretation* 27, no. 3 (1983): 266: "No theologian before or after Luther has celebrated the universal presence of God more than Luther has."

12. For a brief but pointed discussion of the theological uses of paradox, see Sylvia Walsh, "Paradox," in Donald W. Musser and Joseph L. Price, eds., *A New Handbook of Christian Theology* (Nashville, TN: Abingdon, 1992), 346–48.

13. In Luther's case, the language of paradox allows him to speak of God's presence both apophatically—suggesting, for example, that God is nowhere—*and* kataphatically—saying, sometimes in the same breath, that God is everywhere. The word *apophatic* is from the Greek *apophasis*, referring to negation or "saying away." The word *kataphatic* is from the Greek *kataphasis*, referring to affirmation or "saying with." The first has been used by scholarly interpreters to refer to spiritual or mystical experiences of "the ineffable"; the second, to refer to spiritual or mystical experiences of what might be called "disclosures of the fulness of Being.'" See, further, Edward Howells, "Apophatic Spirituality," in *The New Westminster Dictionary of Christian Spirituality*, ed. Philip Sheldrake (Louisville, KY: Westminster John Knox, 2005), 117–19; and Janet K. Ruffing, "Kataphatic Spirituality," in *The New Westminster Dictionary of Christian Spirituality*, 393–94.

14. See Bengt Hoffmann, *Luther and the Mystics: A Re-examination of Luther's Spiritual Experience and His Relationship to the Mystics* (Minneapolis: Augsburg Press, 1976).

15. Bengt Hoffman, trans. and ed., *Theologia Germanica* (Mahwah, NY: Paulist, 1980).

16. E.g., Martin Luther, *Werke* (Weimar Ausgabe) *Tischreden* [hereafter *WA*] 2:1742.

17. Martin Luther, *Luther's Works* [hereafter *LW*], ed. Jaroslav Pelikan et al. (St. Louis: Concordia, 1972), 25:293–94, quoted by Hoffman, *Luther and the Mystics*, 85.

18. Luther, *LW* 29:149, quoted by Hoffman, *Luther and the Mystics*, 163.

19. On occasion, Luther was wont to supplement his paradoxical discourse about the divine immanence, using many prepositions, with abstract language that he inherited mainly from his training in the philosophy of nominalism. Thus he could distinguish between three kinds of divine presence: circumscriptive, definitive, and repletive (for this, see David Steinmetz, "Scripture and the Lord's Supper in Luther's Theology," *Interpretation* 27, no. 3 [1983]: 260). But it appears that the use of these terms was aimed more at his opponents in order to gain debating points, to add still other reasons to support Luther's position. This debating technique was probably an afterglow of Luther's theological training in disputations (e.g., the Ninety-Five Theses). Luther's heart, however, seems to come alive when he discourses about the presence of God, using many prepositions. See Steinmetz's comment, in "Scripture and the Lord's Supper," 261, that "the philosophical argument is not the most important one from Luther's point of view."

20. By insisting that many prepositions must be used, Luther thus achieves what appears to be a highly suggestive integration of the apophatic and the kataphatic. See Luther, *LW* 37:230 (cited by Heinrich Bornkamm, *Luther's World of Thought*, trans. Martin H. Bertram [Saint Louis: Concordia, 1958],190): "Faith understands that in these matters 'in' is equivalent to 'above,' 'beyond,' 'beneath,' 'through and through,' and 'everywhere.'"

21. For this material, see Santmire, *The Travail of Nature*, chaps. 2, 3, 4.

22. True, this kind of conceptuality typically presupposed that there is also a kind of divine overflowing *down* the hierarchy of being, often thought of in biblical terms as the creation and conservation of the world, sometimes richly construed. Augustine, for example, can envision the immanence of that divine overflowing in terms of the multiple use of prepositions not unlike Luther's. But, in Augustine's case, the end or *telos* of the soul is always intended to be *upward*. "Above" is the preposition that finally dominates all the others. See Santmire, *The Travail of Nature*, chap. 4.

23. See Steinmetz, "Scripture and the Lord's Supper," 262:

> Zwingli looks upon the ascension as the final stage of a drama which begins and ends in heaven. . . . The Word comes from heaven to assume human flesh, lives a life of active and passive obedience to God, dies, is raised from the dead and returns to the heaven from which he has come. The ascension means that the humanity of Christ is no longer accessible to me in my space and time. Luther looks upon the ascension as a quite different sort of event. Once having come to us in the incarnation, Christ does not go away. He remains in our space and time. What changes in the ascension is not the fact of Christ's presence but solely the mode of that presence.

24. Julie Canlis, *Calvin's Ladder: A Spiritual Theology of Ascent and Ascension* (Grand Rapids, MI: Eerdmans, 2010). Canlis recognizes that this way of thinking was used by Calvin "to deflect attention away from creation and (upward) to its divine source," thereby risking "emphasizing a salvation *out* of this world" (248). Nevertheless, she recommends and even celebrates this kind of thinking as a great resource for contemporary spirituality. The following is a typical utterance by Calvin, in this respect, according to Canlis: "Believers have no greater help than public worship, for by it God raises his own folk upward step by step. . . . As if it were not in God's power somehow to come down to us, in order to be near us, yet without changing place or confining us to earthly means, but rather by these to bear us up as if in chariots of his heavenly glory, glory that fills all things with its immeasurableness and even surpasses the heavens in height!" (249).

25. In this respect, as others, Luther was at home with the mystical tradition. See the description of Meister Eckhart's discourse by Howells, "Apophatic Spirituality," 118: "Eckhart delights in wordplay designed to move his listeners and readers through affirmation to the negation of their understanding of God . . ., and then to a transforming 'negation of negation'. . . . This is especially evident in Eckhart's *German Sermons*, where metaphors are chosen for their ability to collide with and contradict one another, producing an 'explosion' of language as the meanings fall apart, out of which a new understanding is born."

26. Luther, *WA* 23:134.34–23:136.36, cited by Bornkamm, *Luther's World of Thought*, 189.

27. Luther, *WA* 40:1, 94.

28. Luther *WA* 10:143.

29. Luther, *LW* 21:238. Cited by Bernhard Lohse, *Martin Luther's Theology: Its Historical and Systematic Development*, trans. Roy A. Harrisville (Minneapolis: Fortress Press, 1999), 213.

30. See Kurt K. Hendel, "*Finitum Capax Infinitum*: Luther's Radical Incarnational Perspective," *Seminary Ridge Review* 10, no. 2 (2008): 20–35.

31. Luther was adamant about this theme, particularly in his sacramental disputes, both against the Catholic side and against sacramental views of Protestants such as Zwingli. Luther believed that both the Catholic emphasis on transubstantiation (the replacement of the created substance of the bread and wine) and the Zwinglian emphasis on the Eucharist in terms of what it

signifies (Christ cannot be really present in the sacramental elements and must therefore be in heaven) do not do justice to the goodness of the creation. As Russell Kleckly has observed, Luther held that both groups, the Catholics and the Zwinglians, assumed that "it was undignified for Christ's body and blood to be attached to creaturely elements such as bread and wine," while Luther himself wanted to affirm that the elements of the creation are wholly congenial recipients of the divine presence and action (Russell Kleckley, *Omnes Creature Sacramenta: Creation, Nature, and World View in Luther's Theology of the Lord's Supper*, Dissertation zur Erlangung der Doktorwuerde der Ludwig-Maximilians-Universitaets Muenchen, Evangelisch-Theologische Fakultaet [Columbia, SC: privately published, 1990], 127; see, further, Kleckley's full discussion, 127–41).

32. For a discussion of these matters, see Santmire , *The Travail of Nature*, 127-33.

33. Luther, *LW* 37:57f.

34. Kleckley, *Omnes Creaturae Sacramenta*, 207.

35. Luther, *WA* 26; 339, 25ff., cited by Bornkamm, *Luther's World of Thought*, 188: "It is vulgar and stupid to suppose that God is a huge, fat being who fills the world similar to a sack of straw filled to the top and beyond. . . . We do not say that God is such a distended, long, broad, thick, tall, deep being, but that he is a supernatural, inscrutable being able to be present entirely in every small kernel of grain and at the same time in all, above all, and outside all creatures."

36. Luther, *LW* 37:228, cited by Paul Althaus, *The Theology of Martin Luther*, trans. Robert C. Schultz (Philadelphia: Fortress Press, 1963), 107. Note that when Luther uses the preposition "above" here, he is not using it in the sense that God is at the apex of a grand hierarchy of being, as does the theology of ascent. Luther relativizes that hierarchical way of thinking. "Above," for Luther, is one among many prepositions that he characteristically employs to point to the presence of God here and now, where we are standing.

37. Panentheism also has problems of its own. A major liability, as Ted Peters once pointed out to Sallie McFague at a meeting of the American Academy of Religion, is as follows. What "created world" are we thinking of when we—that is, those who hold the panentheistic view -- imagine either that the world is God's body (McFague) or that the world is enveloped by God (Moltmann). If we are thinking of planet Earth alone as the body or the womb-child of God, then what about the rest of the billions and billions of galaxies? Does God have nothing to do with them? On the other hand, if we are thinking of the entire nearly infinite universe as the body or the womb-child of God, then, given the earth's minuscule place in the whole universe, a infinitesimal speck of cosmic dust, as it were, then God would seem to be so far removed from the earth that the idea of divine immanence would have little meaning.

38. The Christian tradition has been much less reticent about speaking of God reflected in the *human* creature than in nature more generally (a notable exception to this dominant trend is Jonathan Edwards, who envisioned images of divine things in many creatures, not just or not even mainly human creatures; on Edwards, see chap. 6, note 19, above). This is doubtless due, in some measure, to the prominence in Genesis 1 of the *imago Dei* theme. But it is surely the case also that many theologians and masters of the spiritual life have been fascinated with the human creature, not to say fixated on the human creature, and have neglected the greater world of nature or downplayed it in their reflections about the *vestigia Dei*, quite apart from the influence of the *imago Dei* theology of the Book of Genesis. For an comprehensive contemporary discussion of the *vestigia Dei* theme, see David S. Cunningham, *These Three Are One: The Practice of Trinitarian Theology* (Malden, MA: Blackwell, 1998), chap. 3.

39. See Walter Brueggeman, *Interpretation: A Bible Commentary for Teaching and Preaching: Genesis* (Louisville, KY: Westminster John Knox, 2010), 37: "The 'good' used here [Genesis 1] does not refer primarily to a moral quality. It might better be translated 'lovely, pleasing, beautiful. . . . God knows satisfaction and delight in what he has wrought. . . . [God] rests [Genesis 1:31] not because the week ends, but because there is a satisfied, finished quality in his creation."

40. Those who are acquainted with the history of recent Christian theology will recognize that in saying this much I am following the direction of Karl Barth's theology of revelation,

which, for Barth, makes possible a reading of the creation from the side of God's revelation, called by Barth the "analogy of faith" (*analogia pistis*), and rejects any reading of God from the side of the creation (*analogia entis*). More particularly, this is why I am so deliberate about employing the traditional word *traces* and not also giving prominence here to another popular traditional metaphor, understanding nature to be a "book." The latter idea is used often—and not always critically—by Christian thinkers and spiritual writers throughout the ages, for example, by Bonaventure and Calvin. I myself have used this image (as in the prologue to this book) because of its accessibility. The problem with the book metaphor, however, is that it promises too much, at least implicitly: that one can read about who God is by "reading" nature. In the modern era, such thinking was expanded into the idea that there is such a thing as an independent "natural theology." Following Karl Barth in this respect, I do not think that such a theology is possible. It may even, on occasion, be dangerous, as in the case of the mythos of heroic naturalism promoted by the Nazis.

41. Some time after I had written these words, I came upon the book by Bernard Krause, *The Great Animal Orchestra: Finding the Origins of Music in the World's Wild Places* (New York: Little Brown, 2012). Whether or not the thesis of Krause's book is convincing is one matter. Listening to the sometimes symphonic sounds of nature is another, and well worth the time, especially for one who has the spiritual ears to hear.

42. That interdependence between ourselves and trees is, of course, much richer and much more complex than I can indicate here. See this tribute to trees by Jim Robbins, "Why Trees Matter," *New York Times* (April 12, 2012), A23: "We take them for granted, but they are a near miracle. In a bit of natural alchemy called photosynthesis, for example, trees turn one of the seemingly most insubstantive things of all—sunlight—into food for insects, wildlife, and people, and use it to create shade, beauty, and wood for fuel, furniture, and homes. . . . What trees do is essential though not always obvious. . . . A marine chemist [in Japan] . . . discovered that when tree leaves decompose, they leach acids into the ocean that help fertilize plankton. When plankton thrive, so does the rest of the food chain. . . . Trees are nature's water filters, [too,] capable of cleaning up the most toxic wastes, including explosives, solvents, and organic wastes, largely through a dense community of microbes around the tree's roots that clean water in exchange for nutrients. . . . Tree leaves also filter air pollution. . . . Trees, of course, sequester carbon, a greenhouse gas that makes the planet warmer."

43. For a short but illuminating introduction to these themes in Job, see Kathryn Schifferdecker, "Of Stars and Sea Monsters: Creation Theology in the Whirlwind Speeches," *Word & World* 31, no. 4 (Fall 2011): 357–80.

44. See the statement of Christopher Southgate, *The Groaning of Creation: God, Evolution, and the Problem of Evil* (Louisville, KY: Westminster John Knox, 2008), 67f.: "There is within the nonhuman world little sign of costly self-giving to the other, or identification with difference in community. There are some very touching examples of animal behavior, particularly in social animals. Orcas will push an ailing pod member to the surface to breathe; elephants will surround and support a sick member of the family group. But very rarely is there care for the genuinely other. . . . Nonhuman creatures, it might be said, then, offer a kind of 'no' to the example of the triune creator's self-giving love, to the love poured out without the cost being counted. . . . Only hints of this behavior emerge, in the care given to infants in many species, in the mutual protectiveness in social groups. Complex social interactions, containing hints of genuinely altruistic behavior, are seen at their most pronounced in primate groups."

45. See Sarah Coakley, "Evolution and Sacrifice," *Christian Century* (October 20, 2009), 10–11, especially p. 11: "What we now see is that 'Nature red in tooth and claw' has a subtle sustaining matrix of another sort. Let's call it the 'purple line' of sacrifice. . . . . The whole evolutionary struggle has a sacrificial accompaniment, which in certain conditions creatively recurs and forms a vital part of the dynamism of evolutionary development. . . . These phenomena may suggest that cooperation (as mathematically understood) provides a sort of evolutionary

preparation for a higher and fully intentional human altruism that can arise only when the cultural and linguistic realm is reached."

46. Interestingly, John Polkinghorne, *Science and the Trinity: The Christian Encounter with Reality* (New Haven, CT: Yale University Press, 2004), 61, even makes the suggestion that moving from faith in the Trinity to nature also can help us understand the world of nature more fully, from a scientific perspective: "What I claim is not that we can infer the Trinity from nature, but that there are aspects of our scientific understanding of the universe that become more deeply intelligible to us if they are viewed in a Trinitarian perspective."

8

The Works of the Triune God in Nature

Contemplating the Cosmic Ministries of Jesus Christ and the Holy Spirit

During the thirteen years when I was a college teacher and chaplain, pious Christian students on occasion would ask me: "Is Jesus Christ your personal savior?" Sometimes they would also ask: "Have you been baptized by the Spirit?" In an attempt to explore with these students their own spiritual pilgrimages, I would offer the following response.

"Yes, Jesus Christ is my personal savior. Yes, I believe that I have received the Spirit. But Jesus Christ and the Holy Spirit are so much larger than that! Do you know what the word *cosmic* means?" Of course, they did. Then I would begin to tell them about the biblical witness to the cosmic ministries of Jesus Christ and the Holy Spirit. Some of the students took those explorations to heart, even though their initial impulse, when they had first questioned me, had probably been to test whether I was one who lived up to the canons of the piety in which they had been reared.

Many years later now, only all the more eagerly, I want to share with you my passion for the cosmic ministries of Jesus Christ and the Holy Spirit. Yes, it is critically important for a Christian spirituality of nature to be able to affirm *the presence* of the triune God, paradoxically and immediately and wondrously in, with, and under the whole world of nature, as I have tried to do in the preceding chapter. But it is just as important to be able to celebrate *the works* of this God in, with, and under that same world, through Christ and by the Spirit.

To that end, I want to adopt and adapt a now much cited image used by the second-century Christian bishop and theologian Irenaeus of Lyon when he narrated the Christian story of creation, redemption, and consummation. Irenaeus envisioned the Father working everywhere *with two hands*: the Son and the Spirit.[1] This image has appealed to me ever since I first encountered it as a theology student.[2] It suggests to me the openness of God to the whole world, and indeed, the readiness of God to embrace all things with open arms.

Contrast the abstract, geometrical images of the triune God that puzzled me so much as a boy when I encountered them in the liturgical art that was common in American churches in those days: three, overlapping, closed circles, or a single, self-contained equilateral triangle. Such arid images probably inhibited rather than helped my own growth in faith. Encountering the vivid and concrete image of God with two hands was therefore liberating for me spiritually. It dawned on me that, of course, the God attested by the classical faith of the church always has open arms for the whole creation and for every single creature. The God I had come to know and to love had always been a God who had reached out to me and, indeed, to the whole world.

In that spirit, I now want to explore the richness of God's embrace of all things by focusing on the particular ministries of each of God's hands and how they work together in the greater scheme of things. Ponder this thought: the works of the eternal Father are accomplished everywhere, whether in the lilies of the field before us or in the billions of galaxies all around us, whether in the raindrops that hit your face as you hurry to an appointment or in the thunder that you hear resounding in the distance, by the cosmic ministry of the one who is the eternal Gift and by the cosmic ministry of the one who is the eternal Giving, the two hands of God the Giver.

How do we know that?

THE COSMIC MINISTRY OF JESUS CHRIST: A PLACE OF KNOWING

Jonathan Edwards scandalized some of his later interpreters, such as the twentieth-century Harvard historian Perry Miller, by the way he, Edwards, concluded one of his major works, *The History of Redemption*. In that work, Edwards began by considering the eternal decrees of God, then traced the story of redemption, from Adam to Abraham to David and to Jesus Christ, as the culminating moment of redemption history. But Edwards did not end his narrative there. Rather, he traced the universal history of redemption to what he believed to be its very particular conclusion, to the life of the church in the small village of Northampton, Massachusetts, in his own day. That may not be the kind of spiritual vision that can stand up to the canons of the sophisticated academic mind, but that was the only way Edwards could tell the story of redemption as he knew it.

Similarly, whether or not it may sound scandalous to some, I can only conclude my narration of the classic Trinitarian faith of the church, as I understand it, by taking you with me to the life of a single congregation—Resurrection, Boston, Massachusetts—to try to tell you how I have come to understand the works of the triune God through and by "the hands of God": Jesus Christ and the Holy Spirit. I will begin with the story of the Son, the Gift, and then in a later section of this chapter consider the story of the Spirit, the Giving, both from the perspective of one who participates in the life of that congregation in that place of knowing.

I have already told you some things about Resurrection, and now I want to fill in the picture. The congregation was established in an immigrant neighborhood in Boston at the end of the nineteenth century. It was to become the premier Swedish church in Boston for many years. Its stone building still towers over Dudley Square, in the Roxbury neighborhood of Boston. With fits and starts, however, as the heirs of the original Swedish immigrants followed the American dream into Boston's suburbs, the congregation began to take on the color of a new wave of immigrants, African Americans, who had swept into that part of Boston in the first half of the twentieth century. By the time Resurrection had become a majority black congregation, its own neighborhood had long since become the leading African American community in greater Boston.

Toward the end of the twentieth century, yet another in a series of white pastors arrived at Resurrection, but this one brought with him considerable ministry skills that he had honed in the then urban wastelands of Brooklyn, New York. During his tenure, Resurrection became a leading player, along with several historic black congregations, in addressing the social justice trends in the community at that time: the effects of indigenous American racism, rampant poverty, high unemployment, poorly supported public schools, violence in the streets, the drug culture, inordinate numbers of young black men in prison, and many others. As of this writing, things have not changed much, either in the community or in the congregation, even after the arrival of a black pastor and a new generation of black congregational leaders. The congregation still struggles to be faithful, as I imagine most apostolic congregations, established by Paul and others around the Mediterranean basin, struggled in the first century.

But in my experience, the ministry of Jesus Christ is alive and well in the life of this congregation. Let me give you some examples. Several members faithfully distribute large bags of food to the hungry every two weeks. A women in her seventies regularly drives to an isolated, exurban state penitentiary to visit a member of the congregation who is incarcerated there. Several members shepherd two weekly AA groups, one of them Spanish speaking. One member regularly repairs the dilapidated church van, enabling yet another member to pick up scores of children who would not otherwise show up for the Sunday morning children's breakfast and Church School. The pastor maintains an open-door policy in order to speak and pray with street people who frequent Dudley Square. This openness applies also to funerals and baptisms. These critical life cycle rituals are made available not only to members but also to others who have no spiritual home.

Most important of all, perhaps, is the congregation's amazing Sunday liturgy, centered on the Eucharist. I, for one, regularly get carried away by that liturgy, particularly by its global music, from Bach to spirituals, from chantlike songs of the ecumenical Taize community, founded in 1940 in France, to old-time, hand-clapping American Baptist hymns, inspired often by gifted soloists. Here is one sign of who we are: a severely autistic young man, who can barely speak, stands up and dances in place, with his hands waving above his head, while all the rest of us swing through an upbeat Kyrie from Ghana.

Walk with me into this singing fellowship. It's Palm Sunday, also the Sunday of the Passion. As the congregation processes from the streets outside into the sanctuary, singing, we carry the woes of that community with us. Many carry those woes within their own souls. As we walk forward, when the time comes, to receive the bread and wine at the table, I believe we are not alone. Nor have we been alone out on the streets. Like the two disciples on the road to Emmaus after the crucifixion, we have been joined by a companion (Luke 24:13-53).

This is the invisible, resurrected Jesus Christ walking with us. This Christ then serves as the host at the table. This Christ feeds us with his own body and blood. This is the one who would show us the wounds in his hands and feet and side were we to find a way to ask. This is Christ crucified, who dwells in the heart of God and here with us, feeding each one of us with the bread of his resurrected life and the wine of his suffering love, calling each one of us by name as he says, "Given for you." So, the prayers that we uttered during the long, preceding Lenten season, often with the words of that spiritual that has meant so much to me and which I have already quoted, are thus being answered:

When I'm in trouble, Lord, walk with me;
When I'm in trouble, Lord walk with me;
When my head is bowed in sorrow,
Lord, I want Jesus to walk with me.

Jesus, I believe, does walk with us in that liturgy.

If I were asked to choose a single image of what is going on here, for me, in the Palm Sunday procession into the meanings of the Passion Sunday liturgy, I would instinctively know what to say. I would reach into the depths of my own fragile faith, planted there already when I was a child, and into the depths of the historic faith of the church, from its earliest expressions to the present, and lay hold of this image: *Jesus Christ is the Good Shepherd of God.*[3] He is the one sent by God to leave the ninety-nine alone and to search for the single lost sheep—me. Me, a sinner, as I extensively explained earlier in this narrative, but not just me, obviously. Jesus Christ is the one sent by God to lay down his life in behalf of me and all God's creatures, I believe, to hold us all in his arms and to be with us until the eschaton arrives, when he will hand over his ministry to the Father.

In this predominantly black church, when members of the congregation contemplate the central, elevated stained-glass window in the east wall of the chancel, above what used to be the main high altar of the church, they can contemplate the image of the Good Shepherd. This particular figure is caucasian, an irony of our Swedish immigrant history. But I daresay that this image is powerful for all who engage it spiritually: a gracious figure of the risen Lord, holding a shepherd's staff in his extended right hand and a lamb cradled in his left arm. He is looking down at yet another lamb at his feet. As I kneel in my pew, after having communed and then having said my prayers, I often contemplate that stained-glass figure and remember hymns from my earliest days in the church—above all, words like these from "The Lord's My Shepherd, I'll Not Want":

The King of love my shepherd is,
Whose goodness faileth never;
I nothing lack if I am his
And he is mine forever....

Thou spreadst a table in my sight;

Thine unction grace bestoweth;
And, oh, what transport of delight
From thy pure chalice floweth!

And so, through all the length of days,
Thy goodness faileth never.
Good Shepherd, may I sing thy praise
Within thy house forever.[4]

How could this be? How could the one who dwells in the heart of the triune God—the crucified and risen Christ—thus be my most intimate companion here and now? The answer is, of course, that I do not know. I cannot explain the mystery. I can only tell you about it, with whatever imperfect words might be given to me. But I do want to tell you about it because I want to celebrate the whole truth in this narrative about this good shepherd as my *cosmic* Lord and Savior.

THE COSMIC MINISTRY OF THE GOOD SHEPHERD:
THEOLOGICAL HORIZONS

I have already observed that the image of Christ as the Good Shepherd is deeply rooted in the ancient faith of the church as well as in my own particular experience. I want to begin exploring this theme now by identifying some of those ancient meanings, particularly as they emerged in the Gospel of John, since they have been so important for my own faith. I will then try to bind these reflections to the earth by invoking, once again, Luther's immanence theology, telling the story of the crucified and risen Lord, who is both in the heart of God and in, with, and under all things.

These reflections will presuppose this simple axiom of faith: *the ministry of Jesus Christ is larger than the church.* Yes, I believe that it makes good spiritual sense to affirm that the ministry of Jesus Christ is *revealed* within the life of the church, the community in which God's word is preached and where God's sacraments are celebrated. But we must be on guard against an ecclesio-centric view of that ministry. As Jesus himself taught in the parable of the last judgment in Matt. 25:31-46, he is present with the hungry, the sick, and the imprisoned, wherever they may be, within or beyond the community of faith. He may not be revealed there, but he is active there in his latent church, as Jürgen

Moltmann has taught us to say, thereby infusing some traditional theological language with new power.[5] But—as Moltmann has also stressed in a number of his writings on the creation—the ministry of Christ, all the more so, extends throughout *the cosmos*.[6] Hence I think that it is best to speak of *the latent ministry of Christ everywhere*, not just among the poor, as critically important as that biblical theme is also.

THE COSMIC VISION OF THE GOSPEL OF JOHN

In the Gospel of John, we hear, in this vein, a kind of *cantus firmus* celebrating the universal meaning of Jesus Christ. This underlying theme can be heard in the great and sonorous claims for Jesus Christ in the familiar "I am" statements of Jesus himself, among them these: "I am the bread of life" (John 6:35), "I am the light of the world" (John 8:12), "I am the true vine" (John 15:1), and "I am the good shepherd" (John 10:11). This is not the place to explore the many meanings of these statements in any detail. Rather, it is enough to say the following. For the Fourth Gospel, the great "I am" declarations by Jesus, whatever else they may mean, surely hearken back to the name of God, the Tetragrammaton, in the Book of Exodus, the name of the creator and redeemer God, usually translated, "I am who I am" or "I AM who I AM" (Exod. 3:14). These sayings also give expression to the Gospel of John's "word of God theology" or "logos theology." That theology was anchored in the confession of the word-made-flesh (John 1:14), and that aspect made John's theology unique in its own philosophical and theological environment.

Yet the accent on the incarnation of the word—or the logos—was only one of the meanings John meant to convey, as Russell Bradner Norris Jr. explains in a scintillating article:

> Johannine use of the term logos emerges from deep theological reflection on the life of Jesus as the central revelation of God. The Evangelist speaks not of some philosophical abstraction, but of the logos incarnate in human form, who is the logos for precisely that reason. At the same time, John emphasizes more strongly than other New Testament writers the cosmic dimensions of the Word, and specifically the participation of the pre-existent Christ in the creation of the world. It is significant that the Gospel of John begins with the same words found in the first book of the Hebrew scriptures. . . . The evangelist offers a new Genesis account, a new creation story,

one centering in the life, death, and resurrection of Jesus Christ, the incarnate logos of God.[7]

The "I am" statements throughout the Gospel of John further attest to this kind of cosmic meaning, which John wants us to attach to Jesus, the logos in human flesh.[8] This is at least part of what the claim for Jesus made in John 8:58 means: "Jesus said to them, 'Very truly, I tell you, before Abraham was, *I am*'" (italics added). Jesus is here being portrayed as the creator God, whose name is "I Am Who I Am." Hence, when the Johannine Jesus says, "*I am* the good shepherd. The good shepherd lays down his life for the sheep" (John 10:11; italics added), I believe that John is intending us to understand that this is not just testimony to a profoundly personal relationship with Jesus but also a witness to the cosmic scope of the ministry of that selfsame Lord.[9]

Behind all of this, in my view, is the eternal identity of the Good Shepherd, which I believe that John presupposes. In terms of the narrative that we have been following thus far, the Son of God is *eternally* the Good Shepherd, not just temporally. According to the last of the three roughly hewn analogies for the Trinity that we reviewed in chapter 6, the second person of the Trinity is eternally the self-sacrificing savior. It makes good spiritual sense to say, then, that the Son of God is eternally the Good Shepherd.

THE WORK OF THE COSMIC GOOD SHEPHERD

Now consider the work of this good shepherd in the cosmic history of God. Think of this good shepherd, biblically, with the creation story in Genesis (chapter 1) in mind. Imagine this cosmic shepherd graciously gathering all things from the very beginning, calling all things into being in relationship to one another and to himself, as a shepherd gathers his or her flock.[10] Imagine this cosmic shepherd in some sense stepping back, even resting, in accord with the vision of Gen. 2:3, so that every creaturely domain might be on its own and in relationship with all others, as a shepherd on occasion will rest, contemplating his or her flock and taking joy in the growth and uniqueness of individual sheep or, on some occasions, patiently enduring what they are, on their own, making of themselves.[11] (I will return to this theme concerning the being of each and every creature in itself, so created and then re-created by the work of the cosmic Christ, in chapter 9, under the rubric "the integrity of nature.")

Imagine this cosmic shepherd, all the more so, as compassionately bearing with all creatures, suffering especially with those creatures who experience pain, at times singling out some creaturely domains or even individuals for special care and attention, as a good shepherd does when leaving the flock behind and seeking out the sheep that is lost. Luther suggested this kind of vocation for the cosmic Christ, strikingly, when commenting on Heb. 1:3, concerning the word of God *upholding* all things. This is a Hebraism, Luther observed; it expresses "a certain tender and, so to speak, motherly care for the things which he created and which should be cherished."[12]

Imagine, finally, this cosmic shepherd as accompanying the whole cosmic flock one day, accompanying all things, as his last and greatest act of self-giving, through and beyond the valley of the shadows of cosmic entropy[13] to a new and eternal pasture—dreamed of by saints like Perpetua from the earliest Christian centuries[14]—where the lamb will lie down with the lion and where, finally, the cosmic shepherd will bring his gloriously variegated and polymorphic congregation of creatures into the presence of the Giver of every good and perfect Gift, the Giving of the Spirit, so that this God may then be all in all. This is to contemplate the whole cosmos most fully itself, not fallen away into nothingness, nor lost in God as if it were of no account, but united with God and transfigured by God's glory. Carried away in the Spirit by such a vision, would we not then finally comprehend fully the breadth and length, the height and depth, of the cosmic Gift of Jesus Christ?

THE COSMIC GOOD SHEPHERD: SOME SPIRITUAL TENSIONS

I want to say more about this vision of the cosmic ministry of Jesus Christ here because it brings with it some spiritual tensions. This vision shows us Jesus the personal savior, on the one hand, and Jesus the cosmic savior, on the other. What becomes of my intense, personal relationship with Jesus Christ when I affirm that the savior is at once intensely related, in some sense, to every other creature and indeed to the whole creation? Doesn't my personal relationship begin to lose its force when this Jesus, who calls me by name, simultaneously calls every other creature by name? Does not the historical, biblical Christ, with whom I am in intimate communion, now become, in some sense, a vague and uncertain "life force" of the universe? I must answer this question for the sake of those, like my students in years gone by, who ask, from time to time, whether Jesus Christ truly is my personal savior.

Another way of framing this question—if we wish to think in traditional terms about the ascension of Jesus "to sit at the right hand of the Father"—is this: if the biblical, historical Jesus is now to be thought of as everywhere, doesn't Jesus' concrete personal identity begin to fragment? Doesn't his humanity have to be divided, as it were, into billions and billions of pieces, if he is to be the present Lord of every creature? A number of Christians have been troubled by questions like these, perhaps preeminently among them John Calvin.

But if we stay with Luther's vision of the immanence of God, interpreted rightly, I think we can have it both ways: a crucified and risen savior who is for me personal and who is at once the near-at-hand good shepherd of every other creature. Much depends on how we envision the ascension of Jesus in this context. In a three-story universe, a worldview commonly held in biblical times, it made sense to think of Jesus ascending "up" to sit at the right hand of God, who then would be viewed as reigning over all things from above. If that is God's place, so this way of thinking unfolded, the crucified and risen human Jesus must be there, and there alone. For Jesus to be in a personal relationship with me, the Holy Spirit would have to sweep me up, so to speak, to heaven, to the right hand of God. Moreover, according to the same way of thinking, by implication Jesus could *not* be everywhere, seeking out the lost, comforting the downtrodden, healing the brokenhearted, touching the pain of every creature that suffers, close at hand.

Luther, however, broke with that three-story-universe way of thinking. As we have seen, for Luther there is no "up." God is known to us only as the God who is here and now, in, with, and under all things. In service of this vision, Luther made a fundamental claim about the ascension of Jesus Christ—"the right hand of God is everywhere" (*dextera Dei ubique est*)—which was to say: the place where the crucified and risen Lord is located is in, with, and under all things, not sitting isolated in heaven above in some ethereal place, according to the canons of a three-story universe.

Obviously, this is the paradoxical language of faith. But by invoking it, Luther was able to show us the crucified and risen—*and* ascended—Lord dwelling with us here and now, and indeed dwelling with every other creature as well. In a word, my personal savior who dwells with me and all other humans in our affliction, embraces us in our godforsakenness, and bears our pain with us, thus relieving us of its sting, is likewise in a variety of ways the cosmic savior of all other creatures, which also groan in travail in their own manner.

THE COSMIC GOOD SHEPHERD AND THE PROBLEM OF EVIL

This thought touches on an issue that has emerged in this narrative on numerous occasions—the problem of evil. Am I suggesting here that somehow the presence of the crucified, risen, and ascended Christ to all creatures in their pain somehow *justifies* that pain? Once again, my answer to that kind of question is emphatically *no*. I have rejected the idea that evil can be explained away or somehow justified. Rather, I am testifying to the presence of the good shepherd of God, who dwells in the heart of God, here and now in the midst of the distress of every creature that suffers. I am not somehow claiming that that healing and upholding presence justifies the suffering itself. As I have stated at various points along the way, I believe that there is no answer to the theodicy question: we must trust such things to the Lord. But just as firmly, I also believe that God does not abandon his creatures—most particularly, all of animal kind, including humans—in their suffering.

A case in point. Some years ago, I had just walked out of the kitchen door of our summer home in southwestern Maine. My eyes caught the form of an animal, presumably dead, lying a hundred feet up the hill on our country road. I was saddened. Was it a porcupine or perhaps one of our neighbors' cats? No, it was much too big for that. I approached the dead animal cautiously, not knowing what to think, worrying, too, that a car could come speeding over the top of the hill and be upon us both, the dead body and myself, in no time. As I stood over the body, I was astounded. It was a rabbit, but unlike any other rabbit I had ever seen, nothing like the small animals that sometimes nibble the clover on the lawns of Mt. Auburn. It was an elegant, beautiful creature of considerable size. It had black tufts of fir on the edge of its ears and its flanks were white.

I was worried that more cars would soon speed by, further desecrating the body. I ran back to our garage and found a large, flat shovel. I quickly returned and reverently—with some effort—lifted the body and carried it over to the edge of one of the shale shelves on that side of the road. I then gathered armfuls of tall grass that a road machine had left lying there a few days before, and I covered the body. I stood there then, contemplating for some moments what clearly had become to me a sacred site. I did not utter a prayer, but my stance was prayerful. To this day, the sight of that elegant animal lying on the road is vivid in my mind. Later, after I had looked into the matter, I concluded that the beautiful creature must have been a snowshoe hare. Its habits are said to be mainly nocturnal. Perhaps that is why I had never seen one before.

In retrospect, predicated on my fragile faith, I have assumed that that graceful creature did not die alone, as a car or a truck must have come racing over the top of the hill in the middle of the night. In some way appropriate to that creature, I believe, Jesus Christ, the crucified, risen, and ascended Lord, had been present there with it at the time of its death, and before, perhaps as it had taken a frantic turn into what might have been strange territory for it, perhaps as it was being pursued by a coyote or some other predator whose ways are also nocturnal. But that sad killing of that magnificent animal clearly does not stand alone as an isolated incident. In the world of nature, of course, suffering and death run rampant.

What about the woodchucks that I trap in my have-a-heart trap and then later release into the wilds after a long, bumpy ride in my trunk? What about the mice that I, a human predator, trap in my own kitchen? What about the towering moose that once, on a rainy night, emerged in front of our car, barely avoiding being hit and then, unself-consciously, it seemed to me, trotted for some twenty yards in front of our creeping car, a creature that would soon be vulnerable to the state of Maine's hunters, in due season? What about the beautiful moths that flutter at our lighted window at night, some of them soon to be victims of the bats that prey on them?

Then there are all of the collective, humanly induced sufferings of animals in today's industrialized agriculture, the pigs and the chickens especially, which are often prisoners of filth and disease in cramped spaces. In our time, perhaps as never before, the whole animal creation is groaning under massive suffering. Of course, I do not begin to understand all of these things, even less the bloody story of tens of thousands of species in evolutionary history. But I do believe that the crucified, risen, and ascended Jesus Christ is immediately present in the midst of all that pain, comforting where that is possible, ameliorating where that is possible, always upholding every suffering creature as its good shepherd.

THE UNIVERSAL MINISTRY OF THE COSMIC CHRIST

The scope of the cosmic Christ's shepherding is even wider. It extends beyond animal kind to every kind. A text from Ephesians, much beloved by Luther, comes to mind here, referring to the universal reach of Christ's ministry: "He who descended is the same one who ascended far above all the heavens, so that he might fill all things" (Eph. 4:10). The relationship of the cosmic Christ to all things as he fills them is surely differentiated, however, depending on the complexities and the immensities of various creatures. Thus I can imagine Christ speaking personally to me and also being present in some interactive manner with the dying snow hare. But his relationships with other natural creatures will be different, caring for plants, for example, as a shepherd might care for an olive tree, in addition to his or her work with the sheep. But then the metaphor of shepherding must consciously be supplemented by others, were we to think, for example, of his shepherding a comet or a galaxy or families of galaxies.

I find it spiritually instructive, in this respect, to recall another of the roughly hewn analogies I proposed to help us encounter the ineffable being and becoming of the triune God. To this point, in Trinitarian analogies I have suggested, I have been thinking of Christ as the self-sacrificing savior. But here it is also helpful—and, in some sense, spiritually necessary—to recall the analogy of the Trinity as a powerful, torrential flow. Thinking in such terms would suggest the following image of the cosmic Christ: the channeling function of the eternal Son or the logos, akin to the cliffs along the lower Niagara River, channeling the turbulent waters below the Falls.

From such a perspective, I would want to envision the cosmic ministry of Jesus Christ forming and sustaining the being of all creatures, holding each one together, in its appropriate place in relation to every other creature, however immense any single creature might be. Obviously, here—as in every case but all the more dramatically—we encounter the limits of any kind of thinking about God and the works of God through the Son and by the Spirit. But it is necessary to extend the "cosmic rhetoric" (Joseph Sittler) of our thinking in this respect, in order to tell as much of the story about the works of the triune God as our limited minds may permit. This allows us to give some fragmentary testimony, in a Trinitarian manner, to the vision of God's universal history proclaimed by Paul in Romans: "For from him and through him and to him are all things" (Rom. 11:36).

The conclusion of this long cosmic journey of the good shepherd with each and every creature and with all creatures together will be the eschatological consummation, as my fragile faith imagines such things. It is a theme to which I have repeatedly referred, and one that Paul takes for granted in the text just cited: all things are "to him." This is when the day longed for by the ancient prophet, when weeping and tears and suffering of any kind will be over, will have arrived. The lamb will lie down with the lion. The snow hare will romp with the coyote. And little children will play in perfect freedom and safety on every corner of the new earth. The vast reaches of outer space—above all, "dark energy"—will come alive with all the colors of the rainbow. All the dinosaurs and ichthyosaurs and their kin will have new places to flourish forever, throughout the universe. And every tree that ever existed will grow anew eternally throughout the virtually infinite reaches of the renewed cosmos.

All this will then be celebrated with a universal festivity, by each and every creature in its own way, as all creatures enter immediately into the joy of Godself, the image suggested by the first analogy of the Trinity we considered earlier: the festive communal process. The symphony of all things will have reached its glorious climax. The whole creation will have been taken into the joy and the power and the love of the God who is eternally Giver, Gift, and Giving.

THE COSMIC MINISTRY OF THE HOLY SPIRIT: A PLACE OF KNOWING

Now I want to give you some glimpses of what I can see of the ministry of the Father's other hand: cosmic Spirit. I invite you to join me once again in the midst of what is, for me, the spiritual place of knowing for this part of our journey—the life of that small, struggling, but apostolic congregation to which I belong in Roxbury, Massachusetts. Then, in the following section, I will invite you to ponder with me why this very Spirit has been so underattested in traditional Western theology and spirituality while at the same time so richly attested in the Bible. We will see that the Spirit of God, whose cosmic ministry we will be exploring here, is in fact—for faith—the Spirit of nature.

As visitors will immediately notice, at Resurrection, Roxbury, sometimes things aren't done in good order on Sundays. For example, we wait to begin the children's breakfast because the second trip of the church van has yet to arrive. When it does arrive, the children come charging in, shouting. But, in due course, they also pause at their tables and think deeply when asked to tell how Jesus has been with them the preceding week. When it is time for worship, those of us who have come directly to the nave greet one another affectionately and then wait patiently for the liturgy to begin. The typical reasons for the delay can vary: Perhaps one of the musicians, who takes the not always reliable city bus, has yet to arrive. Or on occasion, someone unexpectedly has to go find a new bottle of communion wine because the person who was supposed to bring that wine has had a personal emergency. But regardless, the wait is worth it: the music and the eucharistic celebration of this beset-upon congregation often move me to ecstatic moments of joy, born, I believe, of the joy of God Godself.

Once the liturgy is under way, people continue to arrive, sometimes well into the middle of things. One latecomer, whose story I happen to know, makes her way to her pew, burdened by a personal tragedy and by a body full of arthritis. Another, who arrives from the elevator in a wheelchair, rolls himself down the central aisle to the front as we sing. Yet another, who is a hard-pressed social worker, is always late. Never mind being exhausted by many overtime days during her six-day workweek, she also has to care for her homebound mother on her way to church. People coming in late like her, even during the sermon, make the liturgy feel a little chaotic. Then there are the predictable moments of liturgical disorder. Gathering the children around the font to witness the Baptism, for example, can be like, as they say, herding cats.

Most chaotic of all, perhaps, is the Passing of the Peace. What in many churches is a kind of brief and muted greeting of one's near neighbors in the pews for us turns into a kind of Woodstock of the soul. Everyone swarms around, greeting one another, as all hum "I'm so glad, Jesus lifted me . . ." It's a time for embracing those who are grieving and for hand-slapping those who've experienced some good fortune. Some kids move around, giving oldsters like me high fives. A couple of congregation council members surreptitiously confer about their meeting after the liturgy. Meanwhile, most of the children soon gather up at the altar steps; there, they find a number of percussion instruments waiting for them, and they then keep boisterous time with the upbeat music of the piano and the voices of everyone else as we all mill around. When I reflect about the Passing of the Peace at Resurrection, Roxbury, I sometimes think that the first-century Day of Pentecost might have been something like this—a driven, holy chaos. What were those tongues of fire anyway?

How do my brothers and sisters in Christ happen to gather at Resurrection, Roxbury, every Sunday with such an uncommon spiritual frenzy, even though many of them are so deeply burdened by the cares of this world? The disciples that first Pentecost Day did not just happen to show up to be together, nor did the man in the wheelchair or the kids from the van or I, for that matter, just happen to arrive that Sunday morning at Resurrection, Roxbury, along with all of the other sinners—young and old, rich and poor, male and female, straight and gay, black and white—who arrive on any given Sunday, at any given moment, to worship. People come to participate in these liturgies for many reasons. But from the perspective of the fragile faith that I am sharing with you here, there is only one underlying reason. In words that I learned by heart when I was twelve years old, from Luther's *Small Catechism*: the Holy Spirit "calls, gathers, enlightens, and sanctifies the whole Christian church on earth."

Nor was that holy chaos some random, emotional aberration. The Holy Spirit called us together, I believe, in order to enlighten us and to stir our hearts so that we could be filled with the joy of God Godself, in the knowledge of Christ Jesus. The Holy Spirit gathered us with a kind of resistible but irresistible force, from the places in our lives where we had been bogged down, into this spiritually charged place, where we all are swept up into that sanctifying experience. Again, I quote Luther's words also in his *Small Catechism,* which, for me, have long rung true: "I believe that I cannot by my own reason or strength believe in Jesus Christ, my lord, or come to him; but the Holy Spirit has called me by the Gospel, enlightened me with his gifts, sanctified and kept me in the true faith."

THE COSMIC MINISTRY OF THE LIFEGIVING ONE: THEOLOGICAL HORIZONS

I also came to believe, already as a theological student, that Luther's helpful focus on the Holy Spirit as—in my words—the mother of the church was too narrow and, as a matter of fact, not commensurate with Luther's own understanding of the immanence of God in the whole creation. For me, the calling of the Holy Spirit surely brings me to the place of knowing and stirs me up. But the same Holy Spirit has had much more to show me than the life of the church itself, critically important as that place of knowing is. The Spirit, in my experience, shows me a cosmic vision of the works of both hands of God the Father: the cosmic Christ *and* the cosmic Spirit of Godself.

I now want to show you what I can see, however imperfectly, when I contemplate the works of the Spirit in particular—with special attention to the spirituality of nature. But to do that, I need to acknowledge that I am working within a tradition that has often minimized the works of the Spirit, to the disservice of the church and its mission and to the disservice of Christian spirituality in particular.

THE ECLIPSE OF THE SPIRIT IN WESTERN CHRISTIANITY

Students of Christian theology and spirituality have come to a consensus during the past five decades concerning the place of the Holy Spirit in traditional Western Christian life and thought. That place is highly ambiguous.[15] In this respect, Luther's understanding of the Holy Spirit as what I have called the mother of the church was not that unusual. In Western Christian life and thought, the Holy Spirit has often, if not always, been regarded merely as the handmaiden, the dutiful servant, of the Father and the Son, and chiefly as the mediator of *their* grace within the life of the church. If the Spirit of God did not totally vanish in traditional Western theology and spirituality, the Spirit often faded from significance.[16]

This trend, as many have observed, is especially visible in traditional Western art. Typically, when the Trinity has been portrayed, you can see a vivid image of "the Father" as a bearded, fulsome, and crowned heavenly king, with a still more tangible image of "the Son," sometimes with the Father holding the cross of his suffering Son. Esthetically obscured by that dramatic depiction of Father and Son, a tiny dove—sometimes surrounded with a lightly etched halo—hovers over the head of the Father or elsewhere in the painting. This indicates why classical Western thought and spirituality is sometimes said to be functionally binitarian. The Spirit doesn't seem to be all that important.

Why is that? I first began to think about that question in a course on the history of Christian thought that I took with Paul Tillich when I was an undergraduate. Tillich believed that the Spirit had been driven out of the mainstream of Christian life and thought in the West because the Spirit is "dangerous." The Spirit cannot be controlled by church authorities or their secular allies, said Tillich. The Spirit is democratic, in this rudimentary sense, not hierarchical. The Spirit is available to everyone. Thus so-called "heretics," condemned by the church, typically claimed that they had been inspired by the Spirit.

When he was a young theologian in Germany, he told us, Tillich himself invoked the power of the Spirit in his own life in the form of a *protest* against the established theological and political order of his own time. In his later writings, he would call the theological nexus behind that kind of action "the Protestant Principle." With some colleagues, Tillich took a public stand in behalf of "religious socialism" in protest against the socialism being promoted by the Nazis during the tumultuous years when they were coming to power.

This stance on Tillich's part would bring down the ire of the German religious and political establishment on Tillich and on other religious socialists at that time, and would eventually force Tillich himself to flee the then burgeoning world of the Nazis and take refuge in the United States. But Tillich told that story not to celebrate the place of the Spirit in Western Christianity but to illustrate how rarely the Spirit had been taken seriously, and what the outcome typically had been when the Spirit had become a major theological theme.

I did not realize the full significance of Tillich's interpretation of what might be called the eclipse of the Spirit in traditional Western Christian life and thought until much later. That discovery happened, dramatically for me, when I first read the remarkable theological testament by the Catholic theologian Elizabeth Johnson, *Woman, Earth, and Creator Spirit*, in 1993.[17] It was then I realized clearly that the underlying reason for the eclipse of the Spirit in traditional Western theology and spirituality was not merely because the Spirit is "dangerous," as Tillich had said, but all the more so because the dominant mind of the church had identified the Spirit *with women* and *with nature*. Women and nature had been hierarchically dominated, reduced to a secondary and oppressed status, by the mainstream Christian tradition; hence the Spirit *had* to be reduced likewise.[18]

Thus women, nature, and the Spirit became permanent second-class citizens, or worse, in the theological world espoused by authoritative church teachers and the governing church hierarchy more generally in the Christian West.

That theological eclipse, as Johnson argues, can and must be rejected. This is the key: to move beyond the perspective of sexual dualism and its hierarchical mode of thought, and to celebrate the Spirit and nature, as well as women, in their own right, inspired by a fresh reading of the Scriptures and judiciously informed by the classical Christian tradition's reception of that testimony. To that end, following Johnson's own discussion of these materials, I want to weave together images of the Spirit here, both from the Bible and, cautiously, from the ensuing theological tradition, in order to highlight and to celebrate how the Holy Spirit is, surprising as this may sound to some, in truth the Spirit of nature and is thus to be celebrated. In a word, the Holy Spirit has a cosmic ministry akin to the cosmic ministry of the risen and ascended Christ.

THE ELUSIVE COSMIC MINISTRY OF THE SPIRIT: THE LIFEGIVING ONE

But before I explore some of the biblical testimonials to the Spirit of nature, I want to acknowledge and to underline what must be regarded as the special character of the approach to envisioning the works of the Spirit now before us. In a sense, this way of contemplating the Spirit differs from the ways of contemplating the Father and the Son that we already have followed. The terminology—the *Holy* Spirit—can be taken to imply as much. If we can think of the Father and the Son concretely as the "motherly Father" and the "Good Shepherd," as I believe we can and are indeed well advised to do, how are we to think of the "Holy Spirit"? What images commend themselves?

God as Trinity is "Holy, holy, holy," as a hymn I have sung ever since I can remember proclaims. But, in a sense, the Spirit is *more holy* than the Father and the Son, and less accessible to our imagination than the other two persons of the Trinity. Why else is the Spirit alone called "holy"? This is a good answer, I believe: the Spirit protects the wholly otherness of the immanent triune God, whereas the Son invites us to enter into his own personal relationship with the Father and with every creature. The Spirit is elusive, in a way that the Father and the Son are not.

Biblical testimony to the Spirit, in this respect, is suggestively impersonal. This is not to imply that the more personal images of the motherly Father or the Good Shepherd are not metaphorical. Of course they are. All the persons of the Trinity, in this sense, are ineffable. We have no sure and certain cognitive grasp of any of them. They are beyond comprehension, wholly other, and thus "holy" in that sense. But with the Spirit, the otherness of the immanent God is, in a sense, more striking than in the case of the Father and the Son. Hence our practice of addressing the Spirit alone as holy makes good theological and spiritual sense.

This sensibility is pervasively apparent in the biblical witness to the Spirit and in what is perhaps the most telling identification we have of the Spirit in the classical theological and spiritual tradition, as Elizabeth Johnson has succinctly shown us.[19] According to the Nicene Creed, the Spirit is the "Lifegiver." In order to underline the dynamism to which that term (*zoopoion, vivificatorem*) points, I prefer a parallel English expression, idiosyncratic as it may sound—the "Lifegiving One"—for, theologically and spiritually, this term means, in Johnson's words, that "the Spirit is the unceasing, dynamic flow of divine power that sustains the universe, bringing forth life."[20] The Spirit is richly immersed in the whole creation, as indicated by Ps. 139:7—"Whither shall I go from thy Spirit? Or whither shall I flee from thy presence?" Which suggests, Johnson comments, that "the Spirit is in the highest sky, the deepest hole, the darkest night, farther east than the sunrise, over every next horizon. (Ps. 139:7-12) The Spirit fills the world and is in all things. Since the Spirit is also transcendent over the world, divine indwelling circles round to embrace the whole world, which thereby dwells within the sphere of the divine."[21]

The Spirit as the Lifegiving One is also the *rejuvenating* energy that renews the face of the earth (Ps. 104:30). "The damaged earth," Johnson writes, "violent and unjust social structures, the lonely and broken heart—all cry out for a fresh start. In the midst of this suffering the Creator Spirit, through the mediation of created powers, comes, as the Pentecost sequence sings, to wash what is unclean; to pour water upon what is drought-stricken; to heal what is hurt; to loosen up what is rigid; to warm what is freezing; to straighten out what is crooked and bent."[22] Above all, according to Scripture, the Spirit is the one who empowers the resurrection of Jesus Christ and the new life that flows into the world through the risen Christ.[23]

Perhaps the most widely attested characteristic of the Spirit, according to biblical testimony, is this: the Spirit *moves*. At the very beginning, according to Genesis, the Spirit "sweeps over," that is, *drives*, the primeval cosmic waters.[24] The Spirit is everywhere, moving all things. This is how Johnson suggestively depicts that universal dynamism: "In every instance the living Spirit empowers, lures, prods, dances on ahead. Throughout the process, the Spirit characteristically sets up bonds of kinship among all creatures, human and non-human alike, all of who are energized by this one Source."[25]

Johnson's reference to the Spirit "dancing on ahead" points to another, critically important aspect of the working of the Spirit as portrayed in the Scriptures—*the future*. In Old Testament texts, the motifs of the eschatological bestowal of the Spirit to the Messiah and the eschatological bestowal of the Spirit to the people of God occur alongside each other.[26] In the New Testament, they are combined to give us a vision of the Messiah of the end times who transmits the Spirit to the people of the end times, as is familiarly evident in Luke's account of the Day of Pentecost (Acts 2:1-13), which builds on the prophetic vision of Joel 3:1-5. The eschatological image of the Spirit dwelling in the people as the new temple of God also appears in the New Testament.

All of this presupposes the widely attested New Testament "timetable": with the coming of the Messiah and his people, the new age has dawned; the age of the coming new heavens and the new earth, attested by the Seer of the Book of Revelation, has begun (Rev. 21:1-5). For Paul, for example, the gift of the Spirit is a "down payment" and a sure indication of the redemption yet to come (2 Cor. 5:5; Rom. 8:23) and is thus intended to be a power that links Baptism and eschatological fulfillment. This understanding of the Spirit as the harbinger of the future would later be expressed by early Christian theologians as the Spirit's mission to "perfect" the creation, now and in the age to come.

IMAGES OF THE LIFEGIVING ONE: THE SPIRIT OF NATURE

To describe this immanent life giving and moving of all things toward the future by the Spirit, the Scriptures frequently resort to powerful, impersonal images from nature—above all, wind, fire, and water. Thus the very Hebrew word for spirit—*ruach*—means moving air or *wind*. "The term," Johnson explains, "encompasses all the movements of wind, from the small, gentle breeze caressing our cheek to the mighty storm gale that reshapes the landscape."[27] She instances the wind that blew the waters back at the Red Sea so that the escaping slaves could go free (Exod. 14:21); the wind that blows through the valley of dry bones, breathing life into the vast multitude (Ezek. 37:1-4); the warm breezes of spring that melt the winter ice, producing flowing waters that green the earth (Ps. 147:18); and the mighty Pentecost wind that shakes the house where Jesus' disciples are praying (Acts 1:13-14; 2:1-4).[28]

Fire is another powerful image for the biblical imagination that suggests the presence of God, whether it be a bush that burns but is not consumed (Exod. 3:1-12) or the tongues of fire that descended upon the disciples at Pentecost (Acts 2:1-3). Here is Johnson's vivid description of this image of the

Spirit: "There is no definite shape to fire, and its ever-changing form signifies something that is unto itself, mysterious. It is a dangerous element that sears if you touch it and that can easily escape human control. At the same time, the light and heat that emanate from fire are indispensable to human well-being. It points to the greater fires in the universe, the glowing sun and stars, and the fierce lightning storms."[29]

Finally, *water*. This image is found throughout the Scriptures. To make clean: "I will sprinkle clean water upon you . . . and a new spirit I will put within you" (Ezek. 36:25). The promise of justice and peace: like a cascade of water poured out (Isa. 32:15-18). The Spirit of prophecy: poured out on all flesh (Joel 2:28-29). The love of God: poured into our hearts by the Holy Spirit (Rom. 5:5). Writes Johnson: "As a symbol of the Spirit, water points to the bottomless wellspring of the source of life and to the refreshment and gladness that result from deep immersion in this mystery."[30]

It is impossible, in my view, to think of such images of the Lifegiving One—the energy, the power of rejuvenation, the mover of all things toward the future of God, the qualities of wind and fire and water—without thinking, in one way or another, that the Holy Spirit *is* the Spirit of nature. With a discerning eye, indeed, it is entirely possible for anyone who participates in the liturgy of a congregation like Resurrection, Roxbury, to come to the same conclusion, as he or she experiences the bodily vitality and the personal energy and communal chaos of that sanctifying experience, above all by celebrating the pouring forth of the baptismal waters.

But this is not yet the whole story. I want to remind you here that we have already encountered this cosmic ministry of the Spirit in our earlier reflections about God in Godself. The Spirit is not just the Spirit of nature for us, in our experience. The Spirit is the Spirit of nature essentially, eternally, in the very Trinitarian being and becoming of God. This is not to suggest that nature somehow exists in God eternally. It is rather to suggest this: the second hand of God is intrinsically the Lifegiving One, in the being and becoming of Godself. Recall the second of the three roughly hewn analogies for the Trinity that I have already explored, highlighting the power of God. The Trinity, I said, is like Niagara Falls: the river flowing above the falls, the turmoil and chaos and energy of the waters below the falls, and the cliffs of the river gorge channeling the turbulent waters. The Holy Spirit, I suggested, is akin to the tumultuous waters below the falls, the churning, the apparently chaotic movement, the enormous energies, the driving of the waters toward their future "rest" in Lake Ontario.

These are some glimpses of what I see when I contemplate the cosmic ministry of the second hand of God, the Holy Spirit, in theological perspective. This person of the Trinity is indeed the Spirit of nature. The Lifegiving One is an infinite flow of energy and vitality and rejuvenation, always ready to move forward, akin to the driving wind, akin to the fire that overwhelms as well as comforts, akin to the water that overflows, in tumult as well as in blessing. The Lifegiving One is the eternal Giving of God creating and redeeming and consummating all things, temporally and eternally.

THE COSMIC MINISTRIES OF THE SON AND THE SPIRIT: WORKING HAND IN HAND

I will have more to say about the Holy Spirit in chapter 9, when I will explore some of the meanings given with the third and final petition of the Trinity Prayer. Here, to conclude the current discussion, I want to raise the following question, figuratively: how do the two hands of God that we have just contemplated work together? Surely, this is a case not of one hand not knowing what the other is doing but, rather, of both working with each other harmoniously, so that the will of the motherly Father, the Giver, might be fruitfully and even beautifully accomplished—all while respecting the integrity, the spontaneity, and the particular freedoms of creaturely being and becoming (more about this theme in the next chapter).

A variety of answers have been given to this kind of question throughout the history of Christian thought. Theological and spiritual writers have found this theme irresistible.[31] But identifying the particular ministries of the eternal Son and the eternal Spirit, and the interrelationships of those ministries, is clearly an unsettled theme of theological inquiry and spiritual reflection.[32] Perhaps this is because key biblical texts themselves, such as Gen. 1:1ff. and Ps. 33:6, are so compact; they do not offer clear insights into this question.[33] Nevertheless, this is a subject that wants to be addressed thoughtfully, if at all possible, in order to foster the integration and empowerment of the spiritual life. For me, it is spiritually reassuring and enlightening to know that, notwithstanding all of the ambiguities, we *can* rely on the hands of God working together in cosmic history and then have some sense for what that coworking means.

How, then, to imagine the complementary cosmic ministries of the Son and the Spirit, of the Good Shepherd and the Lifegiving One? Perhaps the best way to envision an answer to this question, in the context of our narrative here, is to recall once again the second of the three roughly hewn analogies for the Trinity—the image of the powerful torrential flow, with the vision of Niagara Falls concretely in mind. All flows from Lake Erie, the motherly Father. Eternally, the Father is the Giver, without ceasing, indeed with constant increasing. Then the cosmic ministries of the Son and the Spirit come into view, the Gift and the Giving.

Akin to the cliffs of the Niagara Gorge, the Son holds all things together, in their current state and in their re-creation, as they flow forward in the currents of creation history. The Son channels all things. The Son's work is to form and re-form, to hold every creature in being and in new being, whenever that is fitting, and always to bear with them, upholding all creatures, especially those that suffer. Then, finally, when the consummation arrives, the Son makes it possible for all things to have new being eternally, in the bosom of the Father.[34]

But when creatures variously begin to lose their identity along the way, ravished by the principalities and powers of death in this world, the forming and re-forming ministry of the Son always becomes a costly ministry of self-sacrifice. Here, the third analogy of the Trinity as the self-sacrificing savior has its meanings to add to our discussion. The realization of new forms of life in the Son often means that the Son is battered and deformed in the process. But the end of such engagement with change and destruction and conflict is indeed new life in the Son.

If the work of the Son is akin to the walls of the Niagara Gorge, the work of the Spirit is akin to the turbulence of the waters below the Falls. In a process that at times is chaotic and at other times is replete with eddies of peace, the Spirit moves things forward toward Lake Ontario, toward the future of God, with energy, power, and vitality. The Spirit destabilizes. The Spirit draws all creatures forward from their present state of being, sometimes in collision with one another, sometimes in conjunction with one another, sometimes slowly, sometimes instantaneously. The Spirit enhances and expands the diversity and the complexity of all of the creatures. The Spirit draws forth the becoming of creation history as a whole. The Spirit hovers creatively over the immensely and incomprehensibly complex currents of cosmic history at every level, from the most minute of cosmic particles to the colossal flow of the galaxies. That, envisioned all too briefly, is the cosmic ministry of the Spirit, the Lifegiving One.

In this way, analogically, we can imagine the two hands of the Father—the cosmic Good Shepherd and the cosmic Lifegiving One—working hand in hand in a richly complementary fashion throughout the course of God's history with the whole creation, constantly establishing the being and constantly eliciting the becoming of all things. This way, too, we can join an ancient tradition of

Christian reflection, predicated on Genesis 1, which gives us this image. We witness the Spirit of God presiding over a majestic and mysterious world that is constantly coming into being, and the word of God speaking in order to give that history innumerable tangible and complexly interrelated forms and to hold all those formed things together as one cosmic whole: "In the beginning when God created the heavens and the earth, the earth was a formless void and darkness covered the face of the deep, while the spirit of God swept over the face of the waters. Then God *said* [spoke the word] . . ." (Gen. 1:1-3a). And then follows the majestic account of the coming-into-being of all the creatures, day by day, each in its own particular form (Gen. 1:3b-2:3).

The contemporary physicist-theologian John Polkinghorne has helpfully recapitulated such ancient meanings this way: "The Father is the fundamental ground of creation's being, while the Word is the source of creation's deep order and the Spirit is ceaselessly at work within the contingencies of open history. The fertile interplay of order and openness, operating at the edge of chaos, can be seen to reflect the activities of the Word and Spirit, the two divine Persons that Irenaeus called 'the hands of God.'"[35]

In the words of the apostle Paul, we do indeed only "see through a glass darkly." A mystical saying of the Christian tradition that I have cited more than once is also most certainly true in this context as elsewhere: "everything comes to rest in mystery" (*omnia exeunt in mysterium*). Faith may seek understanding (*fides quaerens intellectum*), but faith, in this temporal epoch of God's cosmic history, never achieves more than fragmentary understandings. Faith must therefore again and again come to rest, along the way, in praise. Such is our pilgrimage in this narrative, where the *cantus firmus* is always this, the second part of the Trinity Prayer: *Praise Father, Son, and Holy Spirit.* Praise, which presupposes but which also far surpasses understanding, is the heart of any Christian spirituality.[36]

Notes

1. Irenaeus, *Against the Heresies*, 4.20.1-3: "[God] has two hands, for from the beginning He has had at His side the Word and Wisdom, the Son and the Holy Spirit. It is through Them and in Them that He has done everything freely and independently."

2. I am working with the *image* suggested by Irenaeus here. I am not attempting to draw on, and certainly not to reproduce, Irenaeus's own use of the image. For the latter, see M. C. Steenberg, *Irenaeus on Creation: The Cosmic Christ and the Saga of Redemption* (Boston: Brill, 2008), especially 61–100.

3. Between the first and the fourth centuries, the figure of the good shepherd carrying a lamb or a sheep on his shoulders and with two other sheep at his side appears in no fewer than eighty-eight known frescoes. A unique fresco of this kind during this era shows a shepherd

milking a sheep. The same theme was vividly narrated by St. Perpetua at the turn of the third century while she was in prison awaiting martyrdom. There she had what was in all likelihood both an eschatological and a eucharistic vision of an immense garden, in the center of which she saw the tall figure of an old man in the dress of a shepherd, milking a sheep. She reported: "Raising his head, he looked at me and said, 'Welcome, my daughter.' And he called me to him and he gave me of the milk. I received it with joined hands and partook of it. And all those standing around cried 'Amen.' And at the sound of the voice I awoke, tasting an indescribable sweetness in my mouth." The image of Christ as the good shepherd then shaped Christian experience in many tangible ways throughout the ages, in terms of iconography, mystical piety, and hymnody, especially by the invocation of the moving cadences of Psalm 23.

4. "The Lord's My Shepherd," in *Evangelical Lutheran Worship* (Minneapolis: Augsburg Fortress, 2006), 778.

5. See Jürgen Moltmann, A *Broad Place: An Autobiography*, trans. Margaret Kohl (Minneapolis: Fortress Press, 2009), 203: "Christ is there wherever in his name the gospel is proclaimed, people are baptized, and his Supper is celebrated. That is the *manifest* church. But Christ is also in the place where the poor, the hungry, the sick, and the prisoners are to be found: 'As you did it to one of the least of these my brethren, you did it to me.' That is the *latent* church. In the manifest church, 'he who hears you hears me.' In the latent church, 'whoever visits them, visits me.' Here Christ sends—there Christ awaits, and the community of Christ stands between the Christ who sends it and the Christ who awaits it."

6. See further the discussion in H. Paul Santmire, "So That He Might Fill All Things: Comprehending the Cosmic Love of Christ," *Dialog* 42, no. 3 (2003): 257–78. For a short introduction to some of the historical roots of Christian thinking about the cosmic Christ, see Jaroslav Pelikan, *Jesus through the Centuries: His Place in the History of Culture* (New Haven, CT: Yale University Press, 1985), chap. 5 ("The Cosmic Christ"). For a pioneering and still instructive twentieth-century statement of cosmic Christology, see Joseph Sittler, *Essays on Nature and Grace* (Minneapolis: Fortress Press, 1972).

7. Russell Bradner Norris Jr., "Logos Christology as Cosmological Paradigm," *Pro Ecclesia* 5, no. 2 (Spring 1996): 189f.

8. See the discussion by Raymond E. Brown, *The Gospel according to John, I-XII* (Garden City, NY: Doubleday, 1966), app. 4 (EGO EIMI—"I AM"), 533–38.

9. For a survey of the rich symbolism of "the shepherd" in biblical times, much of that symbolism having royal, even cosmic meanings, see the article by Joachim Jeremias in *Theological Dictionary of the New Testament*, ed. Gerhard Friedrich, trans. and ed. Geoffrey W. Bromiley, 6 (Grand Rapids, MI: Eerdmans, 1968), 485–502.

10. See these words of Luther's commentary on the first chapter of John: "God the Father initiated and executed the creation of all things through the Word; and he now continues to preserve His creation through the Word, and that forever and ever. . . . Hence, as heaven, earth, sun, moon, stars, man, and all living things were created in the beginning through the Word, so they are wonderfully governed and preserved through that Word. . . . How long, do you suppose, would the sun, the moon, the entire firmament keep to the course maintained for so many thousands of years? Or how would the sun rise or set year after year at the same time in the same place if God, its Creator, did not continue to sustain it daily? If it were not for the divine power, it would be impossible for mankind to be fruitful and beget children; the beasts could not bring forth their young, each after its own kind, as they do every day; the earth would not be rejuvenated each year, producing a variety of fruit; the ocean would not supply fish. . . . If God were to withdraw His hand, this building and everything in it would collapse. . . . The sun would not long retain its position and shine in the heavens; no child would be born; no kernel, no blade of grass, nothing at all would grow on the earth or reproduce itself if God did not work forever and ever. . . . Daily we can see the birth into this world of new human beings, young children who were nonexistent before; we behold new trees, new animals on the earth, new fish in the water, new birds in the air. And such creation and preservation will continue until the Last Day" (Martin

Luther, "Sermons on the Gospel of John," *Luther's Works* [hereafter *LW*], ed. Jaroslav Pelikan et al. [St. Louis: Concordia, 1957], 22:12.) [AU: add applicable date info?—sh]

11. See Jürgen Moltmann, *The Way of Jesus Christ: Christology in Messianic Dimensions*, trans. Margaret Kohl (Minneapolis: Augsburg Fortress, 1990), 290f.: "God preserves his creation from corruption because, and inasmuch as, he has patience with what he has created. His patience creates time for his creatures. His longsuffering leaves them space. His patience, which is prepared to suffer, and his waiting forbearance are virtues of his hope for the turning back and the homecoming of his creatures to the kingdom of his glory."

12. *LW* 29:112 ("Lectures on Titus, Philemon, and Hebrews"). Among other texts Luther cites in this connection are Isa. 46:3-4 ("Hearken to me, O house of Jacob, and all the remnant of the house of Israel, who are carried by my bowels, and who are borne by my womb. Even to your old age I am he, and to gray hairs I will carry you. I have made, and I will bear; I will carry and I will save.") and Num. 11:12 ("Did I conceive all this people, that thou shouldst say to me: 'Carry them in your bosom, as the nurse is wont to carry the sucking child?'").

13. This theological affirmation presupposes a single universe. If, however, there are in fact many universes, as proposed by a few cosmological physicists, then the statement's scope would have to be extended to a theologically affirmed ending of what would then be our "multiverse." On the other hand, many natural scientists have, for now, concluded that the theory of many universes is suspect, for a variety of reasons. See the summary statement by the Australian philosopher of science Paul Davies, "A Brief History of the Multiverse," *New York Times*, April 12, 2003, A19.

14. For this material, see Santmire, "So That He Might Fill All Things."

15. See the comment of Elizabeth A. Johnson, *Women, Earth, and Creator Spirit* (New York: Paulist, 1993), 19, and the literature she cites: "In unusually colorful language, theologians today describe the Spirit as the forgotten God, something faceless, shadowy, ghostly, vague, the poor relation in the Trinity, the unknown or half-known God, even the Cinderella of theology." As Johnson implies, however, our own era in Western Christian theology has witnessed a flourishing of interest in the Holy Spirit. This has gone hand in hand with the renewal of interest in the theology of the Trinity during the same years. An example of the recent heightened interest in the Spirit is Jürgen Moltmann, *God in Creation: A New Theology of Creation and the Spirit of God*, trans. Margaret Kohl (San Francisco: Harper and Row, 1985). For a more concise approach from the perspective of spirituality, see Lois Malcolm, *Holy Spirit: Creative Power in Our Lives* (Minneapolis: Augsburg Fortress, 2009). The best single systematic treatment of the Spirit and nature is the compact but accessible study by Denis Edwards, *Breath of Life: A Theology of the Creator Spirit* (Maryknoll, NY: Orbis, 2004).

16. The Spirit, of course, is irrepressible. This is one of the reasons, evidently, for the emergence of the so-called "Spiritual Franciscans" as one of the offshoots of the ministry of St. Francis in the thirteenth century and also for the birth and expansion of the Pentecostal churches in our own era, to mention only two of the many historic Christian movements that have self-consciously defined themselves primarily in terms of the works of the Holy Spirit. But it would take me much too far afield to begin to assess these developments, all arising at the edges of the mainstream Christian tradition in the West.

17. Johnson, *Women, Earth, and Creator Spirit*.

18. Johnson, *Women, Earth, and Creator Spirit*, 18f.:

> A certain cosmic alienation accompanies the sexism that pervades classic Christian spirituality and theology. As material and therefore feminine, nature, the body, sexuality, and women are of themselves separated from the sphere of the sacred. Man alone bears the fullness of the image of God, while women only deficiently so, and nature not at all. . . . The path to holiness is marked "Flee the world." To be holy one must escape the prison of the flesh and its transitory desires and seek a higher world where passion and finitude are overcome. The trivialization of nature is the

background against which Christian life, from the spirituality of the individual to the social life of the institution, is shaped by the dualistic legacy of soul over body, man over woman, and God over the world. In every case, it is the dualistically conceived masculine principle *ueber alles*. The influence of this massive heritage sheds some light on the particular neglect of the Holy Spirit in Western Christianity... [So it is that] when most of us say God, the Holy Spirit never comes immediately to mind; rather, the Spirit seems like an edifying appendage to the doctrine of God.

19. Johnson, *Women, Earth, and Creator Spirit*, 42–51.

20. Johnson, *Women, Earth, and Creator Spirit*, 42.

21. Johnson, *Women, Earth, and Creator Spirit*, 42.

22. Johnson, *Women, Earth, and Creator Spirit*, 43.

23. For this theme, see the succinct discussion by Jürgen Moltmann, *The Source of Life: The Holy Spirit and the Theology of Life*, trans. Margaret Kohl (Minneapolis: Fortress Press, 1997), 15f.

24. This word is usually translated "hovers." But Theodore Hiebert has adopted this stronger, more dynamic translation: "sweeps over" ("Air, the First Sacred Thing: The Conception of *Ruach* in the Hebrew Scriptures," in *Ecological Hermeneutics*, ed. Norman Habel and Peter Trudinger [Atlanta: Society of Biblical Literature, 2008], 15.)

25. Johnson, *Woman, Earth, and Creator Spirit*, 44.

26. For this material, see F. W. Horn, "The Holy Spirit," *The Anchor Bible Dictionary*, ed. David Noel Freedman (New York: Doubleday, 1992), 3:260–80.

27. Johnson, *Woman, Earth, and Creator Spirit*, 45.

28. Johnson, *Woman, Earth, and Creator Spirit*, 45.

29. Johnson, *Woman, Earth, and Creator Spirit*, 47.

30. Johnson, *Woman, Earth, and Creator Spirit*, 49.

31. There are at least two traditional points of departure for many recent discussions of this question. The first is Irenaeus in the second century—for example, this statement in his *Demonstration of the Apostolic Teaching*, trans. J. A. Robinson (London: MacMillan, 1920), chap. 5, cited by Celia E. Deane-Drummond, *Creation through Wisdom: Theology and the New Biology* (Edinburgh: T&T Clark, 2000), 125: "In this way it is shown that there is one God, the Father, uncreated, invisible, the creator of all, above whom there is not other God and after whom there is no other God. And because God is rational, he therefore created what is made by his Word, and as God is Spirit, so he disposed everything by his Spirit, just as the prophet says: 'By the word of the Lord the heavens were established, and all their power by his Spirit' (Psalm 33:6). Therefore, since the Word establishes, that is gives body and substance, but the Spirit disposes and shapes the variety of powers, the Son is rightly called Word, while the Spirit is called the Wisdom of God." M. C. Steenberg, *Irenaeus on Creation: The Cosmic Christ and the Saga of Redemption* (Boston: Brill, 2008), 65, summarizes Irenaeus's meaning here in this way: "The Father is he 'of whom' are all things, the Son he 'by whom' are all things, and the Spirit the 'furnisher' of all creation. There is but a single creation wrought by the three, worked differently by each yet unitedly as the one God the Father initiating the one economy through his two hands." The second frequently cited statement about the works of the Son and the Spirit is by Basil of Caesarea in the fourth century in *On the Holy Spirit*, 38 (PG 32, 136B), quoted by Jürgen Moltmann, "The Spirit of Life," in *The Spirit in Creation and New Creation: Science and Theology in Western and Orthodox Realms*, ed. Michael Welker (Grand Rapids, MI: Eerdmans, 2012), 66: "Behold in the creation of these beings the Father as the preceding cause, the Son as the One who createth, and the Spirit as the perfecter; so that the ministering spirits have their beginning in the will of the Father, are brought into being through the efficacy of the Son, and are perfected through the aid of the Spirit."

32. The reader who is ready to deal with the sometimes abstract language of systematic theology and who is particularly interested in exploring how the "two hands of God," the Son and the Spirit, can be thought of as doing their own distinct works in the triune God's history with the

creation can do no better than to consult the compact discussion by David H. Kelsey, *Eccentric Existence: A Theological Anthropology* (Louisville, KY: Westminster John Knox, 2009), vol. 1, chap. 3A, 120–31.

33. See Norman C. Habel, "Geophany: The Earth Story in Genesis 1," in *The Earth Story in Genesis*, ed. Norman C. Habel and Shirley Wurst (Cleveland: Pilgrim, 2000), 40: "The process of creation is introduced in [Genesis] 1:3 with the words of a voice, 'And *Elohim* said. . . .' The primordial setting of the story introduced the presence of *Elohim* in the form of a breath or spirit. In 1:3 the breath of *Elohim* becomes the voice or word of *Elohim*. As in Ps. 33:6, the word and the breath are alternative images to express the presence of God as a creating power; they are two modes of God as Creator. *Elohim* hidden as a breath in the darkness is now revealed as a word that splits the silence and begins to transform the primordial."

34. For those who wish to delve more reflectively into the theme of the complementary cosmic workings of the Son and the Spirit, a good place to begin would be to review the discussion by Christopher Southgate, *The Groaning of Creation: God, Evolution, and the Problem of Evil* (Louisville, KY: Westminster John Knox, 2008), 60–66. Southgate adopts and adapts motifs from traditional Christian thought about the Son, as the Word or *Logos* of all things, which gives every creature, as it were, its own *logos* structure. The Spirit of God, in turn, for Southgate, is the divine power that draws all things forward to new configurations of being and finally to their eternal consummation. Southgate instructively gives expression to this understanding in the language of evolutionary biology: "The works of the 'two hands' of the Father in creation both draws onward the ever-shifting distribution of peaks in the fitness landscape, through the unfolding creative work of the Logos, and encourage organisms, through the power of the Spirit, in their exploration of that landscape, give rise to new possibilities of being a self" (61).

35. John Polkinghorne, *Science and The Trinity: The Christian Encounter with Reality* (New Haven, CT: Yale University Press, 2009), 81.

36. Augustine suggestively worked out the dynamics of what might be called a theology of praise. See the essay by James K. A. Smith, "Between Predication and Silence: Augustine on How (Not) to Speak of God," *Heythrop Journal* 41, no. 1 (January 2000): 66–86. Smith shows that Augustine identified a "third way" of theological knowing, between the extremes of not-knowing (apophatics) and knowing-too-much (kataphatics). This is Augustine, as cited by Smith (67): "And yet, while nothing really worthy of God can be said about [God], he has accepted the homage of human voices, and has wished us to rejoice in praising him with our words" (Augustine, *Teaching Christianity* 1.6.6.). Smith calls this Augustine's "laudatory strategy" (68). For a contemporary theological vision predicated on praise, see Geoffrey Wainwright, *Doxology: The Praise of God in Worship, Doctrine and Life—A Systematic Theology* (New York: Oxford University Press, 1980).

PART IV

Calling on the Holy Spirit

Come Holy Spirit, Come and Reign.

9

Calling on the Holy Spirit
The Integrity and the Travail of Nature

In the words of the popular gospel song, we've come this far by faith. In part 1, we considered the journey before us as well as what it can mean to scythe with God, to practice the Trinity Prayer, and to face the eclipse of God with a fragile faith. In part 2, I invited you to ponder with me the meanings of this petition of the Trinity Prayer: *Lord Jesus Christ, have mercy on me.* I asked you, in particular, to consider the revelation of God in these twilight times and the light of Christ in our midst, and then to reflect about the ambiguous case of one who prays to Jesus. That then led us, in part 3, to the stance of praise: to engage some meanings of the acclamation *Praise Father, Son, and Holy Spirit.* In those chapters, we explored the experience of contemplating the triune God in Godself, the presence of this God in, with, and under all things, and the cosmic ministries of the two hands of the same God: Jesus Christ and the Holy Spirit.

As we now enter part 3, and the final chapters of these explorations, we move from the spiritual stance of *praise* back to the spiritual stance with which we first began our consideration of the Trinity Prayer itself, *petition*, in the strict sense of that word, letting our "requests be made known to God" (Phil. 4:6). We do so with these words before us: *Come Holy Spirit, come and reign.*

I am not sure when this petition first dawned on me as a fitting conclusion for the Christian mantra that I had for some years been thinking of as the Trinity Prayer. Petitions calling the Holy Spirit to *come* were quite familiar to me from my younger years, such as Luther's great hymn, "Come, Holy Ghost, God and Lord." But such calls to the Spirit almost without exception focused on the believer's life or the life of the church more generally, not on the whole created world. As Luther wrote in that hymn: "Come Holy Ghost, God and Lord, / With all your graces now outpoured / On each believer's mind and

187

heart; / Your fervent love to them impart."[1] To my knowledge, only rarely have the church's hymns accented the cosmic ministry of the Spirit.[2] A 1978 hymn by James K. Manley addressing the Spirit is a notable exception: "You moved on the waters, / you called to the deep, / then you coaxed up the mountains / from the valleys of sleep; / and over the eons / you called to each thing;/ 'Awake from your slumbers/ and rise on your wings.'"[3]

COMING TO KNOW THE COSMIC SPIRIT

I myself had been an unconscious heir of that tradition of Western Christian theology and spirituality that in accent had focused on the individual believer or the Christian community as the primary milieu of the Spirit's ministry, as Luther did in his hymn "Come Holy Ghost, God and Lord." I have already discussed the theological and spiritual eclipse of the Spirit in the Christian West more generally. Here, I want to recall how *I* made the transition from that kind of focus on the believer and the community of believers to understand the Spirit more universally, more cosmically. When I now pray "Come Holy Spirit, come and reign," I am envisioning the Spirit coming to all creatures, moving on the waters, calling to the deep, coaxing up the mountains, calling to each thing. I have only recently come to realize *how* in fact I moved—or was moved—from the narrow and, if the truth be spoken, anthropocentric focus on the Spirit that I had inherited in the middle years of the past century to the cosmic vision that I now wholeheartedly espouse. In retrospect, I think that there were two spiritual factors that influenced me the most in this respect.

The first was my longstanding intuition, predicated on my own experience of God in nature, that God has God's own purposes with the world of nature as well as with the world of human history. I had taken it for granted, ever since I began to think about such things, that nature has its own meaning in the greater scheme of things, that it is not just a platform put in place by God so that God could have a history with human creatures.

Already before my teens, I myself had a life of my own life with nature, as I assumed that God Godself did. As a boy, I used to wander in solitude in the large fields and orchards near my home in exurban Buffalo. I would contemplate the redwing blackbirds flying over nearby small ponds, listen to and sometimes see the bullfrogs among the cattails in those ponds, come upon and marvel at—but not disturb—pheasant nests well hidden in the fields, and overturn stones in the flowing waters of the creek that fed the ponds, in order to discover elegantly tiny, lobster-like crayfish. These were the years, too, when

I was intensely involved in family gardening and in traveling with my family to a number of America's great national parks. I do not know when I first heard nature referred to as "the cathedral of the great outdoors," but that was how I entered into nature in those younger years. So, of course, I would later want to say that nature has its own integrity, once I had the language and the occasion to do that.

The second intuition that prepared the way for me to contemplate the full cosmic ministry of the Spirit—an intuition similarly predicated on my own experience of God in nature—was this: the whole world of nature is going somewhere. Call this a nascent eschatological intuition. It never dawned on me to think otherwise, because I was so sure of God's love for the whole world and of God's love for all the creatures of nature in particular. Would God ever abandon the cathedral of the great outdoors? That thought never crossed my mind. But it was only during the years of my theological study that I learned how to give voice to that intuition, instructed most directly by the then-emerging writings of Jürgen Moltmann, beginning with his *Theology of Hope*.[4] I had to wait for his later, more ecological writings to come, but when they then did, I read them avidly. Of particular interest to me along the way was how Moltmann developed his theology of the Spirit in correlation with his ecological and eschatological interests.[5]

That was how my passion for the coming of the Spirit cosmically, and my concern to identify and to champion what I regularly began to call the integrity of nature, unfolded in my own experience, already as a young pastor and aspiring theologian. This direction of my own spirituality also led me then, as it still does, to be poised to take strong issue with an alternative spirituality, historically championed by those who have been called gnostics. I will describe gnostic spirituality later in this chapter. All along, moreover, I found myself constantly wrestling with the challenge of interpreting one of the key texts for any Christian spirituality of nature, where the Spirit also comes to the fore: Paul's reference to the groaning of the whole creation in Romans 8. I will consider that Pauline text at length in this chapter. But in order to explore these themes with you, I first want to take you to a place of spiritual knowing once again.

CALLING ON THE HOLY SPIRIT: A PLACE OF KNOWING

I have in mind the place where I began these explorations, "in the middle of things" (*in media res*), Hunts Corner, but not again the field where I scythe, nor the perennial and vegetable gardens between the field and our house, where Laurel and I labor constantly and joyfully during the summer months. I want to guide you to "the Hidden Garden," a separate place, as the name suggests, set off from the house and the other gardens by a wide swath of goldenrod, glorious when in bloom in the fall, separated from the field beyond by a stand of trees and by the small stream that runs along the near side of the field. The Hidden Garden was Laurel's inspiration more than two decades ago, and I have been smitten by that inspiration with increasing excitement over the years. It is here that I have learned, perhaps more than any other place I know, to call upon the Holy Spirit, which is the theme of this and the following chapters.

By any mundane reckoning, the Hidden Garden just happened. Both of us, preoccupied over the years not just with the field and the other gardens but with raising our children and caring for the house, and with only limited time and resources, just stood in awe of "the great goldenrod field" with the meadowsweet brambles behind it. We never really explored that area early on. We were not even sure that it belonged to us. Then came the time when we purchased more land in the forest to the north and had our property surveyed for the first time. To our amazement, the great goldenrod field, the meadowsweet brambles, and the whole stand of ash saplings behind it were on *our* land. We immediately resolved to get to know the place better.

After that process was well under way, Laurel imagined what the Hidden Garden might be. Her premise was this: clear some space for walking in a kind of oval pattern, and see what might grow at the edges of that space, keeping long established plants, wherever possible, and adding native plantings here and there, none of which would require constant attention, unlike the other gardens. She also made sure that the space was indeed hidden when we laid it out. It could not be seen from the house. The way to enter the Hidden Garden was circuitous, so that the entrance itself was hidden. It had to be approached from below, after walking along the tree-lined stream.

One of the first things we did was plant some highbush cranberry shoots, which I had, rather unceremoniously, yanked from the edge of a great mother bush in an abandoned field down the road. They would be the back border, if they grew. They did. They are now over twelve feet tall, and we have made jelly from their berries over the years. We also added some aromatic lilacs and viburnums and a mock-orange bush to continue the back line. But the big challenge, right from the start, was removing the meadowsweet brambles, a tough project that took several years.

Meanwhile, Laurel set in a number of native plants at the edges of the oval space that was opening up. She gathered lupine seed stalks from all over our land, for example, and, over time, patches of that iconic flower of Maine claimed their own places. We ripped out an old rose bush in a back corner of our field and planted it there; it flourished, as did the several stalks of rugosa roses that we uprooted from behind a stop sign somewhere. To this, Laurel added two wood phlox plants, which produce gorgeous, feathery purple and white flowers in the spring; those plants, thankfully, spread like a wildfire. She also planted other "orphans," some stalks of anchusa, which offer tiny blue flowers throughout the summer and which our daughter found along a deserted rural road, and stalks of penstemons, with tiny yellow flowers and rich maroon leaves, which a gardener in Connecticut once gave us. Both are now flourishing. Then there's the effervescent, pale yellow, bell-flowered foxglove plants that Laurel added to those already there. I also found a place in the shade for two dark-leaved joe-pyeweeds and for some delicate porteranthus plants, with their fine white flowers, all of which are now well established.

As the oval space of the Hidden Garden thus began to become a real garden, and once most of the meadowsweet brambles had been removed, I began to mow that area, some thirty feet wide and sixty feet long. On its own, it became a lawn. All this miraculous greenery, with its multitude of lovely seasonal flowers, tucked around that oval grass space behind the sloping field of goldenrod, basically has taken care of itself over the years, except for a few occasions when we felt called upon to water some seedlings. Once that garden began to blossom, moreover, and the saplings that we originally found there on the far side grew into a small woodlot, we would also witness visitations by a variety of flying creatures, like the hummingbirds and the goldfinches, and the butterflies, such as the monarchs, which sought out the milkweed blossoms here and there.

Laurel's greatest inspiration, however, was yet to come. We would have a swing, a framed wooden garden swing, with a lattice top. But nowhere, in Massachusetts, New Hampshire, or Maine could we find one. One day, while we were driving through the rolling farmlands of northeast Ohio, where we had once lived for eight years, we saw a sign, "Amish Home and Garden Furniture." And there we found Laurel's solid wood swing, with its lattice top. Without a single practical thought, we bought that gracious swing on the spot and had it shipped to Hunts Corner. Later, Laurel planted yellow roses, blue clematis, and a honeysuckle bush around the swing. The honeysuckle has by now grown over the top lattice of the swing, providing shade as well as the beauty of its orange-colored blossoms.

It was my inspiration to extend Laurel's vision from the swing at the top end of the Hidden Garden and the flowers and other plants along the sides. As we sat together on the swing one summer day in the late afternoon, as by then had become our wont, once the blackfly season was over, I looked down the Hidden Garden lawn and saw something that we had not seen before—a vista. Or, rather, the prospect of a vista. Soon thereafter, I cut down a few ash and birch saplings beyond the lower end of the oval and then sawed down two hefty low-hanging branches, each from the two towering old white pines at the edge of the creek. When we thereafter lolled on the swing and caught sight of the variegated flowers, left and right, those magnificent pine trees framed our vista perfectly while we looked down at the stream and the field, where I did my scything, to the forest beyond.

And there is more. Once, when Laurel and I had been walking in the Mt. Auburn arboretum, I told her that the several-hundred-year-old purple beeches that grew there communicated the presence of God to me like no other trees. She said that we should find a way to plant one by the Hidden Garden in Maine. And so we did. It had to be special ordered from a nursery in southern Massachusetts and delivered by truck to Hunts Corner. We planted it at the lower edge of the Hidden Garden, where it would also help to frame the vista, in line with one of the great white pines farther down by the stream. It was some fifteen feet tall then, and now it is more than twice that height.

To keep things symmetrical with the two monumental white pines at edge of the stream, during one winter I chopped out the rootball of a sizable American beech from our forest, dragged it across the frozen field, and, with a pickax, planted it opposite the purple beech in line with the second of the great white pines down at the stream. Miraculously, that so rudely treated tree flourished. We thus are blessed with a marvelously framed—and, to me, mystical—vista anytime we sit on that Amish wooden swing in the Hidden Garden and lift up our eyes toward the forest on the other side of the field.

Do notice, too, the two very much embodied souls on that swing. Luther once observed that the greatest glory of Adam and Eve in the Garden of Eden was the fact that they walked around naked. We are always fully clothed, but I think I know what Luther meant. There was a time when Laurel was a shapely young wife and I was a muscular young husband who could carry her across the marriage threshold when she wanted me to do so. In our elder years, we still will drive on occasion to Maurice's French Restaurant in the thriving western Maine metropolis of South Paris for a truly elegant candlelight dinner and then head back to Hunts Corner to put on some Bach and dance the night away. We love our bodies, clothed or unclothed. True, we are closer to the peasant-stock embodiment that Luther would have recognized, say, Duerer's "Adam and Eve," than to the classical ideal of Michelangelo's "David" or Titian's

"Venus Rising from the Sea." And we have had to learn about our embodied particularities and peculiarities over the course of more than forty years of marriage, not without some serious stress here and there.

But we still hold hands on our walks and, often, on that swing. Perhaps more than ever in these our later years, we are at home in our bodies and at home in our bodies with each other. This may be all the more so the case when one of us falls ill, is disheveled and depressed, and then is cared for by the other. I happen to think that Laurel has the most beautiful smile in the world, under any conditions, as when she woke up from a two-day coma several years ago in the aftermath of a stroke and brightly greeted one of our then-young grandchildren, who was at that moment snuggling with her in her hospital bed. Laurel was radiant at that moment, as she has been many other times in my memory. Her embodiment and mine, I do believe, with Luther, is our greatest glory before God.

And there is still more. As I was wandering in the garden section of a Boston Home Depot store one day, I spied a number of sizable garden figurines, a large frog, some putti, and the inevitable statues of St. Francis, each one with a bird on his shoulder, all made of concrete. As I was passing by, disparaging in my mind the cheap consumerism of much of America's garden pieties, I noticed a small pile of what appeared to me to be Celtic crosses. I pounced on one of them, held it in my hand, and marveled at it. I had written about the great and towering historic Celtic crosses, and they had become important to me spiritually as testimony to the cosmic Christ, the circle around the arms of the cross representing the whole cosmos, I had come to believe.[6] So I immediately purchased that foot-tall concrete cross (for $15.98!) and took it to Hunts Corner, where, once we had found a large field stone as a background, we placed it under the arms of the purple beech, where it stands to this day.

One day, that area will be a memorial plot for us. In recent years, Laurel and I have on occasion talked about our mortality, particularly where we would want to be buried. It did not take us long to come to this conclusion. Our bodies are to be cremated, and we have asked our children to dig our ashes into the soil around that Celtic cross. I was ecstatic when we made that decision, because many of the early medieval Celtic saints, whose stories have been so important to me, thought of their own pilgrimages, whether in uncharted wildernesses or on tumultuous seas, as taking them to "the place of [their] resurrection."

This is what I believe. As Laurel and I glide back and forth on that swing, holding hands, surrounded by the fecund beauties of that Hidden Garden, and contemplating the vista of the tree-lined stream, the field, and the forest beyond, all framed by the purple beech and the American beech and the great pines, we are also contemplating, in that Celtic cross and the earth around it, the place of our resurrection. And, of course, it dawned on me along the way that Jesus himself had been buried and then resurrected, according to the testimony of the Gospels—in a garden. Is it surprising, then, for me to harbor this thought deeply? There is nowhere else in this world that I would rather be, at any given time, than to be swinging with Laurel in the Hidden Garden, contemplating the flowers and the framed vista beyond, but focusing all the more so on that Celtic cross on the earth beneath the purple beech, the place of our resurrection.

And what does the Spirit have to do with all this? I would like to tell you now.

THE SPIRIT AND THE SONG OF ALL THE CREATURES: THE INTEGRITY OF NATURE VERSUS A SPIRITUALITY OF COSMIC DESPAIR

Once, Laurel and I went to a popular "Messiah-Sing" at the Wellesley College Chapel. The soloists and the instrumentalists were accomplished musicians, but most of the rest of us were not. That performance of selections from Handel's stirring work was passable, but the image was, for me, unforgettable. This is what I remember: the conductor facing this "cast of thousands" in the eleven-hundred-seat chapel and presiding over a by no means professional performance, and all the rest of us responding as best we could but with great enthusiasm.

With this image in mind, come with me again to the Hidden Garden. Think of Laurel and me, moving forward and back on the swing, as participants in a great ensemble, with the Holy Spirit as the divine conductor. This is a wonderfully apt metaphor. I have in mind here not so much the sounds of that garden, as we usually think of them—the wind in the branches of the trees, the hum of the honey bees in the goldenrod field, the song of the phoebe emanating from a tree somewhere, the rhythmic squeaking of the swing's chains on the hooks in the trellis above, or the beating of our own hearts—but the baton in the hand of the divine conductor, which coordinates and inspires all the members of that great orchestra of variegated creatures in and around the Hidden Garden, including ourselves.

The metaphor also suggests that the creatures of nature do, in some sense, have their own distinct contributions to make.[7] Is it possible to think of the featherly phlox and the hearty honeysuckle and the homely highbush cranberries and the many other plants as having their own voices?[8] Is it possible to think of the huge white pines, likewise, and of the two newer beeches, the lovely purple and the sturdy American, as joining in the hymn of the whole creation, as their torsos and their limbs and finally their needles or leaves rhythmically give expression to their very being and becoming? Is it possible that our own hearts are soft voices in harmony with that whole chorus? I know that Laurel and I can sing God's praises, because we regularly do that on Sundays and at other times. Can I also imagine such a cosmic concert and, indeed, have a feel for that great chorus as I sit there swinging with Laurel? I can. You have to have ears to hear, of course. Let me try to explain.

THE SONG OF ALL THE CREATURES

As I was working on my studies in the theology of nature in the 1960s, I immersed myself in readings in the Psalms. That powerful creation hymn, Psalm 104—which is a kind of poetic commentary on the traditions that were brought together in the Genesis 1 creation narrative—and other Psalms like it of course drew my attention. But I also kept coming back, again and again, to those Psalms that called on the whole world of nature to sing praises to God.[9] One such of these is Psalm 148:1a, 3–5, 7–10:

> Praise the Lord! . . .
> Praise him, sun and moon;
> Praise him, you highest heavens,
> And you waters above the heavens!
> Let them praise the name of the Lord,
> for he commanded and they were created. . . .
> Praise the Lord from the earth,
> you sea monster and all deeps,
> fire and hail, snow and frost,
> stormy wind fulfilling his command!
> Mountains and all hills,
> fruit trees and all cedars!
> Wild animals and all cattle,
> creeping things and flying birds.

In the years when I was beginning to write, most interpreters simply assumed, without much reflection, that such utterances were matters of poetic license or that they presupposed a kind of "primitive" panpsychism. How, after all, could sun or tree or creeping thing really praise God? But scholarly interpretation of such texts has changed, and changed radically, since those days.

In this respect, ironically perhaps, biblical interpreters in our time have been catching up with St. Francis in the thirteenth century and with his magnificent Canticle to Brother Sun in particular, in which Francis calls upon the whole creation to praise God. I am not sure when I first began to drink deeply from the well of Francis's spirituality. But the witness of the Psalms to the song of the whole creation and the conviction of Francis that all things could sing to God, including the least of them, robustly shaped my own developing spirituality as a theological student and my grasp of the biblical understanding of all creatures' praise of God.[10]

Today, a number of scholars who interpret those Psalms of praise talk about *a real relation* between God and the wild animals and all cattle, creeping things and flying birds, when those creatures are said to praise God. Terence Fretheim is perhaps the most persuasive of all these interpreters:

> The language regarding the non-human as subject cannot be reduced to figurative speech, poetic license or worshipful exuberance. Rather, this language of interresponsiveness shows that God's presence to and relationship with the earth and its creatures is more than external; there is an inwardness or interiority characteristic of the earth and its creatures such that a genuine relationship with God exists. To speak this way does not necessarily lead to a panpsychism or vitalism, only that some kind of internal relationship with God is claimed.[11]

While I am grateful for Fretheim's analysis here, I think we can speak much more concretely of such a real relationship between the praising creatures of nature and the hearing God than Fretheim does.

I believe that *God really hears the voices of all creatures*, just as God really hears human voices, albeit not in the same manner.[12] God hears that symphony of sounds resonating from the microscopic dimensions of nature, from the quarks and the electrons and all the rest, to what may well be the cacophony, the atonal music, of the galaxies and the dark holes and even the incomprehensibly vast world of dark matter. How God hears, say, the disappearance of a star into a black hole we surely cannot know—any more than we can know how God hears the sounds of human voices that, in various ways, praise God.

I am suggesting, then, that the construct of "voice" that many theologians and biblical scholars have taken for granted in modern times has been much too narrow. Why not begin with the assumption that every creature, from the most minute to the greatest, is capable of expressing itself exuberantly in a way that God can in some manner hear?[13] Could it not be the case, indeed, that this was what the Psalmist was struggling to express, poetically and more powerfully than I have been able to describe, when the Psalmist sings of the heavens "telling the glory of God" and the firmament proclaiming God's handiwork, while "There is no speech, nor are there words . . . yet their voice goes out through all the earth" (Ps. 19:1-4). Humans do not hear all this cosmic speech pouring forth. God does. All this, of course, is far beyond our understanding, for we were not there, as the Book of Job says, when God established the foundations of the earth (Job 38:4).

Isn't it a kind of anthropocentric arrogance, moreover, to assume that God can hear only human voices? If God is a hearing God for us, does God cease to be a hearing God for other creatures? God surely is personal and so hears *our* praises personally. But, especially in light of the testimony of the Psalms, why would we not want to say that God also hears, in some sense, the nonpersonal "music of the spheres," the voices of the Higgs boson, the mockingbird, or the Milky Way? Isn't it liberating, indeed, to be able to know that when we humans praise God, we are not a solitary species, unlike any other in the known cosmos, but creatures that stand in solidarity with all others? Our voice is distinct, surely, but not solitary. Our voice partakes in the song of the whole creation that praises its joyful and powerful and loving God, each creature as it is individually gifted so to do.

This brings me back to the Hidden Garden. As Laurel and I sit there swinging, I believe, even though we are not able to hear each other's hearts beating, God can and does hear our hearts, just as God in some manner hears the humming of the honey bees and the song of the phoebe and the rustling of the leaves. Beyond this, the Hidden Garden is, of course, more than it appears to be when we swing there. At atomic and subatomic levels, which we do not experience, of course, there are flows of enormous, even explosive energies, stable, thankfully, but still there. At the microbial levels too, there are innumerable wonders, both marvelous and terrible, all of which resonate with a music of their own.

Then there are the times when Laurel and I avoid the Hidden Garden, such as when the mountain storms arrive, with their awesome lightning bolts and thunderclaps. I once got trapped in such a thunderstorm a few miles from the Hidden Garden, along a one-lane dirt road where I had been walking. As I hurried home, driven by fear, not too far from me a lightning bolt hit a large oak and split it nearly in half. Closer to the Hidden Garden, the stream that I so love to contemplate as we sit there on the swing when the weather is pleasant sometimes becomes, in the aftermath of such storms, a roaring and chaotic torrent, threatening to overflow its banks. We have every reason to believe that the Psalmist also assumed that the Lord heard the voices of such storms, as suggested by the previously cited words of Psalm 148:7-8a: "Praise the Lord from the earth you sea monsters and all deeps, fire and hail, snow and frost . . .!"

THE SPIRIT AND THE INTEGRITY OF NATURE

This is where the Holy Spirit, the cosmic conductor of the voices of all the creatures, comes into the picture. As the Lifegiving One, the Holy Spirit is the power of God that elicits, draws forth, and then conducts the universal symphony of all the creatures of God. In the Book of Deuteronomy, God is often spoken of as the one "who goes before you" (e.g., Deut. 1:30). The Holy Spirit, Moltmann has taught us to say, is "the power of the future," the ultimate divine energy that conducts the symphony of all things, calls them to attention, as it were, and enables them then to praise God, each creature with its own voice.

This is one of the reasons why, since the 1960s, I have insisted on speaking of "the integrity of nature." The universal chorus of all the creatures is not somehow of no account or merely a "warm-up act" for the allegedly main players, the human ensemble. The universal chorus of all the creatures, for God, *is* the main act, including humans. Every creature has an essential part to play, not just humans. And the Spirit is the one who elicits and coordinates that universal praise—its harmonies and its dissonances, its tempi, its keys, its sonorities, and its colors—and ultimately presents that universal praise as an offering to God the Father so that the Father might hear and then rejoice. In the words of the Psalmist: "May the Lord rejoice in all his works" (Ps. 104:31). This is the first reason why it is not only possible but also spiritually necessary to affirm the integrity of nature. All creatures, not just humans, have their own voices. The other reason is eschatological; here, also, the Spirit is the one who is the divine conductor.

The Spirit is the power that draws all things into a process that results in new configurations of being.[14] The Spirit is the power of becoming in the universe. The Spirit is a magnetic force that destabilizes all current forms of being, in a myriad of ways and at widely differing times, in order to draw them into their future, where they receive new being in the Son, where ultimately they will receive the consummated new being of the eschatological new heavens and new earth in the Son. The Spirit is the divine energy that calls forth cosmic evolution, at all levels, from the microcosmic to the macrocosmic. More particularly, the Spirit is the hand of God that sculpts the human body, already in the womb, male and female, and every muscle, every limb, every face.

The eminent theologian of science Philip Hefner, has instructively worked with the categories of the natural sciences to describe the diversity of this universal cosmic process, which I believe is elicited by the magnetic power of the Spirit. Hefner calls it "a drama in five acts."[15] This drama begins with the Big Bang, the first emergence of the world of physics and chemistry, the longest chapter of the universe's 13-billion-year history.[16] The other acts take up only a fraction of the time of cosmic evolution. Act two is the biological, the emergence and the diversification of life on planet Earth. Act three Hefner calls ontogeny. By this, he refers to the emergence of the human species, intricately a part of the physical-chemical and biological dimensions of evolution. The emergence of the human brain then makes possible yet another new dimension of the process of cosmic evolution, culture: "Just as physics and chemistry become biology, biology becomes culture in our brains."[17] We humans are thus biology and culture integrally related to the other, in the midst of and part of the vast world described by physics and chemistry.

Act four begins as the bioculture of humans becomes morality. Hefner describes the phenomenon this way: "When we get to culture, we're talking about a realm of human freedom and decision. . . . We make decisions, we correct our mistakes, we innovate, and in fact *construct* our lives as we go along. . . . *Morality enters the evolutionary process because of our thinking and deciding.* . . . Morality is not an outside intrusion into the evolutionary process, it is inherent, part and parcel, of the process."[18]

Act five Hefner thinks of as the emergence of the spiritual: "We must have visions of . . . the values, ideas, symbols, beliefs, stories of something more that go beyond the here and now and tells us what it can become."[19] This is the dimension of cosmic evolution in the midst of which what we know as religion emerges. In this act, Hefner concludes, we humans "are the playwrights, the poets, who must, like the ancient Hebrews, image, describe, and explain a fuller story of evolution."[20] Since Hefner's own spiritual orientation is shaped by biblical traditions, as, in his view, one among many possible spiritual orientations in the terrestrial evolutionary process, he identifies with the spirituality launched by the Hebrews, who championed a vision of a universal process "created on a moral foundation, tempered by divine love and destined for God's final fulfillment."[21]

If this is a plausible way to understand the evolution of our universe, in consonance with the findings of the natural sciences, as I believe it is, then I want to affirm, on the basis of my own fragile faith, that this whole cosmic process is the handiwork of the Holy Spirit, the eliciting power that moves all things forward, working in, with, and under nature's own spontaneity.[22] The Spirit is omni-active, from the long history of matter (physics and chemistry) to the much shorter time span of the emergence of life on planet Earth (biology), the emergence of human life and our brains in particular (ontogeny, culture), then the appearance of the moral and spiritual world of collective human experience (morality, spirituality), and finally, in Christian perspective, the emergence of the history of redemption and the ultimate consummation of that history, comprehending all things (salvation or soteriology and eschatology).

I particularly want to underline the works of the Spirit in the later chapters of this universal ministry of the Spirit in, with, and under the whole creation. In the midst of cosmic evolution generally, and the emergence of life on this planet and of human life in particular, the Spirit also calls forth a vast profusion of religious and spiritual ways in the history of the human creature, all of which surely have their own meanings in the greater scheme of things. In a book like this, however, it would take me much too far afield to explore the highly complicated question of the meaning of Christianity, in particular, among the many religious orientations of our world.[23] So I want to affirm what I know, immersed as I am, and as Hefner is, in biblical traditions.

In the midst of the variegated religious and spiritual traditions of humankind, therefore, allow me to tell you more explicitly how my vision, like Hefner's, has been focused by biblical traditions of salvation history, beginning with the story of the ancient biblical forerunners Abraham and Sarah, a story that eventually culminates in the narrative of the life, death, and resurrection of Jesus Christ and the outpouring of that same Spirit on the community of believers known as the church.

Still, the history of salvation, thus envisioned, is itself just a beginning. The salvational workings of the Spirit do not end in the coming of Christ and the emergence of his body, the church. From that particular point, the Spirit further and finally carries forth all of the acts of the Spirit's cosmic ministry simultaneously—physics, biology, ontogeny, culture, morality, spirituality, *and* the history of salvation—to that great and final day for the whole cosmos, God's new creation of all things.[24]

It also makes spiritual sense to me to imagine in this context—to use a construct that was important for Calvin in his interpretation of the Incarnation—that the Spirit *accommodates* the Spiritself to all of these dimensions of creation history. Biblically speaking, surely, the accommodations of the Spirit seem manifold, from the cosmic creative "hovering" over—as if giving birth to—the primeval waters of chaos depicted in Gen. 1:1, to a power that was not in the fierce storm which rent the mountains, nor in the colossal quaking that shattered the earth, nor in the dramatic fire that we can imagine might have arisen during a mountain thunderstorm. The same Spirit, rather, was in "the still small voice" that later spoke to the prophet Elijah (1 Kings 19:11-13). On the other hand, never mind that still small voice, the Spirit was the power that drove Jesus out into the wilderness (Mark 1:12) and mightily fell upon the disciples on the day of Pentecost, like the rush of a violent wind, as if with tongues of fire (Acts 2:1-3).

Thus I can imagine the Spirit, whom we earlier contemplated as akin to a torrential flow of power, exercising a kind of raw and creative power from the Big Bang to the era when life was about to emerge on planet Earth, and exercising a kind of raw and creative power all the more so in raising Jesus from the dead.[25] At the same time, I can imagine the Spirit accommodating such uses of raw and creative power to a more magnetic and eliciting kind of energy, with the emergence of life on planet Earth and to a still more persuasive and eliciting kind of power, with the emergence of human life, in particular, and then with the beginnings of human religious history and the history of salvation. I can imagine all those kinds of self-accommodation by the Spirit coming into play, finally, from unimaginably overwhelming raw and creative power to the gentlest touch of love and the softest inner voice, when the Spirit one day will consummate all things by calling forth the new heavens and the new earth, dreamed of by biblical prophets and seers.

This eschatological vision of the Spirit's handiwork throughout the cosmic eons further undergirds and explicates the theme that we are focusing on here: the integrity of nature. The world of nature *is* going somewhere! It means something, ultimately. All the creatures of nature have their own purposes given to them by God—which we humans can barely understand, if at all—and therefore all have their own integrity in the greater scheme of things.[26]

And this integrity will one day—think of this as the eighth day of creation—be affirmed eternally, as all the creatures that ever existed, not just humans, will finally be swept into eternity with the arrival of the day of the new heavens and the new earth. To this, I would add a simple speculation. Call it school-boy spiritual naïveté, if you wish. I believe that there will be room for all creatures that ever existed in the history of the creation in that eternal world of God to come, and room to spare, as a matter of fact, because the cosmos that will be renewed eschatologically is already a world of vast infinitudes. Might I add, whimsically, that one recent scientific report estimated that there are at least 17 billion earth-sized planets in the Milky Way alone? Plenty of room for the many millions of trees and flowers of evolutionary history to flourish and for the dinosaurs and ichthyosauruses to feed and frolic and for the myriad of honey bees to sing and dance and for the billions and billions of ants to run and play.

AGAINST THE INTEGRITY OF NATURE: A SPIRITUALITY OF COSMIC DESPAIR

Now, a warning. The integrity of nature is a theme that must be carefully identified and vigorously defended lest the journey we are on in this narrative be thrown off course. From the earliest centuries of Christian conviction to our own time, the integrity of nature has on occasion been neglected, sometimes even rejected outright.[27] Numbers of Christians have been tempted, and some have given in to the temptation, to envision the universal history of God with the creation as fomenting a kind of metaphysical or spiritual ascent, which humans—or some humans—are called to make toward the ethereal heights of pure spirit above, thus leaving "matter," the basic stuff of the created world, behind. Call this a spirituality of cosmic despair, for in this case there is no hope for nature.

This particular story begins publicly with the speculations of some second-century Christians, who were attracted to the spirituality of Gnosticism, between 130 and 190 c.e. Those who followed this way believed that their journey was rightfully leading them up and away from nature, and in particular, up and away from the human body. Indeed, they believed that the whole world of matter is evil and that salvation must therefore entail escape from this allegedly evil created world. They held, more particularly, that the human body is a particularly heinous evil. The same logic, for them, also applied to the material elements of bread and wine and water in the sacraments, to say nothing of the lilies of the field and the birds of the air. Hence, for them, the notion of the integrity of nature would have been a contradiction in terms. The best thing that could happen to the world of nature and to the human body in particular, from their point of view, would be for everything material to be annihilated.

Contested by church leaders like Irenaeus in the second century, the mature Augustine in the fifth century, and Francis in the thirteenth century, the lure of such a cosmic despair has always hovered at the edges of the life of the church. Even today, its influence is evident in some so-called New Age spiritualities[28] and, in a dramatically different way, in the Left Behind spirituality of some forms of apocalyptic Protestantism.[29] Mainstream Protestantism and Roman Catholicism have also been affected.[30] One literary critic of renown has even argued that Gnosticism is the primary popular religion of contemporary American culture.[31]

So the petition "Come Holy Spirit, come and reign" is not only a prayer for the Spirit to get on with the work of moving the whole world of nature into ever-new configurations and complexities of being in the Son, as it draws the cosmos eventually into the era of the new heavens and the new earth in the Son, and not just an affirmation of the integrity of nature at every step along the way. It is also a call to the Spirit to guide us away from the cosmic despair of gnostic spirituality, which has been an existential temptation for those who seek to claim the Christian faith as their own at many points along the way.

THE SPIRIT AND THE GROANING OF THE WHOLE CREATION: THE TRAVAIL OF NATURE AND A SPIRITUALITY OF COSMIC HOPE

Sometimes when I am working in the Hidden Garden by myself, mowing the grass perhaps, I will give myself a break, and go over and sit on the swing and have a drink of water. That is a wonderful place to let my mind wander, even in the midst of strenuous work on a hot day. When my mind turns away from the chores still before me and the other responsibilities of my retired life, I sometimes do think of that gracious place as a kind of mundane Garden of Eden. There, when it is given to me, I can dream dreams and see visions of this, to me, sacred place, some of which I have recounted in this chapter thus far. But just as the story of Adam and Eve in Eden in their "state of integrity" (status integritatis) was not their whole story, so my account of Laurel and me in the Hidden Garden thus far is by no means the whole story that I want to tell in this chapter, in which we are exploring meanings given with the third petition of the Trinity Prayer: Come Holy Spirit, come and reign.

This is the remainder of my story. Once, when I took refuge on the swing with my bottle of water, thoughts of that place as a kind of Eden kept absenting themselves. On that particular day, as I was mowing, I unintentionally had run over a large toad and had shredded it to death. I couldn't stop thinking about that toad. Over the years, I had taken great care to protect toads from my mower or my spade. On occasion, having discovered one, I would gently carry it to our vegetable garden, with this down-home rationale: the toad would be able to feast on the many insects in the garden and, in that way, the toad would be happy and the plants would prosper. "Brother toad," as I would think of that humble but elegant fellow creature, in a Franciscan mode at such moments, "I will care for you." But at *this* moment, there was that bloody carcass, which I sorrowfully kicked into the high grass on my way to rest and refreshment on the swing.

When my mind is so bent, thoughts about other encounters with the violence of nature and our all-too-often destructive human life with nature sometimes flood into my consciousness. The memory of coming upon that beautiful but dead snow hare on the road. That oak tree, being split down the middle, when the lightning hit it. The nest of wasps that I had cut in half and destroyed with my scythe. Yes, those wasps came after me and inflicted great pain, but I had destroyed their hive. There was no way to put it back together again.

The violence of nature that I experience in Hunts Corner, of course, is quite modest compared to what goes on in some other regions. I once watched a documentary about the migration of the wildebeests in East Africa. They are large cattlelike animals, only much more agile, reminiscent of antelopes. They appear to be magnificent creatures, undoubtedly giving praise to God in their own majestic ways. Every year, more than a million of them migrate over a thousand miles through wilderness areas in Tanzania and Kenya, crossing arid grasslands, large rivers, and treacherous swamplands in the process. In that wilderness march, they are subjected to sometimes unimaginable violence. Accidental deaths, from falls and drowning and illness, occur in great numbers. The wildebeests are bloodied and killed, thousands upon thousands, by such predators as lions, crocodiles, and hyenas. I have not been able to rid my memory of that amazing and shocking documentary.

Then, very much a part of my own experience, there is that beautiful field where I scythe at Hunts Corner, which gives our vista from the swing such a sweeping elegance. I have already observed that this is no ordinary field. Beneath it runs the Portland-to-Montreal oil pipeline, which is part of the global economy, which, in turn, is driving many species to destruction and which may, through the processes of climate change, also drive human life on this planet toward unprecedented disruptions. One time, I noticed what I thought was an oily substances trickling in tiny rivulets down that field. I was horrified but thereafter grateful for my own ignorance. I called in a pipeline official to take a look, and he explained that that black water was in fact natural, an organic phenomenon like the murkiness of swamp water. "Feel it," he said, "there's nothing oily about it; it disappears from your fingers." But it could have been otherwise. That might have been the beginnings of a serious leak, as all too often happens to pipelines around the world, further desecrating the earth.

When such thoughts settle upon my soul as I sit there in the swing, when images of the dark side of nature emerge into my mind and anxieties about the global human exploitation and devastation of the earth flood into my consciousness even more, this is what I sometimes imagine hearing: not the voices of many creatures praising God, which is *nature's first voice*, as when I sit there with my eyes wide open marveling at the garden before me and its vista beyond, but something much more somber and sobering, even sinister. As I think about the carcass of that toad—feeling deeply depressed, if the truth be known—I imagine hearing what the apostle Paul called the groaning of the whole creation. This is *nature's second voice*. I also think of this as the travail of nature, in the language of the King James Bible. This is the experience I want to explore with you now, since it also has to do with calling on the Holy Spirit to come and reign.

INTERPRETING ROM. 8:18-23

To begin these reflections, I propose to consider some of the meanings that I believe Paul is communicating in Rom. 8:18-23, where the now much cited expression "the groaning of the whole creation" has its setting and where the works of the Spirit are very much on Paul's mind. This is to envision what it might mean to hear the second voice of nature, not the praise but the groaning. Here is that text:

> I consider that the sufferings of this present time are not worth comparing with the glory about to be revealed to us. For the creation waits with eager long for the revealing of the children of God; for the creation was subjected to futility, not of its own will but by the will of the one who subjected it, in hope that the creation itself will be set free from its bondage to decay and will obtain the freedom of the glory of the children of God. We know that the whole creation has been groaning in labor pains until now; and not only the creation, but we ourselves who have the first fruits of the Spirit, groan inwardly while we wait for adoption, the redemption of our bodies.

Rom. 8:18-23 is a highly compact and complicated text. In recent decades, those, like myself, who have been interested in ecological theology have sometimes turned to this segment of Paul's intense letter and have drawn simple, sometimes overly simple, conclusions about its implications for us today as we face the global ecojustice crisis.[32] Paul does, after all, refer to the groaning of the whole creation. His words surely do have a contemporary ring.

But Paul's interests at this point in his letter are quite different from what ours generally are today.[33] So we must be cautious about the conclusions we draw when we read Romans 8. I propose this interpretive strategy: to listen to the story Paul is telling, implicitly and explicitly, and then to make some observations that, for me, resonate with Paul's words, but with no claim that I am reporting what Paul actually meant, although with the aspiration to honor Paul's intended meanings in my own reflections and not (I hope) to contradict them.[34] If anyone wants to call this interpretive venture spiritual exegesis, I will not object.[35]

In reading Paul, as with other New Testament writers, it is important to understand the context as well as the text. Although Paul is preoccupied in Romans with a number of particular issues in the church of his time, above all with the relationship between Jews and Gentiles, he also presupposes two grand narratives. The first is the story of the rise and the power of Rome and its claims for ultimacy. The second is the story of the world's creation, human sin, the redemption of all humans, and the consummation of the whole world, the narrative of God's ultimacy. Each of these grand narratives comes to a dramatic focus in the works of its own "lord" or *kyrios*, in Paul's world of thought, Caesar and Jesus Christ.[36] For me, this Pauline juxtaposition of what I think of as the cosmic Caesar and the cosmic Christ makes exciting spiritual sense, particularly when I sit on the swing in the Hidden Garden and ponder the meanings of the Portland-to-Montreal pipeline, on the one hand, and the Celtic cross, on the other.

Consider, first, the public religious aura of Augustus Caesar, during whose reign Jesus of Nazareth was born. Although the Greek poet Hesiod, who wrote at the beginning of the seventh century b.c.e., and others after him, had envisioned a universal history of *decline*, from an original golden age of fecundity and peace to ensuing times of scarcity and war (the silver, bronze, and iron ages), the even greater roman poet of the Augustan era, Virgil, replaced that ideology of decline with a kind of messianic vision of the reign of Augustus as itself *a new golden age*. This is Virgil in his *Fourth Ecologue* (4:11-41):

But for you, child, shall the earth untilled pour forth. . . . Uncalled, the goats shall bring their udders swollen with milk, and the herds shall fear not huge lions. . . . The serpent, too, shall perish, and the false poison-plant shall perish. . . . The earth shall not feel the harrow, nor the vine the prunninghook; the sturdy ploughman, too, shall now loose his oxen from the yoke.[37]

Such ultimate claims for the dawning of a golden age in the reign of Caesar Augustus and his successors were very much "in the air" in the culture of the Roman empire when Paul wrote his letter to the Romans. But the "facts on the ground," Paul and the Roman Christians would have known very well, radically belied such imperial propaganda. In the era of Augustus and his immediate successors, Rome was a ruthless, militaristic culture predicated pervasively on slave labor and vast exploitations of nature. It was no golden age. Both Paul and his audience "could well have thought about how imperial ambitions, military conflicts, and economic exploitation had led to the erosion of the natural environment throughout the Mediterranean world, leaving ruined cities, depleted fields, deforested mountains, and polluted streams."[38]

THE GROANING OF THE WHOLE CREATION

Enter "the groaning of the whole creation." While Paul surely did not have access to any of the scientific knowledge that we take for granted today when we think about our global ecojustice crisis, he and many in his time would have had a sense that something was radically wrong with the way humans were living in the world of nature, under Roman power. Hence the expression "the groaning of the whole creation" is in all likelihood implicitly linked for Paul with the thought of desecration of the earth by the powerful. There also was ample precedent in biblical traditions that would have prompted early Christians to think that the excesses of human greed and power had something to do with whatever it was that was radically wrong with nature.[39]

There was also ample precedent in biblical traditions that would have inclined Paul and other first-century Christians to believe that this kind of situation presupposed a kind of divinely mandated feedback loop—namely, that God judges human sinfulness, in part at least, by "cursing the ground" because of sinful humans, who would therefore themselves have to confront thorns and thistles, instead of the plenty of Eden's garden, where they first had been placed by God (see Gen. 2:17-19). Notwithstanding the difficulty many scholars today have in finding a conclusive reading of Rom. 8:20, in this respect, where Paul talks about God subjecting the creation "to futility, not of its own will," some reflection of the aforementioned biblical themes seems to be implied here. There is no cosmic fall, in other words, but in the aftermath of human sin, as Paul would think about these things, God reshapes the human experience of nature so that that experience is no longer a blessing but a curse, especially under the hegemony of Roman power.

In my own mind, our scientific understanding of an ecological feedback loop—that is, human excess disrupts nature, which, in turn, disrupts human life—and the view that Paul seems to be presupposing here—namely, that God judges human sin by subjecting nature to futility, which, in turn, disrupts human life—amount to the same thing. The parallel between the political and economic excesses of the "powers that be" that in our time cause disruptions in the earth and the Roman excesses that disrupted the earth in Paul's time also seems clear. From either perspective, then, creation groans due to human excesses, especially as those excesses are driven by "the powers that be."

I also wonder whether the groaning of the creation, as Paul and the Christians in Rome to whom he wrote understood it, might not also have referred to a kind of suffering that is endemic to nature, apart from the kind of interventions by the powers of Rome that were so disruptive and so well-known. I arrive at the question in the following manner. I am thinking first of the eschatological expectations of many first-century Christians, which, in some measure at least, were shaped by the prophecies of Isaiah, which, in turn, envisioned the messianic age as a time of cosmic peace, a time when "the wolf shall live with the lamb, the leopard shall lie down with the kind, the calf and the lion and the fatling together, and a little child shall lead them" (Isa. 11:6; see also 11:7-9, 65:25).

I am recalling, too, that first-century Christians would also have known about the promise of cosmic peace that was popularly associated with emperors like Augustus and their alleged "golden age." This was thought to be a peace that, as we have already seen, presupposed the ending of violence among animals, not unlike the peace announced by the Isaianic prophecies. Read against this background, could not "the groaning of the whole creation" also have been understood by Paul and his readers as, in some respects, referring to the suffering wrought by nature-on-nature violence, as well as the suffering brought about by human-on-nature violence? If so, that would perhaps help us to understand what Paul meant by the creation's "bondage to decay" (Rom. 8:21), a phrase that has puzzled many interpreters.

Be that as it may, what are we to make of the groaning of nature itself? Paul's words in Romans 8 do not give us much help in answering that question. Paul appears to take that groaning in itself as a profoundly existential reality and does not explore what the groaning in itself might mean or entail. But I think that, in light of my own previous discussion of nature's first voice, the praising, we can make some observations here about what nature's second voice, the groaning, might also mean.

I begin with the assumption that *both voices of nature are heard by God*, both the praising and the groaning, in some sense. I have already discussed the way in which I think we can understand the first. It makes good spiritual sense to me to understand God's hearing of the groaning in the same manner. We have to do here once again, in other words, with a real relationship between the God who hears and, in this case, the suffering creatures, not merely a metaphorical relationship. Such a conclusion is further strengthened in this case when we examine the word Paul uses for groaning. Considered in itself, it calls to mind the traditional mourning practices of Paul's Jewish heritage.[40] Those practices were communal, public, and often replete with loud cries of grieving. Paul, as a matter of course, attributes the same kind of emotional intensity to the groaning of the creatures. He seems to have a real, public expression of grief in mind. Would the God who hears the praises of all the creatures not also hear their public laments?

We know something about the real relationship between God and the groaning creatures, moreover, in light of our earlier contemplation of the cosmic ministries of the "two hands of God," the Son and the Spirit. As the cosmic good shepherd of God, the Son holds all things together, and as he does that, he, who himself has suffered on the Cross, bears with all the creatures of nature in their varied kinds of suffering. As the Lifegiving One of God, the Spirit also never forsakes any of the creatures whom the Spirit has called into becoming but is constantly moving them, drawing them, eliciting them forward on their journeys toward the day of the new heavens and the new earth, when there will be no suffering anymore. In a word, the hearing Father responds to the groaning of the whole creation by sending the Son to bear with all the creatures so as not to leave them trapped and alone in their suffering, and the hearing Father also sends the Spirit to draw all the creatures constantly onward, again not to leave them trapped and alone in their suffering, toward the day when suffering and death will be no more.

THE GROANING OF THE WHOLE CREATION—IN HOPE

But the groaning of the creation is by no means Paul's only major concern in Rom. 8:18-23. Enter now, therefore, the theme of hope. God, Paul tells us, subjected the creation to futility "in hope" (Rom. 8:20) in order to set creation free "from its bondage to decay" so that the whole creation might "obtain the freedom of the glory of the children of God" (Rom. 8:21). Even more, for Paul, the whole creation itself waits in "eager longing" for the completion of God's work of liberation in God's creation (Rom. 8:19)—just as Paul elsewhere says that he himself has an "eager expectation" for the consummation of his own gospel ministry (Phil. 1:20).

Paul has a two-stage view of salvation here: first, the liberation of sinful humans, and second, the liberation of the whole creation. This reflects the assumptions of the second grand narrative of Paul that I referred to at the outset of this discussion, the story of creation, human fall, the history of human redemption coming to its first particular fulfillment in Christ and in his body, the church, and its glorious, final fulfillment in the consummation of the whole creation. Moltmann has instructively described this universal-to-particular-to-universal vision of Paul this way:

> Creation in the beginning started with nature and ended with the human being [Genesis 1]. The eschatological creation reverses this order: it starts with the liberation of the human and ends with the redemption of nature. Its history is the mirror-image of the protological order of creation. Consequently the enslaved creation does not wait for the appearance of Christ in glory in the direct sense; it waits for the revelation of the liberty of the children of God in Christ's appearance.[41]

How does this two-step Pauline story of hope happen? As with much of his thinking in Romans 8, Paul does not tell us, in so many words. But I believe that the answer to this question is hidden in plain sight. No fewer than fourteen times does Paul refer to the Spirit in Romans 8. And he links the groaning of the creation with the inward groaning of believers, who have the first fruits of the Spirit (Rom. 8:22f.). It makes good exegetical sense, therefore, to conclude that Paul is assuming that the same Spirit is also with the rest of the creatures in their groaning, not just with human creatures. If this is what Paul assumes—as it seems to be—what might we think of the Spirit's ministry both with the children of God, who have the first fruits, and with the rest of the creation, which, as it were, has the second fruits of the Spirit?[42]

This question brings us to what is perhaps the most powerful image in Romans 8. The whole creation is not just groaning, it is groaning "in labor pains" (NRSV) or "in travail" (KJV). The theme of birth pangs is often used in Scripture for the pain of divine judgment.[43] That accent on pain should not be underplayed, as anyone who has given birth or been present at a birth can testify. But that is by no means the whole story of groaning in travail, as mothers who have delivered a healthy child and fathers or others who have been there can enthusiastically attest.

Whether Paul was ever so present seems unlikely. In any case, in Romans 8 he does not seem to have maximized the meanings of his own metaphor. He talks of hope but does not explicitly tie that theme to the powerful metaphor of birthing, as he might easily have done. Best, then, to read Paul's metaphor of travail with its full force, explicitly, through the eyes of the Gospel of John: "When a woman is in labor, she has pain, because her hour has come. But when her child is born, she no longer remembers the anguish because of the joy of having brought a human being into the world"(John 16:21). In this sense, the travail of nature is good news, joyful news, which outweighs all the pain of the groaning, because of its outcome.

The Spirit, I believe, makes all this possible. Just as the Spirit is the divine conductor, who elicits the praise of all creatures, so the Spirit is the divine midwife, who works with the creation to help transform its groaning into joy.[44] My own children were born in hospital settings, so in that sense they did not have midwives in any traditional sense. But the physicians and nurses and technicians who were there, as I encountered them and their work, functioned as intensely caring and deeply knowledgeable midwives. Laurel did most of the work and endured, without medications, all of the pain, as I, overwhelmed, tried to support her. But those "midwives" knew how to ease or, better, channel her intense pain. They knew how to monitor the birth canal and the babies' movements toward their first breaths outside the womb. They knew how to "catch" the babies as their little forms emerged and, thankfully, to hand them gently to me, so that I could, in dumbfounded amazement, hand the newborns to Laurel, to be clutched right away to her breast. I stood in awe of those "midwives."

A SPIRITUALITY OF COSMIC HOPE

In a like manner, only all the more so, I stand in awe of the Spirit's ministry of hope with all creatures. In ways that I obviously cannot understand, the Spirit calls forth the groaning of the creatures so that the motherly Father can hear and empathize, just as the motherly Father hears the praises of all creatures and rejoices in those voices. The Lifegiving One brings forth new life, too, as a midwife, so that all creatures can move ever closer, however circuitously, each by its own spontaneity, throughout the cosmic eons, toward the consummated life of the new heavens and the new earth.

This, emphatically, is *not* to somehow justify the suffering of the creatures along the way. In this narrative, I have consistently rejected the possibility of any theodicy. But I do want to celebrate every sign of new life in this epoch of God's history with the whole creation, from the birth of a fawn to the birth of a star. I also am moved all the more so to celebrate constantly the coming consummation of all things, when the Spirit will, one last and glorious time, bring all the creatures to new being in the Son, and in this case will draw them to their consummation in the Son. And the Son will then hand all things over to the motherly Father.

The works of the Spirit, in such ways, make possible a viable spirituality of cosmic hope in my life, which stands in stark contrast to the gnostic spirituality of cosmic despair I discussed earlier. I often ponder such things when Laurel and I are working together or sitting on the swing in the Hidden Garden. I am a creature of hope, notwithstanding all of the evidence in this world to the contrary. For this reason, inspired by the Spirit, I pray, as constantly as I can: *Come Holy Spirit, come and reign.*

Now, in the next chapter, the last, I want to suggest to you how you might work all this out in practice, how you can venture to pray the Trinity Prayer in many settings and in many ways of your own choosing. These will be suggestions born of years of my own experience, which I hope will help you with your own prayer life as you also stand before nature, engaged with nature, in hope.

Notes

1. "Come, Holy Ghost, God and Lord," in *Evangelical Lutheran Worship* (Minneapolis: Augsburg Fortress, 2006), 395.

2. In addition to the hymn referred to in the following note, I know of only two other instances where the Spirit's cosmic ministry is strongly attested: first, in the nineteenth-century hymn "Eternal Father, Strong to Save," in *Evangelical Lutheran Worship*, 756, st. 3: "O Holy Spirit, who didst brood / upon the chaos dark and rude, / and bid its angry tumult cease . . ."; second, in a twentieth-century hymn, "O Living Breath of God," in *Evangelical Lutheran Worship*, 407, sts. 1—3, e.g., st. 1: "O living Breath of God, wind at the beginning upon the waters; / O living Breath of God, bearing creation to wondrous birth. . . ."

3. James K. Manley, "Spirit of Gentleness," *Evangelical Lutheran Worship*, 396.

4. Jürgen Moltmann, *Theology of Hope: On the Grounds and the Implications of a Christian Eschatology*, trans. James W. Leitch (London: SCM, 1967). Along with Moltmann's theology of hope, I was much taken in those years by that stream of New Testament interpretation that laid bare the eschatological character both of Jesus' own ministry and of early Christian thought and practice more generally.

5. Jürgen Moltmann, *God in Creation: A New Theology of Creation and the Spirit of God*, trans. Margaret Kohl (Minneapolis: Fortress Press, 1993). Another instructive and shorter

treatment of the cosmic ministry of the Holy Spirit is the more recent volume by Denis Edwards, *Breath of Life: A Theology of the Creator Spirit* (Maryknoll, NY: Orbis, 2004).

6. See H. Paul Santmire, *Nature Reborn: The Ecological and Cosmic Promise of Christian Theology* (Minneapolis: Fortress Press, 2000), 111–14.

7. See John Polkinghorne, *Science and the Trinity: The Christian Encounter with Reality* (New Haven, CT: Yale University Press, 2004), 67f.: "Trinitarian theology does not need to see the history of the world as the performance of a fixed score, written by God from all eternity, but may properly understand it as the unfolding of a grand improvisation in which the Creator and the creatures both participate."

8. The idea of nature, or the earth, having its own voice has been given currency recently by Norman Habel and his colleagues in their Earth Bible Project. While I welcome those efforts, I would like to point out how that project and my own differ. For Habel and colleagues, the voice of the earth is primarily an interpretive (hermeneutical) construct. It is employed to open up hitherto unnoticed meanings of biblical texts, a process of retrieval. See Norman C. Habel, "Introducing Ecological Hermeneutics," in *Exploring Ecological Hermeneutics*, ed. Norman C. Habel and Peter Trudinger (Atlanta: Society of Biblical Literature, 2008), 5: "Where we meet nonhuman figures communicating in some way—mourning, praising, or singing—we have tended in the past to dismiss these as poetic license or symbolic language. . . . Discerning Earth and members of Earth community as subjects with a voice is a key part of the retrieval process." My efforts here, however, while they presuppose such a hermeneutic, are more focused on affirming that all the creatures of nature have their own voices and then assessing the spiritual meaning of that natural chorus.

9. I first wrote about such Psalms in my 1970 book, *Brother Earth: Nature, God and Ecology in a Time of Crisis* (New York: Thomas Nelson, 1970), 137f. At that time, I felt very much alone. Mainstream biblical studies in those days were generally not interested in such things. I had to wait for more than a decade to find a seasoned, professional biblical scholar who took this matter seriously, Terence E. Fretheim, "Nature's Praise of God in the Psalms," *Ex Auditu* 3 (1987): 29–30.

10. I would later write about Francis in the *Travail of Nature: The Ambiguous Ecological Promise of Christian Theology* (Minneapolis: Fortress Press, 1985), 97–119.

11. Terence E. Fretheim, "The Earth Story in Jeremiah 12," in *Readings from the Perspective of Earth*, ed. Norman C. Habel (Cleveland, OH: Pilgrim, 2000), 99. See also, more generally, Richard Bauckham, *Living with Other Creatures: Green Exegesis and Theology* (Waco, TX: Baylor University Press, 2011), 147–62.

12. In this respect, I find Calvin's theology suggestive. He believed, as I have already observed, that the infinite, incomprehensible God *accommodates* Godself to us humans in order to *speak* with us. God does this, Calvin affirmed, by becoming incarnate as a human, Jesus, in order to address us in ways that we can understand. Does it not also make sense to say that God also accommodates God's *listening* to a mode appropriate to each and every creature? That would mean that God's listening to us humans, when we address God, is only one form of perhaps a near-infinite number of forms that God employs to accommodate God's listening to all creatures.

13. See the words of Paul S. Fiddes, *Participating in God: A Pastoral Doctrine of the Trinity* (Louisville, KY: Westminster John Knox, 2000), 144: "If human beings are able to respond to God, then it is not unreasonable to think that there must be something at least akin to response to God at all levels of creation, some 'family-likeness' within the cosmos. Even if we cannot describe exactly how this relationship between God and the natural world works, we do have various kinds of language to point to the mystery."

14. I use the word *power* here and throughout this discussion advisedly. It takes on different meanings in different contexts. I will presently suggest the idea of a gradation of kinds of power, from "raw power" of physical force to the "gentle power" of a human touch. The best single discussion I know of the variety of theological meanings of power is by Larry Rasmussen, "Theology of Life and Ecumenical Ethics," in *Ecotheology: Voices from South and North*, ed. David G. Hallman (Maryknoll, NY: Orbis, 1994), 112–29.

15. Philip Hefner, "A Fuller Concept of Evolution—Big Bang to Spirit," *Zygon* 47, no. 2 (June 2012): 298–307. For a book-length exposition of these themes, see Philip Hefner, *The Human Factor: Evolution, Culture, Religion* (Minneapolis: Augsburg Fortress, 1993). Hefner's *Human Factor* can be read profitably alongside a similar study by Charles Birch and John B. Cobb Jr., *The Liberation of Life: From the Cell to the Community* (Denton, TX: Environmental Ethics Books, 1990). Also, for a more cosmic accent, see the widely hailed work by Brian Swimme and Thomas Berry, *The Universe Story: From the Primordial Flaring Forth to the Ecozoic Era—A Celebration of the Unfolding of the Cosmos* (New York: HarperCollins, 1992).

16. "Emergence" has become a key construct for a number of natural scientists and for many theologians in conversation with the natural sciences, like Hefner. See the comment of Denis Edwards, *Ecology at the Heart of Faith: The Change of Heart that Leads to a New Way of Living on Earth* (Maryknoll, NY: Orbis, 2008), 79: "Emergence is a central characteristic of our universe. It appears in the particles found in the first second of the Big Bang, in the hydrogen nuclei formed in the first few minutes, in the stars that synthesize further elements, in the DNA molecule, in the first cells that had a nucleus, in multicellular creatures, and in human brains. At every stage in this process, something that is genuinely new occurs." For a rigorous, technical theological argument that works with the construct of emergence, see Philip Clayton, "The Impossible Possibility: Divine Causes in the World of Nature," in *God, Life, and the Cosmos: Christian and Islamic Perspectives*, ed. Ted Peters, Muzaffar Iqbal, and Syed Nomanul Haq (Burlington, VT: Ashgate, 2002), 249–80.

17. Hefner, "A Fuller Concept of Evolution," 301.

18. Hefner, "A Fuller Concept of Evolution," 301–2, his italics.

19. Hefner, "A Fuller Concept of Evolution," 302.

20. Hefner, "A Fuller Concept of Evolution," 305.

21. Hefner, "A Fuller Concept of Evolution," 307.

22. For a theological discussion of nature's own spontaneity, see Santmire, *Brother Earth*, 133–36.

23. I believe that the whole discussion of Christianity and the religions of the world is of utmost importance, especially in these times of globalizing influences and, sadly, globalizing conflicts. But this is not the place to do that. Still, I hope that my explications of a Christian spirituality of nature here will in some manner be of value to those who are involved in such discussions, at all levels.

24. I am reflecting here a post-Reformation theological theme, taken up in our own time by Karl Barth in his own way—the idea of three dimensions of God's providential activities in the whole creation: (1) cosmic and human history generally, (2) the more particular history of human redemption and cosmic redemption set within and ultimately expanding to encompass the general, and (3) the individual believer's own story respectively set within those wider dimensions (*providentia generalis, providential specialis, providential specialissima*).

25. This is a highly compact statement that presupposes a number of complex ideas. I am thinking here of the Spirit's work in the resurrection of Jesus Christ as in some sense being analogous to the Spirit's originating creativity in the first creation, which was a creation "out of nothing" (*ex nihilo*). The resurrection, however, in partial contrast, is the proleptic beginning (perhaps analogous to the first moments of the originating "Big Bang" of the first creation) that leads to the eschatological new creation of all things. The resurrection of Jesus Christ is thus both the fulfilment of the first creation and the particular inauguration of the new creation. In this respect, the resurrection is *not a creatio ex nihilo*. Yet it presupposes a magnitude of divine power that might even be thought to surpass that of the first creation, which was a *creatio ex nihilo*.

26. See Denis Edwards, *Breath of Life*, 135: "All this suggests an understanding of the universe in which each diverse creature has its own distinct integrity. From the perspective of science, this individuality and integrity are given in all the constitutive relationships that make an entity what it is. From the perspective of theology, each individual creature has its own independent value within an interrelated universe spring from its relationship with the indwelling

Creator Spirit. The Spirit brings forth from within the divine Communion an interconnected and interdependent universe of creatures. But these created relationships bear the limitation of finitude and death. They come to be only within the limitations of time. They come to be only in a process, a process that is incomplete." Edwards elsewhere affirms that that process will only be completed eschatologically.

27. I have traced the coexistence of Christianity and the gnostic spirit at various points in *The Travail of Nature.*

28. See Ted Peters, *The Cosmic Self: A Penetrating Look at Today's New Age Movements* (San Francisco: Harper, 1991).

29. See Barbara Rossing, *The Rapture Exposed: The Message of Hope in the Book of Revelation* (Boulder, CO: Westview, 2004).

30. Philip J. Lee, *Against the Protestant Gnostics* (London: Oxford University Press, 1986). See also the searing analysis by the Catholic New Testament scholar Luke Timothy Johnson, "A New Gnosticism: An Old Threat to the Church," *Commonweal* (November 5, 2004), 28–31.

31. Harold Bloom, *The American Religion: The Emergence of the Post-Christian Nation* (New York: Simon and Schuster, 1992).

32. For a review of the history of interpretation of Rom. 8:19-23, see Cheryl Hunt, David G. Horrell, and Christopher Southgate, "An Environmental Mantra? Ecological Interest in Romans 8:19-23 and a Modest Proposal for Its Narrative Interpretation," *Journal of Theological Studies,* NS, 8:59:2 (October 2008), 546–79, especially 547–55. I have found their overall approach most instructive, alongside the insights of Robert Jewett, "The Corruption and Redemption of Creation: Reading Romans 8:18-23 within the Imperial Context," in *Paul and the Roman Imperial Order,* ed. Richard A. Horsley (Harrisburg, PA: Trinity Press International, 2004), 25–46. I also have learned much from the articles by Laurie J. Braaten, "All Creation Groans: Romans 8:22 in Light of the Biblical Sources," *Horizons in Biblical Theology* 28 (2006): 131–59; and Jonathan Moo, "Romans 8:19-22 and Isaiah's Cosmic Covenant," *New Testament Studies* 54 (2008): 74–89.

33. See Hunt et al, "An Environmental Mantra?," 576: "There is—despite the many passing appeals to this text in ecotheological writing—no easy or obvious means to 'read off' any contemporary ethical responsibilities or policies from Rom. 8:19-23, or indeed any other biblical text. All of the problems we have sketched above should together indicate that drawing on Romans 8 to outline an *ethical* response to our environmental challenges will require an imaginative, theologically, and scientifically informed engagement which goes well beyond what Paul himself might have envisioned"(italics in original).

34. I learned many years ago from Krister Stendahl the importance of distinguishing between what a text meant and what it means. See his still valuable essay "Biblical Theology, Contemporary," in *Interpreter's Dictionary of the Bible* (Nashville, TN: Abingdon, 1962), 1:418–32.

35. It could also be called homiletical exegesis, since it follows the practice of many good preachers who, on the basis of their own historical study of texts, then have to tell their congregations what such texts mean for them. Regarding spiritual exegesis, see further, Michael Pasquarello and Lester Ruth, "Spiritual Reading of Scripture and Liturgical Imagination," *Liturgy* 28, no. 2 (January 2013): 1: "By this [spiritual reading of scripture and liturgical imagination] we mean a personal way of knowing that which is given through divine revelation of the Word by means of the words and images of the Bible. . . . Because the identity of the God whom the church worships is the same as the God revealed in the Bible, the primary form of theological interpretation is telling the Bible's story in the liturgy." Spiritual exegesis, in brief, then, is exegesis that can be preached and prayed.

36. For the Rome narrative, see Jewett, "The Corruption and Redemption of Creation." For the God narrative, see Hunt et al., "An Environmental Mantra?"

37. Quoted by Jewett, "The Corruption and Redemption of Creation," 27.

38. Jewett, "The Corruption and Redemption of Creation," 37.

39. See Jewett, "The Corruption and Redemption of Creation," 41: "The verb *stenazo* (cry out, groan) used here in the compound form of *sustenazo* (cry out, groan together), appears with a

similar meaning in Job 31:38-40, where the link established in Gen. 3:17-18 between human sin and the groaning of nature provides a basis from Job's protestation of innocence. . . . The idea that the earth 'languishes,' 'mourns,' and suffers 'pollution' under the burden of human exploitation also appears in Is. 24:4-7 and Hos. 4:1-3."

40. For this, see Braaten, "All Creation Groans."

41. Jürgen Moltmann, *God in Creation: A New Theology of Creation and the Spirit of God*, trans. Margaret Kohl (San Francisco: Harper and Row, 1984), 68f.

42. See Hunt et al., "An Environmental Mantra?," 569: "Given the way Paul here also describes both the groaning with believers in the Spirit (v. 26), it seems most likely that he here depicts the creation as also bound up with humanity and the Spirit in a solidarity of shared groaning, and, similarly, a shared hope."

43. See Jewett, "The Corruption and Redemption of Creation," 41, for a list of such texts.

44. I am not sure when the image of the Holy Spirit as the midwife of the creation groaning in travail first entered my conscious mind. It may have been in the context of my readings in ecofeminist theologians over the years. In any case, the most recent encounter with the image that I remember was in Denis Edwards, *Ecology at the Heart of Faith: The Change of Heart that Leads to a New Way of Living on Earth* (Maryknoll, NY: Orbis, 2008), 44. I make use of the image here, however, on my own terms, for which I take complete responsibility.

10

Sauntering in the Spirit
Practicing the Trinity Prayer

Thoreau once asserted that the word *saunter* comes from the French *sainte terre*, referring to a medieval pilgrimage to the Holy Land.[1] In making this observation, Thoreau was thinking of two things—first, what might be called a kind of pilgrimage or a mindful walking in wild nature as a world of deep meanings in itself, and second, a rejection of what he considered to be the suffocating world of the city or "civilization." While there is little etymological evidence for Thoreau's derivation of the word *sauntering*, I do find his proposal suggestive on the first account. When you saunter, you are walking mindfully on this earth, on your way toward the new Jerusalem and the new heavens and the new earth. My meaning here is akin to one of Thoreau's own images. He suggests that the saunterer is like a meandering river that seeks the shortest course to the sea.

Over against Thoreau on the second account, however—his rejection of the city or what he calls civilization—I believe that we *can* saunter blessedly in the city as well as in the countryside. I also believe that we can saunter blessedly in the society of the church and its liturgy as well as in solitary adventures in the wilds.[2] That being said, do let us saunter.[3]

Laurel and I love to saunter. We love to walk mindfully in both unfamiliar and familiar places. This may not come as a surprise at this point in this narrative. I want to reflect about this love for sauntering here close to the end, in order to better walk you through some practices I want to recommend to you for praying the Trinity Prayer. All of this falls under the rubric of the third part of that prayer: *Come Holy Spirit, come and reign.* Think of the Trinity Prayer in this practical sense—as sauntering in the Spirit. There is, then, an inner and an outer dimension to sauntering. Sauntering brings with it a certain mindfulness

217

within, along with the critically important movements of your body without, as you explore unfamiliar and familiar places.

SAUNTERING IN UNFAMILIAR AND FAMILIAR PLACES

Laurel and I have sauntered in many unfamiliar places. When we have traveled, we have not been tourists for the most part, in the conventional sense of that word—people who come home from a trip and immediately begin to ask: where shall we go next and what sights should we see? Over the years, we have mostly traveled to unfamiliar places that were in some sense already familiar to us culturally or spiritually, even though they were totally new to us geographically. We have walked mindfully, in that sense.

Typically, Laurel has taken me to visit gardens that she has wanted to see. I have taken her to visit cathedrals or monastic sites that I have wanted to see. And we have taken each other to explore coastal or rural or alpine or urban places that we both have felt driven to visit because of the cultural or ecological meanings already important to one or both of us.

I will resist the temptation to tell you about *all* the unfamiliar places where we have enthusiastically sauntered. But I want to give you an idea of the character of our encounter with such places. Ireland was important to Laurel because of her Scotch-Irish heritage. It was important to me because of my spiritual love affair with the classical Celtic saints and with the towering, historic Celtic crosses, in particular. England was important to Laurel because of her long-standing fascination with that country's gardens, both the great ones of public renown and the cottage plots that one can come upon virtually anywhere. England was important to me, because I wanted to find a way to spiritually inhabit some of that land's great cathedrals, and above all, the Salisbury Cathedral and its gracious setting.

Switzerland was important to Laurel because she had spent a summer in the Alps with a host family as an exchange student in her high school years. It was important to me because, of course, the Alps are one of the great wonders of God's good earth. They were also of interest to me more idiosyncratically because I have long wondered how living in valleys surrounded by such overwhelming heights affects the consciousness and perhaps the unconscious mind of the people who reside and work there.[4] Assisi was important to Laurel because she wanted to see the stunning cathedral that she had studied in college, and the frescoes of Giotto in particular. It was important to me because I wanted to walk in some of the places where Francis had walked.

I could go on. But my chief observation in this context is this: it has been a blessing for us to be able to saunter in all those, and many more, unfamiliar places, rather than to be merely tourists by default. To this day, each of us cherishes the memories of such pilgrimages, and we talk about them often.

I turn, then, to the familiar places where Laurel and I have walked mindfully most regularly. By now, you know two of the most important: the banks of the Charles River and the Mt. Auburn arboretum. We, of course, saunter around Hunts Corner, too, all the time. The first thing we always do when we arrive there from Boston during the day, if the weather permits, is to make our way around the front portions of the land that we hold in trust from the Lord.

We greet old friends, as it were—the trees and the flowers and the vegetables. Along the stream, we look for the first hardy golden blossoms of the marsh marigolds in the early spring or for the golden flowers of the lush ligularia in the late fall. We look, too, to see if any damage has been done to our gardens by other creatures of that place, our more distant friends, the deer, the woodchucks, the voles, the potato bugs, the cabbage worms, the Japanese beetles, the earwigs, or the flee-beetles. We carefully examine signs of damage to the plants or the land wrought by the weather, too. We also celebrate occasional but transcendental surprises, as when one spring day we first saw that the rare and delicate white double trillium, which I had given Laurel for her birthday the year before, had begun to blossom.

At Hunts Corner, moreover, there's nothing quite like a contemplative walk along the graveled Picnic Hill Road, which follows, for several miles, the route that stagecoaches took on their way north from Portland to Bethel in colonial times. Hunts Corner is said to have taken its name from Hunts Tavern, which used to be a way station for those coaches (although I have never come upon any archeological evidence for this). The best time to saunter along Picnic Hill Road, we have discovered, is on a cloudless and crisp winter day when the snow is resplendent with the brilliance of the sun. On such a day, you can indeed see forever, it seems. The Presidential Mountains, among them the venerable Mount Washington, frame the horizon, visible at that time of year in their dramatic, snow-covered grandeur, since there are no leaves on the trees along that forested road to obstruct the view.

During one summer, along the same route, Laurel and I carefully explored a new trail that a local conservationist had carved out, up to the summit of little Round Mountain, just to the north of our land—the very mountain to whose summit Laurel and I once had bushwhacked, with our then young children in tow, many years before.

Along the way to the summit of this, our favorite mountain in all God's good earth, as an elderly couple now, we maximized the inevitable. We made frequent stops along the trail to contemplate the striking mountain vistas to the west, sometimes talking, sometimes just resting in the silence. At our ages, on walks or hikes like that, we do indeed saunter almost all the way. Generally, we don't keep up a pace, because we can't. In this sense, sauntering is now in our very bones and muscles. In truth, we wouldn't be *we* without the sauntering. *Ambulamus ergo sumus.* We saunter, therefore we are.

For me, praying the Trinity Prayer is a kind of inner sauntering that stirs deep within, without which I would also not be me. *Ambulo penitus ergo sum.* I saunter deeply within, therefore I am. I have told you that, by continual repetition, as often as I can, the Trinity Prayer has come to dwell, in some measure, in my subliminal consciousness. Sometimes I am consciously aware of only fragments of the prayer. At other times, the whole prayer surfaces in my conscious mind—but not without working at it, or walking the walk, as they say. I want to tell you more about this inner sauntering now so that sharing some of my own practices may encourage you to think about your own and perhaps enhance your own sauntering in the Spirit, both without and within.

Sauntering and the Wellspring of Singing: A Visceral Interiority

People are different. This truism already gives notice that the recommendation I am about to propose for praying the Trinity Prayer may not work for you. I am a visual person, for example. When I drive in an unfamiliar neighborhood, I will look for landmarks that are familiar to me, in order to give me my bearings. In Boston, that's easy, because there are only a few tall buildings in the center of town and you can almost always locate one of them. My wife is not a visual person. I may tell her to turn left after we cross the bridge over the river and she will respond, "What bridge?" Although we will have crossed over that bridge many times, she will have never consciously noticed it. For this reason, she prefers to use a map in order to find her way. People *are* different.

Hence I have no way of knowing whether the proposal I am about to make will work for you. But with that proviso, I will make this proposal confidently, because it has worked so well for me for so many years. Nor will this proposal surprise you, since I have been making it often in the preceding pages. But here I want to try to close the argument.

Sing the Trinity Prayer. (In the appendix of this book, I will give you some suggestions for familiar hymn tunes that might aid your singing.) We are not all accomplished singers, to be sure. But can I assume that more than a few people are willing to sing in the shower? Or to sing in any place where only God is listening? If it helps you spiritually, imagine that when you sing—or hum—the Trinity Prayer, you will be joining in the song of the whole creation. The loving God who hears the screech owls or the wolves at night will surely not begrudge you your own peculiar voice at any time of the day or night.

When you sing, you will have the company of most of the human race, too. Most people around the globe are musical, whether or not they think of themselves that way. As the distinguished neurologist Oliver Sacks has stated: "The propensity to music shows itself in infancy, is manifest and central in every culture, and probably goes back to the very beginnings of our species. Such 'musicophilia' is a given in human nature. It may be developed or shaped by the cultures we live in, by the circumstances of life, or by the particular gifts or weaknesses we have as individuals—but it lies so deep in human nature that one must think of it as innate."[5] Music seems to have its own location in the brain, too, as we may assume that thinking does; indeed, according to Sachs, that space for music is *larger* than the place occupied by the thinking function. Music is that important physiologically as well as culturally. So, if I may revise an oft-quoted injunction of Luther: be prepared to "sing boldly." Sing the Trinity Prayer, whenever and wherever you can, and as robustly as you can.

THE SPIRITUAL LOGIC OF SINGING

I make this proposal, in part, on the basis of many decades of pastoral experience. As a young pastor in the early 1980s, long before clergy began to be routinely instructed about the dynamics of dementia and related conditions, and long before music therapy had become a popular field in its own right, I discovered for myself a phenomenon that most people in the helping professions today would understand as a matter of course. I once went to visit an older parishioner in a nursing home who, another member of my church had told me, would not be able to speak coherently with me. He was right. Nevertheless, I carefully prepared the Communion Table for her, a lifelong church member. As I did, she began to babble off and on, as if she wanted to speak. Or perhaps she thought that she was speaking.

I was about to offer her the bread and wine when, by some strange inspiration, I paused for a moment and then began to sing: "Beautiful Savior, King of creation . . ." She immediately joined in, and we finished that hymn stanza together: "Son of God and Son of Man! Truly I'd love thee, Truly I'd serve thee, Light of my soul, my joy, my crown." I then opened my book to that hymn, and she—who had sung in the church choir for fifty years—and I then boisterously sang the other three stanzas of "Beautiful Savior" together, to the delight of the nurses in the hall. Music can have that kind of power, perhaps all the more so when it allows a lifetime of faithful spiritual devotion to express itself under severely constricted conditions.[6]

Then there is that wider set of circumstances in which most of us live in these times, circumstances that I described early in this narrative as the experience of the eclipse of God. When I was in seminary, a visiting lecturer from England, whose name I cannot now remember, said that people may not be able to believe the Nicene Creed if they just *say* it. "Try singing it," said that visiting professor. That was good advice. Over the years as a pastor, on numerous occasions, when people would come to me to talk about their crises of faith or related issues, I would often at some point try to find a way to ask them about how they felt when they sang the hymns. Frequently, although not always, this was the kind of response I received: "Oh, I get carried away by the hymns. That's not the problem. The problem is figuring out how I can believe what I'm saying when I confess the Creed." That, for any good pastor, would be an obvious point to begin to explore with the counselee: what the latter thinks "believing" actually means. People can sing their faith sometimes, even though they may be uncertain about speaking their faith.

After years of pastoral experience, and after I had found the conceptual tools to allow me to make a more general kind of spiritual diagnosis, I also came to the conclusion that hymnody, and a sung liturgy more generally, could play an important role in helping many to break with what early on in this narrative, drawing on insights from Richard Baer, I referred to as "the tyranny of the cognitive mind." Learning to sing in church and then singing boldly could function like learning to dance or to speak a foreign language can function more generally, as a way to let the cognitive mind rest and thus to open up the depths of the deeper mind and heart to enter into the faith being announced by the music.

I am sure that this is the way the music of the church has functioned in my own life. Can I really be grasped by the meaning of the resurrection on Easter Day if I'm not given the opportunity to sing hymns like "Jesus Christ Is Risen Today! Alleluia!"? How many times in my life has the dimness of my soul, sometimes even a blanket of depression, been lifted when on any given Sunday I was able to go with the flow of an "old favorite" like "Beautiful Savior"?

In the same vein, think of St. Francis. Was it merely his culture's fascination with the troubadours and his own familiarity with their ways that prompted him to sing his prayers—"the Office," it was called—virtually every day of his postconversion life? Was it only a commonplace for him to sing the Gospel reading at Greccio during the Christmas Eve Mass toward the end of his life when he gathered animals around the Christ-child at the altar for the eucharistic celebration? Was it only accidental that he wrote his great Canticle of Brother Sun *as a canticle*, intending it to be sung, as he himself often did? Francis, indeed, has often been called a troubadour of the Lord. His life was a kind of constant song of praise, exemplary for me, in this way as in many others.

Then there is the example of Luther, whose spirituality, you will already have realized, has shaped my own in many ways, not the least of them his love for music. Luther's celebration of music knew few limits. This "beautiful and priceless gift of God," he said, could "move human hearts through words and song and sound." It could "make the sad joyful, the joyful sad, the timid brave, and the proud humble." Luther urged composers to create "sermons in sound" by "embellishing and ornamenting their tunes in wonderful ways . . ., and so to lead others (as it were) into a heavenly dance." And such commitments on his part, fired by enormous energy and considerable musical talent of his own, helped him to change a whole culture. Whatever else may have made the Reformation the revolutionary historical event that it was—and its causes were many—it was surely fueled, in significant measure, by the music fostered by Luther.[7]

More reflectively now, singing your prayers—in this case the Trinity Prayer—has the advantage of drawing your whole self into the prayer, body as well as mind and soul. Call it a visceral interiority. Disembodied souls cannot sing. Humans need lungs and diaphragms and vocal cords to sing. When you do so exercise your voice, moreover, more often than not you can feel your lungs and your diaphragm heaving and your vocal cords straining. If you are wholeheartedly involved in the singing, furthermore, you may well discover that you need still more from your body, not only the work of your lungs and your diaphragm and your vocal cords. In my congregation in Roxbury, some worshipers joyfully clap their hands when they sing. Others, like me, impulsively swing and sway and sometimes stomp their feet.

And not only in church. Once, on a particularly gorgeous day at Hunts Corner, when I was on my knees in the Hidden Garden, pulling out some grass from around a rosebush, I was so overwhelmed by the beauty of it all that I threw down my work gloves, jumped to my feet, extended my arms toward the Celtic cross nearby, and sang the Trinity Prayer at the top of my voice. Singing that prayer in such a manner can allow your whole self to be carried away, in body as well as in mind and soul. All of which is to say: never mind your current reluctance to sing the Trinity Prayer, if indeed that is your state of mind. Be prepared to sing boldly![8]

SINGING IN EVERY PLACE?

On the other hand, in the spirit of the Book of Ecclesiastes, I do acknowledge that there is a time for everything. You may *not* want to sing at the top of your voice when you are riding on a crowded subway. Still, I have found that a time like that can, contrary to what you might at first assume, offer wonderful opportunities to sing the Trinity Prayer—*in the music of silence*. I once heard the great pianist Arthur Rubinstein interviewed on the radio. He related how he had practiced several hours a day for many years. "Do you still do that?," the interviewer asked the then aging musician. "Yes," he said, "except for times when I practice in my mind."

Over the years, I have taught myself—it did take some practice—to sing silently in my deeper mind and heart. A long ride on the subway is a case in point. There you can turn off the noise of this world so that you can concentrate on singing your prayers within. Likewise, when you are waiting at the airport for a delayed flight or when you are awake in the middle of that long flight to London, when you cannot sleep or read and you are alone with your thoughts in the darkened cabin: sing silently, but sing boldly.

How does one sing silently? Consider that extended subway ride once again. I will on occasion sit there, shut my eyes, and then start silently humming a familiar hymn tune (examples in the appendix), as if I were whispering to myself. I can feel the air of the tune coming up from my lungs and touching the roof of my mouth. Once I am under way with that silent inner tune, I then blend in the words of the Trinity Prayer. Sometimes my lips do move slightly when I give silent musical voice to the words of the prayer. I suppose that if the people sitting opposite me on the subway car would notice me, sitting there with my eyes closed and, perchance, with my lips slightly moving, they might wonder whether I was on some kind of medication. But not to worry, as the train rumbles on, I happily rumble on with my silent song of prayer.

Still, there are times when I am strongly opposed to such praying. When I'm scything at Hunts Corner, for example. That exercise requires my total attention. I can stop swinging the scythe and *then* sing. Perhaps, indeed, the scything in itself is a kind of praying. But that is no time to repeat the Trinity Prayer, either audibly or in the silence of my own heart. I also avoid praying the Trinity Prayer when I am stepping on stones to cross a mountain stream or when I'm having a conversation with my wife about our plans for the week. So I recommend: do avoid praying consciously at such times. I assume, though, that even in such instances, the Trinity Prayer is still within me, that it is stirring in my subliminal mind and heart, when I am not consciously attending to it. As I have already observed more than once, this is how I adhere, in some measure, to the apostolic injunction to "pray constantly."

Be that as it may, my immediate concern here has been to make as persuasive a case as I can to convince you to sing the Trinity Prayer, whenever possible and as robustly as possible, whether silently or aloud. Give voice to this visceral interiority. This is one critically important way to cultivate your inner sauntering, as you also saunter externally through the unfamiliar and familiar places of God's world.

Sauntering and the Cultivation of Sensory Practices: A Spiritual Exteriority

I now want to go into more detail about that outer sauntering. It is not just the walking in familiar and unfamiliar places, or it need not be. The inner voice that emerges from the heart—this visceral interiority—can be complemented by a range of sensory practices in addition to the walking. Call this a spiritual exteriority.

The Sign of the Cross

Perhaps the single most important of these exterior practices, for me, is making the sign of the cross. Others, such as posture and gestures, I will discuss in the epilogue. With some regularity, I make the sign of the cross when I begin and end saying the Trinity Prayer aloud or silently. When I do, I typically press my pectoral cross to my chest. I touch this worn body of mine firmly, with the imprint of the cross, either with abandon, if I am by myself, or more secretly, if I am in public, say, riding on the subway. If I am at home, I also contemplate one of the crucifixes that is visible in several of our rooms. If I am out and around, I form a mental image of my pectoral cross in my mind, as I press it into my chest when I cross myself, secretively.

That pectoral cross is my chief spiritual icon, first among equals of the many crucifixes that are important to me, at home or in the churches I frequent. While over the years I have surrounded myself with stirring iconographical art, I remain an heir of Western Christian crucifix-devotion. Already in my teens, as I noted along the way in this narrative, I fell to my knees before a wooden Spanish crucifix in my uncle's apartment, when I was in the midst of a personal crisis. On Good Friday, I have for many years adopted the practice of bending my knee to kiss the rough, wooden, six-foot-tall processional crucifix, in the chancel of my Roxbury church. In this respect, there is a kind of starkness in my piety, even though I have eagerly explored Eastern Christian iconography over the years, above all in the monasteries of the former Yugoslavia and in the basilicas of Italy and Greece. I have the feeling that I could not get by without my pectoral cross. I misplaced it once, thought I had lost it, and was sick at heart.

This is the story of my pectoral cross. My sister, Mary Kay, bought it for me when she visited Spain. It is made of five simple horseshoe nails, reminiscent, of course, of the nails on the original cross, but also suggesting to me worldly powers, traditionally symbolized by the war horse. The nails of that traditional symbol of terror have thus been transfigured by the cross of Christ. This particular cross has the feel of death for me, of course, but not only in memory of the death of the Savior but also in memory of the death of my sister. She, the apple of my eye and my brother's too, died an untimely death of a rampaging brain cancer in her mid-forties. I have never "gotten over" her death. On the other hand, when I press that cross to my chest, it also has the feeling of life. I can sometimes hear her voice in my heart at such moments, a vivid voice for me from the eternal communion of the saints.

The sign of the cross, as well as that particular pectoral cross, also often calls to my mind my own Baptism, which I highlighted in the first pages of this narrative. Baptized with water, I was. Drowned in the death of Christ, I was. Signed with the mark of Christ's death and the promise of his resurrection, I was. Every day, then, when I make the sign of the cross, when I press that particular pectoral cross into my flesh, I am overcome, subliminally if not dramatically, with the baptismal mysticism that I have already described in this book. This happens not just every day but throughout each day, each of the many times I make the sign of the cross, visibly or secretively.

THE SIGN OF THE CROSS IN MANY PLACES

I want to tell you more about the places where I make the sign of the cross at the beginning and the ending of the Trinity Prayer. I have already alluded to some of these, from the subway to the Hidden Garden, but I want to give a few more examples, so that you will know more concretely what I mean. Think of a slice of life, the beginning and ending of a chapter during any day, every day.

I am in the habit of making the sign of the cross and saying the Trinity Prayer before and after a variety of events on any average day. This is a spirituality for ordinary places.

When I walk to the Episcopal Monastery on Thursday mornings, I make the sign of the cross as soon as I leave my own building, and I keep my hand pressing that cross into my flesh for a long time, as I sing the Trinity Prayer repeatedly at the top of my voice. As I walk along the Charles River all by myself, I sometimes wonder what the geese and the mallards floating in the river think, not to speak of the crews sculling out on the river. Probably, with all the noise of their oars and the water and the shouting of the coxes, those crews can't hear me. The geese and the mallards are another matter. When they cluster at the edge of the river, I do sometimes stop to greet them. So perhaps they are accustomed to hearing my voice when I sing.

Then there's the canvassing Laurel and I sometimes do. Massachusetts has an overabundance of committed Democrats, so we have made it a practice, with many others, to canvass for Democratic candidates like John Kerry, Hillary Clinton, and Barak Obama in New Hampshire. Canvassing, as I have experienced it, is more work than fun, and mostly depressing, if the truth be known. Too much walking and too many people not at home and too many doors slammed in your face. So I have tried to keep things in perspective by reciting the Trinity Prayer now and again, between houses, as I press my pectoral cross against my chest. Asking for mercy is a good beginning. Praising God and celebrating God's purposes help to keep things in perspective. And calling on the power of the Spirit to bring forth some kind of justice out of the whole election process is downright necessary, spiritually.

What about praying before and after a concert? I have done that on occasion, and I can recommend this as a spiritual practice. For me, it works better, I must confess, if the concert is in a church and if the music itself is theologically inspired. So, sitting in one of Boston's cathedrals, I read the program notes for Bach's B-Minor Mass or for Benjamin Britten's War Requiem. I can then focus my soul on the music that is about to be performed when I allow myself, again, to secretly make the sign of the cross and to ask for mercy, to praise God, and to call on the Spirit for wisdom for all present, myself included. When the concert is over, I also sometimes press my pectoral cross to my chest as the crowd exits and once again I inwardly speak the Trinity Prayer.

I don't want to forget cleaning up the kitchen. Making the sign of the cross before I load the dishwasher? I am aware that this may not sound spiritually important to some, but it is to me. This may be an afterglow of my German Lutheran heritage. For the last dozen years, Laurel and I have divided the family chores. She works part-time, does the bills, and cooks. I do the house-cleaning, wash the dishes, take out the garbage, take care of the car, and do the recycling. Such sanctified duties give me numerous occasions to pray. Now and again, I will use the Trinity Prayer as a guide for reflection and prayer when I clean the surfaces and sweep the floor. Who needs my prayer for mercy today? What aspect of God's life as Giver, Gift, and Giving do I want to celebrate in my heart today? Where in the world do I want God to send the Spirit today, to give new life to the broken-hearted and the downtrodden?

Like many others, too, I seize on the beginning and the ending of the day for my prayers, whenever I can, which is most of the time. Even if I am too tired to sing in the morning or the evening, I can always make the sign of the cross and say the Trinity Prayer and say it repeatedly, either silently or aloud. I have found that mornings are an especially good time to invoke that prayer reflectively. Since I usually take the time to do some physical exercises every morning, why not do those spiritual exercises at the same time? As I sing the Trinity Prayer at such ordinary times, moreover, I get in the habit of calling forth themes in my mind and heart, the kind that I have highlighted throughout the preceding narrative. I now want to illustrate how that can happen, as I bring this book to a practical conclusion.

SAUNTERING AND THE VISION OF GOD: SLOWING DOWN TO DREAM DREAMS

In envisioning the pouring out of the Spirit on all flesh, the prophet Joel, quoted by Luke to describe the Day of Pentecost, imagined a time of seeing visions and dreaming dreams, when even slaves, both men and women, would prophesy (Acts 2:17-18). With this text before us, I want to explore what such an experience might be like in our own time for someone who takes the Trinity Prayer to heart and sings it often, as he or she saunters in the Spirit. I will presuppose here, as I have explicitly throughout this book, that the spirituality of that person is immersed in the life of the Christian community, its worship, its disciplines, and its theological and spiritual traditions.

I will also presuppose, as I have implicitly done throughout this book, that the one who prays is entering into a dialogue initiated and sustained by God. We do all the work. God does all the work. That, perhaps, is the chief paradox of prayer. And sauntering helps us to be aware of that paradox, because we are not rushing somewhere to keep an appointment of *our* making. Sauntering, by its very nature, is a slow, reflective pace. It is mindful walking in a place, not hurrying on to some other place. This means that, as we saunter, we can call to mind and heart the idea of God with us and be grateful that God initiates and sustains our praying, even as we also do all the work. But we must be deliberate about this paradox, as best we can. I try to do that regularly by finding a time and a place when and where I can say the Trinity Prayer repeatedly but also allow time and space for my mind to wander and my heart to be open to the inspiration of the Spirit.

But seeing visions and dreaming dreams? What might such an experience be like for someone like me, who has nothing to bring to God but my sins? What might such an experience be like for someone like me, who has nothing but a fragile faith and who must walk in that faith seeing only through a glass darkly? What might such an experience mean for someone like me, who is thoroughly—although perhaps covertly—implicated in an affluent, probably patriarchal, life of worldly comforts and power? Is it possible for someone like me to see visions and to dream dreams, as individual members of that first apostolic community did? I believe that it is.

This is my mundane testimony: practice the Trinity Prayer, in the midst of these twilight times, and by the Spirit you will be enabled to contemplate God anew, however refracted your own vision might be. You may even be enabled to see glimpses of the whole world of nature, your own embodied self included, as a theater of God's glory (Calvin). You also may be enabled to see a vision of this earth, in particular, as a place where all living creatures can flourish, each according to its own ecological niche, even as you are deeply aware that the whole creation is groaning in travail and that you are implicated in that groaning here on earth. What can you do to cultivate such a vision, as you await the Pentecostal tongues of fire to descend upon your life?

Find a time and a place when and where you can slow your sauntering, and your praying of the Trinity Prayer along the way, to a rate as close to stopping as possible. You won't be careening along on the subway, in other words, nor even walking purposely along the banks of a river like the Charles. I'm thinking of sauntering much more slowly than that. Find some place like the Hidden Garden at Hunts Corner, some time when you can repeat the words of the Trinity Prayer no faster than the forward and backward motions of that garden swing. Perchance you will want to separate each of those repetitions by several movements of that swing. Keep the swing moving, in other words, but feel free to sing the three utterances of the prayer, one by one, only after a number of silent movements between each petition. Then you will have the kind of slow time you need to ponder each of the three parts of that prayer and to reflect about each one more than once, perhaps several times. Once you are thus swinging at the slowest possible speed, and allowing thoughts related to each part of the prayer to flow into your heart and mind, it will then be time to wait on the Spirit to inspire you to dream dreams and see visions.

True, if you are new to this kind of devotion, you probably will not be able to do everything at once. It is probably best, for a beginner in such moments, simply to repeat the three petitions of the Trinity Prayer, allowing some silence for reflection between each petition. But let those silences be filled, as that is given to you to do, with spiritual fragments, if you are a beginner, but, whenever possible, with some of the rich kind of images that I have identified in the foregoing narrative. But whether you are just beginning with these kinds of practices or more are comfortable with them, perhaps because of previous spiritual experience, do sing boldly—and then wait.

LORD JESUS CHRIST, HAVE MERCY ON ME

Sing first: *Lord Jesus Christ, have mercy on me.* Then be silent for a spell. Next, repeat this petition, followed by the silence, three more times, for a total of four (I will explain in the appendix why I have chosen the number four). As you move on the swing, so to speak, after each petition let images of Jesus as you have come to know him in the New Testament flood into your mind and heart. The New Testament contains an abundance of such images.

I have already reflected earlier about John's account of Mary Magdalene staring into the empty tomb and then turning to encounter the one who spoke to her, whom she, after some moments, recognized as the risen Lord. In Bonhoeffer's telling Advent image, Jesus opened the door to Mary's world of grief from the outside. Jesus approached her world and loved her. He had mercy on her. And she responded with joy, once she had turned and recognized that it was he. He also made her the first apostle of a new order of things.

That new order of things, however, was not to be just a new order of light. It would soon become evident to first-century witnesses such as Mary that that dawning of the new order of things would also bring with it a new kind of onslaught by the principalities and powers of death, witnessed to by the Johannine author of the Book of Revelation. Jesus would then be dramatically revealed to his followers as the suffering Lamb of God engaged in a terrifying twilight struggle with the powers of "the Beast," powers that were embodied most visibly, according to the Book of Revelation, in the death-wielding reign of Rome. In the language of our own cinematic era, Jesus was thus revealed as the Prince of Peace engaged in an apocalyptic struggle with the Prince of Darkness. Writing in the same kind of first century sociospiritual milieu, the apostle Paul would also take his stand for the lordship of Christ over against the lordship of Caesar.

Reminiscent of the Johannine and Pauline traditions, therefore, we who live in our own twilight times will, when we petition Jesus for mercy, rightly desire to be led into a two-dimensional experience, a double enlightenment. We will want to know the love of God for us personally and the love of God empowering us for an intense struggle with the principalities and powers of this age. The biblical Jesus, as Bonhoeffer never tired of reminding us, is not just given for us but is given also for the whole world, and so all who are touched by this Jesus will at once be sent by Jesus as disciples, as witnesses to his light, into this world of apocalyptic ambiguities.

Often, then, when I slow down the pace of my praying to allow myself to ponder what I am asking for when I call out to Jesus for his mercy, I consciously recall my own sinfulness. And I recognize, in various ways, how implicated I am—given my particular affluent and perhaps also patriarchal existence—in the powers of this world that make for suffering and death for others, particularly for the poor and all the downtrodden creatures of this earth, all of whom are now groaning in travail. So, as I slowly move forward and back on the Hidden Garden swing, and as I take the time to mull over my petition, *Lord Jesus Christ, have mercy on me*, I think of Jesus not only as loving me, a sinner, but also as sending me, now a disciple, to be a peacemaker for the sake of all the creatures of God's good earth, as the Spirit may prompt and lead me. And I dream of a time when all creatures will flourish on this earth and throughout the cosmos, each in its own way, and be at peace with one another in the world to come, when all things will be made new.

PRAISE FATHER, SON, AND HOLY SPIRIT

Sing, second: *Praise Father, Son, and Holy Spirit.* Then be silent for a spell. As you move on the swing after uttering that second part of the Trinity Prayer, let images of the Trinity that you have gleaned from the Scriptures flood into your mind and heart, especially from the Gospel of John where Jesus, the Good Shepherd (John 10:11), says "I and the Father are one" (John 10:30). As an illustration of possible ways of imaging the Trinity, with what I take to be strong biblical resonances, I have shared with you three analogical narratives, each one of which has its own characteristic accent: the joy of God, the power of God, and the love of God.

Further, because I have decided as a matter of practical convenience to sing this petition—*Praise Father, Son, and Holy Spirit*—four times, I can meditate about each of these three accents, joy, power, and love, and then, fourth, about the mystery of God's unsearchable infinity and fecundity. When I bring each of those accents to consciousness, I also find it helpful to bring the originating image back to mind, at least in some fragmentary fashion: for joy, the festival Thanksgiving meal; for power, the torrential flow of the Niagara River; for love, the self-giving of the one who saved my life. Then I conclude, once again, with the fourth repetition, as I ponder the mystery of the fecundity and the infinity of the Trinity.

Since, more particularly, I am constantly concerned to demythologize traditional patriarchal thinking about the Trinity, particularly traditional images of the Father, in those quiet moments on the swing I often reflect about the persons of the Trinity as Giver, Gift, and Giving and, following Luther, about the first person of the Trinity, in particular, as my dear heavenly Father who gives all his children an abundance of good and precious gifts. I also find occasion to think of the Father, in Moltmann's terms, as our motherly Father and as the one who suffers upon losing the Son.

At other times during the silence after repetitions of the Trinity Prayer's second utterance, *Praise Father, Son, and Holy Spirit*, I allow myself to ponder the paradoxical immanence of the triune God, in, with, and under all things. As I swing slowly, I open my eyes to contemplate the world around me, since that is where the God whom I am addressing in the Trinity Prayer is to be found, not lifted up in some other world. I ponder the paradox that the wholly other God is closer to all things than they are to themselves. I see the purple beech in front of me and I know that I am thus, mysteriously and paradoxically, engaged with the God who is in, with, and under all things. I contemplate the monarch butterfly drawing near to kiss the flower of the milkweed, and I contemplate the ineffable presence of God doing the same. I touch the hand of Laurel extended to me on that swing, when she is there with me, and I touch the hand of the wholly other God reaching out to me. But, in all this, what I see is at once just the purple beech, just the hovering of the butterfly, and just the hand of my dearly beloved. God as the Immediate is present in our world only as the Beyond. And all the creatures of God have their own integrity. Still, this is where I engage God, right before my very eyes.

I believe, indeed, that with the eyes of faith, I can cautiously see traces of this triune God inscribed in the world around me, a complex thought that I explored in some detail above but which I also want to underline here. Consider the interdependence of the butterfly and the milkweed plant; the power of that purple beech, which may well grow to be one of those giants in the earth that lives for more than a hundred years; and the self-giving love that Laurel and

I experience when we grasp hands on the swing. Each of these moments, for one who has eyes to see, can be understood to be a trace of the Trinity: the interdependence of the divine persons, the infinite and fecund power of the divine persons, and the self-giving love among the divine persons.

Even more mysteriously, from time to time, between the petitions of the Trinity Prayer, I reflect about those particular creatures—the monarch butterfly, the purple beech, and my wife Laurel—as creatures that have been given being and becoming by the two hands of God, Christ the Good Shepherd and the Spirit, the Lifegiving One. Those created realities are what they are insofar as they are held together by the cosmic Christ, and insofar as they are sustained in their sufferings by the same cosmic Christ, as they may suffer in different ways. The same three creatures of God have also become what they have become because of eliciting powers of the Spirit, drawing them into ever new realizations of being, toward their ultimate eternal fulfillment in God.

COME HOLY SPIRIT, COME AND REIGN

Sing, third: *Come Holy Spirit, come and reign.* Then be silent for a spell. But be ready to be energized. If you happen to find yourself kneeling, as I once did that time weeding around a rose bush in the Hidden Garden, be ready to jump to your feet. If you happen to find yourself sitting meditatively, as I sometimes find myself on the swing in the Hidden Garden, be ready, again, to jump to your feet. Discover that you cannot pray otherwise when you are calling on the Spirit to come and reign. I once thought of this, in an irreverent moment, as sauntering on steroids. There is an inner "high" at this moment, or there can be.

Krister Stendahl used to startle some of his more pious students by referring to prayer as "putting holy pressure on God." Stendahl said that that is a characteristic biblical understanding. You call on God to keep God's promises, with the underlying thought being something like this: "Lord, you have promised to restore the fortunes of Israel, now keep your promise!" A case in point, according to Stendahl, would be the petition from the Lord's Prayer: "Your kingdom come." There you put holy pressure on God to get on with realizing God's eschatological promises. Further, said Stendahl, it is entirely possible, and possibly the best option, to translate the "daily bread" petition in the Lord's Prayer eschatologically, putting holy pressure on God to keep the divine promise for a new heavens and a new earth, without delay: "Our bread for tomorrow, give us today." Stendahl was also wont to observe that a characteristic early Christian posture for prayer was standing on one's tip-toes, arms outstretched to the future, asking God to set things right on earth, as in heaven, and to do so without delay.[9]

Already as a student of Stendahl, I found that that approach to prayer—putting holy pressure on God—could be spiritually liberating. You are a God of healing, Lord; now heal my sister's brain cancer. You are a God of justice, Lord; now bring something good out of this March on Washington. You are a God who loves everything that you have made, Lord; now make this Earth Day the beginning of a revolution in the politics of America. You are a God who notices when every sparrow falls to the ground, Lord; now notice the disappearance of habitats for our brothers and sisters, the birds, in Latin America and North America, and do something about it! You have called your churches to be a light to the nations, Lord; now judge us members of the Body of Christ and set us free to be such a light, in these times when the noise of your good earth's groaning is overwhelming.

For me, petitioning the Spirit to come and reign is such a prayer, putting holy pressure on God. So I always have the impulse, when I so call on the Spirit, to get up from my knees or get off the swing and to stand up on my tip-toes, with my arms extended horizontally before me, to the point on the horizon that I imagine to be the future. And I pray: *Come Holy Spirit, come and reign!* Come Holy Spirit, get on with realizing all the promises of God. Do not wait. Do not hesitate. Do what you are going to do and do it now.

Here we encounter, of course, what might be called the primary conundrum of prayer. If the primary paradox of prayer is the fact that God does everything and that we do everything, the primary conundrum of prayer is that we ask for everything and that God gives us everything, in due course—in God's good time, as my mother used to say—perhaps not until the day of the new heavens and the new earth. But God creates us and redeems us to be petitioning creatures as well as praising creatures. And Jesus teaches us to ask for our daily bread or for our bread for tomorrow, with this question always stirring in the heart of the one who prays, biblically speaking: how long, Lord, how long?! (cf. Isa.. 6:11, Ps. 13:1-2, Ps. 35:17).

CALLING ON THE SPIRIT TO REIGN UNIVERSALLY

With this understanding of prayer in my mind and heart, putting holy pressure on God, I eagerly and sometimes impatiently call on the Holy Spirit to come and reign. When I utter this petition, I also have in mind the different dimensions of God's creation—in, with, and under—where I am urging the Holy Spirit to work. I typically think of these differing dimensions in concrete terms, although sometimes in more discursive phenomenological terms, such as those employed by Hefner in his description of the several "acts" of cosmic evolution, which I reviewed earlier. I think of the history of matter, the history of life, the history of human life, and the history of salvation, all of which interpenetrate one another in various, and sometimes infinitely complicated, ways—and then I call on the Spirit to come and reign. Following are examples of how I call on the Spirit in such ways, referring to that universal and variegated history of the Spirit with all things.

The history of matter. Come Holy Spirit, come and finish the ministry you began with the Big Bang. Empower the countless billions of galaxies in their course. Guide the 50 million earth-sized planets in our galaxy. Keep the continental shelves of planet Earth moving and the Gulf Stream flowing. Call forth the thunder and the lightning in the mountains and bring forth living streams of water from the earth. Flow with the rains and the creeks and the rivers as their waters find their ways to the oceans. Charge the electrons and protons and neutrons in their orbits. Work with power in the vast seas of dark matter.

The history of life. Come Holy Spirit, come and finish the ministry you began with the first emergence of life on our planet. Draw forth new vitalities in the oceans and the plains. Call forth the birds of the air to take to flight and to find safe havens along their routes. Show the downy woodpeckers and the chickadees and all the birds that live in the Mt. Auburn cemetery during the winter where to find food. Engender new springtime life in the bears and foxes in the forests and in the woodchucks and chipmunks of the fields and farms. Hold the mighty sugar maples in place in the midst of the gales that you call forth. Stir inside the seeds of the fields and the gardens, that they may send forth new and living shoots. Strengthen the hearts of the doe and the fawn and the beat of every human heart. Energize and protect the wildebeests in their massive migrations.

The history of human life. Come Holy Spirit, come and gather the lost and forsaken children of Adam and Eve into communities of life. Bring forth good grains and fine fruits from the plains and hills of the earth, in order to nurture our bodies and gladden our hearts. Minister with power in the lives of those people of the earth who struggle against great corporate interests that, out of greed, would destroy the vitalities of the mountains and the streams and poison the soil in the valleys. Call forth prophetic leaders to inspire the citizens of the world to discover and to follow clean energy paths and to curtail those policies that make for the warming of the earth's atmosphere. Bring the citizens of our cities together in order to work for an end to violence in their streets and poisons in their air. Upend the power of those who blink at the incarceration of people of color in huge numbers in our society. Find food for the countless families who do not have enough to eat in this land of abundance. Comfort all the women who are being abused on this earth, and set them free. Let the green places in our cities flourish; and empower the citizens of our cities to demand access to such places in safety. Call forth champions of the wilderness, that those places might be protected and might flourish. Make a way for new generations of tillers of the land to emerge and to prosper, working with the land, in behalf of the common good. Fill the hearts of all artists with creativity, so that many of the children of this earth might be moved in awe and touched with joy.

The history of salvation. Come Holy Spirit, come and finish the history you began with Abraham and Sarah, leading them forth to a far country. As you brought Israel through the wilderness to become a new people in the land of promise and drove Jesus out into the wilderness to become a new Adam to inaugurate a new creation, so inspire the people of the Jesus movement today to be your witnesses to the ends of the earth. As you raised Jesus from the dead to give new life to all things, now instill in the church of Christ a new passion in behalf of the salvation that you are bringing to all peoples and to all creatures, through Christ. Burn fervently in our hearts to preach the Gospel of the forgiveness of sins, life, and salvation. Take hold of our bodies and lead us in the ways of righteousness, helping us to hear the groaning of the whole creation, especially here on earth. Lead us anew to cherish your good earth and fittingly to embrace all its creatures as brothers and sisters. Open our eyes to see the risen Lord gesturing for us to behold the lilies of the field, as messengers of the Father's glory. Create in us a new spirit, that we might rightfully know how to contemplate God as Father, Son, and

Spirit, as Giver, Gift, and Giving, as the source and ground and goal of all things. Teach us, finally, O Lifegiving One, to pray aright, as we stand before nature, engaged with nature, with words like these:

Lord Jesus Christ, have mercy on me.
Praise Father, Son, and Holy Spirit.
Come Holy Spirit, come and reign.

Notes

1. Henry David Thoreau, *Walking* (Memphis, TN: Bottom of the Hill Publishing, 2011), 20: "I have met with but one or two persons in the course of my life who understood the art of walking, that is, of taking walks, who had a genius, so to speak, for sauntering; which word is beautifully derived 'from idle people who roved about the country, in the middle ages, and asked charity, under pretence of going *à la sainte terrer*'—to the holy land, till the children exclaimed, 'There goes a *sainte-terrer*', a saunterer—a holy-lander. They who never go to the holy land in their walks, as they pretend, are indeed mere idlers and vagabonds, but they who do go there are saunterers in the good sense, such as I mean. Some, however, would derive the word from *sans terre*, without land or a home, which, therefore, in the good sense, will mean, having no particular home, but equally at home everywhere. For this is the secret of successful sauntering. He who sits still in a house all the time may be the greatest vagrant of all, but the saunterer, in the good sense, is no more vagrant than the meandering river, which is all the while sedulously seeking the shortest course to the sea. But I prefer the first, which indeed is the most probable derivation. For every walk is a sort of crusade, preached by some Peter the Hermit in us, to go forth and reconquer this holy land from the hands of the Infidels."

2. Further, I think that we can do without Thoreau's infelicitous reference to the Crusades. See the preceding note.

3. What precisely is sauntering? This is one of those constructs that eludes easy definition. Like time, you know what it is, as Augustine once observed, until somebody asks you about it. Sauntering can best be described, rather than defined. Mindful walking is what I usually have in mind when I think of sauntering, in contrast to mindless activity, going through the motions. A simple but not altogether satisfactory example might be this. When I am at the gym, on a stationary bicycle, I can read a magazine when I am just pedaling. But for the last three of my twenty minutes on that machine, when I am pedaling as fast as I can, I have to put my magazine down, grab on to the handles of the machine, and rid myself of any thoughts other than the hope that, thankfully, this exercise will soon be over. The first, longer segment of my riding is akin to what I mean by sauntering. Another example would be two different kinds of movement along a forest path, walking, compared to riding on an all-terrain vehicle. I do not want to sound like a cultural snob in this respect, looking down my nose, at it were, at ATV riders. In southwestern Maine, some participate in an ATV culture that is replete with many virtues, such as community solidarity. But I do think that when you walk along a forest path, you can see things and think about things that you probably would not see or think about were you to be riding through on an ATV. Sauntering is closer to the first than to the second. A third, and final, example I draw from my world of liturgical experience. I have participated in—sauntered through—liturgies that have sometimes carried me away, as if time were of no concern. I have participated in other liturgies that have left me frustrated because they were "rushed," perhaps due to some protestant sensibility that time is money and that therefore an hour for worship is plenty, or perhaps due to some Catholic pragmatism that drives some priests to hurry to finish one liturgy in order to start the

next one promptly. But never mind such examples. I hope you will have a sense for what I mean by sauntering, even though I cannot define it in a satisfactory fashion.

4. The great Karl Barth, author of the multivolumed *Church Dogmatics* and longtime resident of Switzerland, scarcely mentions the Alps in his writings (at least, that was my experience in reading through many of his works), while, in contrast, he finds ways to intensely celebrate the music of Mozart. I don't begrudge him the Mozart at all, but what about his failure to celebrate the Alps at least as much as the Mozart? It has been, and still is, a puzzle to me.

5. Oliver Sacks, *Musicophilia: Tales of Music and the Brain* (New York: Knopf, 2007), x. For a good review of this insightful work, from a theological perspective, see James Clyde Sellman, "Music on Your Mind," *Harvard Divinity Bulletin* 36, no. 1 (Winter 2008): 91–94.

6. See Sachs, *Musicophilia*, 344, writing in 2007: "Familiar music acts as a sort of Proustian mnemonic, eliciting emotions and associations that had been long forgotten, giving the patient access once again to moods and memories, thoughts and worlds that had seemingly been completely lost. Faces assume expressions as the old music is recognized and its emotional power felt. One or two people, perhaps, start to sing along, others join them, and soon the entire group—many of them virtually speechless before—is singing together, as much as they are able."

7. For the quotes from Luther in this paragraph, and for a survey of the considerable historical significance of Luther and the music he championed, see J. Andreas Loewe, "Why Do Lutherans Sing? Lutherans, Music, and the Gospel in the First Century of the Reformation," *Church History* 82, no. 1 (March 2013): 69–89. Loewe concludes his study by citing these words from a poem by Luther, "Fraw Musica" (Lady Music): "For God our loving Lord did music make / to be a proper singer, the master of composers: / Day and night she sings and sounds his praise. / Since nothing will tire her in praising him, / my own song, too, shall honour him/ and give him thanks eternally." For the existential meaning of the church's music more generally, see Jeremy S. Begbie, Resounding Truth: Christian Wisdom in the Word of Music (Grand Rapids, MI: Baker Academic, 2007).

8. I have instanced Luther and his devotion to music as an example of this visceral interiority. Another good example is the music of the Sacred Harp tradition (Shape Notes). From Elizabethan roots, this hymnody spread up and down the Appalacians in America, from the eighteenth century onward. It is reported that, at times, when this vigorous four-part harmony was voiced by a congregation divided by parts on each of the four sides of a meeting hall, singing hours on end, some, if not all, the singers experienced a kind of "high," perhaps induced by hyperventilating (!). Closer to my own experience, African American gospel singing occasionally leads some worshippers to get "carried away' with all manner of bodily expressions. This kind of visceral interiority given with music, strikingly, troubled the great St. Augustine, although he acknowledged the power of hymnody and affirmed its importance, within limits. So he writes in his Confessions 10:33, addressing God: "I admit that I still find some enjoyment in the music of hymns, which are alive with your praises, when I hear them sung by well-trained melodious voices.... I realize that when they are sung these sacred words stir my mind to greater religious fervor and kindle in me a more ardent form of piety than they would if they were not sung; and I also know that there are particular modes in song and the voice, corresponding to my various emotions and able to stimulate them because of some mysterious relationship between the two. But I ought not to allow my mind to be paralysed by the gratification of my senses, which often leads it astray.... So I waver between the danger that lies in gratifying the senses and the benefits which, as I know from experience, can accrue from singing. Without committing myself to an irrevocable opinion, I am inclined to approve of the custom of singing in church...."

9. All of these references to the ideas of Krister Stendahl come from student remembrances, etched in my mind from Stendahl's lectures and sermons and private conversations over a period of many years, when I was an undergraduate and then a theological student.

Epilogue
The Trinity Prayer as Spiritual Exercise

In the preceding pages, I have regularly recommended doing your spiritual exercise—in this case by invoking the Trinity Prayer—as often as you can. Let me recapitulate here. When Jesus says, in the Sermon on the Mount, "Ask, and it will be given you; search, and you will find; knock, and the door will be opened to you" (Matt. 7:7), he presumably is not entertaining the response "How often, Lord?" Rather, he is surely referring to a lifelong rhythm and its promise. The goal, then, is to "pray without ceasing," according to the apostolic injunction that I have referred to a number of times (1 Thess. 5:17).

Still, a journey of a thousand miles does begin with a single step—and it continues with single steps. I have suggested some specific steps in the preceding chapter and have encouraged you from the very beginning of this narrative to *start exercising spiritually without delay*, using the Trinity Prayer. Early on in these explorations, too, I suggested that this is precisely the correct order: start practicing the Trinity Prayer and keep practicing it constantly, whether or not you feel comfortable about it, because while practice does not make perfect, practice can make possible. If you wait for the moment when you will "feel comfortable" with the Trinity Prayer, that moment may never arrive. If you run or jog for exercise, when you first started, you probably didn't feel comfortable about that either. But you kept at it, and that was a good thing.

Then, I also suggested that, as you practice this prayer, you can let your consciousness be suffused with spiritual meanings. The sometimes winding and occasionally steep path we have followed in this book has, I hope, given you the meanings you need to allow you to do that.

This leads me to another, more practical question. How can you possibly call forth *all* of the spiritual meanings we have identified along the way in these lengthy explorations when you pray such a short prayer? The answer is: you cannot. My purpose thus far has been to introduce you to the many and varied meanings that I believe are given with the Trinity Prayer so that they might hover, as it were, in your subliminal mind and heart—not to suggest that all those meanings must somehow gather in your conscious mind when you pray.

239

Still, my hope is that, as you practice the Trinity Prayer, a number of those meanings will emerge, now and again, from your subliminal mind and heart and give your prayer a breadth of awareness that it might not otherwise have. But it is surely sufficient, also, simply just to say the words. Say the words and trust in the Spirit to elicit the meanings in your mind and heart—but do note that you may not grasp those meanings consciously. Keep in mind the words of the Apostle: "The Spirit helps us in our weakness; for we do not know how to pray as we ought, but that very Spirit intercedes with sighs too deep for words. And God, who searches the heart, knows what is the mind of the Spirit, because the Spirit intercedes for the saints according to the will of God" (Rom. 8:26-27).

On the other hand, I have found that some *coded meanings* that are reflective of the long journey of spiritual exploration that we have just completed can be helpful. I don't always consciously rely on these coded meanings. Much of my own praying of the Trinity Prayer is simply saying the words of the prayer and allowing meanings to surface in my conscious mind—or not—as the Spirit may or may not elicit them. But when I find the time and the appropriate place—swinging by myself in the Hidden Garden, for example, or during that long flight to London, or when I stand before the crucifix next to my bed first thing in the morning—I do find that such coded meanings sometimes can be helpful. They offer a way to enrich the mind and the heart at any given moment, without requiring you to be burdened by the thought that you can barely remember the many spiritual meanings that you know are given with the Trinity Prayer. So use these coded meanings or not—or use coded meanings of your own making—as the Spirit may or may not give you occasion.

As I speak each part of the Trinity Prayer, I sometimes consciously call to mind the following coded meanings:

Lord Jesus Christ, have mercy on me. I think how broken and unworthy I am, in these times of crisis.

Lord Jesus Christ, have mercy on me. I think how Jesus is my good shepherd, notwithstanding my sins.

Lord Jesus Christ, have mercy on me. I think how Jesus has given me and everyone else the forgiveness of sins, life, and   salvation.

Lord Jesus Christ, have mercy on me. I think how Jesus has come to liberate me and every creature.

Praise Father, Son, and Holy Spirit. I think of the infinite fecundity and the unsearchable mystery of God.

Praise Father, Son, and Holy Spirit. I think of the joy of God, akin to a festival meal.

Praise Father, Son, and Holy Spirit. I think of the power of God, akin to a torrential flow.

Praise Father, Son, and Holy Spirit. I think of the love of God, akin to a self-giving savior.

ALTERNATE CODE MEANINGS FOR THE MIDDLE PETITION

Praise Father, Son, and Holy Spirit. I think of the motherly Father.

Praise Father, Son, and Holy Spirit. I think of the Son as the cosmic good shepherd.

Praise Father, Son, and Holy Spirit. I think of the Spirit as the cosmic lifegiving one.

Praise Father, Son, and Holy Spirit. I think of the Son and the Spirit as the cosmic hands of the motherly Father, working wondrously together in all things.

Come Holy Spirit, come and reign. I think of the Spirit working throughout the physical cosmos, as in the birth of a star.

Come Holy Spirit, come and reign. I think of the Spirit working throughout the processes of life on Earth, as in the birth of a fawn.

Come Holy Spirit, come and reign. I think of the Spirit working throughout the processes of human history, as when Rosa Parks gave birth to the Civil Rights Movement.

Come Holy Spirit, come and reign. I think of the Spirit working throughout the history of the church, as in my own new birth in Baptism.

However, do not force the matter. Say the words of the Trinity Prayer, and trust the Spirit to take your prayer captive, with or without such coded meanings.

When you grow accustomed to saying the Trinity Prayer in this manner, I hope that you will then be willing to experiment with *singing* the prayer. As I have strongly recommended, if at all possible, those who use the Trinity Prayer should try to sing it and indeed get accustomed to singing it. Those who have musical gifts may want to work this out for themselves, perhaps creating their own tune(s) or chant(s). For those who feel more comfortable with the tunes of familiar hymns, I make some suggestions in the appendix.

Regarding the list in the appendix, I am aware that even such a short selection of hymn tunes may seem formidable. Wouldn't it be better simply to adopt a single, familiar tune, in order not to be distracted by too many choices? Probably, *yes*—and surely at the beginning. For this reason, I recommend for most who want to consider whether regular singing of the Trinity Prayer might work for them to settle upon a single tune and to make use of only that tune for some time. I myself used "the Doxology" (see the appendix) for many years before it dawned on me that my use of the Trinity Prayer might be enriched by weaving it into the fabric of the Church Year.

Once you have formed the habit of singing a single tune, the dimensions of your praying can be enhanced by choosing a tune that reflects where you find yourself in the Church Year (see the appendix for examples). But don't try to do that too quickly. The most important thing is the resonance of your singing. Integrating that resonance into the music of the Church Year is a secondary matter. So, choose a tune, and stay with it as long as you wish. And all the way along—sing boldly.

Next, I want to say something about your *posture* when you say or sing the Trinity Prayer. One advantage of the singing is that your bodily resonance can be very much a part of the experience. That has its own importance, since we humans are thoroughly creatures of nature, and of our own embodiment in particular. I have also mentioned my own swinging and swaying during some hymns on Sundays at my church in Roxbury. I have found that my whole self—body as well as mind and heart—is more fully drawn into the praying experience not only by the singing but also by attending to other kinds of bodily improvisations.

Whether you choose to kneel or to stand, to begin with, is up to you. It could depend on the season of the Church Year, for example, kneeling during Lent and standing during the Easter and Pentecost/Ordinary Time seasons. Your mood may play a part here, too. Sometimes, when life is just too heavy, I kneel as matter of course. Sometimes, when I'm seized by joy, I *have* to stand up—in the mood of the words from *Porgy and Bess*, "I can't sit down." I have even spontaneously assumed the posture of Bellini's St. Francis, as you have seen it on the cover of this book and as I once did in the Hidden Garden.

But usually, whether standing or kneeling, these are the physical motions that I adopt, depending on my location. In public, I adhere to the "secret discipline of faith" (Bonhoeffer) without any visible kind of bodily engagement. In more private settings, when I begin to sing *Lord Jesus Christ, have mercy on me* four times, I contemplate the crucifix that is usually before me and then bow my head and make the sign of the cross, pressing my pectoral cross into my chest to remind myself of the physicality of the cross. When I begin to sing *Praise Father, Son, and Holy Spirit* four times, I shut my eyes, apropos of meditating on the ineffable mystery of the Trinity, and I start swaying, left and right, right and left, as if I am pulsating in harmony with the glorious inner energy of the Trinity itself.

When I sing *Come Holy Spirit, come and reign* four times, I continue to sway left and right, right and left, still with my eyes closed. But I also extend my arms forward toward an imaginary horizon, which, for me, stands for the promised future of God, whence the Holy Spirit has begun to reach back to me in order to draw my singing and indeed my whole self into the future of God. My body moves in yet a different way when I'm pushing myself back and forth on the swing in the Hidden Garden in Hunts Corner, singing the Trinity Prayer, with each petition separated from the next by times of silent meditation. You will have to decide for yourself which motions work best for you and at what times.

Appendix
Possible Seasonal Hymn Tunes for the Trinity Prayer

The following is a list of the hymn tunes that I have used at different times in order to sing the Trinity Prayer boldly. I apologize in advance for the parochial character of this list. These are melodies that happen to be familiar to me. This means that, by definition, they are only a small slice of available options, and by no means necessarily the best slice. Consider them, then, to be a point of departure rather than any kind of canon.

The idea is to repeat each of the three petitions of the Trinity Prayer *four times as a single stanza* of the hymn tune. The first stanza would therefore be *Lord Jesus Christ, have mercy on me*, repeated four times. The second stanza would be *Praise Father, Son, and Holy Spirit*, again repeated four times.[1] Finally, the third stanza would be *Come Holy Spirit, come and reign*, also repeated four times.

ANY SEASON

OLD HUNDREDTH (16th century). LM. Familiar title: Praise God, from Whom All Blessings Flow ("the Doxology")
TALLIS CANON (16th century). LM. Familiar title: All Praise to Thee, My God This Night

ADVENT

VENI EMMANUEL (15th century). 8888. *Adding words of the hymn's refrain to each stanza: "Rejoice! Rejoice! Emmanuel Shall come to you, O Israel."* Familiar title: Oh Come, Oh Come, Emmanuel

CHRISTMAS

VON HIMMEL HOCH(16th century). LM. Familiar title: From Heaven Above

GREENSLEEVES (16th century). 87 87 68 67. *Adding these words to each stanza of four repeated petitions: "This, this is Christ the king,/Whom shepherds guard and angels sing;/Haste, haste to bring him laud,/The babe, the son of Mary!"* Familiar title: What Child Is This

EPIPHANY

DIX (19th century). 77 77 77. *For this hymn tune only, sing each stanza six times.* Familiar title: As with Gladness Men of Old
WALTON (12th century). LM. Familiar title: O Jesus, Joy of Loving Hearts

LENT

ERHALT UNS, HERR (16th century). LM. Familiar title: Lord, Keep Us Steadfast in Your Word
GRACE CHURCH, Ganaoque (20th century). LM. Familiar title: Fight the Good Fight

EASTER

LLANFAIR (19th century). 77 77 and alleluias. *Adding the hymn's alleluias to each stanza.* Familiar title: Christ the Lord Is Risen Today; Alleluia!
TRURO (18th century). LM. Familiar title: Christ Is Alive! Let Christians Sing

PENTECOST/ORDINARY TIME

PUER NOBIS (17th century). LM. Familiar title: O Holy Spirit, Root of Life
OLD HUNDREDTH or TALLIS CANON (see above: Any Season)

Notes

1. Some may wish to use the archaic language—"Praise Father, Son, and Holy Ghost"—rather than the more familiar "Praise Father, Son, and Holy Spirit," for metrical reasons. The single-syllable word *Ghost* seems to flow more freely here than the two-syllable *Spirit,* although the latter also seems to be perfectly serviceable.

Index

Althaus, Paul, 154n36
Analogy/ies, 98-100, 124n6, of being (analogia entis) 155n40, of faith (analogia pistis) 155n40; Roughly hewn narratives as 103, 123, 144-151
Animals: Self-sacrifice of 149; Suffering of 63, 167-168, 203-204, 208-209; Eschatological fulfilment of 201-202
Anthropocentrism, 108, 129, 188, 197
Augustine, St., xxivn19, 94n21, 127n23, 153n22, 184n36, 202, 237n3, 238n8
Augustus Caesar, 206-208

Bach, J. S., 75, 227
Baer, Jr., Richard A., 25-26, 35 n. 8, 222
Baptism, 9-15, 39, 43, 62, 109, 176, 226; Ambiguities of 11, 13-15; and the problematic Trinitarian name 13; and a baptismal mysticism 10-13
Barth, Karl, 38, 39, 41, 65, 94n2, 127n21, 127n25, 154n40, 214n24, 238n4
Bartholomew, Craig G., xxivn18
Basil of Caesaria, St., 183n31
Bass, Dorothy, 33n2
Bauckham, Richard, 69n20, 213n11
Beavis, Mary Ann, 66n2
Before Nature: meanings of xv-xvii
Begbie, Jeremy S., 238n7
Bellini, Giovanni, xii-xiv, xxiiin11
Berger, Peter, xxin2, xxiin3
Berry, Thomas, 214n15
Bethlehem Steel, Lackawanna, NY, 82, 109, 115-119
Billings, J. Todd, 126n16
Birch, Charles, 214n15
Bloom, Harold, 215n31

Body, the human, xiii, xvii, 16, 25, 133, 143, 148, 192-193, 202, 242, See also Spirituality and interiority, visceral and Prayer, bodily involvement in
Bonaventure, St., xxivn19, 29, 105
Bonhoeffer, Dietrich, 37, 46, 49n18, 59, 61, 65, 69n22, 71, 75, 91n1, 93n14, 94n21, 149, 230, 231, 242; and identity issues 82-83; and resistance to Hitler 40
Book of nature, see Nature, book of
Borg, Marcus, 93n16
Bornkamm, Heinrich, 153n20, 153n26
Bouma-Prediger, Stephen, xxivn18, 18n1
Braaten, Laurie J., 215n32, 216n40
Britten, Benjamin, 227
Brown, Raymond, 54, 58, 66nn3-4, 181n8
Brueggeman, Walter, 154n39
Brunner, Emil, 66n7
Buber, Martin, 39, 41, 48n2, 98
Buckley, James J., 34n4
Burrows, Ruth, 34n7
Burton-Christie, Douglas, 48n4

Calvin, John, 10, 55, 126, 139, 141, 153n24, 155n40, 166, 200, 213n12, 229
Campbell, David E., xxin1
Canlis, Julie, 139, 153n24
Case-Winters, Anna, 127n24
Chapel of St. Mary and St. John, Society of St. John the Evangelist, Cambridge, MA, 53-55, 59, 79, 89, 227

Charles River, Cambridge, MA, 39, 41, 47, 53, 54, 89, 105, 130, 132, 142, 147, 219, 227, 229
Chase, Stephen, xxivn16
Christ, *See* Jesus/Christ
Christianity and other religions, 14, 200, 214n23
Clayton, Philip, 49n17, 67n7
Clinton, Hilary Rodham, 77, 227
Coakley, Sarah, 92n9, 93n15, 125n8, 127n18, 155n45
Cobb, John, 214n15
Cosmos, *See* Nature
Cranmer, Thomas, 35n15
Cross/es: Celtic 193-194, 206, 223; Pectoral 225-226; Sign of the 29, 86, 225-228; Wall 86, 225, 226, 240, 242; *See also* Jesus/Christ, cross of

Cunningham, David S., 154n38
Cunningham, Lawrence S., 20n16

Dahill, Lisa, 48n1, 92n8
Daly, Mary, 18n 6, 77
Dante, Alighieri, 139
Dark night of the soul, 72-73, 91; *See also* Twilight of our times
Davies, Paul, 182n13
Dawkins, Richard, 49n 5
Dawson, Christopher, 66n6
Day, Dorothy, 21, 29
Deane-Drummond, Celia E., 183n31
Deism, 136-137
Domitian, 60
Downey, Michael, 126n17
Duerer, Albrecht, 192
Dupré, Louis, 20n16
Dykstra, Craig, 33n2

Earth Bible Project, 213n8
Eating practices, 81, 93n13
Ecojustice crisis, xix, 6, 41
Edwards, Denis, 182n15, 213n5, 214n26, 216n 44

Edwards, Jonathan, 104, 127n19, 154n38, 158
Emergence, cosmic (See: History, cosmic)
Enlightenment, spiritual, *See* Spirituality and enlightenment
"Eternal feminine", *See* Nature and "the feminine"
Eucharist (Communion), 47-48, 62, 143, 160

Faith, *See* Theology of faith
Fiddes, Paul S., 48n3, 69n23, 128n33, 213n13
Francis of Assisi, St., 21, 29, 47, 149, 152n8, 193, 202, 213n10, 218, 223; and Canticle of Brother Sun xiv, xxiin9, xxiin12, 196, 223; and Nature xxiiin12; Legacy of xii-xv
Fretheim, Terence E., 69n25, 196, 213n9, 213n11
Freud, Sigmund, 49n5, 79

Gnosticism, 60, 66n2, 189, 202-203, 212, 215n27, *See also* Cosmic despair and Nature, gnostic view of
God: Accommodating Godself to a variety of creatures 200-201, 213n12; and evil (theodicy) 22, 43, 62-64, 69n23, 69n27, 74, 212, *See also* Jesus/Christ and the problem of evil; as immanent xvii 129-143, 232; as joyful process 104-107, as natural as well as spiritual 108-109, 127n25; as self-giving savior 113-119; as the Beyond and the Immediate, not the Above 136, 142; as torrential flow 109-113; as Trinity *See* Trinity; as wholly other 38, 46, 61, 63, 65, 74, 97, 98, 103, 129, 135, 174, 175, 232; attributes of 104, 127n21; Beyond images of 125n12; Crucified 113-115, 122; Eclipse of 23, 31,

38-39; Fecundity of 105, 148; Immanence of 129-130; Infinity of 104, 148; Mystery of 100-105, 123; Power of 109-113, 200-201; Scything with 8-9; Son of See Jesus/Christ; Spirit of See Spirit, Holy; Transcendence of 129, 134-135, 141-142

Gorringe, T. J., 19n14

Gospel of John: Cosmic vision of 111, 163-164; Mary Magdelene in the 55-58

Gottlieb, Roger, 19n15

Green, Clifford J., 48n1, 69n22

Gregerson, Niels Henrik, 126n16

Gregory of Nyssa, 99, 103, 125n8

Grenz, Stanley J., 127n20

Guiver, George, 35n15

Habel, Norman, 184n33, 213n8

Hall, Douglas John, 64-65, 77nn29-31

Hansen, James, xix

Harris, Samuel, 49n5

Haught, John f., 49n5

Hefner, Philip, 199-200, 214n15, 214nn17-21

Hegel, Georg Wilhelm Friedrich, 67n7

Hendel, Kurt K., 153n30

Hermes Trismegistus, 138

Hesiod, 206

Hiebert, Theodore, 183n24

Hinsdale, Mary Ann, 66n4

History, Cosmic (emergence), 199-202, 214n16, 234-237

Hitchens, Christopher, 49n5

Hitler, Adolf, 37, 39, 40

Hoffmann, Bengt, 152nn14-15

Holocaust, the, 39-41, 43, 62, 63, 74

Hope, cosmic, See Nature and cosmic hope

Hopkins, G. M., 10

Horn, F. W., 183n26

Horn, Henry E., 40

Horrell, David G., 215n32

Howells, Edward, 152n13, 153n25

Hunt, Cheryl, 215n32, 215n36, 216n42

Hunts Corner, Maine, 1-9, 105, 145-195, 204, 219, 223, 229, 243

Hybels, William, xxiin4

Ignatius of Loyola, St., 22

Irenaeus of Lyon, St., 157, 180nn1-2, 202

Janson, Anthony F., xxiiin10

Janson, H. W., xxiiin10

Jenson, Robert W., 126n17

Jeremias, Joachim, 181n9

Jesus/Jesus Christ, 47-48; and the problem of evil 166-169 See also God and the problem of evil; Ascension of 139, 153nn23-24, 165-166; As good shepherd 161-169, 180n3; As cosmic Christ 32, 165-166, 174; Cross of 113-115, 121-122; In Mary Magdalene narrative 55-58; Personal relation to 84-86, 157, 165-166; Touch of 85-87; Universal ministry of 164-169; Voice of 57, 80

Jesus Prayer, 27-28, 30, 35n 9, 35n15, 84

Jewett, Robert, 215n32, 215n36-39, 216n43

John of the Cross, St., 125n12

Johnson, Elizabeth A., xxiin4, 173-177, 182n15, 182nn17-21, 183nn23-25, 183nn27-30

Johnson, Luke Timothy, 215n30

Jungel, Eberhard, 124nn6-7

Kaufman, Gordon, 38, 43-46, 49n9-17, 75

Kelly, Thomas R., 35n16

Kelsey, David H., 92n5, 124n2, 184n32

Kent, Corita, 23

Kenyon, Jane, xxivn17

xvi-xvii; Christianity's ambiguous relation to xiii, 14, 129; Deficit disorder xix; Eschatological fulfilment of 200-201; Integrity of 189, 194-202, 214n26; Gnostic view of See Gnosticism; Groaning of See Nature, travail of; Immensities of 108, 146-148; Love of xii, xx, 5; Meaning of the term 15-17; Spontaneity of 178, 200, 211, 214n22; Stewardship of 16, 19n12; Travail of 189, 203-211; Voice of 194-198, 205, 213n8

Niagara Falls/River, 11, 109-113, 145, 179

Nietzsche, Friedrich, 49n5

"Nones, the" See Seekers

Norris, Jr., Russell Bradner, 163, 181n7

Norris, Kathleen, 92n10

Obama, Barak, 227

Owens, L. Roger, 92n12

Panentheism, 136-139, 142, 154n37

Pantheism, 15, 136-137, 141

Paradox, 137-139, 166

Pasquarello, Michael, 215n35

Patriarchy, xvi, 76-78, 101-102, 114, 232

Paulsell, Stephanie, xxivn17

Pauw, Amy Plantinga, 127n19

Pelikan, Jaroslav, 181n6

Perkins, Pheme, 66n2

Perpetua, St., 165, 181n3

Peters, Ted, 18n5, 19n6, 19n11, 154n37, 215n28

Place/s: Agrarian understanding of xxivn18; of spiritual knowing 1-9, 39, 53-55, 105-107, 109-113, 115-119, 130-132, 158-162, 170-171, 189-194; Theology of xvii-xvii

Polkinghorne, John, 49n17, 156n46, 180, 184n35, 213n7

Practices, spiritual, See Spiritual practices

Prayer, 45, 228-230; Bodily involvement in 223, 226-228 See also Interiority, visceral and Exteriority, spiritual; Difficulty of 21-22; Practice of See Spiritual Practices

Proust, Marcel 31

Putnam, Robert D., xxin1

Rasmussen, Larry, 213n14

"Religion and spirituality", xi, 13, 17, 20n17

Resurrection Lutheran Church, Boston, MA, 88-89, 159-162, 177, 226

Resurrection Lutheran Church, Buffalo, NY, 9, 87

Revelation, Book of, 60-62

Rhoads, David, 19n10

Ricoeur, Paul, 93n16

Robbins, Jim, 155n42

Romans, Letter to the, and creation's groaning, 205-207

Rossing, Barbara, 69n21, 215n29

Rubenstein, Arthur, 224

Ruether, Rosemarie Radford, 77, 126n14

Ruffing, Janet K., 92n11, 152n13

Russell, Robert John, 68n9

Ruth, Lester, 215n35

Saarinen, Risto, 126n16, 126n17

Sachs, Oliver, 93n18; 238nn5-6

Santmire, H. Paul, xxiinn6-7, xxiiin10, xxivn15, xxivn19, 18n6, 19n7, 19nn12-13, 35n11, 66n1, 93nn19-20, 127n22, 134, 136, 151n1, 151nn3-5, 152n7, 152n9, 153n22, 181n6, 182n14, 213nn6-7, 214n27

Sauntering, 217-221

Schifferdecker, Kathryn, 155n43

Schleiermacher, Friedrich, 14

Schneiders, Sandra M., 19n15, 20n17, 66n4, 68nn11-12, 68n14; 69n19
Seasonal affective disorder, 47
Seekers, xiv-xv, xvii, 13, 14, 24, 33n3; The "Nones", xi-xii, 21, 33n1; The "Nones Sympathizers", xi-xii, 21

Self-examination, spiritual, *See* Spirituality and self-examination
Shakespeare, 99
Singing, *See* Music and singing
Sittler, Joseph, 88, 169, 181n6
Smith, James K. A, 94n21, 127n23, 189n36
Society of St. John the Evangelist, Cambridge, MA, 47, 53-55
Soskice, Janet, 124n6
Southgate, Christopher, 69n27, 128n33, 155n44, 184n34, 215n32
Spirit, Holy: as "Holy Ghost" 9, 106, 246n1; as the Lifegiving One 112, 175; Calling on the 187-202; Cosmic ministry of the 170-180, 198-202; Eclipse of the 172-174; of nature 170, 177 Spiritual practices, 22-26
Spirituality: African American 88-90, 93n20; and enlightenment 50n19, 231; and exteriority, spiritual 225-230; and images 230-232; and interiority, visceral 223; and liturgy *See* Liturgy as identity-forming; and practices *See* Spiritual practices; and religion *See* "Religion and spirituality"; and sauntering 217-230, 237n3; and self-examination 71, 74-84; and sexual fantasies 76, 78, 92n9; and the wild 72-73, 91n5, 125n12, 146-148; Apophatic 152n13, 153n2; Bifocal xiii-xvi, xxiiin12, 9; Celtic 89; Kataphatic 152n13, 153n20;

Meaning of the term xxi, 17-18; New Age 66n2, 202, 215n28; of ascent 134-135, 139, 154n36; of cosmic despair 202-203; of descent 136; of ordinary places 73-74, 91nn4-5 *See also* Nature, Christian Spirituality of, Exteriority, Interiority
Steenberg, M. C.; 180n2, 183n31
Steinmetz, David, 152n11, 152n19
Stendahl, Krister, 215n34, 233-234, 238n8
Stoeger, William R., 49n17
Stewart, Benjamin, 18n1
Storz, Martha Ellen, 33n2
Swimme, Brian, 214n15

Tauler, Johannes, 137
Teilhard de Chardin, Pierre, 76, 92n7
Tennyson, Alfred, Lord, 42
Tertullian, 124n8
Theism, 136
Theodicy *See* God and evil
Theology: and science 15, 19n11, 199-202; as human construction 44; Bifocal *See* Spirituality, bifocal; of ascent *See* Spirituality of ascent; of descent *See* Spirituality of descent; of facts 43, 75; of faith xv-xvi, 43, 46-48; of place *See* Place, theology of; of the ordinary 91n5
Thielicke, Helmut, 103
Thomas Aquinas, 70n28, 99
Thompson, Augustine, xxiiin10, xxiiin12
Thoreau, Henry David, xx, xxnn20-21, 15; and sauntering 217, 237n1; and walking in the wilds xvii-xviii
Tillich, Paul, 59, 67, 68, 68n16, 93n16, 103, 110, 111, 124n5, 137, 173
Titian (Tizian Vecellio), 192
Tracy, Thomas, 49n17

Trinity, 97-128, Analogies for *See* Analogy/ies; and patriarchy *See* Patriarchy; and the motherly Father 102, 113-114, 118, 128n29, 174, 211, 232, 178, 179, 212, 241; and the suffering of the Father 113-115; as Giver, Gift, Giving 32, 102, 126n17, 158, 169; Mystery of the 100-105; Name(s) of the 100-105, 126n15; Traces (vestigia) of the 143-151, 232-233; Two hands of the 157-180 *See also* Jesus/Christ and Spirit, Holy; Trinity Prayer xvi, 2, 23, 35n13; as a guide for praying 230-237; as a spiritual exercise 239-243; as a way of spiritual knowing 30-32; Emergence of the 27-28; Heritage and practice of the 28-30; Seasonal hymn tunes for 245-246; Singing the 220-225; with nature in mind 32-33

Tucker, Mary Evelyn, 19n8

Twilight of our times, 38-42, 71-73 *See also* Dark night of the soul

Underhill, Evelyn, 26

Van Gogh, Vincent, 150

Vestigia Trinitatis *See* Trinity, traces of

Virgil, 206-207

Wainwright, Geoffrey, 184n36

Walking *See* Sauntering

Walsh, Brian J., xxivn18

Walsh, Sylvia, 152n12

Ware, Kallistos 35nn9-10

Webb, Stephen H., 126n17

Weber, Otto, 127n25

White, Jr., Lynn, 14

White, Susan J., 35n11

Wiesel, Elie, 41, 48n3, 62

Wildman, Wesley, 49n17

Williams, Rowan, 91n1, 94n21

Wirzba, Norman, xxivn18, 93n13

Wood, Susan K., 34n4

Wright, N. T., 67n8

Wright, Wendy M., 67n8, 91n4

Wuthnow, Robert, xxin2, xxiin3, 33nn2-3

Yeago, David S., 34n4

Zwingli, Huldrich, 139, 153n23, 153n31